THE FILMS OF DELMER DAVES

THE FILMS OF
DELMER DAVES

VISIONS OF PROGRESS IN
MID-TWENTIETH-CENTURY AMERICA

DOUGLAS HORLOCK

UNIVERSITY PRESS OF MISSISSIPPI / JACKSON

For Dominic Sutherland Horlock

The University Press of Mississippi is the scholarly publishing agency of
the Mississippi Institutions of Higher Learning: Alcorn State University,
Delta State University, Jackson State University, Mississippi State University,
Mississippi University for Women, Mississippi Valley State University,
University of Mississippi, and University of Southern Mississippi.

www.upress.state.ms.us

The University Press of Mississippi is a member
of the Association of University Presses.

Any discriminatory or derogatory language or hate speech regarding race, ethnicity,
religion, sex, gender, class, national origin, age, or disability that have been retained
or appear in elided form is in no way an endorsement of the use of such language
outside a scholarly context.

Copyright © 2022 by University Press of Mississippi
All rights reserved

First printing 2022

∞

Library of Congress Cataloging-in-Publication Data

Names: Horlock, Douglas, author.
Title: The films of Delmer Daves: visions of progress in
mid-twentieth-century America / Douglas Horlock.
Description: Jackson: University Press of Mississippi, 2022. | Includes
bibliographical references and index.
Identifiers: LCCN 2021053089 (print) | LCCN 2021053090 (ebook) |
ISBN 978-1-4968-3884-1 (hardback) | ISBN 978-1-4968-3885-8 (trade paperback) |
ISBN 978-1-4968-3887-2 (epub) | ISBN 978-1-4968-3886-5 (epub) |
ISBN 978-1-4968-3889-6 (pdf) | ISBN 978-1-4968-3888-9 (pdf)
Subjects: LCSH: Daves, Delmer, 1904–1977—Criticism and interpretation.
Classification: LCC PN1998.3.D38146 H67 2022 (print) | LCC PN1998.3.D38146
(ebook) | DDC 791.4302/3092—dc23/eng/20220103
LC record available at https://lccn.loc.gov/2021053089
LC ebook record available at https://lccn.loc.gov/2021053090

British Library Cataloging-in-Publication Data available

CONTENTS

INTRODUCTION 3

CHAPTER ONE
The Films of Delmer Daves 11

CHAPTER TWO
Political and Social Values in the Films of Delmer Daves 43

CHAPTER THREE
Race and Civil Rights in the Films of Delmer Daves 82

CHAPTER FOUR
Gender in the Films of Delmer Daves 127

CONCLUSION 174

NOTES 178

FILMOGRAPHY 207

BIBLIOGRAPHY 210

INDEX 226

ACKNOWLEDGMENTS

With grateful thanks to Dr. Stephen McVeigh, associate professor in the College of Arts and Humanities at Swansea University, for his comments, advice, and guidance at every stage of preparing this study.

I am thankful also for the conscientious work of students led by Dr. Maria Fernandez-Parra in the Department of Languages, Translations, and Communication at Swansea University.

I am particularly grateful for the help of Gary Ley in gaining access to important primary sources.

Also, I would like to thank Stephen Sanders and Stuart Horlock for their help in seeking and obtaining copies of particular films.

In addition, I wish to thank the staffs of the following libraries for their help in gaining access to important primary and secondary sources: Swansea University Library, in particular Dr. Ian Glen; the British Library; and the Department of Special Collections, Stanford University Libraries, California, in particular Tim Noakes.

Also providing great assistance were the Columbia Center for Oral History Archives, Columbia University, New York; the Reuben Library at the British Film Institute; and the City and County of Swansea Library at Pontarddulais, South Wales.

I would like to thank my editor, Emily Snyder Bandy, for her continued guidance in preparing this study for publication. Additionally, I thank project editor, Laura Strong, and designer, Pete Halverson. Also, I am grateful to Norman Ware for his meticulous scrutiny and editing of my text.

THE FILMS OF DELMER DAVES

Delmer Daves, ca. 1964. Album / Alamy stock photo.

INTRODUCTION

DELMER DAVES WAS BORN IN SAN FRANCISCO IN 1904. HIS GREAT-GRANDmother had migrated to California in a wagon train after her mother had married an immigrant from Wales, and his maternal grandfather had emigrated from Ireland, fought for the Union during the Civil War, and worked as a wagon master and Pony Express rider, carrying the first mail from Salt Lake City to Arizona. Daves left San Francisco in a refugee train after the 1906 earthquake and settled in southern California. While studying law at Stanford University, he became interested in theater, acting in and directing student productions, and after graduating, he joined the Pasadena Playhouse. He broke into the rapidly expanding silent film industry as a property assistant for James Cruze on *The Covered Wagon* (1924), for which he also designed lettering for inserts. He went on to work as a stunt man and actor in minor roles and as an assistant in special effects and editing departments. After working with director Sam Wood on *Queen Kelly* (1929), and because Daves had recently been a student, Wood asked him to write the first sound film to be set on a college campus, and thus he received his first screenwriting credit for *So This Is College* (1929). During the 1930s and 1940s, he provided stories and scripts for a range of genres including musicals such as *Dames* (1934), comedies, romances, and dramas. He completed noted screenplays for *The Petrified Forest* (1936), *Flirtation Walk* (1934), and *Love Affair* (1939), the latter two nominated for Best Picture Oscars. His screenplay for *Love Affair* was filmed largely unchanged for *An Affair to Remember* (1957) and also formed the basis of the 1994 remake of *Love Affair*.

From 1943 to 1965, Daves directed thirty feature films including Westerns, war films, adventure and crime films, romantic melodramas, and a biblical epic, and he directed major stars such as Clark Gable, James Stewart, Humphrey Bogart, Henry Fonda, Frank Sinatra, Cary Grant, Alan Ladd, and Gary Cooper. *Spencer's Mountain* (1963) spawned the popular television series *The Waltons*, and Jacqueline Nacache suggests that *Dark Passage* (1948) may have inspired the successful series *The Fugitive*.[1] Having spent his entire career working within the studio system, Daves did not enjoy the status of postwar directors such as Elia Kazan and Martin Ritt, who were highly regarded because of their earlier work in theater, or directors such as Sidney Lumet and John Frankenheimer after their innovative work in television. He received no Oscar nominations during his career but may be considered unfortunate in this regard, as he contributed to the original story for *Love Affair* but received no formal credit. While *Love Affair* was nominated for an Oscar for Best Original Story, the screenplay was not recognized. Daves revealed that the love affair of the title was developed from his own personal experience of a shipboard romance, but in order to ensure equal recognition for the film's four writers, the official credits distinguished between story and screenplay.[2] The absence of such formal acknowledgment may in part explain the diatribe of the literary critic in *Youngblood Hawke* (1964), who derides the Pulitzer Prize–winning novel of the protagonist, listing the writers of classic works of American fiction who had been "ignored" by the Pulitzer jury. Only a Directors Guild nomination represented recognition of any significance,[3] and the conclusion of Daves's career coincided with the collapse of the studio system, with Jack Warner relinquishing executive powers at Warner Bros. in 1966 and Sam Goldwyn producing his last film in 1959. As such iconic symbols of the studio system were replaced, Daves made his final film in 1965 at the relatively early age of sixty-one.

In advocating an auteur theory of criticism, Ian Cameron concedes that films are produced collectively but still maintains that it is possible to detect the "stylistic fingerprints" of an individual artist and that a film may be considered the expression of a director's vision.[4] Although he believes that this approach has overcome a traditional neglect of American directors, he writes dismissively of the films of Delmer Daves, claiming: "His pictures may be trivial, dishonest, immoral. . . . [His] movies have every fault in the book."[5] Jim Kitses justifies omitting any discussion of Daves's Westerns, the genre for which he is most remembered, declaring that they are insufficiently distinctive.[6] Yet in his reflections on films that inspired his love of cinema and influenced his own work, Martin Scorsese includes *The Red House* (1947) among films that he believes have been inexplicably neglected and lists Daves as a director who has been sadly forgotten.[7] In fact, there is sufficient evidence from commentary on a significant number of Daves's films to suggest that Cameron's view is extreme. *Destination Tokyo* (1943) and *Pride of the Marines* (1945) achieved Top Five ranking in the *New York Times* Ten Best lists for their respective years.[8] *3:10 to Yuma* (1957) was nominated for a British Academy Film Award for Best Film from Any Source, and in 2012 it was selected by the US National Film Registry as historically and aesthetically significant and of enduring importance to American culture.[9] Four of Daves's Westerns were placed in the Ten Best Westerns lists of twenty-seven French critics in the journal *Le Western*,[10] and philosopher and Slovenian presidential candidate Slavoj Žižek lists *3:10 to Yuma* in his top ten films in a British Film Institute international poll.[11] Žižek also argues that *The Hanging Tree* (1959) was critically ignored and deserved more serious consideration.[12]

Auteurism has secured prominent critical recognition for numerous Hollywood directors such as Douglas Sirk, Samuel Fuller, Budd Boetticher, and Vincente Minnelli and also a renewed admiration for the work of Howard Hawks, John Ford, and Alfred Hitchcock. However, Daves has remained largely overlooked in scholarly literature and film retrospectives, with much of his work disregarded and his contribution to well-received films undervalued. Darryl F. Zanuck, head of Twentieth Century Fox throughout much of Daves's career, attributed the success of *Broken Arrow* (1950) to "an amazing script, a powerful story, spectacular scenery, a great human quality and several outstanding performances."[13] He gave no credit to Daves, whereas Richard Whitehall notes that the project was originally offered to John Ford and suggests that images of American Indians would have been different if Ford had accepted.[14] In praising *The Hanging Tree*, Homer Dickens commends the production values of Warner Bros., the acting, the music, Dorothy Johnson's original prize-winning story, and the work of the cameraman, editor, and art director, but he does not mention the director.[15] Similarly, Gérard Legrand writes that *Dark Passage* is "a multi-level masterpiece" but then questions how David Goodis's worthy novel had been turned into a work of such splendor by "the ordinary Delmer Daves."[16]

Edward Buscombe expresses surprise that his own selection of the hundred most important Westerns includes five of Daves's films, a total that is second only to John Ford and ahead of Anthony Mann, Howard Hawks, and Clint Eastwood.[17] Although he concedes that Daves is a better director than has been acknowledged, he feels that this distinction is due as much to factors other than the quality of his direction, such as outstanding acting or the significance a film may have within its genre. This seems to discount the possibility that Daves's direction may have contributed to the standing of particular films or to the performances of actors. Both Whitehall and Charles Burnett, for example, praise the performance of "B" movie actor Rory Calhoun in *The Red House*, with Burnett suggesting that no other director was able to exploit the ability that Calhoun demonstrated in this film.[18] Similarly, both Robert Nott and George Morris claim that in *Pride of the Marines*, John Garfield gave his finest performance to date, in conveying a range of emotions from charm and humor to anger, bitterness, and self-pity in the intensity that he brought to key scenes.[19]

Yet in an obituary for Daves, Dominique Rabourdin claimed that while he was responsible for some of the most beautiful scenes of American cinema, there have been few opportunities to consider his films.[20] While a number of Hollywood filmmakers have been championed by auteurist critics, Daves's reputation has not benefited to the same degree; for instance, although François Truffaut recognized that Daves's work is not without interest,[21] critic and director Bertrand Tavernier concludes that he is "the most forgotten of the American directors."[22] He has received more attention in European countries. The National Museum of Cinema in Turin recognized Daves's work in 1966, alongside the films of Hitchcock, Ritt, and Henry Hathaway, which were similarly recognized during the 1960s. Haden Guest notes that a rationale for Bologna's Il Cinema Ritrovato festival is the discovery of obscure and neglected films and filmmakers.[23] He praises the showing of *Jubal* (1956) at this festival in 2010, commenting on Daves's innovative use of CinemaScope and noting that it is a tense, marvelously intimate and quiet film. However, the only substantive retrospectives of Daves's work to date were screened at the 1972 Oberhausen Film Festival and the 1999 Amiens International Film Festival, but this did not stimulate more sustained critical attention from European critics other than that of Tavernier and a series of short essays published for the Amiens festival.[24] Until 2016, only Michael Walker, writing in English, examined Daves's work in depth, albeit just his Westerns, finding evidence of personalized themes.[25] The only other volume devoted to Daves consisted of extracts in French compiled from other published sources.[26] Other than *Dark Passage*, *Broken Arrow*, and *3:10 to Yuma*, Daves's films had received little critical consideration.

While there has been no major retrospective of Daves's films in English-speaking countries, in recent years restored prints of a small number of his films have been screened at festivals in London and New York and at Harvard University. This indication of increasing interest in Daves has been substantiated with the 2016 publication of the first major volume devoted to Daves's films.[27] A compilation of essays edited by Matthew Carter and Andrew Nelson, it represents an important contribution to greater appreciation of his work. Fran Pheasant-Kelly's analysis of Daves's visual style in *3:10 to Yuma*, including rising crane shots, tracking shots, acute camera angles, and framing devices that enhance perception of characters' inner psychology, is more detailed than any previous analyses.[28] *Jubal* and *Spencer's Mountain* are examined at a similar level, and, other than in Walker's study, films such as *Drum Beat* (1954) and *Cowboy* (1958) had not previously received the standard of attention achieved by the Carter and Nelson volume. Of particular note is the judicious reference by five of the authors to Daves's personal papers, a source that hitherto had not been used extensively. Deeper understanding of the films and valuable support for the authors' arguments are achieved as a result.

A number of these authors highlight the progressive elements in Daves's films. Fernando Berns identifies Daves's focus on a more tolerant and caring society and the possibility of social improvement as key concerns.[29] John White argues that his Westerns demonstrate "that Daves was the ultimate liberal," and his discussion is unusual in viewing *The Badlanders* (1958) as more than just a remake of a classic heist movie.[30] This depth of analysis has not traditionally been associated with Daves's work: more customary has been David Thomson's conclusion that he made only "non-reflective action movies."[31] Pheasant-Kelly suggests that Daves portrays women as independent and resourceful and so questions established gender roles,[32] and Joseph Pomp argues that *Spencer's Mountain* pursues a feminist agenda that challenges the patriarchal basis of Earl Hamner Jr.'s original novel.[33] This is significant, as Daves has not been regarded as a filmmaker who focused on issues of gender and has never been considered in any sense a "women's director." A number of authors in the Carter and Nelson volume discuss Daves's portrayal of American Indians. *Broken Arrow* was considered revisionist at the time of its release: in his review of the film, Robert Hatch felt that it offered "new insight" and was "beautifully photographed, staged with taste and a decent regard for history."[34] However, this view has been reexamined in more recent scholarship, with suggestions that Daves's presentation is more conservative and reflects a wish to extirpate Indian identity.

The issues raised in the essays in the Carter and Nelson volume stimulate deeper insights into Daves's films. Twelve films are discussed in depth, and as the editors recognize, these are his better-known films, which, in the main, are Westerns. They go on to accept that, as an edited collection, their volume can only go some way toward rectifying Daves's hitherto neglected status, and some contributors recognize the need for evaluation of his "forgotten" films. Collectively they support the conviction that Daves was more than a competent studio employee and that more sustained critical scrutiny is warranted. Consequently, in this study, these issues are examined in the depth that a monograph permits. Due note is taken of Peter Wollen's contention that "it is only the analysis of the whole *corpus* which permits the moment of synthesis when the critic returns to the individual film."[35] Although it should not necessarily be assumed that Daves adopts an antiracist stance from the evidence of just one film, Luc Moullet is overly cynical in suggesting that Daves does so in *Broken Arrow* because his contract so stipulated.[36] In an interview, Daves emphasized the importance of understanding other cultures and religions, and after university he spent several months living on a Hopi Indian reservation.[37] However, in this sense, knowledge and understanding of a body of work may well stimulate a more thorough consideration of individual films. Thus, while taking note of Jean-Pierre Coursodon's comment that "[p]erhaps one day someone will attempt a reappraisal of Daves's late period,"[38] all Daves's films are considered in order to assess his ability to create personal films of substance within conventional Hollywood genres.

Furthermore, attention is given to seventeen of Daves's screenplays for other directors, in the main written for films prior to his directorial debut in 1943. Coursodon states that other than for *Love Affair*, these screenplays are mostly negligible and hardly indicative of what would develop in the 1950s.[39] However, many of the themes and ideas introduced in the screenplays are developed more fully in his films as director. Additionally, I examine the Delmer Daves Papers, archived at Stanford University.[40] Comprising scripts, notes, and sketches as well as Daves's correspondence and working papers from 1930 to 1965, this source provides significant supporting authority for key issues in this study and raises questions with regard to conclusions in published literature. Also, I refer to the Albert Maltz Papers at the University of Wyoming.[41] Another primary source utilized is Daves's contribution to an oral history program, now retained at Columbia University, New York.[42] This consists of sixty-six pages of unpublished reminiscences in which Daves reflects on his experiences in the film industry, the power of the studios, and working with particular producers, technicians, and actors, as well as discussing his filming of important scenes. This is supplemented with reference to interviews with Daves. Although he gave few extended interviews for publication in English, Daves gave detailed interviews for French, German, and Spanish journals in which he discusses his experiences in Hollywood and his intentions and methods as writer and director.

Despite his working within the confines of a restrictive studio system, Daves's films deserve to be examined as the work of a serious artist of the cinema. Although Andrew Sarris pays little attention to his work, he identifies three key criteria—"technique," "style," and the "interior meaning"—by which films may be judged according to the extent to which the vision of directors transcends the system in which they worked.[43] The controversy over his implementation of these criteria is well documented, including the elitism and subjectivity of his ranking of directors and the conflation of views of a film's quality with that of any significance it might have within a director's body of work. However, John Belton states that, in proposing that directors of popular entertainment films might express a personal vision and explore social and ethical issues, Sarris stimulated a reevaluation of American cinema and encouraged Americans to take their own cinema seriously.[44] He adds that Sarris provided the opportunities "for others to follow, add to, correct, and challenge."[45] In their introduction, Carter and Nelson provide an account of how these opportunities have been embraced; Bernard Dick, in his review of the essay collection, suggests that their discussion should be compulsory reading in any film theory course, further stating that he had yet to read a better analysis of authorship.[46] It would be difficult to disagree with this conclusion. Sarris wrote that his ranking was based on directors' total rather than occasional achievement.[47] However, Carter and Nelson argue strongly that his appraisal of Daves's work "is less original insight than a restatement of a critical consensus arrived at largely, if not solely, on the basis of the director's most recent films."[48] Therefore, there is an implication that a more thorough implementation of his criteria would result in a more reliable judgment.

English historian Edward Hallet Carr wrote that "[a]ll history is contemporary history,"[49] as it involves interpreting the past in the light of the issues and concerns of the present. The same principle can be applied to analysis of film authorship, and Carter and Nelson emphasize the dynamic nature of this aspect of criticism.[50] Citing authors Pam Cook and Richard Slotkin, they categorize the concept of authorship as a "discursive subject," with the reader (viewer) equally responsible as the author for determining meaning. For example, having claimed that he did not believe in women directors,[51] it is unlikely that Sarris would have concurred with the feminist perspectives in *Spencer's Mountain* and *Jubal* identified by Pomp and Carter, respectively.[52] Thus, over time, interpretations and analyses will be reassessed and revised alongside developing social and political interests and concerns. Carter and Nelson note also that although Jim Kitses accepts criticisms of the auteur theory because of the industrial and ideological concerns that work against personal expression, he believes that a genre such as the Western still allows the communication of a personal vision. Additionally, they note Richard Maltby's pragmatic observation that much of film criticism continues to envisage the director as an author.[53] Therefore Sarris's criteria may be reapplied. Both White's identification of themes in Daves's Westerns and Pheasant-Kelly's textual analysis of *3:10 to Yuma* are essentially applying his criteria of interior meaning and style, respectively. It is noteworthy that while Sarris expressed seemingly unconventional opinions on films such as

The Searchers (1956), *Vertigo* (1958), *Rio Bravo* (1959), and *The Night of the Hunter* (1955), his conclusions now constitute critical orthodoxy.

Robin Wood argues that inherent in and reinforced by the classical Hollywood cinema are the values and assumptions of American capitalist ideology.[54] He refers to the importance of the right of ownership, the primacy of private property and the settling of the land, highlighting an implicit justification for the overcoming of obstacles to their achievement and protection. Together with the institutions of marriage and family, these ideals were presumed to define the fundamental constituents of civilization, alongside the assumption that in America, difficulties could be resolved and "the pursuit of happiness" was possible without the need for fundamental change. Traditionally, Westerns, for example, have tended to reinforce a patriotic certainty in the exceptional nature of American social and political beliefs, and it is easy to assume, as does Judith Wright, that such films act as conservative reaffirmation of the dominant tenets of an existing political structure.[55] However, Jean-Loup Bourget argues that they have the capacity to make subversive statements about current issues.[56]

In *The Wizard of Oz* (1939), Dorothy concludes that "there's no place like home," whereas in L. Frank Baum's original stories, Oz is real rather than a dream and Dorothy and her family leave Kansas to live there. However, the protagonist in *Dark Passage* can only escape from a threatening and oppressive urban postwar environment by leaving America to live in Peru after being wrongly accused of murder. Conventionally, he would fight to clear his name, but he chooses to leave the country, and the heroine is content to join him in exile. In *Kings Go Forth* (1958), a white woman marries a Black man who has achieved educational and economic success in America, but they decide to raise their daughter in France, where they find "a beautiful blindness to color." Similarly, the young woman in *Rome Adventure* (1962) sails from America, passing the Statue of Liberty, to gain freedom from puritanical attitudes. Despite Daves's willingness to work within Hollywood's studio system, his films present a coherent challenge to the conventions of popular Hollywood genres. In the following chapters, I examine the nature and consistency of the vision and ideals revealed in his films, alongside the practices and values of Hollywood filmmaking as embodied in the Production Code to which the studios adhered. Also, I discuss themes that feature prominently, with reference to the observations, analyses, and research findings of contemporary commentators and social scientists.

CHAPTER ONE

The Films of Delmer Daves

THE CAREER OF DELMER DAVES: CRITICAL RESPONSES TO HIS FILMS

THE MAJORITY OF DAVES'S FILMS WERE COMMERCIALLY SUCCESSFUL, WITH *Destination Tokyo* (1943), *Hollywood Canteen* (1944), *Broken Arrow* (1950), *Demetrius and the Gladiators* (1954), *3:10 to Yuma* (1958), *A Summer Place* (1959), *Parrish* (1961), and *Spencer's Mountain* (1963) among the top-grossing films of their respective years, and although critical reception was conflicting, incidental testimony suggests that his work merits greater attention. When contributors to the journal *Cinema* were encouraged not to be restricted by established taste and fashionability when nominating their "10-best films," Roger Huss listed *The Hanging Tree* in his selection.[1] Blake Lucas refers to Daves's "masterly" direction of *3:10 to Yuma*,[2] and when *Pride of the Marines* was released, critic Howard Barnes commented that the war scenes may have been the finest to have appeared in a Hollywood production.[3] However, this level of judgment was not always forthcoming, and Bertrand Tavernier submits that Daves continues to retain an unfairly low critical status.[4]

David Quinlan suggests that *To the Victor* (1948), *Youngblood Hawke* (1964), and *The Battle of the Villa Fiorita* (1965) should be considered the worst films of their respective years.[5] Yet, one review of *To the Victor* concluded that "it would be impossible to praise too highly the script, the direction and the work of the entire cast."[6] Allen Eyles points out that *Youngblood Hawke* was heavily abridged for general release in Great Britain, noting that it was cut from 136 to 91 minutes,[7] and his review of the complete film is more positive than Quinlan's. Eyles concludes that it is well acted, stylish, and enjoyable, and he praises Daves's direction if not his adaptation of the novel by Herman Wouk.[8] The visual exteriors are memorable: while the sights of New York are very familiar to audiences, Daves captures the awe and enthusiasm of a first-time visitor, and the shots of Hawke alone by the river, set against the misty city skyline, intimate his loneliness and disillusion as his ambitions are collapsing. While some critics felt that the acting of James Franciscus was solid and plausible,[9] his performance was regarded as a major weakness, particularly as Warren Beatty had been offered the title role. Franciscus fails to convince that his character has the ability to be an intelligent writer, and as Eyles observes, his performance is weak when he needs to act or react without speaking.[10] There is less disagreement over the performance of Suzanne Pleshette as Hawke's literary editor and eventual love interest. Just as in *Rome Adventure*, Daves was able to elicit a performance that conveys an understated but obvious passionate nature and sensuality together with sophisticated intelligence, integrity, and generosity of spirit.

Quinlan suggests that any reputation that Daves does enjoy as a director depends on a very small number of good films.[11] He then goes on to make positive comments such as "memorable," "compelling," "commendable," and "extraordinary" about eight of his films, while it is arguable that the critical reputation of Francis Ford Coppola rests largely on just three films.[12] Certainly some of Daves's work, while popular on release, is easy to dismiss. Described by Tavernier as a "hopeless failure,"[13] *Never Let Me Go* (1953) is typical of the more simplistic of Hollywood's Cold War films, which portrayed a perceived communist threat to American institutions. For another critic, *A Kiss in the Dark* (1949) was mediocre and silly.[14] However, in his discussion of the auteur theory, Andrew Sarris concedes that "even the greatest directors have their ups and downs"[15] and that it is inevitable that there may be disagreement about the relative quality of directors' individual films. For William Meyer, *Dark Passage* is weak, illogical, and contrived.[16] Yet for Dominique Rabourdin, it is one of the masterpieces of film noir.[17] Similarly, Peter Bogdanovich believes that John Ford's *The Man Who Shot Liberty Valance* (1961) is one of the best films ever made,[18] but for Bruce Beresford, the film constitutes evidence of Ford's creative decline.[19] While critics have disagreed about individual films directed by Ford, there has been little dispute about his standing as a major figure in the history of cinema.

David Thomson writes that *3:10 to Yuma* does not deserve a prestigious reputation, largely because of its contrived action scenario.[20] However, predominately a tense psychological drama, it takes place in the confines of a farmer's home and then in the claustrophobic space of a hotel room. Many scenes in *Broken Arrow* and *Bird of Paradise* (1951) have a static quality, with relatively small proportions of the films' length taken up by action. Darryl F. Zanuck complained that some dialogue scenes in *Broken Arrow* were "hopelessly slow," with characters "merely moving up to the camera and talking."[21] Nevertheless, he wrote that "the intimate scenes have been directed and staged magnificently," including scenes with Tom Jeffords and Cochise in the wickiup that "are real masterpieces."[22] Unusually for Westerns, key issues emerge from characters talking and even debating fundamental matters of prejudice. In *The Badlanders*, the characters' reactions highlight such issues. After being saved from ridicule and assault by a white man, a woman asks: "You knew I was Mexican when you fought for me. Why did you bother?" The man's expressions and body language reveal his basic instincts for natural justice; a corrupt businessman, on the other hand, uses different body language and declares, "I don't trust Mexes."

For Thomson, another weakness of *3:10 to Yuma* is the inability of its star, Glenn Ford, to be "nasty."[23] Yet in an earlier publication, he credits Daves for the film's skillfully created tension and claims that the experiment of portraying Ford as an articulate villain works extremely well.[24] Early in the film, he ruthlessly and without any apparent regret shoots one of his own gang members as well as killing a stagecoach driver. The scene is effective in the surprise it engenders and is a forerunner to the famous scene in *Once Upon a Time in the West* (1968), now regarded by some as one of the greatest of Westerns, in which the killer, played by Henry Fonda, normally the epitome of American integrity, shoots a defenseless young boy. Although the degree to which director Sergio Leone may have been influenced by Daves's film is uncertain, it is noteworthy that rather than being taken to the local jail, Cheyenne is transported to a prison in Yuma. Additionally, the sequence in which Fonda's gang seeks to ambush him evokes Daves's scene in which the gunman is taken to the train station. The respective gangs stalk their targets amid the long, dark shadows that are cast across the empty streets. Leone's rising crane shot, which shows the chaotic activity of a growing town accompanying the building of the railroad, is reminiscent of the opening shots of *The Hanging Tree* in which the protagonist views the rapidly developing mining community from high on a cliff. Daves's slow, panning crane shot captures the hopes and desperation of "gold fever" and the chaos of hastily constructed buildings and tents as miners, their families, gamblers, and prostitutes journey from all directions. More specifically, the sequence in Leone's film in which Cheyenne places his hand on a woman's behind and suggests that she may allow others to do the same evokes a scene in *Jubal* in which the hero gives advice to his boss on appropriate attitudes to women: "She's just fed up with being whacked on the rump."

Tavernier feels that the decline in popularity and regard for the Western helps to explain the relatively low esteem in which Daves is held.[25] However, this reasoning is not consistent with, for example, the increasing critical interest in the Westerns of Anthony Mann, nor with the continued admiration for those of Hawks and Ford. Additionally, Tavernier feels that the decline in quality of Daves's later films, which Jean-Pierre Coursodon describes as "dangerously close to artistic suicide,"[26] may also explain the lack of interest in his work. *Spencer's Mountain* was a financial success, but for its star, Henry Fonda, the sentimental charm of this portrayal of a modern frontier family's tribulations and joys "set the movie business back twenty years."[27] One review concurred, believing Daves's "rose-tinted rural Americana" to be heavy handed and irrelevant to the 1960s.[28] The issue of relevance will be considered, but for Eyles, the film had much that was genuinely poetic.[29]

Certainly, a number of the films Daves made after the commercial success of *A Summer Place* received some unfavorable reviews. He wrote and directed three further romantic melodramas, with a British review that dismissed *Lovers Must Learn* (released in the United States as *Rome Adventure*) as a "glossy tasteless fantasy" typifying the response.[30] However, while Robin Bean's review finds the plot to be trite, he concludes that the film is a very professional and polished production in which Daves demonstrates his talent for cinematic interpretation.[31] Philip Strick's review of *Susan Slade* (1961), while suggesting that Daves was wasting his talent with the material, nevertheless refers to "the Daves inspirational style."[32] This is perhaps Daves's weakest film: it is set along the northern California coast, and while Strick comments on the beautiful photography, he concludes that the film is "superficial rhubarb all the same." Daves admitted to Tavernier that the story had little quality and that he undertook the project only to help Jack Warner, who had purchased novels that were proving difficult to adapt for the screen.[33] He acknowledged that he had made some films that he wouldn't have normally selected, but had done so out of loyalty to Warner, who had given him the opportunities to be a screenwriter and later a director and producer.[34] The limited acting range of Troy Donahue and Connie Stevens is a major weakness, while Daves's screenplay wastes the talents of veteran actors Lloyd Nolan and Brian Aherne. Daves's characters constantly use erudite, weighty, and profound phrases, but the effect is dialogue that is pretentious and mannered. For example, after Susan has nearly drowned, her father remarks to her doctor: "She's learned a bitter lesson too young. In the midst of life we are in death," and her mother's advice is given in perfectly crafted but stilted prose: "There will come a day, a great and joyous day when you'll know some man to whom you are heaven and earth." Nevertheless, there are memorable moments that engage the viewer's feelings. The shot of a pregnant young woman whose lover is avoiding contact, alone on a San Francisco street, sharply captures her desolation and desperation, and the wordless shots of Susan, later playing with her child, are poignant and moving. Particularly effective is the brief scene in which a father tries to keep his emotions in check as he announces the death of his only son: his understated grief is more heartfelt because of the intensity of his expression and the slight movements of his hand while he has difficulty holding the telephone.

Parrish was commercially successful but was not well received by critics. One review referred to a superficial and cumbersome plot, forgettable acting, and absurd dialogue.[35] At 138 minutes the film is overlong, but in fact it benefits from some convincing acting, notably in the quiet integrity of Dean Jagger and the controlled ruthlessness of Karl Malden. Bean finds that the theme of the ethics of business methods and rivalries is interesting but believes that it is made too subservient to the love affairs of the title character and that the film succeeds or fails on this portrayal.[36] By common critical consent, the stilted and expressionless acting of Troy Donahue seems totally inadequate, particularly when the original intention was to star Warren Beatty as Parrish with Jane Fonda as one of his romantic involvements. Therefore, Tavernier may be correct to suggest that Daves's perseverance with Donahue has contributed to his lack of critical recognition.[37] Lawrence Quirk notes Daves's belief that Donahue possessed unexploited depth and sensitivity, and his determination to develop the actor's potential beyond his physical appeal.[38] Daves felt that the experience of working with actors such as Malden and Claudette Colbert would help in this regard, but in fact their acting only exposed Donahue's weaknesses, and his career declined rapidly after *Rome Adventure*, his last film with Daves. In *Parrish*, Donahue fails to convey the initiative or ability to reach the level of success that the character achieves or to gain the loyalty of others. Similarly, the instant attraction of the three young women with whom he has relationships is not convincing because of his complete lack of charisma or charm.

Although these films received mixed reviews, the level of authority Daves exercised as writer, producer, and director should necessitate their inclusion in any consideration of the issue of authorship. Just as Douglas Sirk has gained a lasting critical reputation for melodramas that were poorly regarded when released, Daves's later films are more meaningful than critical opinion has recognized and warrant similar reassessment as critiques of American society as the social upheaval of the 1960s approached. They were dismissed as soap operas, but one review of *The Battle of the Villa Fiorita* felt that Daves had produced "a superior soap opera" and that the film was "an old-fashioned enjoyable entertainment."[39] While Quinlan denigrates this film, another reviewer comments on Daves's professionalism and praises his sense of humor and flair.[40] The film examines, sympathetically, themes of marital breakdown and the conflict between personal fulfillment and duty toward children, issues that were to become the focus of significant social concern. For Rumer Godden, author of the original novel, Daves's script "is so nearly perfect ... warm, alive, funny, often touching."[41] The film's star, Maureen O'Hara, also felt that it was a beautiful love story with an excellent script by Daves but was ruined by poor editing and enforced casting difficulties.[42] In fact, it is such studio-imposed constraints and compromises that contributed to the relative lack of regard for American cinema of the 1950s and 1960s, including the films of Delmer Daves.

FILMMAKING IN HOLLYWOOD: DAVES AND THE STUDIO SYSTEM

For British actor Sir Cedric Hardwicke, Hollywood was a community dedicated to making money by producing pictures within a system that he described as a "sausage factory" that played down "to the lowest common multiples of human taste."[43] Although strongly expressed, this conclusion does tend to reflect perceptions of an industry that seemed to be organized primarily to create profit. It is a view that is emphasized by anthropologist Hortense Powdermaker, who in 1946 spent one year interviewing filmmakers and observing production methods. She concluded that Hollywood had "permitted the businessman to take over the functions of the artists" and that, because the demands of business were regarded as paramount, Hollywood films were formulaic, based on the premise that, "if phoniness brings in money easily, why bother about the details of honesty?"[44] Thus, films tended to maintain a conventional narrative structure, and the content of productions such as Westerns, gangster films, and musicals generally conformed to audience expectations and rarely strayed from proven formats or narratives.

The degree of control or autonomy exercised in the choice of subject for a film and in its treatment may be regarded as a key criterion for evaluating the work of a director. However, the power of the major studios in this context has been well documented by numerous authors including Thomas Schatz, Richard Maltby, and Pam Cook. A key aspect of studio organization was the implementation of a "factory system," which involved a strict demarcation of skills and division of labor with regard to casting, writing, shooting, editing, and scoring. After a studio had acquired a story, the original author would have no influence over its treatment, and after submitting a script, a screenwriter would have little control over how it was filmed. Similarly, as director Frank Capra concedes, most directors would start on the "assembly line" after the screenwriter had left and would be expected to shoot screenplays as written, with no influence on casting, and on completion of filming, they would have little involvement in editing.⁴⁵ A film started by one director could be finished by another, and after previews, retakes might be shot by another director. Although Victor Fleming is the credited director of *Gone with the Wind* (1939), the film retains scenes shot by George Cukor before he was replaced, as well as scenes shot by Sam Wood and producer David O. Selznick. Key to the success of this assembly line was the power of the studio heads, who controlled all aspects of production and retained absolute power to assign personnel to any project or loan them out to another studio. An actor or director would be expected to undertake any project allocated, and refusal could result in contractual suspension.

This system impacted Daves's work. In order to make innovative use of the handheld Arriflex camera and photograph action from the subjective point of view of the hero in *Dark Passage*, Daves had to justify this use and seek permission from Jack Warner. Zanuck claimed that the success of *Broken Arrow* was in large part due to his reediting: "We edited a triumph, in spite of everything.... I don't believe any picture has benefited by editing as much as *Broken Arrow* did."⁴⁶ Zanuck ordered Otto Preminger to film additional scenes for *Treasure of the Golden Condor* (1953) after Daves had finished shooting and been loaned out to MGM to prepare *Never Let Me Go*. There is clumsy editing, if not clumsy direction, in *Jubal*. After Jubal's first encounter with the wagon train, several characters refer to "his girl." Yet there is no indication that he has even noticed the girl in question, and it is obvious that the single shot suggesting her attraction to him had been taken from a later scene, as she is wearing a different dress.

Further restrictions on filmmakers' freedom existed, because the absence of First Amendment protection meant that the content of films could be subject to regulation. From 1934, all films required a Seal of Approval before release, and under the leadership of Joseph Breen, the Production Code Administration (PCA) exercised increasingly strict control. Fundamental to the Code's principles was that no film should lower the moral standards of audiences, that "correct" standards of life should be promoted, and that the sympathy of audiences should not be directed toward any form of crime, wrongdoing, or "sinful" behavior. The sanctity of marriage had to be upheld, and adultery or illicit sex could not be explicit or justified. Pressure and condemnation from activist groups such as the Catholic Legion of Decency acted as further restraint so that filmmakers were less likely to examine controversial themes or contemporary social issues. As a result, studios invariably deferred in advance to the fact that, for example, some states approved films with characters of color only if their roles were subservient. Two versions of *Kings Go Forth* were released, with the print viewed in the South omitting usage of the word "nigger" and an army lieutenant's admission of racial prejudice.[47] The initial script for *Pride of the Marines* included servicemen of different races sharing recreational facilities, but this was vetoed by producer Jerry Wald, who also limited Daves's intention to include Black female defense workers in *The Very Thought of You* (1944).[48] Similarly, Daves was dissatisfied with the ending of *Bird of Paradise* in which a relationship between interracial lovers ended tragically.[49] Although Zanuck agreed, he still felt obliged to accede to the dictates of the Code.[50]

Directors such as Ford and Hitchcock, admired for their "authorship" of their films, did not enjoy unrestricted freedom. Zanuck "interfered" in Ford's films, for example imposing different endings on *The Grapes of Wrath* (1940) and *My Darling Clementine* (1946). Similarly, Hitchcock revealed that he had no choice over the leading cast members of *Saboteur* (1942), and, because of RKO's concern over the "image" of Cary Grant, he was not permitted to develop the plot of *Suspicion* (1941) as he wished, with Grant as a murderer.[51] These features of Hollywood film production have tended to undermine an appreciation of the importance of the director in the creative aspects of filmmaking. English-language criticism, while committed to the idea of a director's personal vision, generally found greater individuality and integrity in this regard in European cinema, as directors were perceived to have had more artistic control. Daves had sufficient authority to insist that Edward G. Robinson should replace Charles Laughton in *The Red House*, even though the latter had been contracted, but this film was made by independent producer Sol Lesser rather than a major studio. Daves was reluctant to make *Treasure of the Golden Condor* and *Bird of Paradise* when under contract to Fox, as they were remakes of earlier popular films, but he risked suspension if he refused.

In conversation with Heinz-Gerd Rasner, Reinhard Wulf, and Wolf-Eckhart Bühler, Daves recalled that he resisted Jack Warner's demand that he accept a seven-year contract as a scriptwriter.[52] As a writer and then director, he signed only contracts that committed him to a set number of films, but this still restricted his freedom to choose projects. He admitted that "we cannot always choose our screenplays: we are under contract with producers who require us to make films about particular subjects of little interest."[53] When discussing these aspects of filmmaking, Daves did wonder how films of quality could be made.[54] However, he accepted that without the support and resources of the studio system, he would not have been able to make as many films as he did, and that *Broken Arrow*, *Cowboy*, *3:10 to Yuma*, and *Dark Passage* may never have been made.[55] While relying on satisfactory commercial returns for the majority of their projects, studios were willing to take risks surprisingly often, even when under pressure not to make films such as *The Grapes of Wrath* and *Citizen Kane*. Schatz argues that the relationship between money and creativity need not be malign and that the two may interact, with one enabling or enhancing the other, just as the absence of constraints does not guarantee quality.[56] He uses André Bazin's phrase, "the genius of a system," to argue that films of genuine quality and artistry were made, and he accepts that there have been directors with authority and style who, as well as proving to have talent, could work successfully within the studio system.[57]

While Powdermaker writes that "Hollywood is engaged in the mass production of prefabricated daydreams,"[58] she also acknowledges that there have been popular and profitable films of quality that have demonstrated "[t]ruthfulness in the portrayal of characters," and that "help humans understand themselves and their complicated world."[59] Her examples of such films include *Pride of the Marines*. Powdermaker goes on to suggest that such cinematic achievement is due to "someone with power enough to leave his stamp on a film[,] ... [who] really cared for and respected mankind" and who is capable of synthesizing the diverse elements of words, music, sound, and visual images.[60] Howard Koch, cowriter of *Casablanca* (1942), is in no doubt: "It seems incontrovertible to me that the writer is the primary creative source."[61] This may be a valid conclusion with regard to films such as *The Wizard of Oz*, which had four directors, and also *Casablanca*, as, during its filming, neither director nor stars knew from day to day how the story would develop or how the issues would be resolved.

The screenplay that gave Daves the greatest satisfaction was *Love Affair*, but it is significant that he accepted that director Leo McCarey deserved at least equal credit as "author" of the film, and more generally he conceded that his scripts were often improved by other directors.[62] In the same way, Daves makes clear that as director, he made what he felt to be necessary changes to the scripts of all his films.[63] For example, Andrew Nelson notes that the shooting script for *The Hanging Tree* indicates Daves's responsibility for merging and amending the drafts of Halstead Wells and Wendell Mayes.[64] Similarly, the final script for *The Badlanders* is credited "by Delmer Daves," with an added handwritten note, "I waived writing credit."[65] Daves suggested that his choice of location could impact the screenplay, as passages may need to be changed to adapt to the chosen settings. He recalled that while the screenplay for *3:10 to Yuma* was the first script he had read that he would be willing to film unaltered, rewriting was still necessary in order to develop the narrative from different viewpoints and to exploit locations and ensure that sets and props were period appropriate.[66] His attention to detail is indicated in the mechanics of opening and keeping open the hotel window.

The fact that Daves retained the fine, sparse dialogue of the screenplay for *3:10 to Yuma* did not inhibit further creativity. In the powerful love scene, when the outlaw expresses his preference for blue eyes, the barmaid's eyes look down wistfully as she refers to her brown eyes. The framing emphasizes their growing closeness, and Fran Pheasant-Kelly describes her "exquisitely poignant upward glance," with eyes wide open and with longing, as he replies: "They don't have to be blue." Pheasant-Kelly attributes the intensity of this scene "entirely to Daves's direction."[67] In the same film, the request by the captured killer for fat to be cut from his meat was improvised on the set and is a brief moment that enriches the portrayal of the character. These lines are not in the early versions of the screenplay but appear as Daves's handwritten additions in the margins of the revised final draft.[68] It is a sequence that, with minimum dialogue but with eye movement, expressions, and glances across the kitchen table, conveys the unspoken thoughts and motivations that determine the actions to come. The charm and confidence of the outlaw induce the rancher's wife to have thoughts of a life with less drudgery, but also guilt over her feelings of disloyalty toward her husband, who fears that he is losing the respect of his family. There is a moving scene in *Destination Tokyo* in which some men listen to a recording of a dead crew member's message from his wife. Initially, John Garfield's effusive character jokingly anticipates "racy" dialogue—"We could do with a laugh"—but the restrained anguish in his facial expression and the slow, downward eye movement as he hears her dignified and heartfelt words convey a richer sense of the character behind his outward bombast.

Daves's style is unpretentious and economical but also rich in detail. For example, the opening fifteen minutes of *To the Victor* centers on a car chase along the streets and across the bridges of postwar Paris, with a young woman seeking refuge in a hotel. With precise cutting between close-ups and angled long shots, this is an exciting sequence. However, there are also intimations of the arrogance and ruthlessness of the surviving Nazis, the cynicism of black marketeers, and the protagonist's callous attitude toward women. Furthermore, in snatches of barroom conversation, there are hints of emergent Cold War prejudices. Daves admitted that only when he became a director did he realize that his earlier scripts had been too long and overwritten and needed editing by directors,[69] and he recalled lessons from his days in silent films when communication was achieved through expression and the eyes in particular.[70] This is illustrated more explicitly in *Dark Passage* when the hero has undergone plastic surgery and his face is hidden by

"Some men you see every day for ten years and never notice. Some men you see once and they're with you the rest of your life." *3:10 to Yuma*. Felicia Farr, Glenn Ford. Photo 12 / Alamy Stock Photo.

bandages. His ability to speak is restricted, and initially he can communicate only by blinking. When he finds his friend murdered, and later when the heroine confronts him when the killing is reported in a newspaper, the depth of his emotions is expressed through the movement and intensity of his eyes, showing his confusion and horror. Filming *The Hanging Tree* with Maria Schell, whom he believed to be the finest actress with whom he had ever worked, Daves shot what he considered to be one of his best scenes.[71] The character's sense of pride turns to despair and then anger as she realizes that her hard work has been devalued by deception. This is achieved with impeccable transition from master shot to accusatory and then reaction close-up and with a minimum of movement and dialogue, but with intensity of expression and eye movement.

Albert Maltz's screenplay for *Pride of the Marines* was widely praised and was Oscar nominated. Yet David Gerber claims that Maltz objected to the significant changes that Daves made to his early drafts and was dissatisfied with the final screenplay.[72] However, he did not refuse his Oscar nomination or ask for his name to be removed from the credits, as he did for *The Beguiled* (1971) because he was dissatisfied with Don Siegel's treatment of his work. Daves indicated that Maltz asked him to "take over the 'sentiment and humor' re: writing"[73] as this was not his strength, and Joachim Kreck notes that Daves was responsible for the love scenes.[74] Furthermore, Maltz emphasized that his eighteen pages of suggested improvements were intended to be constructive and that he had not itemized all "the excellent things he [Daves] had done to the script.... [T]he list is too long to remember."[75] Maltz praised Daves's writing of specific scenes and went on to comment that "whenever you [Daves] substitute a scene topper for mine, it is invariably much better."[76] Discussing *Destination Tokyo*, Joan Mellen specifically ascribes the status of auteur to Maltz rather than the director, despite the fact that Daves received joint writing credit with Maltz.[77] Barbara Zheutlin and David Talbot emphasize that Daves was solely responsible for the first draft and that Maltz was brought in to add elements of social commentary, which proved to be the elements that attracted controversy.[78] Zheutlin and Talbot conclude that Maltz's additions did not alter the fundamental structure or character of Daves's screenplay, which was undoubtedly enhanced by his empathy with the naval crew and understanding of submarine warfare, learned after spending a month at sea aboard a naval submarine. It was this knowledge that persuaded Jack Warner to ask an initially reluctant Daves to accept his first directorial assignment, and it is the authenticity of technical and personal details of life on a submarine that was admired and that proved useful to the navy for training purposes.

Although disagreement over the primacy of the director has impacted the nature and orientation of film criticism, these differing views need not be contradictory or mutually exclusive. A. J. Reynertson distinguishes between two kinds of film directors.[79] Some directors will consider a script or producer's instruction as something inviolable, to be faithfully presented and translated in visual and aural terms. Such a director allows the material to dictate his method. However, a director's creativity need not be limited to the skill required to realize the intentions of a writer or producer, and Reynertson argues that some directors use a script as a vehicle for the expression of their own ideas and attitudes: they transform rather than translate the material. For example, identical speeches in the Laurence Olivier (1944) and Kenneth Branagh (1989) versions of *Henry V* present very different perspectives on the nature of leadership and the conduct and purpose of war. Similarly, Paul Rotha contends that producing a good fiction film requires "the stern insistence of a director having the guts and faith to stick by his intentions."[80] It is significant that Daves wrote the screenplays for many of the films he directed, but he also stated that as a director, he was able to exercise a certain control over the films for which he did not write the screenplay, "(what you call *director's polish*) in order to make them conform to some of my ideas."[81]

Glenn Ford considered the three Daves films in which he starred to be among his most satisfying, and he remarked that "Del was a very fine director.... He was always prepared and he knew what he wanted.... Nothing happened in a Delmer Daves film that wasn't intentional, from the camera set-ups to the wardrobe."[82] As well as indicating the degree of authority he exercised, Matthew Carter and Andrew Nelson's scrutiny of the Delmer Daves Papers, which contain handwritten notes, annotations, and sketches added to his shooting scripts, confirm the meticulous detail of his planning and preparation. His papers for *3:10 to Yuma* include notes on character motivation and action as well as camera angles and movement, alongside precise sketches of ranch and township settings, with details of the ideas and effects he sought to convey.[83] Oscar-winning actor Ernest Borgnine, who also made three films with Daves, claimed that he was one of the finest directors he had worked with,[84] and supporting actor James Drury felt that his time working on *The Last Wagon* (1956) was "just a wonderful experience. ... [H]e was a wonderful, kind, gentle man ... just a wonderful director."[85] In his documentary film about his sister, Maria Schell, actor and director Maximilian Schell claimed that filming *The Hanging Tree* was one of the most enjoyable experiences of her career, even though she had worked with highly regarded directors such as Anthony Mann, Luchino Visconti, and René Clément.[86] Daves directed two of the very few post-*Shane* (1953) films of any quality made by Alan Ladd. Both Ladd and Gary Cooper asked him to direct for their respective production companies, and he was one of the very few directors with whom Humphrey Bogart would work without prior approval of a project.

DAVES AS "AUTHOR"

The creativity and personality of directors are important factors in considering the degree to which they can be regarded as the author of their films and the extent to which they have been able to impose their personal standpoint on a collaborative and hierarchical system. Sarris suggests that "[n]ot all directors are *auteurs*. ... [M]ost directors are virtually anonymous,"[87] and he dismisses Daves's films as light and merely likeable, finding no evidence of any meaningful coherence in his work that might have been imposed by a strong directorial personality.[88] Schatz suggests that the directors who succeeded as "author-artists" were those who maintained a level of antagonism to the studio hierarchy and who were often considered to be "difficult to handle," thus giving the appearance of independence.[89] However, Daves has been described as the most open, popular, and easygoing of directors in Hollywood.[90] In particular, producer Walter MacEwen notes Daves's "affinity for authors and ability to please them" with his adaptations of their work.[91]

A feature article on Daves notes that he was regarded by studios as reliable in terms of keeping to the budget and shooting schedule, and that the "production office [didn't] have sleepless nights" when he was working on a film, to the point that Daves worried that when studios and producers acknowledged his "niceness," "[t]hey allow it to sound a little resentful."[92] He accepted that studio heads had the legal right to make final decisions and that it was important to harden oneself to the multiple factors that may impact filmmaking. He seemed to be more tolerant of the constraints on creative expression imposed by the assembly-line methods of production, for example objecting to the use of such negative phrases as "studios tampered with" in this context and the implication that this process necessarily violated an individual's work.[93]

Importantly, however, Peter Wollen writes that American cinema is worth studying in depth and that masterpieces were made under the studio system not only by an elite group of directors but also by a wider range of artists whose work had been dismissed or ignored.[94] Rasner, Wulf, and Bühler suggest that because of his pragmatic and nonconfrontational approach, Daves gained the trust of producers and executives and actually enjoyed a higher level of independence as a result.[95] For example, Columbia head Harry Cohn had criticized the use of deep shadows in *On the Waterfront* (1953), feeling that it was difficult for an audience to view the totality of the action. However, when filming *3:10 to Yuma*, Cohn accepted Daves's decision not to use light reflectors to brighten shaded areas, thus enhancing the depth and richness of the long shadows formed in the Arizona winter.[96] Therefore, Daves was able to heighten the contrast with the white parched earth and emphasize the arid landscape devastated by drought. Similarly, in the campfire scenes in *Cowboy*, Daves does not use lighting, so that an audience sees only faces revealed by firelight. He uses rich shades of blackness to evoke the nights as experienced on the prairies, rather than the bluish Technicolor twilights common in "day-for-night" shooting.

It is interesting that Daves's son Michael, who worked in the film industry and was certainly an admirer of his father's films, felt that the wide range of projects undertaken precludes consideration of Daves as auteur.[97] Yet this has not prevented serious analysis of the films of John Ford. Douglas McVay suggests that the majority of filmmakers who demonstrate a consistent and recognizable personal style have worked regularly with the same actors and technicians.[98] If not as renowned as the John Ford "Stock Company," arguably several actors completed their best work in Daves's films, including Glenn Ford, Felicia Farr, John Garfield, Dane Clark, and Suzanne Pleshette, and Daves regularly cast Eleanor Parker, Debra Paget, Douglas Kennedy, Richard

Jaeckel, and Kent Smith. Ernest Borgnine and Anne Bancroft worked for him several times early in their careers, and Glenn Ford referred to Charles Bronson as a member of the Delmer Daves "Stock Company."[99] Daves recalled that this strategy helped in his attempts to instill a "family" community and cooperative ethos, which he felt benefited the creative process of filmmaking.[100] He refers specifically to "on-set" discussions when filming *The Hanging Tree*, which resulted in reviewing scenes and script changes: "We worked with such complete rapport on that picture." Jerry Hartleben, who as a ten-year-old acted in *3:10 to Yuma*, remembers that Daves respected and involved the cast including himself in decisions and also recalls in particular the creative way that Daves worked with Glenn Ford, which resulted in improvised action and dialogue.[101]

If the importance of the working relationship between director and cinematographer is axiomatic, it is significant that Charles Lawton Jr., who had worked with Orson Welles and John Ford, photographed six of Daves's films and refers to the very close collaboration on the visual style and photographic texture of their films.[102] Composers Max Steiner and George Duning scored many of his films, and Duning relates how Daves was sensitive to background music and on *3:10 to Yuma* shot scenes to the mood and timing of Duning's melodies. He had clear ideas as to how the music could enhance the film's themes, for example to emphasize the outlaw's thoughts when he observes the devotion between the rancher and his wife.[103] However, regularly working with artists is only an indicator of the possibility of "authorship."

On the basis that a "great director has to be at least a good director,"[104] the most basic criterion is the ability to produce a film that has clarity and coherence, and there is substantial evidence that in developing his narratives and themes, Daves displays an intelligent and creative technique. In *Pride of the Marines*, the hero's first meeting with his future fiancée in total darkness after an electrical failure anticipates his blindness and her role in helping him overcome his reluctance to confront his fears and accept his condition. Later, as she moves restlessly around her home and stares out of the window into a strengthening storm, the thunder and lightning merge into the sound and fury of warfare. In *Kings Go Forth*, an army lieutenant realizes that he is losing the woman he loves to another soldier. Outwardly he remains composed, but the chaos resulting from the destructive German bombing that follows reflects his inner turmoil. Carol Donelan notes a similarly effective transition sequence in *Dark Passage*.[105] The hero confronts his blackmailer with the Golden Gate Bridge in the background. The imposing girders and suspension cables of the bridge dissolve into the patterned latticework in the door that separates the faces of Humphrey Bogart and Agnes Moorehead.

Tavernier writes that the battle scene in *Pride of the Marines* is among the most powerful in the genre.[106] It is certainly more realistic than many contemporary war films, which tended to mix studio-bound shots with rather obvious back projection of actual war footage. Daves's low-angle shooting and double printing with positive and negative images effectively evoke the horror of combat at Guadalcanal. Unexpected shots such as a close-up of a huge crab seeking its prey further reflect the men's deepening vulnerability and anger. The scene is made more nerve wracking by enemy voices emerging from the darkness, which anticipate the trauma of the protagonist's blindness, and by the shock of a grenade explosion that fills the entire screen. Later, the hero recalls this experience in a dream in which he returns to the station where he and his fiancée earlier declared their love. The terror of his nightmare deepens as the superimposition of photographic negative images of himself as a helpless blind man disturbs the vision of her loving greeting. Alarmed by his appearance, she runs away as he screams after her.

Daves emphasized the importance of using a range of lenses to create different visual effects, for example the use of revolving multiple lenses to film Bogart going under anesthesia in *Dark Passage*.[107] After experimenting with lenses for *The Red House*, he ordered the use of red filters for *3:10 to Yuma* to bleach out shades of color and so heighten the visual effect of a barren landscape devastated by searing heat.[108] Therefore, the desolate environs become part of the drama rather than the mere backdrop, with the real hardships of frontier existence starkly conveyed. At the beginning of *3:10 to Yuma*, Daves used wide-angle distancing lenses, thus highlighting the relationship between individuals and landscape and objectifying the action. He achieved a similar objective tone in *Broken Arrow* through use of master shots rather than close-ups, which allowed audiences to observe and judge attitudes and behaviors, therefore raising moral issues more effectively. However, as the drama in *3:10 to Yuma* becomes more confined and intense, he explores motivation and silent thoughts from different perspectives using lenses that allow piercing close-ups. His choice of lenses in *Destination Tokyo* effectively compressed action within a tight frame, thus enhancing the sense of a claustrophobic existence aboard a submarine.

Although Zanuck commented that Daves's talents lay mainly in intimate scenes and stories, he described the "rushes" of *Demetrius and the Gladiators* as superb, in particular the composition of and action in the gladiator school scenes. He commented that "[t]he photography, direction and action were outstanding" and went on to conclude that "the picture is good enough to stand on its own—and not just as a sequel."[109] Although released after *The Robe* (1953), *Demetrius and the Gladiators* was filmed concurrently, using some of the same actors and sets. Both were filmed in CinemaScope, one of the technological innovations designed to reverse the decline in cinema audiences attributed to the popularity of television. In his study of the relationship between new technology and style, Barry Salt concludes that early use of CinemaScope tended to be visually unimaginative, with directors keeping action to the central area of the frame.[110] With the screen being two and a half times as wide as it was high, this shape was used effectively in *The Robe* in isolated scenes, such as in the composition of the Crucifixion sequence and when four white horses pulling a wagon gallop in close-up across the full width of the screen. Overall, however, director Henry Koster failed to exploit this screen ratio imaginatively. Compositions are rather static and almost "theater bound" in scenes with dialogue. Characters occupy the center of the screen with empty expanses on either side or are positioned at opposite ends of the screen with inexplicable space between them.

Daves made clear that save for scenes of spectacles, he disliked CinemaScope, and this led to arguments with Zanuck, who had determined that this process should be used for all Fox films.[111] Nevertheless, Daves's use of the wide screen proved to be more effective, despite the fact that the new process was as novel and untried as it was for Koster. Salt comments that Daves was unnecessarily modest about his use of this process, noting that a number of compositions and groupings make full use of the CinemaScope frame, with Zanuck later acknowledging "the perfect handling of CinemaScope" in particular scenes.[112] The opening shots in *The Robe* were intended to demonstrate the potential of the wide screen and to convey a sense of the grandeur of Rome: the curtains behind the opening credits open to reveal a crane shot of a crowded gladiatorial arena. However, this was originally shot by Daves for *Demetrius and the Gladiators* and added to *The Robe* in postproduction.[113]

Daves demonstrates originality and flexibility in composition, and with careful placement of groups and individuals in the foreground, middle, and background, he creates different focal points of interest across the wide screen while still guiding audience attention toward the principal figures or action by means of lighting, positioning, sound, or camera placement. He shows skillful use of light and shadow to exploit the rectangular screen shape, framing key action by the deliberate positioning of rocks, pillars, or doors. The crowd scenes, particularly those set in the gladiator camp, are very effective, as is the shot of a tiger leaping across the full length of the screen. Similarly, the slaying of the tiger in the arena demonstrates the powerful framing of close-up action in CinemaScope; particularly striking is the final sequence in which three men walk toward the retreating camera, framed by rows of pillars. Reviews of *Drum Beat* praised Daves's use of CinemaScope, not only for exteriors in capturing the feeling of the hot sun and dust of the plains and in scenes of conflict, but also for the composition of interiors.[114] In an early scene set in the White House, characters are framed by doors and pillars, and with the positioning of characters carefully placed across the full width of the drawing room decorated in deep shades of red, those merely listening seem to be participants in the action.

Commenting on American cinema's capacity to experiment with an original stylistic technique while not detracting from narrative or commercial requirements, Jacqueline Nacache gives the use of the subjective camera in *Dark Passage* as an example.[115] Robert Montgomery has been credited with its first usage in *Lady in the Lake* (1946), with private detective Philip Marlowe seen only when reflected in mirrors or when briefly addressing the cinema audience. However, Carter and Nelson show that it is very probable that during the period of delay because of Jack Warner's initial opposition, Daves discussed his ideas with Montgomery, who then asked if he could use the subjective camera in his film.[116] This is highlighted in the Delmer Daves Papers, which also detail his painstaking experimentation with the technical and organizational aspects of the equipment and different strategies to effect the movements of the camera "acting as a person."[117] Based on this research, Carter and Nelson suggest that Daves may warrant the status of unacknowledged innovator and quote his claim that his work anticipated the "'Nouveau Vague' some fifteen years later in France."[118] However, there were unenthusiastic critical comments. A British review felt that Daves had made a "not altogether successful attempt to emulate the first person camera technique adopted by Robert Montgomery," but "[f]ortunately he gives this up at the end of the first few reels."[119] Bosley Crowther commented that Daves's use of the subjective camera interspersed with more objective long shots and establishing shots was confusing.[120] Therefore, the contribution of this "innovation" to the quality of *Dark Passage* should be considered.

The purpose of this subjective narration is to allow identification with a protagonist to the point of feeling personally involved in the action, and it is questionable whether Montgomery achieves this effect. The viewer can only infer his presence from the conduct of other characters and the occasional awkward appearance of his hands or feet or rising cigarette smoke. There is little insight into Marlowe's feelings, for example his unpleasant attitude to women. Montgomery's use of subjective narration seems little more than a gimmick, which adds nothing to the narrative. Instead, it slows down the action due to the absence of cutting, particularly with the movement of Marlowe's eyes, unconvincingly represented by excessively slow panning. For

The use of the subjective camera in *Dark Passage*. Moviestore Collection Ltd. / Alamy Stock Photo.

example, when Marlowe opens a shower door, his eyes go to the top of the cubicle and then move slowly down the wall before seeing a body. Daves's use of the narrative technique in the early reels of *Dark Passage* is more purposeful, and contemporary reviews, which indicated a rigid division between the use of the subjective and the conventional camera, are simplistic. In the first thirty minutes, the first-person technique predominates, but there are more objective shots in scenes when the hero is covered up in a car, when his face is in shadows.

Bernard Dick argues that the subjective camera should not dominate an entire film but should be used when demanded by the plot.[121] Used only at times of vulnerability, the subjective camera emphasizes the fear and loneliness of the fugitive, played by Humphrey Bogart, in an environment where he is uncertain about whom he can trust. The accusatory looks and rapid questioning by the driver who stops on the road for the escapee create the feeling that it is the viewer who is being investigated: "Where're you from ... where're you going ... whereabouts in San Francisco ... why are you going to Frisco?" It is only when the hero finds refuge and support that Daves reverts to the conventional objective camera. To avoid capture, the fugitive undergoes plastic surgery, and his face is not seen until his bandages are removed. This enables his voice to be used throughout, thus avoiding a weakness whereby a different actor is used prior to a character's metamorphosis, as for example in *Seconds* (1966). Furthermore, the movement of the eyes is more effectively suggested by the "whipping movement" of the subjective camera rather than orthodox cutting: the camera darts and swings round, reflecting the fear and apprehension in response to unexpected sounds.

Barry Salt acknowledges that Daves was the first director to use, in a feature film, recently captured German handheld Arriflex cameras, which had previously been operated in combat.[122] The subjective camera sequences are particularly enriched. Filming Bogart in the streets and on a cable car with this lightweight camera attracted less public attention and was more realistic than using back projection, just as Bogart's character had to reach his destinations without being detected. To escape from San Quentin, he had hidden himself in a steel drum on a truck. Having forced the drum off the truck, it tumbles down an embankment. With the camera placed in the drum, the viewer experiences his distorted vision as the spiraling movement gathers speed. His sense of disorientation when he crawls out the drum depicts the desperate nature of his plight. Later, when taken into an apartment, rapid eye movements reflect his uncertainty, too quick to notice what he "sees," but as he becomes more relaxed, his movements are more steady. For Pedro Poyato, Daves's application of this technology in *Dark Passage* is innovative.[123] He likens Daves's focus on Bogart's hands as he shaves, turns the taps, and then moves the shower head to the idea of hands with "a life of their own," as in Luis Buñuel's work and in Robert Wiene's *The Hands of Orlac* (1924). As Bogart showers, the water spurts into his face, and thus also the viewer's face, a shot that Alfred Hitchcock replicates in his famous shower scene in *Psycho* (1960). Similarly, the crop-dusting sequence in Hitchcock's *North by Northwest* (1959), in which Cary Grant throws himself to the ground when attacked by a biplane, is reminiscent of a shot in *Task Force* where the approach of a similar plane is too low and a sailor must fall to the deck of an aircraft carrier. When Bogart's plastic surgery begins, his fear is expressed as the camera focuses on the shriveled face of the surgeon with his razor. As he is anesthetized, warped images of faces and piercing eyes multiply and revolve to the sound of frenzied laughter. The hallucinatory quality of these distorted close-ups evokes the expressionism of films such as Jean Cocteau's

La Belle et la Bête (1946): as "Beauty" enters the Beast's castle, there are dissolving mirrors and candelabra held by human arms on the walls as she is observed by the gaze of live statues.

In interviews, Daves seems to dismiss the notion of a clearly defined "Daves style," stating, "I much prefer the audience not to know that there's a director" and making clear that he adjusted his methods to meet the demands of the story.[124] Nevertheless, his work exhibits distinct and identifiable characteristics that express similar insights and attitudes whatever the genre or content of a film, and as such satisfy Raymond Durgnat's definition of an artist's style.[125] Certainly, Sarris's accusation that Daves has "stylistic conviction in an intellectual vacuum" may be challenged to show that, contrary to Sarris's conclusion, Daves was able to "transcend" rather than merely "mingle" with his material.[126] Distinctive stylistic features such as the use of crane shots, which Sarris dismisses as attention seeking and debasing,[127] were more than cinematic gimmicks and in fact enhance the narrative and exposition of themes. Daves believed that the crane allowed increased artistic freedom, especially for exploring gracefully and without abrupt cutting, human relationships within the infinity of space surrounding them.[128] In this context, Michael Walker suggests that in *3:10 to Yuma*, the crane shot sweeping downward to meet the rancher's wife running toward the camera to greet her husband is an initial and lyrical intimation of the closeness of their relationship, which is to be tested by events to come.[129] More generally, crane shots with long shadows and interspersed with expressive close-ups create the claustrophobic atmosphere central to the intensity of this film. The crane shots in *Kings Go Forth* enrich the drama of liberation, showing the coordination of artillery and infantry involved in attacking a German defensive position. Such shots contrast with telling close-ups of involvement in battle, in particular that of an elderly woman's exultant expression as she offers wine to liberating troops. A rising crane shot in *Drum Beat* reveals the strength of Modoc mountaintop defenses, and another such shot illustrates the weak strategic movement of soldiers and volunteers as they attempt an advance in a long line against the tribe. A retreating camera shows the scale of the army's rout, and this is followed by shots of a diagonal line of defeated and wounded soldiers withdrawing in the dust of twilight, an image that is as evocative as similar scenes in Ford's cavalry films.

Daves pioneered the use of a more flexible camera crane that allowed 360-degree panning and vertical crane shots, which he felt better enabled "revelations of beauty."[130] In *Spencer's Mountain*, the camera lifts up from the singing at a graveside to create a profound link between the death of a pioneer and the land that he had loved. The initial loneliness of the hero in

Broken Arrow is emphasized by extreme long shots of bleak canyons and desert, and a fugitive's desperation and vulnerability at the beginning of *The Last Wagon* is intensified by dramatic crane shots of his running amid the rugged and inhospitable parched brown terrain. The opening of *The Badlanders* is set in Arizona State Prison at the end of the nineteenth century. Inmates' treatment is powerfully conveyed by wordless crane shots of prisoners chained together and tracking shots of their forced robotic walking in line after exiting their cells, with the only sounds being the rattling of their chains, the whipping of a prisoner being punished, and the harsh commands of the guards. The film is a remake of *The Asphalt Jungle* (1950), which was set in a contemporary urban landscape, and it retains elements of film noir. With troubled and angry characters and corrupt institutions and officials, and with much of the narrative set in confined spaces, unlawful conspiracy and deception are planned behind locked doors. However, the wide-screen crane shots of Mexican American workers in bright sunlight, running from different directions to act together to overcome their oppressors, emphasize with a sense of exhilaration their common purpose and unity.

Although Zanuck commented that Daves "should never go on a location picture nor ever be associated with large-scale crowd scenes,"[131] he later described the "rushes" of *Treasure of the Golden Condor* as "breathtaking ... photography superb.... Daves has done an outstanding job on location."[132] More generally, his films are noted for the visual beauty of the exteriors. Set in the red-rock canyons of the Sedona area of Arizona or the mountain ranges of Wyoming and Montana, the landscapes in Daves's Westerns are as visually impressive as those in Ford's films. Even poorly reviewed films have been praised for outstanding photography, such as in *The Battle of Villa Fiorita*, the California landscape in *Susan Slade*, and the opening of *Parrish* with a ferry crossing in the mist. However, his locations are integral to the narrative rather than just settings for the action. A month's first-unit shooting in San Francisco for *Dark Passage* replaced the customary use of stock studio footage serving as a backdrop. Panoramic views of magnificent city buildings, busy streets, and beautiful familiar sights in bright sunlight evoke a sense of postwar contentment. However, beneath this surface complacency exists a darker, seamier, and more shadowy world that the protagonist must inhabit. As Bogart walks along a dimly lit street, the subjective camera captures movements in the shadows, momentarily visible alongside streetlights or the sudden flare from a lighted match. In the dark streets and back alleys there is violence, blackmail, and covert and illegal acts such as unlicensed medical practice. The openness of the city images are disturbed by the bleak lighting of studio filming, which intensifies a sense of oppression, just as developing anticommunist frenzy begins to subvert this sense of national optimism.

In *Bird of Paradise*, an interracial love affair begins in an idyllic Polynesian setting, but the landing on the black sand beach of a volcanic island is a portent for the tragedy to come. Ford's shots of pioneers in a valley or cavalry alongside a butte in Monument Valley suggest the naturalness of their presence and that theirs is almost a spiritual as well as physical journey in bringing civilization to the West. Daves focuses on the dangers of an alien landscape, encountered on a cattle drive in *Cowboy* or on a wagon train, difficulties that may not be overcome unless individuals adapt and learn. Giving *To the Victor* as an example, Tavernier comments on Daves's attention to landscape, noting that he often personally supervised material usually left to second-unit directors.[133] Unusually for this time, much of this film was shot on location in Paris and Normandy, and these settings add to the topical quality of the narrative and help to ensure that the observations on the immediate post–World War II world are both provocative and compelling. Particularly with a poignant rendition of "La Vie en Rose," the scenes of Paris capture the atmosphere of postwar confusion and increasing despondency that the better world that war had promised might not be realized, with characters seeking to profit from this confusion and with hints of a more destructive war to come. This cynicism is heightened when set against the love between a black marketeer and a suspected collaborator, which develops alongside the solitude of Omaha Beach, still scattered with the wreckage of liberation, a reminder of sacrifices made and the hope for fulfillment of that better world.

In addition to stylistic consistency, a distinctive directorial voice may be detected in recurring motifs and thematic preoccupations on the basis that a director's personal vision of the world is embodied in his or her total oeuvre, irrespective of the type of film. What Sarris terms "interior meaning" can be expressed in a brief moment or sequence in a film, and there are such moments in Daves's work. In *Broken Arrow*, the delicacy of emotions is encapsulated as Daves's camera gracefully follows the American Indian maiden stepping out from the river, walking toward, and silently lying down beside the white hero, where they declare their love and happiness. In the background, majestic bluffs and mesas rise up against the blue sky, taking on the force of immutable moral principles set against the racist hatred of many white settlers. It is this same landscape that provides the background to the credits for *Drum Beat*, in which a former Indian fighter gains a deeper understanding of the culture and history of another race and reconsiders his long-held instincts that it should be vanquished. The hero's violent actions in the opening scene of *The Last Wagon* take place against the same imposing geological features and set in motion the events that highlight the ethical issue of the tension between justice and the rigidity of man-made laws.

In *The Hanging Tree*, a fast tracking shot follows a woman out of a cabin to the cliff edge after her sight has been restored, emphasizing her isolation from the mining community. In *Task Force* (1949), the loneliness of command is conveyed by a slow dissolve to a long shot of an officer in silhouette against the moonlight and lengthening shadows, walking alone toward the camera along the length of an aircraft carrier. A sustained tracking shot along a Pasadena, California, street in *The Very Thought of You* captures the initial shyness of a young couple who have just met and also observes their increasing confidence and warmth as they relax in each other's company. *3:10 to Yuma* is memorable for moments of delicate and discreet eroticism, seen in the understated but sustained love between a married couple and the intense sexual attraction between a murderer and a saloon girl. With minimum dialogue, both tenderness and longing are implied through the exchange of looks and facial expressions in close-up. Although just one brief encounter, the latter relationship is profound in the feelings awakened in the characters, and their farewell is moving in its openness and lack of regret. The poignancy of the moment is conveyed in the powerful reverse crane shot as the stagecoach moves away, leaving the woman standing alone in the street, one senses with her view of her life irreversibly changed: "Some men you see every day for ten years and never notice. Some men you see once and they're with you the rest of your life." This scene exemplifies Daves's ability to evoke the joys of desire with great feeling and simplicity. Equally tender is the final scene in *Dark Passage* as hero and heroine are reunited: as she approaches him in the restaurant, he rises, and without speaking they take each other in their arms and, as Tavernier notes, begin dancing to the music "Too Marvelous for Words."[134]

However, Daves may also be so judged on the extent to which his work is more than the sum of memorable moments. Screenwriter Cesare Zavattini argues that "the artist's task is not to make people moved or indignant . . . but to make them reflect . . . on what they and others are doing," and that this requires "a search for the most deeply hidden human values."[135] While Daves has commented on the importance of accuracy with regard to aspects of locale and period, he has also referred to his intention to tell stories with elements of universality that examine ideas and values that are timeless.[136] In imposing his personality and ideals on his material, Daves does not merely reflect the conventions of Hollywood in the 1940s and 1950s but challenges the boundaries of acceptability demanded by the Hollywood Production

Code of that period. In so doing, his representation of America and the values inherent in these images evince a consistent and principled moral vision and notion of personal integrity that anticipate social, political, and intellectual developments yet to impact fully on society's mores.

THE PROGRESSIVE VISION OF DELMER DAVES

While the demands of the studio system did act to temper the potency of Daves's vision, Carter and Nelson acknowledge the liberal and progressive elements in his films.[137] Although Daves worked with different screenwriters, John White identifies "a distinct and consistent liberal imprint" in his Westerns. With the use of phrases such as, "Daves (or is this Maltz?) is not unaware," he suggests that Daves may have been strongly influenced by the interests and convictions of screenwriters Albert Maltz and Dalton Trumbo.[138] The Delmer Daves Papers indicate no professional contact with Trumbo until relatively late in Daves's career with *Cowboy*. However, he worked with Maltz on two of his most important early films. Furthermore, Daves asked him to work without credit on the script for *The Red House* because, according to Maltz, "he was the only man in town he [Daves] could trust to work with him easily and do a good job."[139] Therefore, it should not be surprising that Maltz may have had some influence on Daves's view of the world, which, if so, does suggest that Daves, as a declared Republican, remained open to different ideas, in this instance those of a known member of the American Communist Party.

White does accept that Daves could have played a larger role in their screenplays. Interestingly, Daves's son claims that Maltz's final script for *Broken Arrow* was unmanageable and that his father had to undertake substantial revisions without credit, cutting Maltz's 215 pages down to 120 pages.[140] In *Pride of the Marines*, as the Japanese attack is announced on the radio, a puzzled protagonist asks, "Where's Pearl Harbor?" His coworker replies, "Down Jersey coast, near Atlantic City," and his fiancée replies, "I was never very good at geography." This is definitely Maltz's writing: he was critical of schools because "they don't teach geography today as they should," and of an intelligent son of a friend, he commented: "He doesn't know the world in which he lives."[141] The high school teacher in *Spencer's Mountain* reminds her audience of the "opportunities for growth, learning, and achievement" offered by the world outside. This sentiment may reflect Maltz's influence on Daves. However, White also recognizes that it is just as likely that, despite opposing party allegiances, they shared a similar political perspective. There is a consistency of outlook across the wider body of Daves's work, including screenplays he wrote before his association with Maltz. It is noteworthy that, as reported in the Stanford University newspaper, Daves and some fellow students met to form a Liberal Party at Stanford to campaign for greater democracy at the university and to establish principles to which it should adhere.[142] Furthermore, after graduating, he spent several months living with Navajo and Hopi in the Arizona desert. At a conference that discussed the accuracy and significance of the Western genre, including images of Indians,[143] he spoke warmly about this period, a time "of great importance to me" that "filled me with joy,"[144] because of the depth of knowledge and understanding engendered by his experiences and the resulting influence on his work.

While the narratives and themes developed in his films are examined in more detail in the chapters that follow, more generally I argue here that Daves's stories and their exposition reflect his inherent optimism with regard to human potential and for American society, at the heart of which is a belief in the innate worth of fellow human beings. Even as the protagonist in *Dark Passage* is relentlessly pursued, he is able to reflect, "It's better to have something to look forward to." More specifically, Daves's vision is consistent with the political and social ideals of progressivism, which was a movement that had its roots in the 1890s, came to prominence in the years before World War I, and reemerged later in the twentieth century. By the end of the nineteenth century, increasing industrial innovation and factory efficiency were transforming America into a world economic power. Yet prosperity was unevenly distributed, and a sense that the promise of American ideals was unfulfilled was increasingly being articulated by the progressive movement, which campaigned for greater social justice. Focusing on early twentieth-century California progressives, writer George Mowry shows that most were not opposed to the fundamental principles of an economic and industrial system based on capitalism, but rather to the impersonal abuses of the concentration of privilege and monopolistic power and the resulting corruption of public life.[145] Issues of priority included improvement of working conditions, women's employment, child labor, and alleviation of poverty. Furthermore, the reforming spirit of the progressive movement impacted the arts. The fictionalized, collectivist utopia in Edward Bellamy's *Looking Backward* (1887) inspired a vogue for utopian and dystopian literature. The theme of Frank Norris's *The Octopus* (1901) is the titanic struggle between the wheat farmers in the San Joaquin Valley of California and the powerful railroad company that controlled transportation and ruthlessly exploited its monopolistic power.

In their analysis of Hollywood films as social criticism, Terry Christensen and Peter Haas show that early silent films that coincided with the rise of the progressive movement were willing to criticize aspects of contemporary life.[146] *The Ex-Convict* (1905) treated crime as a social problem, *The Eviction* (1907) condemned ruthless landlords, and *The Politicians* (1915) exposed corruption in political party machinery. Christensen and Haas go on to argue that this willingness was further demonstrated in the 1930s, with films such as *I Am a Fugitive from a Chain Gang* (1932) and also *Our Daily Bread* (1934), which highlighted effects of the Depression. Similarly, with the decline of the Code's influence and with more liberal issues gaining political attention, 1966–1976 is a period when films became more critical of American society. Earlier, films tended to portray a confident society with definite values, and these films therefore tended to reassure rather than question. Specifically, Joan Mellen writes that in the 1950s, "Hollywood conformed to the orthodoxy of the moment," and films were devoted "to the glorification and reinforcement of individual success and crass material gain, and to the most straitlaced adherence to puritan values."[147] This tendency may be regarded as reflecting postwar optimism and confidence in America as an economic, industrial, and military global power; J. Ronald Oakley concludes that many Americans during the 1950s were satisfied with themselves and viewed their country as the greatest in the world, and a very good place to live.[148]

However, Oakley goes on to point out that if the 1950s was the best decade in the history of the republic, this was true primarily for white, middle-class Americans and in particular for white males. He emphasizes the paradox of increasing prosperity and great poverty, pride in the ideals of democracy and equality alongside the practice of racial and sexual discrimination, as well as the glorification of family values while there was evidence of increasing marital breakdown and changing moral attitudes. President Dwight Eisenhower was hesitant about the advancement of civil rights, urging that African and Native Americans should show greater patience[149] and taking decisive action only when federal authority was challenged directly, such as with refusal in Arkansas to admit Black students to segregated white schools.

With respect to gender issues, despite the fact that, post-1945, many women were forced to leave wartime employment, by 1952 economic expansion increased the demand for low-paid workers in service, sales, and office employment, and such jobs when filled by women generally did not interfere with their domestic roles. In the main, it was higher-paying, more responsible jobs that had been lost to them. Thus, Oakley notes, 1950s Hollywood portrayed women stereotypically as being happy with their domestic role or content with undemanding employment until they got married.[150] Also, William Chafe observes that most Hollywood films celebrated a male culture of courage, strength, and decisiveness[151] at a time when Arthur Schlesinger Jr. discusses "the decline of the American male" and an uncertainty as to how men could assert their masculinity.[152] Furthermore, Chafe writes that central to the political environment in which such issues arose was an intense anticommunist hysteria.[153] Declining box-office receipts and increased pressure for consensus and conformity resulted in a significant reduction in the number of films that dealt with serious social issues or controversial subject matter.

The central tenets of the progressive agenda in the postwar years, and of the Progressive Party led by Henry Wallace, emphasized both the importance of labor movements in serving the interests of working people and the end of Jim Crow laws in the South, advocating the values of racial equality and social justice. Also, Clayton Koppes notes that as President Franklin Roosevelt's secretary of agriculture, Wallace expressed appreciation for Native American spiritual life and community ideals.[154] The Progressive Party also proposed women's equality in the workplace, in terms of opportunities and compensation. It rejected the concept of American hegemony and advocated greater global cooperation to solve the problems of hunger and inequality. It was during this period that Daves directed his thirty feature films that were confined to traditional Hollywood genres. Daves was a Republican, but in the late 1940s and early 1950s polls indicated that Progressive ideas and propositions attracted the support of 15 to 20 percent of the population, irrespective of party loyalty. Arthur Link and Richard McCormick conclude that the "essence of Progressivism lay in the hopefulness and optimism which the reformers brought to ... the high moral purposes in which they believed."[155] In the same way, Daves's films, within the framework of traditional genres, defied the tendency toward conformity, focusing explicitly and implicitly on contentious political and social issues and evincing a strong faith in progress and justice.

A common criticism of Daves's work is that the endings of several of his films are weak, disconcerting, or illogically happy in relation to preceding events.[156] In the novel on which *Youngblood Hawke* is based, the hero's acute pneumonia proves fatal, and ruthless businessmen profit from his writing. However, in Daves's film, the character survives and finds happiness with a woman who maintains her love for him despite his dishonorable behavior. At the conclusion of *3:10 to Yuma*, a killer rejects the opportunity for certain escape, saves the life of his captor, and allows himself to be taken to prison. Bosley Crowther describes this as incongruous,[157] just as he finds the conversion of the cynical black marketeer protagonist to patriotic hero in *To* the *Victor* to be artificial and contrived.[158] Thus, for a number of critics, the impact of the sincere intentions at the center of Daves's work is diminished. In presenting American Indians as sympathetic human beings, *Broken Arrow* has been regarded as influential in transforming cinematic attitudes toward Native Americans. However, M. Elise Marubbio argues that the killing of the hero's Indian bride is too convenient, just as the Apache chief is portrayed as a figure of intelligence and honor only in ways that make him acceptable to white audiences.[159]

Screenwriter Albert Maltz believed that the ending of *Pride of the Marines*, imposed by Daves, was too conventional and was "spoiling an honest film with a dishonest ending,"[160] in avoiding the issue of the continued severity of the difficulties faced by those with disabilities such as blindness. It is possible that such decisions were in part commercial, made in the belief that happy or hopeful endings are more popular with audiences than those that are downbeat. However, Maltz accepted that the incident when the hero partially recognizes the shape and color of a taxi did actually occur. At that time of the incident, his sight was severely impaired, with limited vision in one eye only, and even this deteriorated quickly until he became totally blind. Similarly, while the reconciliation of an estranged couple with children in *The Battle of the Villa Fiorita* may be consistent with the Production Code's precepts, the return of an adulterer to her husband is more ambiguous with regard to long-term prospects for the happiness of the family. Andrew Howe notes that the fictional Commander Jonathan Scott in *Task Force* expounded similar views about the importance of military air power as Brigadier General Billy Mitchell, who served during World War I.[161] He suggests that Daves was able to make the story palatable for audiences, providing a happy ending in which Scott is praised, unlike Mitchell, who was court-martialed and died before the accuracy of his views on air warfare and the Japanese threat to Pearl Harbor became clear. To view Scott as a stand-in for Mitchell is a reasonable assumption. However, in his preparatory interviews with navy personnel, Daves pinpointed Rear Admiral Clarence Wade McClusky, a naval aviator and hero of the Battle of Midway, as "an excellent prototype for our lead."[162] Certainly there are similarities in the age, experience, and naval service records of Scott and McClusky.

Mowry emphasizes that central to the Progressive manifesto was the belief in the fundamental goodness of the individual, that evil could be overcome so that good may triumph.[163] Despite the tragic events in his novel *The Octopus*, ultimately Frank Norris is hopeful: "Greed, cruelty, selfishness, and inhumanity are short-lived. . . . [A]ll things, surely, inevitably, resistlessly work together for good."[164] This optimism is encapsulated in the hero's voice-over narration at the end of *Drum Beat*, which recognizes that although the struggle for peace would be difficult, it would cost "plenty" and leave "scars," it is achievable. "It showed the country something it had to learn; that among the Indians as among our people, the good outnumber the bad." In *Broken Arrow*, Cochise's thoughts and General Howard's words of comfort for Jeffords express optimism that tragedy will persuade antagonists to reexamine their beliefs and actions: "Your very loss has brought our people together and the will to peace. Without that will, treaties are worth little or nothing." Specifically, the townspeople's acceptance that the white racists responsible for a senseless killing of an Indian maiden must be brought to justice was obviously radical in terms of nineteenth-century values, but it was also an important statement in the context of mid-twentieth-century racial attitudes and events.

While Sarah Pearsall acknowledges the significance of *Broken Arrow* in Hollywood's representation of racial diversity, she goes on to criticize the film for its portrayal of an American Indian bride as a good 1950s housewife who is content to prepare food, wash, and clean for her husband.[165] Indeed, Yves Kovacs writes that despite some exceptions, Westerns represent gender in a conventional manner, with women generally reduced to a passive, virtuous, and angelic role, and describes Felicia Farr's roles in Daves's Westerns as little more than prizes for male warriors.[166] However, I propose that Daves focuses on the intolerance of those who adhere strictly and without compassion to traditional beliefs. Even in his early scripts, he expresses a less conventional viewpoint, and images of masculine and feminine roles are less stereotypical than has been suggested. Furthermore, in his later, largely ignored films, his advocacy of greater understanding and compassion for those who experience family or relationship difficulties began to challenge Hollywood's usual presentation of gender roles and expectations.

Included in the Delmer Daves Papers is a list of philosophers' reflections on "goodness," including those of Confucius, Seneca, and Cicero. A quotation by sixteenth-century philosopher and statesman Francesco Guicciardini—"There is no evil in human affairs that has not some good mingled with it"[167]—encapsulates the core of Daves's beliefs, just as in his preparatory notes for *The Last Wagon*, he writes that the story is about "the bad man becoming a good man in the eyes of those who hated him intensely."[168] Crowther finds *To the Victor* distasteful because of the despicable nature and actions of the black marketeer and collaborator protagonists.[169] Certainly the postwar cynicism of the majority of the characters is highlighted by Taggart (Dennis Morgan), who dismisses the bravery and commitment that brought about the "empty victory" of World War II and ridicules wartime hopes and promises as "some tomorrow." He is heavily involved in the black market of postwar Paris with the highest profit his only motive, whatever the aims or scruples of those with whom he deals. His relationships with women are equally amoral: "Did you care who the woman was?" He agrees to help Christine (Viveca Lindfors), who is attempting to escape from surviving Nazis who wish to prevent her from testifying against her traitorous husband, but only because she is attractive. However, the film emphasizes the potential and the importance of moral redemption. There are mere hints at the suffering Christine had endured that compelled her to collaborate, but her courage and integrity, and her honesty in admitting her misdeeds, force Taggart to examine his own actions and conscience and reawaken in him a sense of purpose and direction. This transformation is fully realized when the couple escapes to Normandy and their love is acknowledged, framed by the wreckage of invasion and symbols of sacrifice on Omaha Beach.

There are very few unambiguous villains in Daves's films, and the few who exist tend to be exaggerated and unconvincing. Pinky in *Jubal* is an obvious example. Overall, characters exhibit little evidence of outright evil but rather conduct themselves in response to social or political circumstances and resulting prejudices. In *The Hanging Tree*, the protagonist is secretive, exploitative, and egotistical, and he demonstrates ruthlessness in his repeated shooting of Frenchy. Because of his behavior, his wife leaves him for his brother, whom he then kills after her suicide. Yet he also shows tenderness, loyalty, and courage and readily disregards the puritanical gossip about his relationship with the blind heroine and when helping a prostitute, allowing her to die with dignity, despite protests. Frenchy is crude and lecherous but is a skilled and conscientious worker and is clearly an uneducated product of his environment. The tribal chief in *Drum Beat* is a vicious killer, but he displays pride in his race and culture and does not regret his attempts to defend his homeland, whatever violence that might involve. In *3:10 to Yuma*, the killer's attraction to a barmaid and his demonstration of tenderness hint at his increasing dissatisfaction with his violent existence, and his yearning for a different life becomes clearer as the film progresses. In this sense, his sudden submission to justice may represent an existential decision to begin life anew. In *A Summer Place*, Bart is an inadequate husband and an embarrassment to his family. He uses binoculars to spy on others, and he is an alcoholic. However, there are hints of an earlier, more purposeful time in his life. He speaks French fluently and cleverly exposes another character's pretentious usage of the language. He recalls with pride using his binoculars during his wartime service in the navy, and, in a poignant sequence as he leaves to go to the hospital, where he will die a lonely death, he puts on his old navy uniform in remembrance of a more honorable past. In the same film, Helen is overzealous and hysterical, and her treatment of her daughter could be interpreted as vicarious sexual abuse. Nevertheless, Daves noted that "Helen has to show a human side."[170] She genuinely wants her daughter to have opportunities denied to herself, but she is overbearing and selfish in the way she behaves.

Daves's stories are about physical or spiritual regeneration and redemption, and how characters can be fulfilled and benefit their community as well be served by a society that has the potential for tolerance and benevolence. His films focus on the innate goodness of humans and their potential to make the world a better place, bringing together communities and individuals separated by prejudice and intolerance. The chapters that follow argue that his examination of bigotry and irrational fear, and his vision of institutional and personal morality and freedom, enabled him to present a consistent and revisionist exploration of themes associated with traditional Hollywood genres, which in turn testify to the presence of an individual artist and filmmaker with a distinct and coherent vision.

CHAPTER TWO

Political and Social Values in the Films of Delmer Daves

PRODUCED DURING WORLD WAR II AND THE COLD WAR ERA THAT FOLLOWED, Delmer Daves's films examine, either directly or implicitly, the political and social issues of the times. To support President Roosevelt's conviction that Hollywood could make a useful contribution to the war effort, studios submitted scripts to the Office of War Information (OWI) for approval and followed the guidance provided. It was expected that films should affirm a sense of national purpose and convey an understanding of the reasons for the Allies going to war. Films emphasized the need for commitment, decisive action, and unity rather than an advocacy of isolationism and even Anglophobia common in prewar films. Good Germans are distinguished from evil Nazis, and in *Mission to Moscow* (1943), Russia is shown to be governed by a benign and avuncular Stalin. The conflict tended to be portrayed as a "people's war" with images of the courage of ordinary and united people at home and at the front, working together and willing to make sacrifices for ultimate victory. While the overall tone and substance of Daves's wartime films concurred with such sentiments, his films were less stereotypical and jingoistic than was usual with regard to the portrayal of enemies and the experiences of those in conflict and at home. Furthermore, the postwar resurgence of conservatism and intolerance of dissent that impacted Hollywood's output is not evidenced in Daves's body of work.

DAVES'S CONTRIBUTION TO THE GENRE OF MILITARIST MUSICALS

Militarist musicals were designed to reinforce the moral certainty of American policies as well as providing enjoyable entertainment for audiences at home and serving abroad. *This Is the Army* (1943) and *Up in Arms* (1944) were typical in emphasizing the respect in which the armed forces were held and in featuring a parade of popular stars, lighthearted military comedy, sentimental ballads, and well-drilled marching to patriotic songs. Daves's support for the validity of America's participation in World War II is indicated in his screenplay for *Stage Door Canteen* (1943), which narrates the exploits of a group of servicemen in their last few days in New York before leaving to fight overseas. More significantly, Daves wrote and directed *Hollywood Canteen*, which is less synthetic than similar films as it reflects the activities of the actual servicemen's club of that name founded in 1942 by Bette Davis and John Garfield. Centered on the arrival of the millionth serviceman to attend, the film celebrates the work of the club, which offered opportunities for embarking and returning servicemen to mingle and dance with stars, who, as well as providing entertainment, also cleaned, prepared and served food, and raised funds for the wounded. Besides Davis and Garfield, the film featured Jack Benny, Roy Rogers, and Joan Crawford, who also volunteered at the real-life club. Dane Clark, Dennis Morgan, and Eleanor Parker, who had all worked with Daves previously, also featured, and the entertainment included songs by Cole Porter and E. Y. Harburg.

The similarities in the structure and content of *Stage Door Canteen* and *Hollywood Canteen* are obvious, and Daves's screenplays for both films present a similar mix of sentiment, humor, and patriotism. However, directed by Frank Borzage, principally with a static camera and with mainly medium-range shots, *Stage Door Canteen* has little energy or pace; it does little more than record a succession of performances. Thus, Katharine Hepburn's rousing speech about the need to create "that kind of world where we can live in peace and happiness" seems like just one of these performances: it seems out of place amid the music and dancing. In *Hollywood Canteen*, Daves ensures that the viewer feels part of the club's proceedings. His moving camera, particularly in the dance and band sequences, adds excitement and vibrancy to these scenes, and incisive cutting synchronized with the music highlights soloists and sections of the orchestras. Daves effects a smooth transition between comedy, musical numbers, and dialogue between stars and servicemen, with crane shots emphasizing the energy of the dancing and the unity of the patriotic choruses. In contrast, striking close-ups and varied camera angles heighten the impact of lyrics and enhance moments of quiet intimacy, with telling phrases such as "my stomach sort of jumped up into my heart" encapsulating the conflicting senses of enjoyment and inner turmoil experienced by those soon to embark.

The film's patriotic message is integral to the musical performances rather than an awkward addition. Dennis Morgan, singing "You Can Always Tell a

Yank," asserts that "what makes a nation as great as the USA" is a determination "to defend a thing called democracy and save the world from tyranny." He invites the members to join in, and Daves's camera moves throughout the audience, showing servicemen of different races singing these words together and with enthusiasm. Although whites represent the majority, Latino, Asian American, and African American soldiers sing alongside them. On the film's release, critic Kate Cameron accused Daves of showing a lack of restraint or humor throughout.[1] Certainly for the modern viewer, the repetition of phrases such as "I think you're wonderful, Miss Davis" and "Imagine me standing right here and talking to Barbara Stanwyck" may seem irritating, although this does reflect the awe in which stars were held at that time. However, other than some rather mawkish moments such as when a soldier "romances" Joan Leslie, his "dream girl," the typical sentimentality that characterized such films is restrained, with the respect for those in harm's way conveyed with simplicity and dignity by Bette Davis's final words, spoken directly to the camera: "Wherever you go, our hearts go with you."

The patriotic sentiments of *Hollywood Canteen* are more temperate and meaningful than in most films in this genre, notably in terms of recognition of different groups of Americans, and the dry sense of humor in much of the dialogue reflects Daves's style of writing in many of his films. Reviews of his early screenplays identified a sense of humor as a strong virtue,[2] and Bosley Crowther's review of *Return of the Texan* (1952) notes its sincere direction and considerable consistency of humor and charm.[3] Similarly, the fast-paced and sparkling dialogue in *You Were Never Lovelier* (1942), particularly spoken by Adolphe Menjou, remains fresh and witty to a modern audience. However, instances of Daves's humor were criticized on the grounds of taste. Alvah Bessie, his cowriter on *The Very Thought of You*, censured his insertion of "off-color gags,"[4] an example being a scene in which two wartime servicemen and their girlfriends are staying in a motel. The protagonist describes a room as only functional, to which the other's girlfriend replies, "For what I need it, it functions fine." A similar instance occurs in *Destination Tokyo*, in which John Garfield plays a submarine crew member who boasts regularly about his success with women. When recalling one supposed encounter, he jokes, "The minute I saw her I says, 'up periscope!'" For this time, such dialogue was rather risqué and, as expressed by a main character, could be deemed close to defying the dictates of the Production Code with regard to portrayal of sexual matters. Yet there is a sense that this is the dialogue of "real" people, women as well as men, particularly during the uncertainty and loneliness of wartime, and such talk also contributes to the presentation of multilayered characters. One review of *The Very Thought of You* commented on "the diary-like insight into how today's people feel and what they do."[5] Cameron's comment that *Hollywood Canteen* maintains a patronizing manner echoes a more disdainful view of the stars' efforts, expressed by a soldier in combat: "It was as though we'd been taken into a millionaire's home, treated like uncouth fools . . . then sent back, dazed by the splendorous kindliness of the mighty."[6] However, Cameron also notes the gracious and welcoming nature the film shows, and it is the presence of the stars as "real people" that distinguishes this film from others in the genre. As a result, the words spoken by a soldier about the importance of democracy, as exemplified in "big shots listening to little shots," carry conviction; the film is more overt than most in this genre about the nature of the better society for which war was being waged.

DISTINCTIVE FEATURES OF THE WARTIME FILMS OF DELMER DAVES

Daves's early screenplays are supportive of the role and conduct of America's armed forces. A review of *Flirtation Walk* writes of audiences "howling with patriotic fervor,"[7] and John Davis refers to this film, *Miss Pacific Fleet* (1935), and *Shipmates Forever* (1935) as recruiting posters for the navy.[8] He describes *Destination Tokyo* as "an adventure in applied Americanism": significantly, it was made with full navy cooperation. However, Daves's films also present a more realistic and balanced view of wartime experiences. Daves referred to *Hollywood Canteen* as "a work of charity rather than a proper film,"[9] with the profits used to help wounded veterans. His attitude may in part be due to the blocking of his original intentions, which did not shirk the reality of fatalities and serious injuries. His first draft of the screenplay begins amid the pain and horror of jungle combat and has specific instructions for the camera to cut to shots of weary and wounded servicemen.[10] Sherrie Tucker shows that the OWI objected to such scenes,[11] and instead, the film begins with aerial shots of Hollywood as the camera closes in on servicemen assembling by the canteen's entrance. His first draft also had directions to show men and women of color dancing and relaxing in each other's company, and included a scene with Humphrey Bogart and Dooley Wilson performing together. However, the PCA discouraged the inclusion of some scenes that could be interpreted as advocating equality in social relations between races.

While Daves's intention to portray the activities of the club in the context of such truths was frustrated, his resolve is evidenced in his other wartime films. He believed that he had contributed to the introduction of a documentary style to Hollywood: his wartime films demonstrate this approach, and he may be considered an innovator in this regard.[12] One review of *Task Force* notes that Daves captures the tension of battle as well as including "eye-filling documentary detail," and that the accuracy of the action sequences places *Task Force* "among the most authentic war pictures ever made."[13] In preparing *Pride of the Marines*, which focuses on the experiences of blinded marine Al Schmid (Garfield) and his fiancée, Ruth (Eleanor Parker), Daves filmed at Schmid's home, place of work, and the station from which he left for war. Also, he researched Schmid's treatment in the hospital, discussing details of his therapy with his doctor and nurse and how he was taught to manage his condition, such as "eating by the clock."[14] While noting that filmmakers were showing an increasing interest in the use of documentary techniques to enhance examination of social themes, Dorothy Jones states that it was not until well over a year after the war that "social document" films appeared, giving William Wyler's *The Best Years of Our Lives* (1946) as an example.[15] In fact, Daves claimed that Wyler showed *Pride of the Marines* to his crew before filming, saying, "Here is the type of film that we should be making."[16]

Daves declared that after viewing the work of British documentary makers' films about the Battle of Britain and the war in the Atlantic, he was determined that in *Destination Tokyo*, the image of warfare at sea should be as realistic as possible.[17] He selected a cast that, apart from Cary Grant and Garfield, was made up of relatively unknown actors, and unusually for a Hollywood film he insisted that the actors wear no make-up. Joe Morella, Edward Epstein, and John Griggs interpret *Destination Tokyo* as a "morale-booster" and a patriotic tribute to the submarine service.[18] Led by Captain Cassidy (Grant), the submarine *Copperfin* leaves San Francisco with secret orders to transport a meteorologist from the Aleutian Islands to Tokyo Bay to gather data in preparation for the Doolittle Raid on Tokyo in 1942. The craft survives an attack by Japanese planes, an unexploded bomb lodged in the deck that has to be defused, and attacks by destroyers with depth charges during which time it sinks an aircraft carrier. Most of the action is confined within the submarine, and despite the film lasting 135 minutes, Daves manages to hold the viewer's attention, with key scenes effectively constructed and directed. Acute tension is created as the submarine passes through a minefield, and the scene in which a pharmacist's assistant performs an emergency appendectomy is appropriately nerve wracking. There is a surfeit of stirring patriotic music and moments of rhetoric and excessive sentiment, such as when the crew exchange Christmas presents and sing carols in perfect harmony.

Nevertheless, *Destination Tokyo* was the first Hollywood film to show, realistically, detailed aspects of on-board submarine life and convey an understanding of the importance of vital technology and the affiliated routines and responsibilities of crew members. Daves's camera positions allow detailed observation of procedures for surfacing and submerging, and for attack and defense, while also focusing on the crew's emotions, ranging from excitement to fear and vulnerability. Based on his own research and time spent on a submarine on active service, Daves supervised the accurate construction of a replica submarine in the studio, which enabled him to show the crew's adaptation to cramped and claustrophobic conditions at times of tension and danger as well as during periods of inaction. This is conveyed by Daves's use of angled shots, which emphasize the low ceilings and generally depict the constant, oppressive sense of the danger of life on a submarine. His level of technical accuracy in the details of submarine warfare resulted in the film being used for training purposes; Robert Eberwein notes that the navy was in fact concerned that the film's oscilloscope shots demonstrated excessive knowledge of the detection devices used.[19] The film helped to establish conventions that were duplicated in future such productions, including attacks by depth charges, the strain of long periods of silence, avoidance of booms and mines, and the use of periscopes in observation and the firing of torpedoes. Alongside technical details, Daves, in his real-life experience, also observed how naval crew members and officers relate to each other in different, difficult situations; Jeanine Basinger highlights the film's emphasis on the concept of family and social existence within the enclosed world of submarine combat.[20] The crew is presented as a group of mixed personalities with different beliefs and roles, but who must work as a cooperative and self-supporting unit for survival, which contrasts with the rugged and heroic individualism that typified Hollywood action films of the time. It is a philosophy that characterizes Daves's body of work.

Frank Wetta and Martin Novelli note that the realism of the battle scenes in *Pride of the Marines* led one contemporary commentator to suggest that it could serve as a training film to demonstrate how to use the .30-caliber machine gun.[21] Bosley Crowther wrote that Daves directed the film "with brilliant pictorial realism and emotional sympathy" and commented on his "masterfully authentic style."[22] Daves's approach also demonstrated a willingness to confront issues of controversy. Bernard Dick identifies Hollywood's "Slap the Jap" policy as characteristic of most American war films of the era,[23] for example portraying Japanese hara-kiri tactics as cowardly, while Americans willing to face death were shown as heroic. Daves portrays the Japanese enemy as intelligent and resourceful rather than almost subhuman.

In *Destination Tokyo*, it is suggested that "big business" had pressured politicians not to interfere with Japan's pre–Pearl Harbor militarization, and *Pride of the Marines* raises issues of unemployment and racism. Even while the war continued, Daves presents instances of low morale: in *Pride of the Marines*, there are complaints about lack of cleanliness, food, and equipment—"no sleep, no food, no mail, no smokes . . . there wasn't enough of anything"—and the central character's motives for enlisting are neither patriotic or noble. One marine's question, "Got any dope?," must be one of earliest cinematic references to the use of drugs to relieve the stress of conflict, a fact not really acknowledged in films until the Vietnam War.

The Very Thought of You does not hide the realities of wartime at home. Brief snatches of dialogue in early scenes focus on a seemingly unpleasant and fractious family, which one contemporary reviewer labeled "one of the most quarrelsome and obnoxious families the screen has spawned."[24] Only Janet (Eleanor Parker) displays commendable qualities. She works in a factory making parachutes, which, although essential work, is ridiculed by her sister Molly—"Where's parachute girl?"—who is having affairs while her husband is fighting abroad. Their brother, Cal, has managed to be declared unfit for active service on dubious grounds, and there are references to his involvement in black market activity that exploits wartime shortages. He complains: "I'm getting tired of turkey." A battle-weary soldier (Dennis Morgan) is made to feel awkward and unwelcome, particularly when Cal expresses a wish that the war should continue because of the opportunities for profit that result. After Molly intercepts the soldier's love letters to Janet from the front line, Janet leaves the family home. Although the romance is the central focus, the film examines the loneliness, insecurities, and temptations of women as the war continued, and the realism of its view of life on the home front is enhanced with location shooting in Pasadena, California.

Task Force adopts a similar approach in narrating the story of the navy from the 1920s to World War II as seen through the naval career of Commander Scott (Gary Cooper). The film focuses on his determined efforts to persuade his reluctant superiors of the importance of naval air power. The eventual success of the airmen is celebrated with a sudden switch to glorious Technicolor with scenes of their combat victories, demonstrated in a skillful merging of actual wartime footage with fictional reconstruction. In fact, there is relatively little combat action: instead, the film focuses on procedures for launching aircraft, the difficulties of safe landing, and the different mechanisms and skills involved in navigation, radar operation, and the tracking of enemy planes and vessels. More importantly, it exposes the political maneuvering that impeded change. Despite a rather verbose screenplay and moments of excessive sentiment as Scott articulates his vision and overcomes obstacles to its realization, *Task Force* starkly reveals how conservatism and entrenched political thinking within government and military bureaucracies can frustrate innovation.

DAVES'S FOCUS ON THE TREATMENT OF VETERANS

As victory in World War II approached, there was growing anxiety about potential threats to social order and stability posed by the sudden demobilization of servicemen. Contemporary sociologist Robert Nisbet, referring to "the lost generation" of men alienated from society after World War I, warned that "it would be folly to minimize the problem that will confront us," as "[p]ersonal adjustment will be difficult in all cases, impossible in some."[25] Attitudes to and treatment of veterans, including those with disabilities resulting from their service, had proved to be a controversial issue after World War I. Many ex-servicemen experienced unemployment and poverty and were reduced to begging, with veterans' anger encapsulated in the song "Brother, Can You Spare a Dime?" In 1932, marchers from all over America, including many disabled veterans, congregated in Washington to demand the early payment of World War I bonuses promised by Congress, as compensation for wages lost during their service. The Senate rejected the veterans' requests for recognition and help, and their demonstrations were put down by armed soldiers on presidential direction.

While wartime films did not ignore the reality of casualties, their focus tended to be on the bravery and nobility of soldiers' necessary sacrifice, with little attention to the resulting difficulties. Daves's concern for this issue is evidenced in the folder of newspaper reports and unemployment statistics in his papers,[26] and is reflected in his films. The hero in *The Go-Getter* (1937) has had a leg amputated after an accident while on active service. In the story on which the film is based, the difficulties he faces are encompassed in one line: "I haven't had a very good time the past three years."[27] However, Daves's screenplay develops this theme with reference made to the inadequacy of disability pensions for those who served in the armed forces. He focuses on the difficulties that the protagonist experiences in finding employment in San Francisco when jobs were scarce. Some rejections are polite, but others are more brutal: "You're a cripple." In *Pride of the Marines*, one serviceman remembers that his father was forced to sell apples on street corners, while another insists that there must be "no more wars ... no apples, no bonus marches."

Daves examines the issue of disabled veterans in *Pride of the Marines*, in which the protagonist, Al Schmid, is blinded during the American campaign to occupy Guadalcanal in the Solomon Islands and secure supply routes to Australia and New Zealand. The film focuses on the fears and uncertainties of combatants and anticipates the problems of readjustment when "all soldiers come back different," particularly those with serious injuries. Thomas Doherty writes that *The Best Years of Our Lives* is the first close look at a disabled American in mainstream Hollywood cinema.[28] However, the problems of readjustment and the difficulties in reestablishing a relationship are clearly anticipated in Daves's film. The words of the veteran in Wyler's film, "All I want is for people to treat me like anyone else, instead of pitying me," directly echo Schmid's worry about his fiancée, whether "she'll pity me." Harold Russell, double amputee and actor in *The Best Years of Our Lives*, remembers: "When the war was over, disabled vets would be a dime a dozen"; and further, "I lay awake for hours ... hoping against hope ... [h]ow could any woman love a cripple?"[29] In Daves's film, the marines express deeply felt concern not only for their domestic life but also for their employment prospects after the war. Daves captures the mood of uncertainty and anxiety in the convalescent ward as the wounded discuss their hopes and fears for the future. One marine reflects, "Now that I'm going home, I'm scared. I wasn't half as scared on Guadalcanal as I am now."

Although Martin Halliwell feels that Daves resorts to homespun sentimentality, he acknowledges that his representation of the experience of such injuries and their treatment is entirely realistic, with audiences for the first time made aware of the medical consequences of modern warfare, with details of hospitalization and rehabilitation.[30] The film captures the sense of disorientation experienced by such veterans; research indeed suggests that even 78 percent of veterans *without* physical disabilities experience severe adjustment difficulties.[31] Daves powerfully dramatizes Schmid's sense of isolation and loss of self-respect, which cause him to feel that he would be a burden to friends and to his fiancée, Ruth. In this regard, the attitude of family is a crucial dimension in a veteran's adjustment, as made clear by George Pratt, a wartime army psychiatric examiner, writing that one of the most distressing adjustment problems is fear of rejection by family: "[T]hey cannot wholly rid themselves of the horrid fear that perhaps these persons will now find them repulsive and that as a consequence their affections may cool."[32] *Pride of the Marines* is notable for its focus not only on the physical disability of blindness but also on the psychological effects of injuries and the level of support for veterans, with research indicating that 40 percent of casualties at Guadalcanal suffered from "neuro-mental" conditions.[33]

This represents a significant departure from Roger Butterfield's biography of Schmid, from which the film was adapted.[34] Virtually three-quarters of Butterfield's account details Schmid's life before his loss of sight, including his earlier life in Philadelphia as a foundry worker, his developing relationship with Ruth, and the early battles with the Japanese. There are few references to his medical treatment, with mention made only of the removal of shrapnel from one eye and the need for the doctors to persuade him of the importance of removing his left eye.

The film presents a detailed and authentic depiction of the rehabilitative treatment that Schmid received in the San Diego hospital, as an exemplar of the medical attention that a veteran deserves in an enlightened society. In her major study of the social history of blindness in America, Frances Koestler argues that American policies for preparing men blinded in World War I for future productive lives compared unfavorably with those of Great Britain and its empire, where specific and more generous resources enhanced rehabilitative and residential care, which enabled men to "learn to be blind."[35] She contends that American provision was less generous in disability compensation and less sensitive to the difficulties and traumas experienced by men with such wounds. The Bonus Marches provided testimony to the inadequacy of preexisting policies, and Daves's film reflects the more progressive, interventionist approach beginning to be developed during World War II. This involved initial steps taken in the hospital toward learning independence in eating, walking, and dressing and then beginning the use of special devices for reading and writing, followed by care in a rehabilitation center for intensive vocational retraining. The film illustrates the importance of a caring and supportive ethos in attempting to alleviate the despondency common to newly blinded veterans, and also of psychological support to encourage optimism, but also the need for firm, high expectations within a full program to leave little time for self-pity. Schmid proves to be a difficult and reluctant patient, but as well as a caring ethos, the film emphasizes a tolerant but firm approach, as adopted by the doctors and the nurse, Virginia Pfeiffer: "I want to say something important too, straight and tough," consistent with a more purposeful treatment of injured veterans.

The important roles of the nurse and Ruth in the film lead Halliwell to conclude that such films may be enlightened with regard to the implications of serious injuries, but "their gender politics reveal blind spots" in showing how therapy is removed from the hospital into the home, particularly with the restorative power of love suggested.[36] After providing care for Schmid, Pfeiffer writes to Ruth: "I've done my part; now it's up to you," and Ruth does seem to exhibit the devotional female characteristics needed for the task, as indicated in her expression of pride when Schmid is awarded the Navy Cross. John Bodnar also develops this view from a feminist perspective, arguing that films such as *Pride of the Marines* and *The Best Years of Our Lives* place the responsibility for veterans' welfare not in the hands of the government or society but in the hands of loved ones who can render care and understanding.[37] Although the war had brought newfound opportunities to women, there was an expectation that they should be willing, when needed, to sacrifice any personal ambitions in order to support the physical and emotional security of veterans. Social historian Sonya Michel highlights the efforts by social workers and the military to advocate the importance of women taking responsibility for veterans' readjustment, particularly those with psychiatric behavioral difficulties. She notes that wartime nurseries and after-school programs that enabled women to work were closed immediately after hostilities ceased, and she concludes that, for women, "the legacy of WWII was not a set of permanent social entitlements, but instead a cluster of new social and psychological family responsibilities."[38]

While Daves's film does not provide a riposte to this interpretation, there is a significant shift in tone when compared with earlier films such as *Random Harvest* (1942), which focuses entirely on the love story rather than the effects of shell shock and combat fatigue. Daves is reflecting a broadly accepted expectation that a badly injured man would be supported by his wife and that adaptation in their domestic circumstances would result. Indeed, David Gerber refers to interviews with blinded veterans who testified to the strong debt they owed to their wives for emotional and practical support.[39] Significantly, however, Daves shows that while love and care are important, excessive sympathy or pity may impede the regaining of independence and self-reliance. This approach is encapsulated in Pratt's advice to families that, where possible, the injured man should resume the performance of activities formerly pursued; above all, "[d]on't absolve him from all duties and responsibilities and ... do not make him dependent."[40] Even when Schmid grows more content and willing to return to Philadelphia with Ruth, and as the film moves toward a happy ending, Nurse Pfeiffer urges him: "Don't stop fighting Al, don't." Ruth assails him with the accusation, "You want to be helpless," and challenges him to "show enough pride to face the truth," to accept the challenge of his injuries and thus reduce his dependence on her. Ruth accepts that the direction of her life to a large extent will be dictated by Schmid's condition, and, importantly, this is what actually happened with the real-life couple. Furthermore, with greater female participation in active service, and in harm's way, in more recent times, it is probable that the male partner of an injured female veteran would be prepared to make such adjustments, and it is unlikely that society would judge that his position in his relationship had been emasculated. It is only more recently that such a scenario has been tentatively explored, in *Home of the Brave* (2006), in which a young woman, after an explosion during her service in Iraq has resulted in the amputation of an arm, returns home and forms a relationship with a male schoolteacher who has not served abroad. Such a scenario is anticipated in *Pride of the Marines*, when Ruth asks Schmid if he would abandon her if it had been she that was disabled.

The essence of the interpretations propounded by Bodnar and Halliwell is that such stories do not pose political or cultural questions about societal attitudes and values. Referring to the work of Sonya Michel, Halliwell suggests that the "problem" of veterans points to the failure of the political system to protect all its citizens.[41] Therefore, in emphasizing the importance of family as well as the individual, the responsibility of society is diminished, with the danger that such stories are reduced to a narrative of "'sick soldier' versus 'healthy society.'"[42] In this sense, Schmid's reaction to his blindness is more of a problem than the blindness itself. He is responsible for his isolation from friends and family while he remains defiant in his resentment and bitterness. He is aggressive with doctors, spurns help from staff, and refuses to return to Ruth, fearing that she will reject him. He throws away his braille alphabet and thwarts the hospital staff's attempts to teach him to feed himself. He is properly "adjusted" and can look forward to the future only when he realizes that his place is in the family and when he accepts Ruth's love, encapsulated in the last line in the film, in which he instructs the taxi driver to drive home.

While Daves's film can be analyzed in this way, societal responsibility does not escape examination. The servicemen express concern not only about going home to wives and families but also about their standing in society and whether their service and sacrifice will be forgotten. As they discuss their worries and aspirations in the film, they hope that their experience will be different, that conditions will not return to the inequities of the 1930s, and that particularly through measures such as the provisions of the GI Bill, there will be no impediments to equal opportunity for all in postwar America: "Don't tell me we can't make it work in peace like we do in war.... We need a country to live in where nobody is booted around for any reason." In the hospital scenes, Daves portrays the quality of care and treatment that the government should provide in reality, and Koestler shows that provision for the 1,400 American servicemen blinded in the European and Pacific war zones indeed improved, with hospitals in Pennsylvania and California designated to provide immediate specialized medical treatment for blinded veterans.[43] However, particular concerns remained. Lee Diamond, Schmid's

Jewish friend, warns him that he may experience prejudice: "Sure, there'll be guys who won't hire you even when they know you can handle a job." The film exposes the complacency of official statements such as, "There is hardly a community or an industry that is not cooperating in ... giving the break [veterans] have earned,"[44] and it recognizes the reality of a *New York Times* report of 1945 that refers to the lack of business opportunities and support networks for returning veterans.[45]

In *Washington Merry-Go-Round* (1932), a politician is asked to address the Bonus Marchers. Although a veteran himself, he condemns their actions as unpatriotic and urges greater personal responsibility and patience. There is no such caution in *Pride of the Marines*: a marine vows to enter politics, insisting that "when I get back into civilian life, if I don't like the way things are going ... I'll stand on my own two legs and holler. If there are enough of us hollering, we'll go places." The film celebrates improvements in government action and medical care but also emphasizes the need for the support of community employers. Daves's screenplay for *Stranded* (1935) indicates that the voluntary sector was inadequate to meet the needs of the poor and unemployed, and his preparatory notes for *The Go-Getter* and *The Stuff of Heroes* (1940) include details of unsatisfactory housing provided by the private sector and inadequate pensions for the disabled.[46] While Daves does not present an overt challenge to conventional American political assumptions, he does consider the consequences of an unfeeling and illiberal implementation of social and economic practices.

POSTWAR HOLLYWOOD: RESPONSES TO THE COLD WAR

Following from the above, Paul Carter's criticism with regard to wartime films, that "Hollywood has always been chicken-hearted about social and political controversy,"[47] should not be levied at Daves's films. Carter's view that "[t]he Cold War reinforced these intrinsic tendencies" is equally inapplicable. America emerged from World War II as the world's supreme economic and military power, but with the rapid disintegration of wartime alliances and the challenge to America's monopoly of the atomic bomb, the Soviet Union was soon perceived as a threat to the nation's security. This was enhanced by Soviet policies in Eastern Europe, the rise of Communist China, and the exposure of Soviet spies in America and Britain. It was this postwar suspicion and fear that led to a series of House Un-American Activities Committee (HUAC) investigations into potential communist infiltration into a range of areas of American society that included unions, government departments, universities, and the arts. This campaign perhaps reached its zenith in 1950, when Wisconsin senator Joseph McCarthy claimed that he had proof of communist infiltration in the US State Department, encapsulating historian Bruce Jentleson's conclusion that "[t]he whole country was consumed with paranoia."[48]

More significantly and perhaps deliberately, McCarthyism confused those who may have had nefarious motives with a far greater number of people who were involved in the constitutionally guaranteed activity of free speech. Jentleson observes that as a result, the manner in which anticommunism was pursued "took a profound toll on civil liberties and created an environment inimical to the openness of a democratic society."[49] Those investigated included members of the Hollywood Anti-Nazi League as well as liberals, advocates for civil rights, feminists, pacifist groups, and New Dealers. Often ignoring the rules of evidence or the constitutional rights of witnesses, communist witch hunts led to the blacklisting of government officials, union officials, university professors, and scientists. In 1951, as president of the Screen Actors Guild, Ronald Reagan claimed that "the real aim of the Communist Party is to try to prepare the way for Russian conquest of the world."[50] This conviction impacted on filmmaking and the treatment of Hollywood personnel.

Russell Shain notes that between 1948 and 1962, there was a consistent anticommunist focus in the 104 Hollywood films he identifies that deal with aspects of the Cold War.[51] Films such as *The Iron Curtain* (1948), *I Married a Communist* (1949), and *I Was a Communist for the FBI* (1951) focus on Soviet plots to obtain atomic secrets, spread dissension and disruption by instigating industrial strikes and racial riots, and use sex to blackmail young men into working for the party to undermine the American way of life. Perhaps the film that is most noted for its anticommunist paranoia is *Big Jim McLain* (1952), in which John Wayne, playing an FBI agent, foils a plot to bring Hawaiian shipping and communications to a state of paralysis. The original rationale for the Production Code was to ensure that mass entertainment was moderated by morality and decency, but by 1947 its scope had been extended. The Motion Picture Alliance for the Preservation of American Ideals (MPA), with Walt Disney as vice president, declared that films should not smear the free enterprise system, industrialists, wealth, or the profit motive. In addition, the MPA emphasized: "Don't smear success.... America is the land of the self-made man," nor glorify the collective or "deify the 'common man'... the phrase is one of the worst slogans of communism."[52] Such edicts had a chilling effect on the content and tone of mainstream films; Steven Ross concludes that any examination of aspects of capitalism virtually disappeared from the screen.[53] These attitudes impacted films of different genres.

In the prologue to *The Ten Commandments* (1956), Cecil B. DeMille as narrator invites the audience to consider, "Are men the property of the state or are they free souls?" He adds, "This same battle continues throughout the world today." In *California Conquest* (1952), nineteenth-century advocates of American freedom must thwart Russian attempts to prevent California from joining the United States by establishing Russian "protection" contrary to the wishes of the people.

Industry leaders adopted what Shain labels "pragmatic capitulation."[54] Besides restraints on content, in the 1947 Waldorf Declaration,[55] studio executives agreed that they would not employ any known communist or anyone who did not cooperate with HUAC. The results have been well documented. Hundreds of actors, writers, and producers came under suspicion, and many were barred from working in Hollywood, with some never working in films again. HUAC hearings gave witnesses the opportunity to testify to their detestation of communism and "name names" of those whom they believed had communist sympathies. The failure of "the Unfriendly Ten"[56] to answer questions about their political beliefs and affiliations led to their imprisonment for contempt of Congress, while protests against HUAC, such as that led by the Committee for the First Amendment, quickly dissipated.[57] Also, there existed what Larry Ceplair and Steven Englund refer to as an unacknowledged and secretive "gray list" of those with actual or rumored liberal beliefs, affiliations, or associations.[58] Such practices were justified in Hollywood films. In *My Son John* (1952), the parents of a communist agent believe that their son "has been poisoned" and that in informing the authorities, they are "[f]ighting on God's side." John's mother screams, "You have to be punished John," and begs him to "[g]ive up. Name names." Similarly, the opening scenes of *Big Jim McLain* praise the work of HUAC and condemn the use of the Fifth Amendment to avoid answering the committee's questions.

DELMER DAVES AND THE COLD WAR

As a Republican, Daves never denied the possibility that communism might pose a threat to America.[59] After the breakup of the Soviet Union and with the availability of Soviet archives as well as US government papers, M. Stanton Evans has found evidence of Soviet schemes to penetrate various branches of the US government and organize spying and subversive projects.[60] However, Daves made clear that he was firmly against the detention of the Hollywood Ten, and he criticized the existence of what he called "the terror of the blacklist," which he acknowledged "caught" many more than just communists, as "[e]ven the slightest contact with [communists] was already regarded as evidence of guilt."[61] In his screenplay for *The Petrified Forest*, there is a line of dialogue that is not in Robert Sherwood's play from which the film is adapted:[62] "Everybody's entitled to their own way of thinking," thus highlighting the basic freedoms of thought, speech, and association. John Garfield, who had made three films with Daves, was "gray-listed" after refusing to name names when he appeared before HUAC. His sympathies were on the left, as were those of many of his friends, but in writing about Garfield, Daves makes clear that he had no idea whether Garfield was a communist and that politics was not an issue between them.[63] He emphasizes instead the strength of their lasting friendship and his admiration for Garfield's qualities as an actor, for his overcoming the difficulties of his upbringing during the poverty of the Depression, and in particular for his hatred of prejudice and injustice and his loyalty to his friends, irrespective of politics or race.

Daves believed that those with opposing political convictions nevertheless should still adhere to classic American values of fairness and decency in the way that people relate to each other. Daves cowrote *Love Affair* with Communist Party member Donald Ogden Stewart, who left the United States before being subpoenaed by HUAC. In his autobiography, Stewart recalls the pleasure he felt when working on this film, that Daves and director Leo McCarey were "a delight to work with," and that political discussions were "smothered in laughter."[64] In fact, Daves worked with several left-wing and communist writers including four times with Albert Maltz, with one screenplay written during the time when Maltz was blacklisted and working under a pseudonym. Daves praised additional scenes written by Maltz for *Destination Tokyo* as important and meaningful and insisted that Maltz receive cowriting credit when he could have retained sole credit.[65] Alvah Bessie, later to be blacklisted and imprisoned, wrote an initial treatment for *Pride of the Marines* as well as working with Daves on the screenplay for *The Very Thought of You*. The relationship was not always harmonious. Both Warner and Daves rejected Bessie's initial script for *The Very Thought of You*, which Daves rewrote in order to focus on a wartime love affair. Daves emphasizes that he did not object to Bessie holding communist views but rather to the fact that expressing such views seemed more important than the story.[66]

Thus, Daves's approach is more compatible with that of Maltz, who did not accept that, "*unless* art is a weapon ... serving immediate political ends, it is worthless."[67] In "What Shall We Ask of Writers?" (1946), Maltz argues that because of such a position, "much of left-wing artistic activity—both critical and creative—has been restricted, narrowed, turned away from life."[68] Nevertheless, Bessie did acknowledge that Daves agreed enthusiastically that one female worker in a Pasadena parachute factory should be a Black character: "That's great! I want to show that all kinds of people are working to win the war,"[69] an idea that Bessie describes as "subversive," albeit criticizing the final print because he felt that the character was rather light skinned and her time on screen had been reduced. Although brief, the sequence is effective: the character, interestingly named Hope, is shown working harmoniously and as an equal with white women, and there is no suggestion of the workplace segregation that was prevalent in factories in the earlier part of the war. Also, Daves cowrote *White Feather* (1955) with Communist Party member Leo Townsend, and Dalton Trumbo, perhaps the most famous writer-victim of the Hollywood blacklist, worked anonymously on the script for *Cowboy*. The screenplay for *The Badlanders* was prepared by Richard Collins, who had been blacklisted but later revealed the names of fellow communists to HUAC.

Daves believed that, even if justified, the blacklist was superfluous for the purpose of controlling the content of films. He recognized that of greater significance was the power of producers and studio executives to check, filter, and edit content inserted by writers or directors to ensure that the "studio line" was maintained.[70] This view is supported by Dorothy Jones, who conducted a year-long inquiry into the content of more than three hundred films made by four major studios.[71] She concluded that the degree of control exercised by studio executives negated any attempts by a small number of writers to incorporate content that might appear to serve the interests of communism. Similarly, Thom Anderson concludes that HUAC "failed abjectly in its effort to demonstrate Communist influence on movies."[72] Numerous directors, writers, and actors had been party members but for only a short time, many becoming disillusioned after the Stalin show trials in 1936–1937, the Soviet-Nazi pact in 1939, and Nikita Khrushchev's 1956 revelations about the Stalin era. In fact, Anderson argues that "Hollywood Communists were not really Communists"[73] but American radicals who believed in justice, fairness, equality, and democratic rights. Similarly, Barbara Zheutlin and David Talbot conclude that Maltz's scripts were laced with "Rooseveltian" visions that emphasized democratic values, economic security, religious freedom, and world peace.[74]

Józef Jaskulski gives details of a meeting of the Screen Directors Guild in October 1950 during which Daves made an emotional and angry response to the attempts of Cecil B. DeMille to depose Joseph Mankiewicz as president, and to DeMille's calling into question Mankiewicz's political affiliations and displaying xenophobic prejudice against numerous directors, particularly those who were foreign born.[75] As revealing is Daves's reaction on learning that MPA members had criticized scenes in *Pride of the Marines* as "un-American." Of Daves and Jerry Wald, Albert Maltz recorded, "they hit the ceiling. Daves says this is the chance to smack into those MPAers."[76] It is probable that Daves came under some suspicion at this time. When asked if he had encountered any difficulties with HUAC, he referred to "small problems" that he had experienced, particularly because of his working collaboration with those such as Maltz who were under investigation. He gave no details, and the sense is that he was reluctant to discuss these issues, describing the events as "a period of hysteria ... water under the bridge" and concluding: "Now it's all gone and people can go in freedom."[77] Because it permitted desegregated dancing, the Hollywood Canteen was subjected to FBI surveillance during World War II. Sherrie Tucker's examination of FBI files reveals details of agents' observations and that those who supported such dancing were deemed to be radicals, either communists or fellow travelers.[78] Throughout *Hollywood Canteen*, there are shots of a multiracial dance floor with audiences and dancers of different nationalities and races in close proximity. Tucker shows that, as a result, many people involved in the film were spied upon.[79] There is no specific reference to Daves in this context, but Tucker does refer to missing pages and the significant quantity of redacted material, including names, in the files. Moreover, it would be surprising if the writer/director of the film escaped consideration.

HUAC hostility was also directed toward a sequence of dialogue in *Destination Tokyo* during which an unexploded bomb has been wedged under the submarine's superstructure after an attack by Japanese planes. After a tense scene in which the bomb is defused, the captain shows the detonator cap to the crew and observes that it was made in America. The captain comments sardonically that the bomb has "[m]ade in USA stamped on it ... the appeasers' contribution to the war effort." This was a clear criticism of America's prewar attitude to the rise of fascism and imperialism, a criticism advocated by the American Communist Party, and the film was rebuked as a result. This had been an issue of public and political controversy: some politicians and pacifists had criticized the fact that up to 1940, America had supplied Japan with 90 percent of its scrap iron and steel for the manufacture of bombs, which were then used to attack China and very probably Pearl Harbor. Although this dialogue was written by Albert Maltz, who was employed to introduce elements of contemporary commentary, it was approved by producer Jerry Wald and by Daves, who states categorically: "I wrote the final screenplay for *Destination Tokyo*."[80] Similar suspicion was directed toward Daves and Maltz with regard to *Pride of the Marines*. Records of FBI analyses of films of this period state that they "had the actors say everything possible to 'provoke doubts' concerning representative government and free enterprise; they accused employers of everything from racial prejudice to a conspiracy to scuttle the GI Bill of Rights."[81] Given some of Daves's prewar interests and associations, it is perhaps not surprising that he felt some threat. He had lived in the Edendale district of Los Angeles[82] and was an active supporter of its artistic community, which had initially been a commune founded by Mexican communists. He joined sketching sessions and hosted meetings to bring together artists, composers such as John Cage, sculptors, and architects. Also, he provided financial support to maintain buildings and provide security to some of the artists to allow them to maintain their artistic freedom. However, Daniel Hurewitz points out that many members of the community were more politically engaged, organizing campaigns and educational activities to promote civil rights and the ideals of a more humane world based on radical and socialist principles.[83]

THE COLD WAR IN THE FILMS OF DELMER DAVES

Apart from his films made during World War II and shortly thereafter, the majority of Daves's work was produced during the most intense periods of the Cold War. As a Republican, Daves might be expected to adopt a conservative stance on political and social issues. The protagonist in his screenplay for *Shipmates Forever* is initially reluctant to follow a family tradition of service in the forces but comes to appreciate the importance of honor and integrity, and the belief in service to the country. In addition to liberal and communist writers, Daves also worked with Leo McCarey,[84] who later directed *My Son John* and who, along with John Wayne, Ronald Reagan, and Walt Disney, was a leading figure in the MPA as well as a friendly witness before HUAC. Furthermore, Daves shared a writing credit for *The Last Wagon* with James Edward Grant, who worked on twelve scripts for John Wayne including *Big Jim McLain*. However, he did reject significant sections of Grant's contributions, which he felt were confusing and illogical in terms of character development.[85]

Never Let Me Go, Daves's only film that deals explicitly with Cold War issues, takes a conventional anticommunist stance. Susan Carruthers identifies the film as an exemplar of a distinct subgenre of Hollywood's Cold War output, specifically showing the dangers faced and ingenuity needed in effecting an escape from Soviet Europe.[86] The protagonist is an American foreign correspondent (Clark Gable) who marries a Soviet ballerina (Gene Tierney). She is forcibly prevented from leaving for America with her husband, who is being expelled for criticizing Russian limits on freedom. The story involves the execution of the correspondent's plan to sail across the Baltic to rescue his bride, despite the efforts of dozens of trained Russian army officers to stop him. Elements of the plot strain credulity, but François Truffaut's review does note that even to move to another district in order to marry could prove problematic for a Russian woman.[87] Therefore, the central premise that thousands of people, including ballet stars, risked imprisonment or persecution to move to the West is valid, as are references to censorship and phone tapping. However, Daves's film affirmed a typically simplistic representation of Soviet officials and agents, disparagingly referred to as "Uncle Joe's hatchet men," as overly bureaucratic, simpleminded, overbearing, or duplicitous.

This may be one of Daves's weaker films, but there are some effective scenes that add to the tension of the climactic episode. For its time, the car-chase scene is well constructed and convincing; and in another scene, as the ballet *Swan Lake* is being performed, the grace of the dancing and melancholy of the music is interwoven with the startled faces of audience members as they turn toward the penetrating torchlight of the security guard until it rests on the desperate face of the protagonist. Furthermore, as an adventure film, the representation of Soviet Russia is not as crude as in many films of this era, such as *Prisoner of War* (1954), the purpose of which seemed to be to educate the American people about the "evils" of communism. An intelligence officer (Ronald Reagan) goes behind enemy lines and witnesses communist torture and indoctrination: "We're going to teach you all we can about communism. . . . You'll need to know all that." Daves's perspective in *Never Let Me Go* essentially reflects orthodox anti-Soviet, Cold War thinking. However, he held no particular attachment to the film, agreeing to direct it purely as a favor to his friend Gable, the lead actor. "I loved shooting in London . . . wonderful people—but the story."[88] Also, he was dissatisfied with the script, particularly when the studio reinstated scenes that he had cut and had refused to shoot.[89] He had no influence on editing. In attempting to effect the heroine's escape from the Soviet Union, the hero meets her at a Baltic port, but the explanatory scene in which this is arranged was inexplicably cut after shooting had been completed and Daves had moved on to another project.[90]

With their focus on the defense and advancement of civilization and a determination to resort to force if needed, it is no coincidence that Westerns constituted a large proportion of Hollywood's output in the postwar years.[91] Westerns can be seen to reflect a time when Americans were still largely in agreement about the justifications for war and when there was a perception of an enemy with whom compromise, or negotiation, was difficult. Michael Walker considers a Cold War interpretation of *Drum Beat*, with the "Red Men" taking the place of the "Reds" of the Soviet bloc.[92] He highlights the significance of McCarthyism in creating a political climate that was intolerant of a liberal or moderate view of the world and in promoting an extreme or even confrontational approach to international diplomacy. Because of the failure of the attempts to seek peace (liberalism) due to the deceit of Modoc chief Captain Jack (totalitarian treachery), who instigates the murder of unarmed members of the peace delegation, a more hawkish attitude toward an enemy is justified, including resorting to military action if needed. John Lenihan develops this interpretation further.[93] He suggests that when former Indian fighter John MacKay (Alan Ladd) tells Captain Jack that "people will fight for peace and even give their lives," the underlying message is that Americans are willing to stand up to whoever threatens their values and way of life. MacKay's assertion that allowing Jack to keep the Lost River territory would only encourage him to make further demands evokes fears of appeasement and the dangers of the "domino effect" so prevalent in the Cold War thinking of the 1950s. Thus, Bob Herzberg concludes that while *Broken Arrow* advocated peace, *Drum Beat* strove for war.[94]

After his interview with Daves in 1973, Lenihan recalled that Daves had indicated that he may have developed *Drum Beat* according to assumptions about the Cold War.[95] However, John Tuska came to no such conclusion in his own conversation with Daves,[96] and he sensed that Daves had no apparent intention to convey a pro–Cold War viewpoint. Furthermore, Andrew Nelson finds evidence in the Delmer Daves Papers that his first drafts for *Drum Beat* (titled *Modoc Ambush* and then *Warpath*) were written by 1940, before the Cold War.[97] Lenihan does suggest that Daves's allusions to Cold War assumptions may have been unconscious. If this is the case, one can interpret Mackay's plea to his fellow whites to try to overcome traditional distrust and hostility, for otherwise "[t]he land will be filled with hate," as an analogy for the divisions in American society that resulted from the excesses of McCarthyism and Cold War rhetoric. In this way, the Cold War mentality of confrontation is condemned, and a yearning for peaceful coexistence and the desirability for negotiation is expressed. MacKay warns fellow whites of the dangers of violent conflict and proposes peaceful coexistence with the Modocs: "More killing means war. . . . In war, only one side wins. In peace, both sides win." MacKay, as well as Dr. Thomas and General Canby, are willing to go unarmed to achieve peace with Jack: "If it is God's will that I give my life for peace, I am willing to do so." This is consistent with sentiments in Daves's unrealized project of 1951, in which homesteaders and Blackfeet Indians agree that "a means of understanding must be found between both peoples—or both will suffer."[98]

While there is ambiguity in *Drum Beat*, *White Feather* and *Broken Arrow* are more clear in recognizing the importance of sustained effort and patience to overcome the difficulties that opposing sides face in making peace. In *Broken Arrow*, the white American is willing to make the first move toward dialogue at considerable risk to his own safety. The film was released shortly after the outbreak of the Korean War, when political candidates such as Richard Nixon, running on a Cold War, anticommunist platform, achieved electoral success while accusing opponents of being soft on communism. However, if the Apaches and white settlers are seen to represent Cold War adversaries, the film questions the merit of aggression in solving problems and advocates a policy of tolerance and peaceful accommodation based on greater understanding and respect for a traditional enemy. One of the white traders who want to clear the area of Apaches is willing to admit, "I don't know.... I don't claim that a white man's always done right." The film emphasizes that needless and ruthless violence had been perpetrated by both sides and that long-standing hostilities between Apaches and whites had begun because of the duplicity of US army officers. Daves expressed these values at a time when, as Michael Coyne states, the Western genre justified territorial expansion, the dispossession of Indians, and the use of violence to solve problems, before the more revisionist period of the late 1960s and 1970s.[99]

When Tom Jeffords (James Stewart) comes across an injured Apache, his humanitarian instincts outweigh any political or racial concerns. He does not "pass by on the other side," despite the ongoing enmity between the two peoples. After a scheme to trick Cochise fails and he attacks a wagon train, the townspeople ignore the duplicity of the army colonel and ask: "How did Cochise know we had men hidden in the wagon?... Who's telling him, who's his spy?" This moment parallels the contemporary paranoia with regard to Soviet infiltration, and the readiness of the majority to threaten Jeffords can be seen as condemnation of the ease with which anger toward alleged communist sympathizers could arise. The film is prophetic in that it emphasizes that the US army had been fighting a lengthy war with the Apaches in which decisive victory for either side seemed unlikely. As action in Korea in the early 1950s developed into a lengthy and costly war of attrition, the conflict became increasingly unpopular. Just as the white settlers in *Broken Arrow* demand increased action against the Apaches, General Douglas MacArthur's demand for decisive action against North Korea and China, despite the risks of escalation, seemed attractive and popular. Similarly, President Harry Truman's policy of seeking a negotiated peace and his dismissal of MacArthur attracted public criticism, just as Jeffords's plea for peace with the Indians was mistrusted by the settlers. Democratic presidential candidate

"If you don't fight against them, you're with them." *Broken Arrow*. Will Geer, James Stewart. AF archive / Alamy Stock Photo.

Adlai Stevenson wrote, "negotiation—a word that in some frantic circles seems to have become a synonym for appeasement."[100] With his opponents accusing him of being soft on communism, his presidential campaigns in 1952 and 1956 failed.

Broken Arrow recognizes that Indians were attempting to protect their traditional homelands and customs. However, because of his attempts to encourage dialogue and coexistence with the Apaches, Jeffords is regarded as a traitor within his community and is nearly lynched. The film hints at the offensive doctrine of "guilt by association" of McCarthyism as Jeffords is confronted with the aggressive assertion that "[i]f you don't fight against them, you're with them." Just as Stevenson wondered "if we do not understand the limits of our own strength,"[101] *Broken Arrow* suggests that the army is complacent about its capacity to defeat the Apaches: "In six months the war will be over and we'll have Cochise up by his neck." It is necessary for Jeffords to point out that, as the Apaches have a more detailed knowledge of the region and can employ more appropriate tactics with a greater network for intelligence, the army's action is doomed to defeat. Daves shows that the lack of trust that characterized relations between Apaches and whites damaged peace initiatives. Similarly, defensive measures taken by either side in the Cold War were invariably seen as aggressive by the other, thus deterring conciliatory statements or policies. Soviet rejection of the American

Baruch Plan to establish international supervision of nuclear weapons was regarded with suspicion, as was US intervention in Lebanon and Iran to support regimes friendly to the United States and extend military bases throughout the world.

Stanley Corkin broadly recognizes *Broken Arrow*'s sincerity in its advocacy of nonviolence but believes that this sentiment lacks conviction because of the portrayal of Oliver Howard, nicknamed the Christian General, who seeks to persuade Cochise to agree to a formal peace treaty.[102] Corkin equates the strength of Howard's Christian zeal with the imperialist image of nineteenth-century missionaries, who, while attempting to convert "heathens" in Asia and Africa, also disparaged traditional cultures and customs. Corkin perceives Howard as representing a military force that sought to dictate terms of peace, just as America, after World War II, sought political and economic influence and power throughout the world. Yet Corkin concedes that when contrasted with the other officers, who wished to exterminate Indians, Howard's humanitarian instincts are evident. Howard makes clear that he's "not here on active military duty," and his motives in seeking reconciliation and accommodation seem sincere. He is brightly lit and shot from an angle that emphasizes his full height, and Daves thus hints at his innate strength and dignity; there is no suggestion that he wishes to impose his values or terms for peace. He invites Jeffords to define these terms and respects Jeffords's vow that he "will not sell Cochise down the river." John White notes that after the Civil War, the real-life Oliver Otis Howard headed the Freedmen's Bureau, which was founded by Abraham Lincoln to give legal and educational assistance to former slaves, and also established Howard University in Washington, DC, which admitted students of all races.[103] Similarly, Donald Worcester presents a touching picture of Howard playing with Apache children and senses that he was a good friend to the Chiricahua.[104] In negotiations with Cochise, he was willing to acknowledge the Apaches' point of view and envisaged a treaty that guaranteed preserving political and cultural integrity. Significantly, in Daves's film, in expressing admiration for the way Howard applied biblical teaching, Jeffords is convinced of his sincerity—"Read your Bible for me, I like the way you read it"—and Daves reintroduced the character in a similarly empathetic role in *The Last Wagon*.

Therefore, in indicating a belief in the importance of trust and reconciliation, Daves's body of work is more pacific and integrationist in outlook than Lenihan has suggested. Very early in the Cold War, philosopher and political theorist James Burnham argued that "[t]he Third World War began . . . in the Spring of 1944, and has thus already been going on for several years."[105] In *To the Victor*, Daves acknowledges such postwar cynicism. An American expatriate writer bluntly warns of the dangers of ideological conflict—"Now they're getting us ready for the third [world war]"—and predicts an intensification of "the war of nerves ... the hate propaganda." The belligerent contention that communism should be resisted with the bombing of Moscow is challenged by a former army pastor, who points out that war did not rid the world of fascism and that "you can't get rid of an idea with a bomb: you've got to provide a better way.... We don't have much time." The dangers of the abuse of atomic power and the need for dialogue are expressed symbolically in a museum, set against skeletons of dinosaurs, which had "disappeared from the earth because they could not live together, but only against each other ... their brains were too small."

Certainly Daves was proud of America and its traditions, and the fact that his ancestors had played a part in the nation's past. However, his vision is closer to the views of critics of the extremes of America's Cold War policy, such as Adlai Stevenson, who contended: "The reservoir of good will and respect for America was not built up by American arms or intrigue; it was built upon our deep dedication to the cause of human liberty and human welfare."[106] Daves's personal papers contain detailed notes on Roosevelt's foreign policy,[107] emphasizing the principle that no nation should impose its will on the affairs of another. Roosevelt established official ties with the Soviet Union, and his "Good Neighbor" policy with regard to Latin America effectively repudiated the Monroe Doctrine and its 1904 Corollary. At the end of *Demetrius and the Gladiators*, the emperor's edict to Christians, that "[a]s long as they commit no acts of disloyalty to the state, they have nothing to fear," relates to two of Roosevelt's "Four Freedoms," those of worship and from fear, and also echoes Roosevelt's definition of freedom of speech as "freedom to express one's self as long as you don't advocate overthrow of government."[108]

It is these principles that characterize Daves's response to the existence of blacklisting and the witch hunt in Hollywood. The playing of the song "Someone to Watch over Me" in *Dark Passage* may refer to the care the hero receives from the woman who helps him, but it could also hint at an atmosphere of unforgiving surveillance during a time of growing anticommunist hysteria. Unable to prove his innocence, the protagonist is relentlessly pursued and persecuted. His sense of isolation is highlighted by the comment of a bus passenger: "There was a time when folks used to give each other a helping hand." In this context, the film is prophetic in that, ultimately, his only alternative to imprisonment is exile, a fate that was forced on many Americans by the climate of fear that HUAC fostered. In *Jubal*, Daves shows how easily secretive insinuations can incite dangerous emotions, with demands for murderous retribution against Jubal (Glenn Ford) after a rival has informed

"Treason is everywhere.... Who can be trusted?" *Demetrius and the Gladiators*. Jay Robinson. Allstar Picture Library Ltd. / Alamy Stock Photo.

upon him, resulting in two violent deaths. In *Demetrius and the Gladiators*, Caligula is a witch-hunting dictator persecuting Christians, whom he regards as subversive and who are forced to meet in secret cells. He gives orders to "take hostages, kill them, torture them, you'll find one that will talk . . . I'll find out," just as HUAC witnesses were bullied into giving names. Martin Winkler identifies clear modern overtones in postwar Hollywood films set in ancient Rome.[109] He highlights the theme of the inevitability of power leading to corruption and intolerance of opposition in which Rome is analogous to modern dictatorships. In *Ben-Hur* (1959), a Roman commander asks contemptuously: "What do the lives of a few Jews mean to you?" The same commander demands that Ben-Hur provide the names of Jews hostile to Rome, and Winkler suggests that this may be a reference to the activities of HUAC and the pressure to reveal names.[110]

In *Demetrius and the Gladiators*, filmed five years earlier, the emperor Caligula, in his madness and his obsession with Christians, rants that "treason is everywhere.... Who can be trusted?" Just as he rages about "philosophers, their brains ... full of mildew," anticommunist paranoia was essentially anti-intellectual and in part directed against those Americans who were in positions of power or influence. This is reflected in Caligula's specific accusation of "spies at court. . . . No one in the palace can be trusted," in his fear of an alternative set of beliefs that will "come back to rule the earth." Just as HUAC gave witnesses the chance to "confess," Caligula allows Demetrius a similar opportunity: "Do you renounce your false god?" Because of a crisis in his faith after the apparent death of Lucia (Debra Paget), he replies that "there is no other king but Caesar." To Messalina (Susan Hayward), Caligula shouts: "I'll give you witnesses to your treachery. . . . You; you'll swear that she's guilty," which is followed by hurried and anxious affirmative responses by senators. This abuse of law and the Senate can be seen as analogous to the use of "friendly witnesses" to name names and also may be a reference to the failure of the Supreme Court to protect the constitutional rights of the Hollywood Ten under the First Amendment. The court refused to hear their appeal, which resulted in their imprisonment. After the death of Caligula, the first act of Claudius, the new emperor, is to articulate a more enlightened "constitutional" position vis-à-vis dissent and freedom of association and worship, stating that "[m]en do not kill what they despise, only what they fear."

DAVES'S FILMS AS CRITIQUE OF AMERICAN CAPITALISM

In *The Last Wagon*, the wagon master leads the travelers in prayer, asking God to help them "share with our fellow man Thy bounty, Thy infinite goodness, each according to his needs." This may be an expression of human kindness and fellowship, but it could also reflect a progressive social and political outlook encompassed in an important objective that Daves, when a student, helped to secure for the Stanford University Liberal Party: the need for "leveling living group differences toward the end of establishing a more democratic campus."[111] Also, the wagon master's sentiment is at odds with the individualism and self-reliance associated with the conventional Western hero. Daves praised the "unblemished community spirit" of the American Indians who worked on his films, noting that they neither signed contracts nor received payments as individuals but took their earnings for the tribe to improve community facilities.[112] It was this "collective" nature of Indian communities that Senator George Malone of Nevada identified as "natural Socialist environments."[113] However, Daves was more interested in what draws people together for the benefit of the community. The nurse in *Pride of the Marines* emphasizes that "[n]obody stands alone," just as the cooperative warmth of the Apache community transforms Jeffords's outlook after his admission that "all my life I've been mostly alone." Similarly,

Daves's preparatory notes for *The Girl from Bali* include details of Balinese customs and beliefs that emphasize the cooperative nature of this society, as exemplified in a sentence that Daves had underlined: "The Balinese world is his community."[114] In 1950, he drafted a script for this project, but it was not filmed.

Albeit within the confines of conventional Hollywood genres, the ideals promoted in Daves's films indicate a more skeptical approach to the MPA's directive as to the inviolability of free-enterprise capitalism. His story for *Dames* is slender, and his screenplay does little more than provide opportunities for Busby Berkeley's elaborately staged musical set pieces. Nevertheless, the opening montage of shots of banking, insurance, and utilities providers emphasizes their detachment from the interests of ordinary people. Daves's screenplay for *The Go-Getter* includes critical social commentary on the hardened attitudes of big business and its "every-man-for-himself" philosophy. Daves contrasts this with the integrity and loyalty of the protagonist, who, despite his severe injuries, is cruelly exploited by his boss. More significantly, Daves wrote the screenplay for *Stranded*, in which Mack (George Brent) is superintendent of construction of San Francisco's Golden Gate Bridge. Interspersed with actual footage of work on the site, the film shows the pride taken by the workers in the quality of their engineering and construction work. Mack is a principled manager, employing only union labor and adhering to union rates and conditions, and so the film implicitly condemns the practice of exploiting the economics of the Depression by paying lower wages and weakening the influence of unions. This pro-union stance is further indicated when the solidarity of the union workers helps Mack defeat the criminal intentions of the protection racketeers who seek to disrupt the work on the bridge. This was at a time when, after its formation in 1933, the Screen Writers Guild experienced considerable resistance and opposition from the major studios, including accusations of communist motives. Although Daves criticized the restrictive practices of some unions because they detracted from the cooperative "family" ethos he sought to create on set, he emphasized that he supported the raison d'être of unions.[115] For many years, he was on the negotiating committee of the Directors Guild, and, prompted by attempts by Louis B. Mayer to arbitrarily reduce studio salaries, he became a charter member of the Screen Writers Guild[116] and in 1951 became its president.

Stranded hints at the need for public intervention and remedial action to alleviate the sufferings of those who had fallen victim to the Depression and cycles of laissez-faire capitalism. It highlights the value of systematic attempts to relieve suffering, in particular by finding jobs and organizing shelter for the homeless. The film's heroine, Lynn (Kay Francis), is devoted to her work in helping the destitute, those living in poverty, broken families, the homeless, and penniless immigrants. No moral judgment of their circumstances is made; she provides consolation, understanding, and assistance to an unmarried, pregnant young woman who has been abandoned, as well as to orphans, the dispossessed, and the lonely. This help might involve dealing with politicians or with welfare, legal, or religious personnel; or it could mean just listening to individuals' worries or the reminiscences of the elderly. This intervention, independent of the state, is organized by the group Lynn leads, but the film hints that, on its own, this may be inadequate. In response to the criticism that "you don't really think you do any good in this silly business," she replies: "Sometimes we help a lot," but also concedes that "sometimes we fail." Importantly, however, the group's support is offered without condemnation, in contrast to the initial attitude of Mack, who believes that such individuals are "misfits" and that such support is "based on a phony premise. You're working with material that has a flaw in it. It's not up to standard; it should be thrown out. That's hard, but it's sense." His view is consistent with the extremes of unfettered capitalism and is antagonistic toward the concept of social security, maintaining that if individuals had any worth, "they'd get out of their own jams." However, despite his initial views, with Lynn's influence his ideas change, and he shows a willingness to make job offers to give a second chance to those who had made mistakes or were victims of economic circumstances.

The director of *Stranded* was Frank Borzage, who is noted for portraying moving and poignant portraits of life set during the Depression era, and this film does make reference to the desperation of the homeless and jobless. However, several critics have concluded that Borzage was an uncompromising romanticist[117] and that his stories are melodramas about the power of love to create "heaven on earth" out of the deprivation and destitution of the period. In *Man's Castle* (1933), Borzage makes reference to the Depression and to the fact of twelve million unemployed. Bill (Spencer Tracy), who inhabits an inner-city shantytown, asserts that "[n]obody ever has to be hungry again, anywhere." However, the soft-focus shots of Bill and his lover, Trina (Loretta Young), and the rather artificial back-projection shots of the city seem to isolate the protagonists from the realities of the time and suggest that they are not part of the same world. In arranging an ordered domestic environment in which she washes, cleans, and cooks, Trina builds a metaphorical drawbridge that separates and protects their "castle" from the poverty and squalor of the Depression. She calls the shack "a safety-zone, like a clearing in the forest where everything is quiet and peaceful."

This sense of spiritual protection is explicit in Borzage's *Mannequin* (1937), in which a factory girl (Joan Crawford) lives for Saturday night, when she can dream of a life that "shuts out" her immediate world of poverty and violence. Sitting on a beach, she draws a circle in the sand and says to the man she loves, "You and I have this little space all to ourselves, and what we feel for each other shuts out all the rest. So, what more do we need?" When her husband (Spencer Tracy) loses his wealth due to the uncertainties of capitalism, there is no conception of the realities of mass unemployment: "You go back to work; start tomorrow morning." The strength of their love is sufficient to triumph over earthly misfortunes, prompting Frederick Lamster to conclude that Borzage's characters exist outside of the real or material world.[118] However, in the very first scene of *Stranded*, there is an immediate introduction to the realities of the Depression. After his resigned whisper, "I don't know what to do; where to go," and too proud to continue to accept charity, a native-born San Franciscan commits suicide. The political issues that impact the characters relate directly to the economic and social conditions of the Depression and therefore demand remedial action. A loving relationship in itself cannot ameliorate such adverse conditions, and Lynn is willing to forgo her love and disregard society's expectations of a woman's role in order to contribute to addressing these circumstances. The film suggests that something more than love or mere sympathy for the dispossessed is needed to overcome hardship, and it is these aspects of the screenplay that are unusual in a Borzage film and therefore may reflect Daves's views.

Filmed a year later, *The Petrified Forest* was cowritten by Daves and reflects on darker aspects of American capitalism. In order to conform to the strictures of the Hollywood Production Code, the film makes clear that the escaping murderer, Duke Mantee (Humphrey Bogart), is recaptured and killed, while in the original play this is more ambiguous: "They'll never catch Mantee in my car."[119] For the same reason, the line spoken by the young waitress in Sherwood's play, "I asked him to let me go away with him, and live in sin,"[120] does not appear in the film. However, because of the film's overall fidelity to its source, it is difficult to evaluate the relative contributions of the writers and that of the director, Archie Mayo. For David Thomson, Mayo's record at Warner Bros. was not impressive,[121] and David Quinlan feels that the film lacks any real personal touches from the director.[122] A contemporary review comments that the direction was respectful but static, and the fact that the film is animate and vital is due to thoughtful writing.[123] Therefore, it is possible that the substance and tone of the film was determined by the interpretation of Sherwood's play as conceived in the screenplay of Daves and his cowriter, Charles Kenyon.

Kenneth Bindas notes that many observers feared that Hollywood would alter much of Sherwood's play in order to appeal to a wider audience, pointing out that Daves's screenplay omits Sherwood's references to Marxism and statement that "in Russia ... [they] ... are building something new." However, Bindas acknowledges that the film preserves the tone of Sherwood's dialogue.[124] At the play's beginning, set in a roadside café, two telegraph linemen discuss the appeal of the system in Russia and the need "to finally get some kind of equality they talked about in the Declaration of Independence ... do you call *this* freedom?"[125] This sentiment is not expressed explicitly in the film, and the line "Certainly it's Revolution. And that's exactly what we got to come to"[126] is omitted. However, Alan Squier, the film's protagonist (Leslie Howard), who longs for "something to believe in, worth living for," regrets that he was born "too soon for the new order"; and a lineman expresses the view that "[t]he Republic's in bad need of saving ... a fine excuse for a Republic we've got." More specifically, the lineman feels angry that his work, involving the construction of telegraph poles, allows bankers to "call some guy in Los Angeles to say he's washed out." The irony of the play's dialogue—"Rugged individualism! Every man for himself! That's the kind of Liberty we've been getting"[127]—is implied in the film when Squier refers to "destiny closing in ... [on] the world of outmoded ideas." Having traveled abroad, Squier returns home to find that American capitalism has resulted in exploitative social restraints that dehumanize the individual. Hitherto orthodox social and economic doctrines and ideas are fossilized; "they're all so many dead stumps in the desert.... [Y]ou're obsolete, Duke [Mantee], just like me." The downfall of Mantee and the death of Squier as he sacrifices himself to ensure the realization of the young waitress's potential represent the demise of the relevance of the philosophy of unrestrained free enterprise, which had failed in the years of the Depression.

In *Stranded*, brief snatches of a half-heard background conversation—"You take this guy Roosevelt"—hint at an interest in the New Deal and a different approach to political and economic issues. This intimation is affirmed in Daves's preparatory notes for *The Stuff of Heroes*, which was never filmed.[128] His notes include a quotation from Roosevelt's radio broadcast of January 19, 1940: "If any child lacks opportunities for home life, health, protection, education on moral and spiritual development, the strength of the nation and its ability to cherish and advance the principles of democracy are thereby weakened."[129] In the original story and silent film version, his responsibility for his brother's children forces the protagonist to reassess his life, resulting in greater commitment and success at his workplace.[130] In effect, his "heroism" brings greater profit to his employer and leads to his promotion and romance. Daves's treatment adopts a very different position that reveals his own response to Roosevelt's words, which is included in his papers: "We can hope for the day when the poor will have elbow room and the kids will have a chance to survive and breathe and see the sun."[131] The hero's concerns are directed toward "the problems of raising children on a meager salary ... the problem of forty percent, at least, of Americans today."[132] More specifically, he undertakes "a crusade to clear slums, to give people like himself and their kids a chance to live and grow."[133] He discovers that his employer is responsible for the worst of the slum conditions, and his campaign confronts political corruption and landlords who charge rents beyond the earning levels of the tenants, who will be summarily evicted. Daves's treatment condemns those who ignore this injustice, such as a city official, who, in answer to the hero's question, "Have you ever seen the slums?" replies, "Sure ... in one of those Dead-End Kid pictures."[134] The reason why Daves's screenplay was not filmed is suggested in a letter from producer Hal Wallis, in which he stated: "I particularly don't like the business of slum clearances.... I don't know why writers persist in this sort of treatment."[135] The seriousness that Daves attached to this issue is indicated by his files of newspaper cuttings dealing with housing conditions and slum clearances in Los Angeles and the concern that slums would be replaced by housing only for those who could pay higher rents.[136] He advocated public intervention, and his attitude to such expenditure through taxes is unambiguous: "[W]e all grouse about them ... but they pay for the privilege of living in America."[137]

These explicit and implicit values are later reflected in films that Daves directed. Adrian Danks notes that "the rituals of work" are a preoccupation of Daves's Westerns, showing details of ranching, mining, and the cattle drive.[138] However, Daves also examines the relationship between labor and capital. In *3:10 to Yuma*, he shows the devastating effects of drought and hints at the farmers' dependence on the "largesse" of corporations and speculators. Fran Pheasant-Kelly quotes David Murdoch's contention that "those who controlled water rights dominated the Western economy and its society," and therefore farmers and workers were "at the mercy of market forces."[139] Similarly, White notes that the gang leader reflects, "You gotta have money behind you."[140] Anger and frustration at the family's vulnerability is expressed by the farmer's wife: "You have to do something. You can't just stand by and watch. You worked so hard." In *Cowboy*, the determination to maximize profit engenders selfish and callous attitudes in the cowhands: "This calf is worth $20 in Chicago. How much are you worth?" They are reluctant to help a coworker in trouble, as delay would result, and they show indifference when a death occurs because of their horseplay. "A man's dead and that's that." Even the actions of some Indians who try to avoid them is expressed in business terms: with their protected reservation, "[t]hey got a better deal." In *Broken Arrow*, it is a seemingly respectable businessman who believes that he is bringing "civilization" to the West by selling clothes, carpets, and household goods. He is frustrated by Jeffords's peace initiatives and is anxious to maximize profits—"I've got a wagonload of first-class whiskey waiting for me in the East. I could sell that at a dollar a bottle if it wasn't for Cochise"—and he advocates aggression toward the Apaches. Thus, the motive of achieving profits justifies the means, which may involve violence. Walker notes also that the film exposes the traditional myth of violent Apaches intent on taking white peoples' scalps.[141] One of the white men who had wanted to usurp the Indians' territory and was subsequently killed had three Indian scalps in his possession. The film establishes the fact that white men are willing to pay "many dollars" for such scalps.

At the root of the emperor's paranoia in *Demetrius and the Gladiators* is his fear of his growing unpopularity, in large part due the inequality in the distribution of grain: while ordinary citizens grow more hungry, the plentiful supplies of grain are withheld for the elite, namely those on whose support the emperor depends to retain power. Daves's critique of American capitalism is more explicit in *Parrish*, for which the tobacco industry of Connecticut provides the setting. Central to the narrative are the actions of unprincipled tobacco tycoon Judd Raike (Karl Malden), who controls "more land and more dollars and more people than any other firm in the valley." The film exposes the ruthless methods he employs to establish a virtual monopoly and destroy any competition to his power and influence: "He thinks he owns everybody." With the use of informers, his unscrupulous business practices take advantage of the misfortunes and suffering of others and define the unrestrained excesses of capitalism that "drive decent men from their own land." He tries to stop workers from helping Parrish, who threatens his monopoly: "My father never forgives a man who forgets who he works for.... Any Raike employee who works for Parrish McLean is finished in the valley." His intentions are recognized by the workers—one young woman challenges Raike's son, who is listing Parrish's workers: "What are you starting, some sort of blacklist?" The hero realizes that the injustice and the "wall of fear," bred by Raike's blacklisting and abuse of power, must be defied: "There comes a time when you realize if you close your eyes just once too often to what is right and decent, you'll never open them again, you'll be lost." Daves's images evoke the nobility of the workers in the fields, with some singing, "There's a man going around taking names." He emphasizes their unity, as white and Black workers travel and labor together, taking pride in their work and their willingness to work longer for an enlightened employer who joins them in the field when the crop is threatened. The shots of the workers walking home alongside a riverbank, as the shadows lengthen in the setting sun, recall the paintings of Jean-François Millet in suggesting the spirit and harmony within the group. This unity is indicated further in Daves's final retreating crane shot showing the vast area under cultivation, with the workers together under protective covering.

Youngblood Hawke also comments on the unscrupulous tactics of those willing to exploit and cheat, even with family members as victims. More specifically and in what also may be a comment on developments in Hollywood that followed the breaking up of the studio system, the film shows the increasing power of agents and financiers in the publishing industry and their readiness to manipulate and control the contracts, expectations, and business affairs of writers. However, this theme is less convincing due to the rather stereotypical portrayal of these characters—particularly the cigar-smoking businessman, the insincere agent, and his vacuous girlfriend—and Daves's failure to control the overacting of the supporting cast in these roles. Furthermore, because of Daves's excessive focus on Hawke's rather tedious and predictable affair with the married Frieda, although Geneviève Page does give a very powerful performance in this role, the potency of this critique of modern business is diluted further, and it is this aspect of Daves's script that Warren Beatty identified when turning down the title role just five days before filming was due to begin.[142]

By the time that *Parrish* was released, the effects of McCarthyism and blacklisting were beginning to wane, but the impulse in Hollywood to conform was still prevalent. Mervyn LeRoy's *The FBI Story* (1959), for which J. Edgar Hoover had script and cast approval, uncritically traces how the FBI had made "this world of ours a safer place in which to live." When trailing a suspected communist spy on a Sunday, an FBI agent (played by James Stewart) uses a phrase that encapsulates Hollywood's traditional antipathy to communism: "Since he was a communist, we know he wasn't going to church." Gay and Robert Zieger conclude that it was not until the late 1970s that films such as *Norma Rae* (1979) conveyed genuine empathy toward workers who tried to organize action against harsh working conditions.[143] In fact, *Salt of the Earth* (1954) is the only film from an earlier period that set out to champion workers and organized labor. This film is based on events in New Mexico in 1951–1952, when accidents caused by inadequate safety provisions in a zinc mine, and racial discrimination with regard to wages and working conditions, provoked a bitter and lengthy strike organized by the International Mine, Mill, and Smelter Workers Union. Directed, written, and produced by blacklisted Hollywood artists[144] and financed by the union, the film details the efforts of the strikers and their wives to resist attempts to break the strike.

Due to the film's content, it was denied access to Hollywood's technical facilities during filming, which was regularly disrupted by anticommunist vigilantes and others threatening cast and crew members. After completion, the film was denied commercial distribution. Deborah Rosenfelt writes that the film endorses gender and racial equality and advocates more control for workers over their own lives.[145] In the film, the miner Ramón asks his wife Esperanza: "Have you forgotten what is was like ... before the union came? When Estella was a baby, we couldn't afford a doctor when she got sick"; and in a very powerful sequence, shots of strike leader Ramón being subjected to a violent beating are interspersed with close-ups of Esperanza in painful childbirth after medical attention has been refused by the mining company. Although some commentators regarded *Salt of the Earth* as an honest film about working people, opposition was exemplified by film critic Pauline Kael, who viewed it as "a clear piece of Communist propaganda" designed to denigrate capitalism and convince "the rest of the world that there are no civil liberties in the U.S.A."[146]

This comment cannot be applied to the more commercial production of *The Badlanders*. However, in showing the potential for exploitation by mine owners, Daves's film does encourage the viewer to consider similar political and social issues, albeit less explicitly or substantially. When Peter Van Hoek (Alan Ladd) and John McBain (Ernest Borgnine) are released from prison, circumstances bring them together to rob a gold mine, after which they are helped by Mexican American laborers and their families. The film rejects the stereotypical images of Mexicans that Westerns have conventionally presented. Rather than presenting images of large families living in relative poverty but with a cheerful acceptance of their lives and their subservient status, *The Badlanders* examines the reality of working people's lives. McBain learns that Anita, his newfound love, had earlier lost a baby in childbirth because of lack of medical help: "I was alone and when I cried out for somebody ... there was nobody." McBain has to assist Anita with the delivery of a baby of a young Mexican girl who has insufficient money to pay a doctor—"There is no money for doctors here"—and he learns that this situation is not uncommon for Mexicans.

As Daves's camera tracks the arrival of the stagecoach into the township, a revealing crane shot shows the segregated areas in which Mexicans and whites live and indicates the disparity in the living conditions therein. From the stagecoach, Van Hoek comments: "On the left is the Mexican part of town. The mine owners brought them in as cheap labor," and it is clear that the town's wealth from the gold mines has not benefited Mexican workers. In this sense, at a time when American capitalism had developed the world's strongest economy and greatest level of affluence, the film raises the question of how this position should be maintained. Rosenfelt contends that the prosperity of the American Southwest was built on the availability of cheap Mexican labor,[147] and Daves's film alludes to the reality of the exploitation of the workforce: "The boss-man; he's a slave-driver." In this sense, the film anticipates changes in the American economy in which US companies outsource jobs to developing countries with the intention not specifically of helping the economies of those countries but rather of maximizing profits whatever the working conditions or the consequences for jobs back home. In this regard, Donald Barlett and James Steele reveal the high costs in business closures and loss of jobs in the United States as a result of deregulation and relocation of production, not only to ensure lower wage costs but also because of federal encouragement to relocate through tax breaks.[148]

In *Salt of the Earth*, the miners and their families are roused to action: "We want equality with Anglo miners—the same pay, the same conditions," and to achieve this they realize that "there was only one answer ... solidarity." Because of the setting of *The Badlanders*, the unionization of the workers is not an issue. However, their unity is not in doubt. As White notes, rather than the Mexican flag, the French colors are flown as symbols of revolution and freedom.[149] Their solidarity is demonstrated when they are inspired to act together to overcome their oppressors and in the supportive nature of the community, particularly when someone is in need. After Anita has been the subject of ridicule and abuse from white townsmen and McBain helps her, she informs him that "my friends know what you have done; they are now your friends."

The film shows that the laborers are exploited not only in terms of wages and conditions but also in the willingness of white townsmen to abuse women who are forced into prostitution to support their families. Just as the workers in *Salt of the Earth* know that "the mine owners would stop at nothing to keep them from getting equality," Daves shows, in the persons of the mine owners and the sheriff, the potential for corruption in unrestrained capitalism, viewed seemingly as a series of attempts by the powerful to bribe, cheat, or outmaneuver and increase their wealth at the expense of others. As McBain observes, facing the camera (and the audience), "Seems like everybody around here is stealing from everybody else," which White suggests "is as near to 'ownership is theft' as you are likely to get in a Hollywood studio film."[150] Thus, the film is reflective of Keith Buchanan's severe critique of

American capitalism. He argues that American economic success is increasingly dependent on the penetration and subversion of the economies of other nations, including exploitation of the resources of Third World countries, to the extent that American prosperity is undermined if such countries begin to utilize their assets to improve living standards for their own people.[151] It is this principle that explains covert CIA interventions in Iran in 1952 and Guatemala in 1954.

The plot development and denouement in *The Badlanders* are less conventional than in *The Asphalt Jungle*, in which a gang executes a bank heist, and its societal critique is less labored than in *Salt of the Earth* because the issues are set within a tightly controlled and more vigorous Western narrative structure. In John Huston's film, audience sympathy lies with the gang, despite Doc's sexual proclivities for young girls. Ciavelli is a devoted family member with a sick child, and Dix has been the victim of financial and personal misfortunes and seeks to regain property lost to his family. Nevertheless, after being double-crossed, the gang members do not succeed. Dix dies as he reaches the beloved farm that he had dreamed of recovering. In *The Badlanders*, Van Hoek plans the robbery because he was earlier swindled out of his contracted share of the gold that he had found as a geologist and engineer and framed for a crime he had not committed. McBain agrees to take part to finance his dream of raising cattle after having been cheated out of his land, which included the gold mine. Similarly, in Daves's *Treasure of the Golden Condor*, Frenchman Jean-Paul (Cornel Wilde), when a young boy, had lost his estates to his corrupt uncle. This raises the issue of the potential for big business to exert power by means that may be legal but is nevertheless of questionable morality, just as in *Salt of the Earth*, Esperanza makes clear that "[t]he land where the mine stands; that was owned by my husband's own grandfather. Now it belongs to the company."

Although Van Hoek's plans would seem to have greater justification than they would in Huston's film, the demands of the Production Code would be expected to dictate that the robbers could not benefit from their actions, which involve the theft of private property and during which McBain kills a deputy marshal (albeit in self-defense, and albeit a corrupt marshal). In Huston's film, the gang members are either caught or killed and the corrupt detective is apprehended, and in keeping with the values of the Code, in the penultimate scene there is a homily to the hard work and effectiveness of the police. However, in *The Badlanders* the theft succeeds. McBain is shot but not seriously wounded, and they are able to escape with the gold despite being double-crossed, while the corrupt marshal remains in office. Walker comments that in this sense the film is more radical than *The Asphalt Jungle*, as there is no punishment for the criminal action, thus presenting a direct challenge to the Production Code, and he notes also that, just as in *Dark Passage*, the protagonists must leave America to be happy.[152]

The Red House begins in a tranquil pastoral setting, with a narrator reflecting on the confident values of small-town America. However, the movie was filmed during the year that the HUAC hearings started, and there are soon ominous hints of hidden menace below the surface complacency. The increasing madness of the farmer (Edward G. Robinson) mirrors the developing paranoia of McCarthyism, seen in his increasing demands for unquestioned obedience, threats of punishment, and warnings of impending catastrophe: "It will follow you all your life." Daves's films exhibit his respect for those who may have differing views. In *Rome Adventure*, the young assistant librarian decides to immerse herself in another culture when she leaves her job at a college after being censured for introducing a student to an "unsuitable" book. Daves's heroes are open to new moral perspectives and thus embody Adlai Stevenson's vision of America's role in the world: "We shall have to listen as well as talk; learn as well as teach. . . . We can encourage the acceptance of our ideas only as we are willing to accept the ideas and suggestions of others."[153] The teacher who speaks at a high school graduation ceremony in *Spencer's Mountain* expresses pride in the American system of government but also reminds her audience to learn about "the enormous world outside."

Daves was reluctant to film *Treasure of the Golden Condor*, as it was a remake of *Son of Fury* (1942). The latter had been a more lavish production with a more prestigious cast and had been a popular success, but for Daves it was old-fashioned, with an improbable story.[154] Nevertheless, one review of *Treasure of the Golden Condor* praises Daves's crisp script and direction and notes its period authenticity and adherence to realism not often found in this genre.[155] Furthermore, as writer and director he was able to imprint intimations of his beliefs and values onto the narrative. The film is an eighteenth-century adventure story centered on a search for treasure by Jean-Paul and a Scotsman that encompasses conventions of the genre including a sea voyage, an ancient ruined city, collapsing caves, and the dangers of the jungle, such as poisonous snakes and murderous tribesmen. The Scotsman had intended to use the treasure to buy a castle and a title, while Jean-Paul was determined to reclaim his estates. Yet having discovered the treasure in Guatemala, their thoughts then revolve around how to use it for good, including building schools for the native community in Central America and French peasants back home. They come to realize that "there's more to this journey than the gold and emeralds we found," just as the journey of the young people in *The Last Wagon* is a fundamental maturing and learning experience. The Scotsman realizes that he doesn't need a castle or an aristocratic title, and Jean-Paul, having regained his estates, gives up his wealth and property to the community and frees all his bonded servants. Both decide to live in the native Guatemalan community, where they have found peace and contentment; their feelings are certain: "I've never known a place like this.... Have you noticed the happiness in these people?" In the penultimate courtroom scene, Jean-Paul is found guilty of the capital offence of attacking his master when he was still regarded as a bond servant, and he is set to hang. However, natural justice prevails. In his final testimony to the court, Jean-Paul condemns a society in which "injustice makes chattels of human beings" and in which those who are "broken in soul and spirit [are] without hope of redress within the law." These words and Jean-Paul's final declaration encapsulate Daves's vision of a just society that is deserving of defense when threatened, and more specifically a vision that reflects his emotional and political response to the extremes of Cold War ideology and its impact on Hollywood: "The day will come when the Frenchman, whatever his worth, will be both free and equal with full rights over his own person, his work, [and] the expression of his ideas."

CHAPTER THREE

Race and Civil Rights in the Films of Delmer Daves

AN IMPORTANT STRAND OF AMERICAN POSTWAR FOREIGN POLICY WAS directed toward containing communism by building alliances with Asian, Latin American, and African countries. However, there was an increasing realization that world attention on racial difficulties at home undermined the legitimacy of America's self-designated position as "leader of the free world." The view that any impetus within the political establishment to implement civil rights was motivated by pragmatism rather than moral concerns is consistent with Harry Benshoff and Sean Griffin's conclusion that the classical Hollywood narrative form "encourages all spectators, regardless of their actual color, to identify with white protagonists."[1] Their exemplification of this assertion is that Native Americans were encouraged "to root for white cowboys battling evil Indians." Also, they highlight the practice of "tokenism," in which nonwhite characters in supporting roles were included to deflect any accusation of racism. However, the importance of the belief that discrimination is incompatible with American ideals should not be underestimated. *Brown v. Board of Education* (1954)[2] became one of the most celebrated civil rights cases in American history and paved the way for racial integration in public schools, and there is little doubt that *Brown* and subsequent decisions energized a movement that was inspired by a moral commitment to equality.

Broken Arrow has been credited with beginning a cycle of Westerns that challenge the stereotypical portrayal of Native Americans in Hollywood films. In fact, in one of Daves's earliest screenplays, *Clear All Wires* (1933), a war correspondent in Morocco deliberately panders to ill-informed public preconceptions of Arabs fighting the French Foreign Legion as uncivilized savages. Yet he observed their leaders to be educated and sophisticated: "I have never met more considerate, more courteous, more intelligent officers and gentlemen." Issues of race feature prominently in Daves's films, and this was groundbreaking for its time in that his acknowledgment and celebration of diversity encouraged viewers to confront their consciences and prejudices as well as contemplate a more inclusive perspective on America's past.

ATTITUDES TO RACE IN DAVES'S NON-WESTERN FILMS

In *Demetrius and the Gladiators*, the Black actor William Marshall plays Glycon, a Nubian king who had been taken as a slave and trained as a gladiator. Marshall's screen appearances tended to exploit his powerful physique and emphasize his characters' prodigious strength and passionate desires. In *Lydia Bailey* (1952), the contribution of Marshall's character as an eighteenth-century revolutionary leader in Haiti is diminished in favor of the actions of the white hero. His costumes expose his powerful body, which is invariably glistening with sweat, and his potency is indicated by his numerous wives and mistresses. Marshall's contemporaries such as Woody Strode were similarly presented: only in Ford's *Sergeant Rutledge* (1960) did his character display heroic qualities of courage and dignity. These stereotypical images are consistent with earlier representations of African Americans in Hollywood films. Despite Paul Robeson's formidable academic and sporting record and his success as a singer and stage actor, his films did little to elevate the status of Black people: typically, he was at the service of white men, often inculcating the values of the British Empire. In *The Emperor Jones* (1933), he does assert pride in his race, but he is punished for his "sins" when he is hunted down and killed.

Although Marshall had the necessary physique for a gladiator, Daves's camera does not dwell on his body or focus on his physical prowess. He emphasizes instead his thoughtfulness and intelligence and the genuine friendship that this non-Christian offers to Demetrius, the Greek hero (Victor Mature). He helps to ensure his physical survival at the gladiators' camp, and when Demetrius rejects his faith and his sense of morality weakens, Glycon exhibits a willingness to take responsibility: "I suppose I should blame myself for what has become of you." Glycon's dignity and integrity—"I won't obey that order. You are my superior, but I choose my friends"—are crucial qualities in the moral reawakening of his "master." The strength of his values and the sincerity of his words provide moral guidance to the hero and set a standard against which the actions of other characters may be judged.

Although the contribution of scriptwriter Philip Dunne must be acknowledged in taking this stance, it is significant that Dunne also coscripted the aforementioned *Lydia Bailey*, whereas the values inherent in *Demetrius and the Gladiators* are consistent with Daves's wider body of work. For example, *Spencer's Mountain* is set in a traditional Western landscape usually associated with Hollywood's celebration of the progress of white "civilization" and the ideals of the "American Dream." Yet for the scene at a traditional school graduation, Daves chose a Black actress to sing "America the Beautiful" as the high school teacher extols the virtues of American democracy. Critic Judith Crist finds this to be patronizing tokenism and doubts Daves's sincerity, pointing out that there are no other Black characters in the film.[3] Even if Crist's condemnation is in any way justified, it must be significant that Daves made this selection at the height of the civil rights campaigns in 1963. While Earl Hamner's novel on which the film is based is set in the 1930s, Daves chose to set his story at a time of controversy, when racial segregation in schools and colleges had been declared unconstitutional but enrollment for some students of color remained problematic. Such moments, while memorable, are not indicative of the central themes of these films but nevertheless provide pointers to Daves's vision and his interest in the principles of social change.

In World War II–era films, the participation of servicemen of different races and ethnicities was portrayed positively as symbols of the inclusiveness of American democracy. Jeanine Basinger describes the combat unit in *Bataan* (1943) as representing the American "melting pot," with individuals of different races, classes, and levels of education, although she notes that a Native American character, present in initial drafts, was eliminated in the final screenplay.[4] In *Guadalcanal Diary* (1943), the unit includes Jewish and Hispanic marines, and their mutually supportive cohesiveness is emphasized. However, apart from the single Mexican American marine (Anthony Quinn), they do not share in the camaraderie of victory, and the Jewish cantor must show a willingness to take part in a Christian service. More meaningful inclusiveness is demonstrated in *Pride of the Marines* in which Jews, Hispanics, and Native Americans fight and socialize together, with several film critics noting that the Jewish marine makes an equal contribution to America's cause.[5] This inclusiveness is encapsulated in the trench scene, in which the machine gun is decorated with a Star of David as well as a shamrock. Furthermore, Daves is willing to recognize that anti-Semitism is not confined to the enemy. A Jewish marine testifies to prewar difficulties, particularly in finding jobs: "There's guys who won't hire me because my name is Diamond instead of Jones, because I celebrate Passover instead of Easter." K. R. M. Short points out that it would be a further two years before such an articulate Jewish war hero would be portrayed on the screen, when John Garfield appeared in *Gentleman's Agreement* (1947).[6] While the group of injured marines in Daves's film demonstrate cohesiveness and friendship, they wonder whether there will be the same opportunities after the war for the comradeship of equals that they have shared.

Hollywood Canteen also reflects an intention to downplay racial divisions during World War II. For actress Andrea King, the Hollywood Canteen was "one of the earliest instances I can remember when a night club was racially mixed."[7] After the club's directors voted to permit mixed dancing and audiences, despite concerns about reactions from southern servicemen, Bette Davis recalls that very few difficult incidents occurred.[8] However, Kevin Starr notes that the degree of integration was limited in that "black and white servicemen tended to remain in their own groups and space."[9] There were examples of couples who exercised the freedom to dance "across" race, but this was relatively infrequent. The film's jitterbug sequence clearly shows dancers of different races on the floor at the same time and in close proximity, but dancing with a partner of the same race. Furthermore, no person of color speaks directly to the camera, and there are sequences with Black actors in Daves's original screenplay that were not filmed, with some instructions to focus on Black couples not followed.[10] Nevertheless, servicemen and hostesses of different races, in audiences and dancing, were shown side by side and in close-up at a time when the armed forces were segregated. Also, Sherrie Tucker observes that the dance floor in the film is vastly more integrated than images in wartime newsreels and magazines more generally.[11]

Daves's overall inclusive stance is indicated by the words of the millionth serviceman to attend the Hollywood Canteen: "I represent every man in the room. I might have been a Russian friend, a colored boy, or one of our South American neighbors. I'm all of you rolled into one." The film is more inclusive than many others in this genre. Twentieth Century Fox acknowledged the wartime contribution of African Americans with *Stormy Weather* (1943), with stars such as Lena Horne and Fats Waller. However, this was a segregated, all-Black musical in which the lead actresses are lighter skinned than other cast members. In *This Is the Army*, Black soldiers are not seen marching with the white forces led by Ronald Reagan, and they are not visible as the massed forces sing on stage. Only one brief shot shows boxer Joe Louis, and only with Black men in the same frame. In *Stage Door Canteen*, the inclusion of different groups of Americans seems limited. There are Black singers and musicians, but only one visiting Black soldier is seen in the foreground. The song "That's What the Well-Dressed Man in Harlem Will Wear" presents stereotypical images of a Black minstrel show with deep Black faces, exaggerated smiles, bright lips, and white eye makeup, the performers wearing outrageous costumes. In contrast, Daves's film provides a Black quartet performing the film's most sincere and melodic song, "The General Jumped at Dawn," reminding the audience that "remember we gotta win the war," and that to do so requires "Black men, white men—a real solid old American team ... every creed and color and belief." The song also includes a line expressing the readiness of Black pilots to fly, at a time when they were deployed on escort missions but were not permitted to serve as bombardiers.

Daves deals with the issue of prejudice against African Americans more directly in *Kings Go Forth*, in which Lieutenant Sam Loggins (Frank Sinatra) meets and falls in love with Monique (Natalie Wood) as the US army advances through France in 1944. When he learns that her parents are American and her deceased father was Black, he is forced to confront his own prejudices: "A lot of people need somebody to look down on—or think they do." Their growing closeness is shown as they face each other in delicate medium shot, but by means of a wordless closeup the viewer shares Sam's despair as Monique is increasingly attracted to the unit's charismatic radio operator, Britt Harris (Tony Curtis). When Monique criticizes the way Sam drinks wine, his resignation and despondency are conveyed with subtle movements of the eyes and mouth, and then his feelings show with just one line of dialogue: "Yeah, I'm a slob." After spending the night with Monique, Harris refuses to marry her because he regards her as "Black." The core of Daves's beliefs is encapsulated as Monique's mother (Leora Dana) speaks into the camera with great tenderness, dignity, and pride of her husband's achievements in overcoming major obstacles to become president of a Philadelphia insurance company.

On release, one critic concluded that the film "doesn't come close to having the guts of the book by Joe David Brown."[12] The language of racism is less blatant and callous. When Britt makes clear that he is no longer interested in Monique, he says only that he has never been involved with a girl who is not white, whereas in the novel, Britt's language is more crudely misogynistic and racist: "I've learned that she had a nigrah pappy.... It wasn't a bad piece of tail after all."[13] In fact, Karen McNally notes several changes made in the transition to film. Britt is from a privileged Eastern background rather than the South, and Sam was raised in a Harlem slum.[14] Conventionally, Hollywood presented racial discrimination as a feature of southern culture, but in extending the recognition of racism beyond the South, McNally implies that Daves presents a more severe indictment of American prejudice. This is emphasized further as Daves's camera moves slowly into a close-up of Monique. Perhaps because of her experience abroad, she is more scathing when she refers with distaste to the expression "nigger," when the term was not held in the same universal contempt as in more recent times, and it is only with Americans that she feels she must be secretive about her parentage: "I guess nigger is one of the first words you learn in America." In the novel, Monique commits suicide, while in the film she lives but remains emotionally scarred. After the death of her mother, she finds some satisfaction in providing a home and school for war orphans. Daniel Leab predicts that Sam and Monique will marry, suggesting that only a disabled or disadvantaged white man would contemplate a mixed marriage.[15] However, the film implies that she will continue to live alone, just as Sam, whose war wounds have left him physically disabled, albeit less so than in the novel, will also be alone. When Sam's commanding officer emphasizes that "the worst thing in the world [is] loneliness," it is clear that it is racial prejudice that has brought about this unhappiness.

With Roosevelt's plea for Americans "to bury in oblivion all internal differences," and with advice from the OWI that "[p]roperly directed hatred is of vital importance to the war effort,"[16] Hollywood war films typically emphasized the racism of the Japanese enemy in the interests of achieving unity at home and in the forces. Reviews of *Guadalcanal Diary* commented on its realism and honesty in portraying modern warfare.[17] Yet the Japanese are presented as sinister stereotypes: their tactics are shown to be unscrupulous and devious, and they are described as "apes," "monkeys," and "dwarfs." Thus, Daves's antiracist stance seems in doubt in *Pride of the Marines* as Al Schmid uses terms like "slinky" and "slanty eyes" and describes Japanese soldiers as "yellow-bellied, dirty, stinking, slimy pigs." David Gerber claims that Albert Maltz did not want such expressions in the film, but for commercial reasons, Daves and producer Jerry Wald inserted this language in order to exploit the deep-seated wartime antipathy to Japan.[18] Maltz insisted that "[w]hat makes Japan our enemy has nothing to do with slant-eyes" and that "[t]his is a backward approach."[19] Yet in the same memorandum, Maltz acknowledged that the final script reflects Schmid's actual racial prejudice, which continued after the war. Roger Butterfield's biography of Schmid, which was based largely and uncritically on his reminiscences, makes clear that "Al hated the way [the Japanese] talked and everything about them."[20] It is possible that the producer/studio decided to exploit anti-Japanese sentiments, but there is no evidence that this reflected Daves's views. Maltz does not explicitly make this accusation, and on at least two occasions, navy personnel complained to Jack Warner that Daves's portrayal of the Japanese was too favorable.[21]

Furthermore, Daves made clear his opposition to anti-Japanese and anti–Japanese American sentiment particularly on the West Coast during and after World War II, and he recounted an incident when he refused to sign a petition to force a Japanese family to leave the neighborhood where he lived. Instead, he made and remained good friends with the family, and their children played in each other's homes.[22] Despite Schmid's anti-Japanese remarks in *Pride of the Marines*, he acknowledges the skill and effectiveness of their infiltration tactics: "They were good at it, too good." Daves's view of Japanese soldiers is more compatible with War Department advice given to US soldiers.[23] This perpetuated some stereotypical elements, such as small stature and protruding teeth. However, this guidance also emphasized the courage, loyalty, discipline, and skill of the enemy as well as the extent and rigor of their training. A naval officer in *Task Force*, albeit filmed when Japan was no longer an enemy, exclaims in reference to the attack on Pearl Harbor and the way in which the Japanese forces evaded American detection, "Who said the Japs weren't smart?," and the film also acknowledges prewar American complacency and lack of preparedness. *Task Force* was one of the most popular foreign-made films shown in Japan in the postwar years. Sandra Wilson discusses the fact that Japanese-made films about World War II were very popular in Japan in the 1950s as, unlike Hollywood films, they portrayed situations where Japanese showed admirable discipline, courage, and skill; and that there were Japanese heroes.[24] Daves's film shows the intensity of attacks from both sides at the Battle of Midway, recognizing Japanese strengths, and Wilson states that Japanese audiences appreciated and applauded the film's acknowledgment that their forces fought well.[25]

Director Francesco Rosi claims that "a film should be made to touch the conscience and intelligence of the spectator."[26] He emphasizes that it is important to be honest about the past and be aware of painful as well as glorious episodes. Benshoff and Griffin suggest that it was not until the postwar period that mainstream Hollywood began to explore racism in the context of the reasons for which war was fought, with films such as *Gentleman's Agreement* and *Body and Soul* (1947) dealing with anti-Semitism and *Home of the Brave* (1949) examining racism in the armed forces.[27] Daves's *Pride of the Marines* predates these films and is unusual in that it acknowledges the existence of division and discrimination while the war continued and Hollywood usually sought to emphasize national unity as Nazi racism and Japanese imperialism were still being confronted. This is not just attributable to Maltz's screenplay, as Frank Krutnik and colleagues imply,[28] but is redolent of Daves's view of the world as expressed across his body of work. When another combatant fears that his peacetime job will have been taken by a Mexican, the others make him feel ashamed of his remarks, particularly as he has spoken in the presence of a wounded Mexican American soldier who had shown courage and self-sacrifice. This was a controversial issue of that time. As the demands of war on industry and the armed forces highlighted systemic inefficiencies and waste of manpower, the machinery of segregation and discrimination began to be challenged, with wage differentials based on race outlawed in 1943, despite opposition from southern Democrats. Nevertheless, Thomas Guglielmo shows that despite attempts by the Texas legislature to satisfy the increasing demand for labor by ensuring that Mexican and Mexican American residents had full and equal privileges, they generally received lower wages while working in more unpleasant jobs.[29] They experienced segregation in housing, education, and public amenities, and Daves returned to this subject of racial and economic exploitation of Mexican Americans in *The Badlanders*.

Certainly Daves celebrates the values of American democracy: in *Pride of the Marines*, as "America the Beautiful" plays on the soundtrack, Al Schmid, as narrator, reflects with pride on symbols of freedom such as Independence Hall and the Liberty Bell in his hometown of Philadelphia. However, his films express a genuine liberal concern over the social and political realities that may detract from that vision of America. As in many Hollywood films of this and earlier periods, a train porter in *Pride of the Marines* is played by a Black actor, and this reflects the reality of the age. Appearing in two scenes, which screenwriter Maltz acknowledged were written by Daves,[30] his portrayal is neither stereotypical in the way that he speaks nor unduly servile in his dealings with the white passengers. He is presented as a dignified and conscientious individual, and relations are characterized by mutual respect; the Black porter in Daves's script for *Stranded* is similarly portrayed. *To the Victor* expresses the danger that a cynical post–World War II world might set "race against race, religion against religion, hemisphere against hemisphere," and Daves's vision is encapsulated in the final shots of *Demetrius and the Gladiators*, in which three men of different creeds and race walk together as equals in common purpose, forward to fulfill their destiny.

Bird of Paradise explicitly confronts the subject of racism in the opening scene, with the bigoted arguments of a white racist trader filmed menacingly in partial shadow. His tone and expression as he rants against any form of integration is contrasted with the innate dignity, tolerance, and intelligence of Tenga (Jeff Chandler), the Polynesian chief's son, and his community's willingness to welcome visitors despite previous experiences of disease and violence that had resulted from contact with foreigners. Just as Tom Jeffords's experience is transformative in *Broken Arrow*, the European hero André (Louis Jourdan) observes and, with Tenga's explanations, learns how the community's customs and traditions are appropriate to its beliefs and needs. He appreciates the importance of the key values of generosity and kindness in this self-supporting society, following a way of life where there is no accumulation of private property. André realizes that there is something missing in his life despite his wealth and sophistication, and he is attracted to the simplicity and honesty of this lifestyle: his acceptance of its customs and values and his love for Tenga's sister (Debra Paget) are demonstrated in the tenderness and beauty of the marriage ceremony. Filmed before the Production Code was strictly enforced, an early version of *Bird of Paradise* did not address issues of racism. It was a romantic melodrama noted for shots of nude swimming and erotic rather than culturally accurate dancing. Daves's film, in tone and viewpoint, is the antithesis of Richard Walton Tully's play,[31] which was the original source material for both film versions and which Christopher Balme feels is "resonating with eugenic philosophy"[32] and is antagonistic to racial intermarriage and miscegenation.

HOLLYWOOD'S PORTRAYAL OF AMERICAN INDIANS

Toni Morrison writes: "Deep within the word 'American' is its association with race."[33] She argues that the classic heroic qualities celebrated in American fiction are those of self-reliance, independence, and control and that these virtues are dependent on the presence of racial inferiors on whom control can be exerted. Philip Deloria also recognizes that "Blackness ... has been an essential precondition for American whiteness."[34] He highlights the association of Indians with children and the belief that, as children of nature, Indians were capable of savagery and therefore needed to be controlled.[35] He goes on to submit that attitudes to "control" have ranged from segregation from whites to the assumption that Indians could be assimilated into "American" society, with resistance to these "solutions" to be countered with force.[36] Lakota scholar Vine Deloria adds that because the African American labored, he was considered to be "a domestic animal," whereas the Indian occupied large areas of land and was considered "a wild animal,"[37] and so the breaking of treaties and extermination could be justified. Consequently, "Christianity thus endorsed and advocated the rape of the North American continent."[38] In this context, he emphasizes that despite feelings of guilt over past treatment of Indians, there was no understanding of what it is like to be an Indian or of the experience of being held in contempt.[39]

While Morrison's focus is on African Americans, she refers more generally to "non-whites," and in exemplifying her discussion of characters of color in fiction, she comments that "they are Tontos all, whose role is to do everything possible to serve the Lone Ranger."[40] This conviction reflects her perception of the American dream of flight from oppression and limitations on freedom as a "move from discipline and punishment to disciplining and punishing; from social ostracism to social rank."[41] Thus, at the core of American history is the belief that different races and societies may exist at different points on an evolutionary scale from savagery to civilization. It is this premise that illuminates policy and attitudes to those of color as well as perceptions of America's role in the world. It is a perspective consistent with nineteenth-century observations, such as those of traveler Edward Freeman, who noted that although Indians were "less ugly than the Negroes ... they were repulsive from their utter lack of intellectual expression."[42]

Furthermore, this is a reflection of the values articulated in a paper presented to the American Historical Association in 1893 by Frederick Jackson Turner.[43] In his thesis, Turner argues that the essence of the American character and identity and the exceptionalist nature of American democratic institutions developed as a result of the movement of the frontier and contraction of free land. As settlers and pioneers spread westward and adapted to hostile conditions at "the meeting place between savagery and civilization ... little by little [they] transform the wilderness."[44] Just as Turner perceived that "the Indian was a common danger demanding united action,"[45] Theodore Roosevelt felt that the subjugation of the different tribes ensured that civilization would progress "over the world's waste spaces,"[46] as he described lands inhabited by Indians. These attitudes were espoused in presentations such as "Buffalo Bill" Cody's Wild West Shows and in popular fiction. Two characters in Laura Ingalls Wilder's novel *Little House on the Prairie* (1935), considered to be wholesome educational reading material for children, believe that "[t]he only good Indian was a dead Indian."[47] Although one character recognizes that "it's his path. An Indian trail, long before we came," he also states: "When white settlers come into a country, the Indians have to move on." Another emphasizes: "Treaties or no treaties, the land belongs to folks that farm it."[48]

Such beliefs were reflected in Hollywood films. John O'Connor notes that although there are several standard plot variations, the classical Western narrative involves human conflict between those who are outside society and those inside, with the latter showing themselves to be morally superior and stronger, ultimately triumphing over the inherent weakness of the former.[49] More specifically for Richard Slotkin, at the heart of these human conflicts is the opposition between wilderness and civilization, with Indians seen as acting outside civilized society, functioning as "the special demonic personification of the American wilderness."[50] Angela Aleiss does point out that more positive images of American Indians were not uncommon in the silent film period.[51] She refers to early films of Cecil B. DeMille and D. W. Griffith and Thomas Ince's *The Indian Massacre* (1912), which shows the persecution of a peaceful Indian community by avaricious and brutal white men who slaughter buffalo and shoot Indians for pure enjoyment. Nevertheless, Aleiss maintains that such films did not overcome dominant cultural values and could not withstand the demand for stories in which cowboys defeat uncivilized aggressors.[52] Indeed, as early as 1911, an Indian delegation traveled to Washington to protest to President William Taft about the inaccurate portrayal of Indians in films. In fact, these same directors also reinforced stereotypical racist images of Indians as synonymous with hostility and evil. In *Custer's Last Fight* (1912), Ince presents Custer as a hero of the West and the Sioux as an impediment to the advance of civilization.

In the sound era, some directors of "B" movies tended to enjoy more freedom, provided they kept within a very tight budget. Some of the Gene Autry and Roy Rogers Westerns recognized that Indians fought only when their lands and food supplies were threatened.[53] Similarly, both *Indian Uprising* (1952) and *Ride Out for Revenge* (1957) show the duplicity with which white men broke peace treaties, encroached on Indian land, and tolerated the brutal murder of peaceful Indians. However, the dominant themes in Westerns have traditionally focused on the transformation of a vast, empty desert into a fertile "garden," achieved because of the sense of mission, courage, and self-reliance of pioneers. O'Connor suggests that to give the Indians a more complex role than that of noble primitives or savages would result in unacceptable moral ambiguity in the narrative and go beyond the confines of audience expectations, which might threaten a film's box-office appeal.[54]

In the novel from which *Northwest Passage* (1940) is adapted, the Harvard-educated protagonist comments that "Indians are supposed to be more savage, cruel, treacherous, cowardly, short-sighted than any other race. Yet I doubt that an Indian at his worst can outdo white men."[55] However, in the film, the same character observes Indians who are drunken, childlike, and unreliable allies or murderous savages. He learns that "Injuns is peculiar people; you can't judge 'em like white folk" and accepts the need to "kill every fighting Indian, kill 'em quick, kill 'em dead." The increased critical and popular recognition of Westerns after the success of *Stagecoach* (1939) encouraged studios to produce "A" Westerns that predominantly celebrated the "civilizing" of the West, with Indians portrayed as obstacles to that civilization. They were seldom articulate, usually uttering little more than fierce shrieks, grunts, or at best very limited vocabulary: they usually adopted a scowling expression and an unnaturally stiff body stance. They were presented either as bloodthirsty heathens who slaughtered white settlers or as misguided, primitive, and sometimes noble savages who would have done no harm but for the evil influence of white villains. Steven Leuthold suggests that such stereotypes have been perpetuated in more recent non-Westerns.[56] For example, in *Taxi Driver* (1976), Robert De Niro's violent character is told by an adversary to go back to his own tribe, and he cuts his hair in a Mohawk style as his savagery begins.

It is a racial image that is central to John Ford's *The Iron Horse* (1924), in which there is little regret for the killing of Indians who attempt to prevent the construction of the first continental railroad, and to *Drums along the Mohawk* (1939), in which the Indians must be overcome to enable young families to build homes and communities. The raising of the American flag at the close of both films serves to validate these beliefs and acts as a symbol of the rectitude of American exceptionalism. Even in *Soldier Blue* (1970), which is sympathetic to their plight, the Cheyenne are essentially anonymous, presented as a tribe of helpless victims rather than as individuals with a distinct way of life and culture; the chief is portrayed only as muscle-bound and virile. Aleiss argues that in Ford's *Fort Apache* (1948), the Apaches hold firm to their distinct identity and culture and resist white encroachment and the racism of the colonel (played by Henry Fonda). However, this position is weakened by the final homily to the army and the importance of belief in heroes, irrespective of the truth. In the same way, Philip French feels that in *Little Big Man* (1970), the focus on General Custer as a crazed psychopath dilutes the film's condemnation of American society's treatment of Indians.[57]

DAVES'S PORTRAYAL OF AMERICAN INDIANS: *BROKEN ARROW* AND *WHITE FEATHER*

While Hollywood Westerns tended to conform to the conclusions articulated by Deloria and Morrison, Daves's Westerns, despite ambiguities, evidence a more nuanced approach to issues of race and to America as a world power. Melvyn Stokes writes that "*Broken Arrow* introduced major changes in how Indians were represented on film,"[58] and arguably it was the first major film of the sound and color era to challenge conventional stereotypes. Recognition of the significance of *Broken Arrow* was not total. Bosley Crowther's review noted its "honorable endeavor" but argued that Indians "merit justice not patronage" and that in this film, "Indians act like denizens of the musical comedy stage."[59] However, other reviews attached greater significance to the film, focusing on the proposition that Apache society "is the match of any civilized culture ... in social organization, community service and morality."[60] In suggesting that the Apaches could be thoughtful, kind, and considerate, as human and civilized as white people, the film paved the way for a continued reexamination of cinema's treatment of American Indians. In this sense, the film meets the criteria for what André Bazin refers to as a "super-western" in having a sociological or moral dimension extrinsic to and enriching of the genre and by which the film makes a lasting critique of its traditional subject matter.[61] Furthermore, its commercial success suggests greater audience receptiveness to its stance. It reached number 6 in the list of the year's top-grossing films, although its highest grosses tended to be in northern and eastern cities rather than in the South.[62]

The film tells the story of the friendship of Civil War veteran and scout Tom Jeffords (James Stewart) with Chiricahua Apache chief Cochise (Jeff Chandler), set amid the brutality and hatred that existed between the races. Jeffords lives with the Apaches and learns about their customs and values. During this time, he marries Sonseeahray, an Indian maiden, but as a direct result of the racist actions of some white townspeople, she is killed. With Cochise, who proves to be a shrewd and farsighted leader, and with General Oliver Howard, Jeffords is determined to establish peace between the two peoples, despite the risk to his safety. Edwin Sweeney records that the historical Jeffords was the subject of a smear campaign and was heavily criticized in the press, and he quotes General Howard, who testified to Jeffords's bravery and to the injustice of the slander against him.[63] The film depicts Indians as figures of intelligence and dignity with their own traditions and standards of integrity, and where hatred existed, there were reasons that needed to be understood. Daves explored this theme in different ways in *Drum Beat* and *The Last Wagon* and as screenwriter in *White Feather*. The latter film is based on a short story by British historian and screenwriter John Prebble[64] and recounts the relationship between Prebble's great-aunt Appearing Day (Debra Paget), a Cheyenne, and surveyor Josh Tanner (Robert Wagner), set against ongoing peace talks between the US army and the Cheyenne and Sioux nations. Unlike the fictional romance in *Broken Arrow*, this was a real-life relationship that resulted in marriage.

The respective narrations by Jeffords and Tanner enable audiences to appreciate and understand what these characters learn about the reality of the frontier experience, as their recognition of the humanity of their "enemies" effects a reexamination of traditional racial assumptions. After Jeffords's life is spared by the Apaches because he has saved the life of a young warrior, his reactions to witnessing the mutilation of white victims indicate that he had previously accepted the stereotype of Indians as "just animals . . . more dangerous than a snake." Yet he "learned many things that day," noting that the white victims of Indian torture had Apache scalps among their belongings. He realizes that "an Apache woman would cry over her son like any other woman" and that "Apache men have a sense of fair play" and keep their word. He learns their language and customs, appreciating that "it is good to understand the ways of others." Typically, in Hollywood Westerns, the white characters show very little regret when an Indian is killed during a skirmish with the army or pioneers. The significance of *Broken Arrow* in this regard is illustrated in Daves's composition in one brief sequence as Apaches clash with the army. While the fighting is ongoing in the middle and background of the scene, the body of a dead Indian lies in the foreground. The Apaches outwit the army on this occasion, but with the dead Indian's hair blowing in the swirling dust of battle, this shot points to the eventual fate of the American Indian tribes.

In a 1972 interview at Stanford University, Daves stated, "I'm a documentarian at heart."[65] He emphasized that out of respect for his pioneer ancestors and after the time he spent with the Hopi and Navajo Indians in his youth, he wanted to present a more honest picture of the West.[66] In *Broken Arrow*, Jeffords exclaims: "Let's get the facts straight," when arguing about responsibility for the Indian Wars; and *Jubal* and *The Hanging Tree* provide incidental background details of the lives of ranchers and miners, respectively. In *3:10 to Yuma*, Daves presents a barren and unromantic West where there is an unceasing struggle against a harsh environment, and he intended *Cowboy* to present a realistic impression of life on a cattle drive. A contemporary review of *Cowboy* found that it was an "exceptional Western that will not soon be surpassed for authenticity.... [A]ll of its action arises naturally out of the habits and customs which constituted life on the trail."[67]

Yet there are significant factual inaccuracies in *Broken Arrow* that contradict the opening narration's claim that events "happened exactly as you'll see it." Cochise had sought peace before he met Jeffords, and the importance of their relationship is emphasized at the expense of the role played by Cochise's two brothers, in particular that of Coyuntura, whom Terry Mort describes as Cochise's "confidant, advisor, and protector, literally a brother in arms."[68] Frank Manchel notes that Cochise and Jeffords appear in the film as contemporaries, when in reality Cochise was an old man when he knew Jeffords, who outlived him by forty years.[69] Manchel argues that the film exaggerates the authority that Cochise exercised over the Apaches and underplays the disease, devastation, and disruption caused by Euro-Americans to Native Americans, while also ignoring the courage and determination of pioneers. The romance between Jeffords and Sonseeahray (Debra Paget) is fictional, and although the relationship appears in Elliott Arnold's novel *Blood Brother*, on which the film is based, O'Connor suggests that this story line was included for commercial reasons.[70] That may be the case, but historians generally believe that Jeffords did have a relationship with an Indian woman.

In fact, Daves's primary purpose was not exclusively to record accurately. He concluded, for example, that *Task Force*, in recounting the struggle to develop naval air power, is "almost too much of a documentary,"[71] just as for Michael Walker, *Cowboy* is the weakest of Daves's Westerns because its narrative is rather slender due to the documentary nature of its focus on cowboys' experiences.[72] However, Jean-Loup Bourget submits that the freedom of directors is not measured by what they can do openly within the Hollywood system but rather what they can imply about society.[73] While identifying factual errors and misrepresentations, Manchel nevertheless recognizes the revisionist stance of *Broken Arrow*, concluding that it presents the real-life characters and events "not as they were, but as we wanted them to be."[74] In this sense, the utopian societies depicted in *Bird of Paradise* and *Treasure of the Golden Condor*, as well as that in *Broken Arrow*, draw attention to the fact that the viewer's own society may fall short of such ideals. When Cochise outlines the difficulties that Jeffords and Sonseeahray may face together, Jeffords replies: "What he says does not have to be." Daves's films present a vision of what should be possible, consistent with Graham Greene's view that the true subject matter for film as an art form is the antithesis between life as it is and life as it ought to be.[75] It is the nature of such reflections and the values espoused in Daves's films that strike a chord with an audience and express his expectations of a wealthy and educated society that purports to guarantee freedom and that rests on an assumption that individuals are entitled to justice and to be treated with respect.

With Jeffords doubting customary assumptions about who is to blame for the interracial violence and exclaiming, "Cochise didn't start this war," Daves challenges the myths that were common in conventional Westerns and that were yet to be seriously examined by mainstream historians. John Higham argues that only by the early 1970s was it possible to conclude that "today's Americans are losing Turner's underlying faith in the relevance of the pioneer heritage."[76] He contends that initially this "debate" did not spread beyond the confines of universities. Indeed, images of Indians as bloodthirsty heathens in films such as *Northwest Passage* were utilized in teaching American history in schools in the 1940s and 1950s. It was significantly later that John Price, in discussing the stereotyping of Indians, pointed out that very few tribes regularly rode horses, wore elaborate feather headdresses, or hunted large game.[77] Most were farmers or fishermen, wore woven robes rather than tailored hide clothing, and lived in permanent housing rather than temporary hide tents. Similarly, Robert Utley and Wilcomb Washburn show that Indian attacks on forts, stagecoaches, or wagon trains, central in Westerns such as *Stagecoach* and *Drums along the Mohawk*, were relatively rare.[78] They dismiss the convention that the US army was usually victorious unless overwhelmingly outnumbered or when a victim of deception, and they emphasize that small groups of Indians were often successful because of their skillful guerrilla tactics. In *Broken Arrow*, it is the army that tries unsuccessfully to deceive Cochise. Jeffords refuses to cooperate with an attempt to lure Cochise into a trap, and the soldiers are routed by superior Apache preparation and tactics. Utley and Washburn also regard as fiction the view that the army or settlers attacked Indians only after whites had been subjected to motiveless violence. In fact, peaceful Indians were invariably victims of indiscriminate attacks.

In both *Broken Arrow* and *White Feather*, the main characters gain a more balanced understanding of the causes and conduct of violence between whites and Indians. Jeffords learns that the bloody ten-year war with the Apaches started when an army lieutenant abused and dishonored a "flag of truce" and executed Cochise's brother and other Indians when acting under that flag. He recognizes that the Apaches had been fighting against those who wished to take their land and that the "whites have done great wrong to the Indians." This is consistent with the real-life General Howard's record in which he recognized the responsibility of whites in starting the wars and also that Indians were often allocated reservation land that was too poor to work.[79] Similarly, as a surveyor employed by businessmen to lay plans for a town that would inevitably remove Indians from their traditional territory, Tanner learns that whites have committed violations of a tentative agreement over territory, while "the Indians have kept to their side."

Dee Brown provides numerous examples of ruthless and callous actions against Indians.[80] For example, General Custer exceeded orders to kill only men when attacking the village of Chief Black Kettle and the Southern Cheyenne in 1868. Of the 103 Cheyenne killed, only 11 were warriors, yet he was congratulated for "efficient and gallant services rendered" by General Philip Sheridan, who famously said, "The only good Indians I saw were dead." In *Drum Beat*, although his parents and sisters had been killed in an Indian massacre, MacKay, a Buffalo Bill–like Indian fighter (Alan Ladd), recognizes that the wars had resulted from motiveless violence from whites. Indians in *The Last Wagon* conform to Hollywood stereotypes in that they are unseen, threatening figures who attack in the dark and are ready to kill innocent women and children, but it is clear that their attack is revenge for the slaughter of more than one hundred Apache women and children, just as the hero (played by Richard Widmark), a white man who has lived among the Comanches, takes revenge for the murder of his Comanche family. While Westerns often focused on the threat posed by Indians, Hollywood did not always show Indian families similarly threatened or Indian actions explained.

John Belton criticizes *Broken Arrow*, suggesting that Cochise is portrayed as a victimized saint rather than as an authentic frontier inhabitant, implying that this rehabilitation of the Indian goes too far in the opposite direction.[81] In fact, the film presents Cochise more realistically as a multilayered human being with faults as well as strengths. He is a strong and dominant personality, invariably filmed standing as an equal with whites, in close-up, from a low angle, and against the sky or lit from behind, thus emphasizing his authority. He is seen as intelligent and honorable and as one who keeps his word, in contrast to the intolerance and hatred of some whites. He demonstrates effective communication skills, for example with his potent analogy trying to persuade tribesmen to accept his plans for peace: "If a big wind comes, a tree must bend or be lifted out by its roots." He shows shrewdness in overcoming the deviousness of the army general but also ruthlessness in the way that he crushes army troops and in his summary shooting of Nahilzay, who breaks an Apache promise to the townspeople when he tries to kill Jeffords.

Cochise displays a sense of humor, for example as he comments affectionately on Jeffords's weak attempts to impress Sonseeahray with a bow and arrow: "Never mind, by the time he's a grown man, he'll know how." This aspect of Indian behavior was rarely shown in Westerns. Even when sympathetic to their history, films tended to portray Indians as rather solemn or imposing figures. In his Stanford interview, Daves stated that Hollywood films did not show "the great sense of humor I found among the Apache," and went on to say, "Indians have the greatest sense of humor I have seen."[82] He emphasized that he addressed this neglect in his films. In *White Feather*, the Cheyenne laugh uproariously when Little Dog struts pompously wearing Tanner's Stetson. They also enjoy Tanner's humorous response as he combs his hair and encourages Little Dog to reciprocate. Speaking of their two encounters, Little Dog says, "I will remember both days with laughter." In *Drum Beat*, on the morning of his execution, the Modoc chief listens to the visiting preacher, who assures him of the wonders and beauty of heaven. He replies, "You like it so much, you take my place out there."

Daves's portrayal of Cochise is consistent with Mort's analysis of eyewitness accounts that refer to Cochise's gravitas, honesty, and dignified implacability and his obvious authority among his people, but also to his capacity for cruelty.[83] General Howard also recognized his honesty, hospitality, and wisdom as well as his ruthlessness and capacity for violence.[84] In his journal, Lieutenant Joseph Sladen, Howard's assistant who helped to negotiate with

Cochise, testifies to Cochise's dignity, intelligence, good humor, and generous hospitality as well as his anger and violence.[85] Howard describes the warmth and closeness of Apache families,[86] and Sladen's expression of surprise at the cleanliness, friendliness, generosity, and humor of the Apaches[87] suggests that he underwent a similar revelatory experience, as does Jeffords in the film. While Cochise in *Broken Arrow* demonstrates that he is a realist in appreciating that whites are getting stronger while the Apaches are becoming weaker, he shows also a degree of naïveté in assuming that whites will keep their word, unlike Broken Hand, who agrees to sign a treaty only with heavy resignation and stoicism in *White Feather*.

Just as Jeffords is exposed to racist arguments such as those of a trader—"We'll have peace when every Apache is hung from a tree"—so Tanner encounters similar hatred from the shopkeeper from whom he rents a room. However, Jeffords's experiences lead to a developing friendship based on mutual respect with the decent and proud Cochise. This relationship of trust is instrumental in his acting as an intermediary in bringing about a peace treaty. Tanner has held no strong views about Indians, but his attitudes develop as, through friendship with and respect for Chief Broken Hand and his son Little Dog, he begins to understand Cheyenne customs and traditions and respects their strong family values. Jeffords's opening narration, echoed by Tanner in *White Feather*, explaining that an Indian will speak in English "so that you may understand him," reflects Daves's belief, expressed in interviews, in the importance of understanding different peoples.[88] This sentiment encapsulates his advocacy of the universality of basic human values, and with his main characters gaining in such understanding or ensuring that others may so learn, audiences are encouraged to make the same journey of discovery.

DAVES'S PORTRAYAL OF AMERICAN INDIANS: *THE LAST WAGON* AND *DRUM BEAT*

As well as directing, Daves received collaborative credit for the original story and screenplay for *The Last Wagon*; Richard Whitehall writes that it is "one of the most continuously exciting Westerns ever made."[89] John Wakeman agrees that it is exciting but feels that it is less reflective as a result.[90] However, the fast-paced action sequences stimulate reflection as well as create momentum. Walker suggests that *The Last Wagon* continues from the point where *Broken Arrow* concluded, with "Comanche" Todd taking revenge for the rape and murder of his Comanche wife and the killing of his children, a revenge to which Jeffords was initially inclined but against which Cochise argued persuasively.[91] As in *Broken Arrow*, Daves conveys a sense of morality and idealism through the actions and development of the characters and the interaction between them. After Todd's capture by a brutal and racist sheriff, the pair join a wagon train of Christian families to travel through Indian Territory, as had Daves's grandfather after the Civil War. Because of his life with the Comanches and his violent revenge for the murder of his family, Todd encounters reactions ranging from sympathy to suspicion and extreme hatred from the travelers. However, after Apaches slaughter the majority of the group, the young survivors are dependent on Todd to lead them to safety. Their trek into the unknown becomes a journey of ethical maturation during which their sense of justice and morality is tested and developed through their responses to the dangers they experience: "Billy's grown quite a lot on this journey. Maybe you have too."

It becomes clear that the young people must learn to trust Todd and rely on his knowledge and competence in the "ways of the Indian" to survive. Daves expressed amusement at comments that Todd's character is modeled on Nazi ideals of leadership, as Todd demands absolute obedience, insisting that the end always justifies the means. Daves emphasized that the group must turn to a person with experience, as would happen in any emergency situation, and that for Todd, there is a sense that there may be something more important at stake than his own survival.[92] The selfless nature of his status as a teacher and savior of the group, for which he is ready to put at risk his own freedom, is suggested further by the fact that, before the Apache attack, he was manacled to a wagon wheel with his arms outstretched and deprived of sustenance, as if being crucified, an image that is sustained in the shot of Todd being "raised up," arms still outstretched, from the foot of a cliff after the attack.

The issue of racism is addressed directly through the attitudes and experiences of the young survivors, in particular the two half-sisters who were traveling with their white father. Valinda is sickened at the thought of her father with Jolie's Navajo mother—"It was something filthy when my father took your mother as his woman"—and so displays disgust toward her sister. As Walker suggests, the venom in her veins after a rattlesnake bite is an expression of the poison of her racism.[93] In sucking out the poison, Todd saves her life, and his conduct, as well as that of Jolie (who sacrifices her rations when Valinda is ill), are instrumental in her reflecting on her behavior. She recognizes her own racism and the need to change when she gives Todd the key to unlock his manacles. Her statement at his trial, "He made me grow up," could be applied to the moral journey of all the young people.

Furthermore, Jolie overcomes her sense of inferiority, cultivated by the way she has been treated. She gains self-respect because of the support she is able to give Todd on their journey as well as his encouragement for her to value her Navajo ancestry: "He gave me pride in myself."

Todd also influences the attitudes of General Howard, the judge at his murder trial (based on the historical Oliver Otis Howard). Consistent with the Production Code, Howard's initial view is that a killing must be punished, despite understanding Todd's reasons. Todd alludes to the fact that the general has been given medals for killing Indians and therefore challenges the inflexible implementation of the law. The general's convictions with regard to the conventional concept of absolute right and wrong are shaken by the submission that Todd's moral debt to white society has been paid by his saving of many more lives, together with his reference to the validity of Indian law: "Ain't it justice that counts? Everywhere on earth peoples, peoples got laws that may be different from their neighbors', but justice don't change nowhere." This echoes a character in *It All Came True* (1940), to which Daves made an uncredited contribution to the screenplay. The comment that "the law's awful cockeyed sometimes" mirrors Todd's role as teacher in illuminating the essence of the biblical text "Christ hath redeemed us from the curse of the law,"[94] and in contemplating a vision for the future based on forgiveness and redemption. As the judge is the same "Christian General" seen in *Broken Arrow*, it is possible to suggest that, in thematic terms, his debate with Todd influenced Howard's attitude to American Indians as well as his conceptual understanding of justice, which in turn may account for his beliefs and conduct demonstrated in the earlier film. In this way, Daves introduces the concept of restorative justice as an alternative to retributive punishment, which is symbolized by a "hanging tree" in every community. Fernando Berns makes a similar point regarding *The Hanging Tree* in which Doc Frail saves Rune from the mob and gives him the opportunity to make a fresh start.[95]

Based on the true story of the Modoc Indian wars of 1871–1873 on the California-Oregon border, *Drum Beat* explores similar themes, but while White refers to a liberal stance that is "remarkably consistent throughout" Daves's films with Native American characters,[96] he does not discuss *Drum Beat*. Józef Jaskulski feels that this is a more reactionary film that retracts the progressivism of *Broken Arrow*.[97] He indicates that this may in part be due to the "staunch conservatism" of Alan Ladd, the film's producer, who was well known for being very conscious of his image and for avoiding controversy.[98] This does seem credible. Bryan Forbes, for example, recounts that when working on the script of *The Black Knight* (also 1954), he was not allowed to have Ladd's character take a horse without the owner's permission, even to foil a Viking plot against England.[99] That said, as Daves wrote the script and contributed to the original story as well as directing, the fact must be addressed that the narrative appears to undermine the values espoused in *Broken Arrow*. Despite his initial doubts, MacKay (Ladd), a former Indian fighter who is proud of his past, is asked by President Grant to persuade the tribe to return peacefully to their reservation. The naïveté of Dr. Thomas, who sympathizes with the Modocs, is ridiculed when he refers to anti-Modoc discrimination, and MacKay, who finally defeats Captain Jack, the Modoc leader (Charles Bronson), eventually seems to align himself with a racist storekeeper after a white peace delegation is deceived and murdered.

As Walker emphasizes, Dee Brown's account of these events is very different.[100] The film does not show the deception of the army general or his rejection of the Modoc leader's pleas for compromise to retain dignity and pride. It ignores Jack's belief that the races could live together: "I want no more war ... I have always tried to live peaceably ... I liked to be with white people."[101] Jack's statement in the film that he wants whites "to come and settle in my land" is countered by MacKay's view that lives could have been saved "if you hadn't grabbed country that wasn't yours." This seems to be an unambiguous reflection of the racist dimension of Turner's "Frontier Thesis." Because of the labor expended in taming a wilderness, the dispossession of Indians was therefore morally right and inevitable, as proclaimed by the Swedish hero in Jan Troell's *The New Land* (1972) despite his knowledge of the genocide inflicted on the former Indian possessors of that land: "I've earned a right to my ground." Daves's declared intention was that *Drum Beat* should present the point of view of the white settlers.[102] Describing the film as a virtual documentary on the Modoc wars, he explained that to present a historically accurate account, much of his screenplay was based on contemporary accounts and on actual transcriptions of the peace conferences and the trial of Captain Jack.[103] However, such official records do not reflect the Modoc perspective that Dee's account attempts to present, and Walker fears that the Native American viewpoint has been expunged.[104]

Therefore, there would appear to be a lack of consistency with the vision of *Broken Arrow*. However, in his discussion of the potential subtlety of conventional Hollywood genres, Bourget suggests that the visual and aural language of film creates opportunities for irony, or implicit and sophisticated comment, that may penetrate behind or provide distance from the explicit elements of the narrative.[105] In short, he feels that the camera's (or the director's) viewpoint may not coincide with that of the main characters, just as it is not axiomatic that the racist comments made by Al Schmid in *Pride of the Marines* must reflect Daves's beliefs. While the predicament, views, and aspirations of whites are clearly presented in *Drum Beat*, there is implicit ambiguity that allows a different perspective of events to challenge the more explicit stance. As with *Broken Arrow*, there are comparatively few battles scenes, and relatively little actual violence is shown. The discussions and negotiations pertaining to councils of peace play a more substantial role, as do scenes of the aftermath and effects of violence, which present a direct challenge to a rigid insistence on peace only "with honor."

MacKay only enters an alliance with a racist when he feels that the actions of Captain Jack have made dialogue impossible and when some of Jack's own men turn against him. The tenor of the film is not against the Indians as a race, emphasizing that most are generally honorable and peaceful when allowed to live without conflict. When questioned, MacKay states that he has no objections to interracial marriage, and in the presence of the president he voices approval of the growing number of such marriages, the result of greater contact between the races at the edges of the frontier. His rejection of Toby (Marisa Pavan) is due to his love for another: he is respectful and sensitive when he could have taken sexual advantage. The narrative makes clear that the Modoc uprising was initiated by the racist actions of a white man, and as Walker notes, it is significant that when MacKay and Nancy come upon a farm destroyed as a result of an Indian revenge attack, Daves avoids inserting conventional reaction close-ups of horror, thus mitigating feelings of anger toward the Modocs even though Nancy's relatives have been killed.[106] Despite his Indian-fighting background and his initial pessimism about the likelihood of a peaceful outcome, MacKay tries to calm feelings against the Indians and the desire for vengeance after a white woman has been killed. In effect, the film repudiates the extremes of a Cold War mentality based on the pursuance of decisive victory. While MacKay listens to settler outrage at proposals for peace with their families' killers, he also recognizes Modoc grievances and anger. He comes to accept that with war, "the land will be piled high with hate," and he strives for peaceful coexistence. He acknowledges that to secure peace, agreement must be reached with an enemy, despite memories of "sins" committed in the past and the difficulties and objections that arise.

DAVES'S PORTRAYAL OF AMERICAN INDIANS: RECOGNITION OF INDIAN CULTURE AND CUSTOMS

While there is obvious ambiguity about Daves's perspective in *Drum Beat*, his body of work counters the view that his attitude to Indians and their beliefs and customs is paternalistic. Vine Deloria argues that the problem of stereotyping and condescension is primarily one of limited knowledge and perspective.[107] However, Daves had revealed a special interest in American Indians, and after college graduation, he joined an archaeological and ethnological study of early Hopi culture. He spoke of the friendships he formed with the Hopis and said that, despite their dislike of tourists, they invited him to stay in their pueblos and, unusually, observe their Snake Dance and Antelope Dance.[108] Importantly, *Broken Arrow* is concerned with Apaches who value and wish to preserve their culture and customs. Furthermore, the fact that these traditions are presented with respect and a high degree of accuracy is consistent with Daves's other Westerns. At a Western Movies: Myths and Images conference organized to coincide with the US bicentennial celebrations in July 1976, attendees leveled criticism at conventional Hollywood stereotypes, emphasizing that there were few instances of "real" Indians in Westerns. Attendees included younger directors such as Clint Eastwood as well veteran directors including Daves and King Vidor, and authors Vine Deloria, Richard Slotkin, and Jim Kitses. Participants agreed that "Hollywood" Indians obliterated ethnic and cultural distinctions between tribes, imposing a stereotype derived from popular fiction.[109] However, the conference recognized *Broken Arrow* as an exceptional film and commented that its tone, detail, and texture were rich in its noncondescending approach to and respect for Indian dignity, customs, and mores.

Ken Nolley agrees that, traditionally, Hollywood has not shown respect for the significance and uniqueness of Indian tribes or their respective cultures and histories, and that the language, rituals, and beliefs of one tribe are frequently attributed to another.[110] However, Daves's interest in and celebration of cultural differences is demonstrated in the care taken in films such as *Broken Arrow* and *Drum Beat* to offer more authentic insights into the point of view and culture of the Apache and Modoc Indian tribes, respectively. Aleiss gives examples of Daves's attempts to portray Apache customs faithfully, and his papers emphasize the importance he attached to accuracy regarding details of clothes, equipment for horses, jewelry, and games played by Apache children,[111] with his use of Morris Opler's major ethnographic study of the Chiricahua.[112] *Broken Arrow* avoids the elaborate feathers and beadwork that Ralph and Natasha Friar point out are either fake or inaccurate,[113] just as the beaded headband is a Hollywood invention. Artifacts such as tools and domestic implements including work baskets and Indian paintings on deerskins, as well as details in domestic scenes in dwellings, are authentic. For example, Edward Buscombe notes that the Apache wood and grass wickiups are ethnographically accurate, in contrast to Hollywood's usual tepees.[114] Similarly, a semi-underground Modoc lodge with an entrance in the roof is accurately re-created in *Drum Beat*. Significantly in this context, Daves invariably utilized the knowledge and advice of Indians employed as extras: for *Broken Arrow*, he benefited from the memories of Lambert Stone, a 104-year-old Apache who had joined Geronimo in breaking away from the main tribe. He also ensured that details of cavalry formation and tactics were accurate, as well as styles of lettering in street signs.[115] His papers show that for a brief scene in *Never Let Me Go*, he ensured that details of traditional Russian weddings were accurately portrayed.[116]

Broken Arrow's score contains actual music and dance of Apache traditions and rituals such as that of hailing the Mountain Spirit during a girl's puberty rites, and studies by Opler and James Haley confirm that the film recognizes the importance of this ceremony to the Apache culture as well as ensuring accuracy in dress, location, and proceedings.[117] There are details of a social dance that provides opportunities for men and women to become acquainted, with a woman taking the initiative by touching her chosen man on the shoulder; Aleiss acknowledges that such detail is consistent with authoritative studies.[118] However, the representation of an Apache wedding is entirely fictional: it is highly romanticized, and neither Opler nor Haley were able to describe such a wedding. Nevertheless, details provided by both historians show that the film accurately reflects courtship and preparation practices as well as the custom of a man preparing a secluded site where he and his bride might stay alone for several weeks before returning to the community.[119] Just as the opening credits of *Broken Arrow* show examples of Indian art and artifacts, the credits in *Bird of Paradise* not only exhibit Polynesian signs, religious symbols, and artifacts but specifically state that the film reflects actual nineteenth-century rituals and customs. In *Bird of Paradise*, Daves's camera views in detail the preparation of foods, the importance of plants, and the significance of music and dance, and the film examines the legal system and the importance of courtship before marriage. In *Treasure of the Golden Condor*, part of which is set in Guatemala, the opening credits emphasize that the native Mayan rituals and costumes depicted are authentic.

After more recent films such as *Dances with Wolves* (1990), *Broken Arrow* has been criticized for its use of white actors to portray American Indians; Stokes refers to this as a "limitation."[120] Furthermore, several critics have noted that it is the "villainous" Indians in *Broken Arrow*, such as Geronimo, who are played by Native American actors, while white actors portray the "good" Indians who can be trusted.[121] Some sympathetic characters in *Broken Arrow* were played by Indian actors such as Billy Wilkinson as Juan, Jeffords's teacher, and Chris Willow Bird as Noihalo; and a factor in the hiring of actor

Nick Thompson for *Drum Beat* was his knowledge of tribal customs and language.[122] Nevertheless, these comments are warranted, and it is undeniable that although Daves filmed *Broken Arrow* with "the intention of completely overhauling the characteristics of the genre,"[123] his casting, in the main, is rather conventional. Thus, Aleiss concludes that the overall impact is to erase cultural differences and transform Indians into model white men and women instead of doing justice to their distinctive character.[124]

While this criticism can be applied to many Westerns of this period, the ethnicity of actors was not an issue for Daves: his papers show that he auditioned numerous Indian actors and judged them purely on ability.[125] He initially considered Jay Silverheels for the part of Cochise but decided he wanted a taller man: "I wanted Cochise to be able to look Tom Jeffords in the eye—a real man to man confrontation."[126] He emphasized that his main concern in casting Jeff Chandler for the role was finding an actor who best conveyed the different facets of Cochise's character.[127] Price contends that even the acting of good white actors is usually unsatisfactory for such roles because of their lack of knowledge of Indian behavior and culture.[128] Arguably, however, Chandler's acting is sensitive and intelligent, and his Oscar-nominated performance is successful in conveying his character's innate dignity and wisdom, as well as his anger and humor. Interestingly, Chandler does bear some physical resemblance to Edwin Sweeney's description of Cochise, which is based on eyewitness accounts, and also to Cochise's son Naiche, who was photographed and who is said to have resembled Cochise.[129] Lawrence Quirk believes that because of Chandler's bone structure, as well as his acting, he did not look out of place in this role.[130] Kevin Brownlow notes that "Iron Eyes" Cody,[131] who acted in many of Ford's Westerns as well as in *Broken Arrow* and *Devil's Doorway* (1950), recognized that because there was no American Indian tradition of acting at that time, few such actors were available.[132] Price adds that only from 1966 were serious attempts instigated to promote the training and use of Indian actors with the formation of an Indian Actors Guild,[133] and Nobel Chissell describes workshop activities led by Jay Silverheels designed to contribute to wider aspects of education as well as develop acting skills.[134]

Stokes feels that a further limitation of *Broken Arrow* is that the Indians only speak English,[135] and for Aleiss, this reflects the process of blurring of cultural differences.[136] However, Vine Deloria attaches less importance to casting and argues that an important contributory aspect of stereotyping is the judgment of people on the basis of their ability to use the English language.[137] He points out that even in films that present an Indian point of view, Hollywood Indians usually speak in limited or broken English and are therefore more likely to be deemed backward by an audience. Furthermore, the use of Native American actors and languages in itself does not guarantee accuracy or balance or the avoidance of stereotypes. Daves makes clear that in terms of the narrative they spoke Apache, but in English only for the convenience of the audience. For Daves, this was key to the film,[138] and in this way, he emphasizes the intelligence of the Indians through the sophistication of their language.

Rick Worland and Edward Countryman argue that not until *Dances with Wolves* (and other "new" Westerns) was a proper level of cultural respect achieved, with the presentation of the Lakota nation as an alternative and meritorious society.[139] For Stokes, at the heart of the film is a narrative of discovery in which an army lieutenant learns that "[n]othing I had been told about these people is correct.... They're not the bogeymen they have been made out to be," an opinion for which he is beaten by fellow cavalrymen. However, the experiences of Tanner and Jeffords in *White Feather* and *Broken Arrow*, respectively, are just as transformative and profound, and Jeffords is similarly attacked by townspeople. With its use of Native American actors and the Lakota language, *Dances with Wolves* was praised as a revisionist Western. However, Alexandra Keller argues that by 1990, the year it was released, its theme was hardly radical, and therefore she questions its revisionist status.[140] *Broken Arrow* developed the same theme four decades earlier and can therefore be regarded as more innovative. After *Broken Arrow*, it was increasingly unusual for Hollywood to produce, with conviction, "A" Westerns in which Indians merely provided a "test" for the white hero to overcome to secure the progress of civilization. Of the major Westerns that followed, only *How the West Was Won* (1962) presents the history of the West as an enactment of Turner's "Frontier Thesis." There are no Black or Asian characters even in the sequences based on the Civil War or the building of the transcontinental railroad. Seemingly unmotivated Indian attacks on white pioneers provide obstacles to the movement westward to areas of "free land," although a later sequence does refer to treaties broken by white people.

RACE RELATIONS IN DAVES'S FILMS

Some critics have expressed a preference for *Devil's Doorway* over *Broken Arrow*. Slotkin argues that Anthony Mann's film is more radical in its view of racism expressed from the Indian's perspective and is more innovative in the ways it reflects contemporary issues.[141] For Don Miller, its stark monochrome photography evokes a sense of impending and unavoidable tragedy, and its uncompromising statement about the treatment of an American Indian Civil War hero who loses his land because of the Homestead Act is an allegory of the treatment of Indians, including servicemen, in the twentieth century.[142] In contrast, a review of *Broken Arrow* referred to the softening of its portrayal of discrimination, with its breathtaking Technicolor scenery and excessive focus on the love story impacting negatively on the film's sense of realism and unorthodoxy.[143] Certainly *Broken Arrow* is more optimistic. Before her death, Sonseeahray hopes that "in times to come we will see our children ride white horses, maybe." In *Devil's Doorway*, the hero retains loyalty to his race and traditions. However, the underlying theme of the film is critical of a society that prevents him from realizing his desire to be treated as white, including the right to own property. In condemning such a closed society, the film envisages the assimilation of Indians into the dominant culture. For much of the film, the hero is unrecognizable as an Indian but for his headband (ironically a Hollywood invention). He uses his Americanized name, Lance Poole, rather than Broken Lance, to which he reverts only when he has abandoned his desire for acceptance. In this regard, *Broken Arrow* is more radical because Jeffords wishes to adopt Apache customs.

Lary May's analysis of Hollywood films indicates that the postwar years witnessed an increase in films featuring villains of different ethnicity, alongside a decline in the number of admirable or heroic characters of color.[144] Thus, whatever limitations may be perceived by modern viewers, Walker is right to conclude that *Broken Arrow* is a genuine attempt to view sympathetically the plight of American Indians.[145] The film may be regarded as progressive for its time in its readiness to portray interracial relationships; indeed, Daves's films may be similarly regarded even by the norms of present-day mainstream Hollywood. With the decline of the studio system, the influence of the Production Code also diminished, and it was formally abandoned in 1968. Nevertheless, Murray Schumach feels that the Code had a longer-lasting, pervasive influence and that Hollywood filmmakers continued to censor themselves in order to appeal to the broadest possible audience.[146] Even in *Dances with Wolves*, the Pawnee Indians, as enemies of the peaceful Lakota, are portrayed as stereotypical murderous savages; and despite the hero's developing respect for the Indians, the story introduces a white woman so that he may find love with one of his own race. However, in *The Last Wagon*, the hero, having saved white people by adopting Indian tactics and strategies, argues his case successfully in court according to Comanche principles, showing no regret or repentance for having broken the white man's law. Thus, Daves challenges the application of the Production Code, dramatizing that even the most serious of crimes should not automatically require summary punishment without a prior examination of context.

Some commentators have questioned the extent of Daves's nonconformity in how he presents Indians, perceiving his treatment of interracial marriage as conservative. In *Broken Arrow*, Sonseeahray is killed shortly after her marriage to Jeffords, while in the original novel, *Blood Brother*, she becomes pregnant first. In *Drum Beat*, Toby, the Indian maiden who loves the white hero, is killed, and a similar fate befalls the Polynesian woman who has married a European in *Bird of Paradise*. Thus, Stokes argues, the difficult issues of mixed-race children and how such families would be accepted in white society can be avoided.[147]

In *Broken Arrow*, Cochise warns the lovers about the difficulties they will face when married, and for Jaskulski, this represents conservative thinking that seeks to discourage interracial relationships.[148] White, however, believes that Daves stretched the boundaries of the Production Code as far as possible. He suggests that Cochise's warning is purposefully realistic about the difficulties that interracial couples will experience in postwar America but that this does not diminish the film's support for such unions.[149] Certainly Daves made it clear that he found it revolting that interracial lovers had to die: "I do not understand why in racial stories two lovers can never be united, especially in this day and age."[150]

Additionally, Jaskulski feels that *Drum Beat* "seems to possess an underlying tone of miscegenation anxiety," particularly with the overt eroticism of Toby's behavior.[151] For the same reason, Walker suggests, Nancy, the white heroine, feels a sense of duty to save MacKay from the evil of miscegenation, and he rejects the advances of a Modoc woman who genuinely loves and respects him.[152] The exigencies of the Production Code made it difficult for a film to show a white leading actor marrying a woman of color. Thus, the implication is that there is no fundamental difference of principle between such narratives and those of earlier films such as DeMille's *Union Pacific* (1939), in which the heroine pleads that she should not be taken alive, and Ford's *Stagecoach*, in which a man prepares to shoot a young white woman to "save" her from Indians. Yet Daves's conviction that miscegenation need not warrant reproach presents a further challenge to the Production Code.

Certainly white heroes in films by other directors have chosen American Indian women in preference to white women. In *Across the Wide Missouri* (1951), the couple have a child before the Indian wife dies and the other pioneers mourn her death. However, she is accepted in the community only after she has taken part in Christmas celebrations, and their marriage is recognized after a Christian ceremony, with the presumption that the children will be raised as white. In films such as *The Big Sky* (1952) and *The Indian Fighter* (1955), the interracial relationships are lasting. However, William Indick emphasizes that they are initiated with the white hero forcing his attentions on the Indian woman, just as whites took Indian land by force.[153] The fact that the Indian women remain with the heroes willingly in a sense absolves whites of guilt over their aggression or conquest. There is no such aggression in the relationship between Jeffords and Sonseeahray. Their love is declared and later consummated alongside a river with its life-enhancing freshness serenely flowing through the green and fertile valley. It is celebrated particularly in the tender wedding scene, with the beauty of the verse, "now there is no cold, one is warmth to the other; now forever there is no loneliness," enhanced by Daves's low-angled shot as they enter their marriage wickiup, leaving a final image of two white horses standing beside the river. It is a scene that respected British reviewer Caroline Lejeune found to be unforgettable and unbearably beautiful.[154] Thus, miscegenation is viewed positively, and despite Sonseeahray's death the film ends optimistically. She is shot beside a river now fast-flowing, but the most racist of the townsmen is killed and swept downstream, as if his "sins" have also passed away, offering hope for the future.

M. Elise Marubbio argues that such deaths of Indian women were necessary because of the need for the white dominant culture to prevail: their deaths free the white man to propagate his race and culture, with the woman "punished" for seeking to challenge this principle.[155] In fact, after the death of Sonseeahray, Jeffords rides away alone: he does not return to white society and marry a white woman, as takes place in Arnold's novel. Marubbio's view seems inconsistent with the delicate and touching tone of the portrayal of the relationship in *Broken Arrow* and the film's sympathetic picture of Apache culture. Such an interpretation is also not consistent with similar scenarios in Daves's other films. In *White Feather*, Tanner's love for Appearing Day also develops beside a peaceful riverbank, while the uncertain future of the Cheyenne is decided alongside a dried-up riverbed. Their relationship is presented with affection and their marriage survives, which, as Walker notes, is certainly progressive for the 1950s.[156] Even the fact that the real-life couple remained married did not stop studio head Darryl F. Zanuck from expressing surprise when he read Daves's draft screenplay: "I was astonished when our leading man ended up with the Indian girl."[157] In *The Last Wagon*, Valinda expresses a hostile attitude to miscegenation in describing her father and Indian stepmother "acting like a pair of animals" at her half-sister Jolie's conception, and by her hateful remarks about Jenny's attraction to Todd.

Walker suggests that her invectives are a projection of her self-disgust at her own attraction to an Indian.[158] Her father is proud of his marriage to a Navajo woman, while anxiety over miscegenation is represented by Valinda's maliciousness. Comanche Todd, although born white, is regarded by both races as Indian, and thus Jenny's developing love for Todd is unconventional because it endures: its consummation challenges the norms of the Production Code. Todd does not behave as a typical white American hero. His references to sex are more erotic than those of the standard hero of the 1950s: he asks Jenny if she has been "broken in yet," as "girls and ponies both, the younger you break them in the better." The love scene is explicit for this period, and Jenny clearly feels that she is making love to an Indian: "I didn't know Comanches kissed like this." She is open and proud of this relationship and is not "punished" for her actions as she abandons her plans for a conventional marriage.

Buscombe maintains that while the portrayal of white men taking Indian wives was problematic for studios, social attitudes of the 1950s presumed that at least the wife would take a subordinate role to the husband and therefore be assimilated into a more "civilized" way of life.[159] The assimilation of a white woman's values into those of an Indian male was less acceptable. Thus, the forced miscegenation of a captured white girl who wishes to return to her own community could be forgiven, as in *The Searchers*, but a woman who prefers the Indian way of life was invariably "punished," usually by death, as in *The Charge at Feather River* (1953). Joanna Hearne argues that Mann's *Devil's Doorway* offers a bolder depiction of a cross-racial romance than does *Broken Arrow*, as it involves a white woman and American Indian man.[160] However, this relationship is not consummated, nor is any real physical contact seen. While actual physical contact between interracial partners tended to be minimal in Hollywood films in the 1950s, White points out that in *Broken Arrow*, Daves shows Jeffords and Sonseeahray embracing intimately and lying fully outstretched together across the screen.[161] While a degree of ambiguity is acknowledged in these films, Daves's instincts are revealed in a project that was not filmed. In his treatment, a white woman is reunited with her natural family after being raised by Indians. Although loved and well treated by her birth family, she chooses, and is allowed, to return to the tribe to marry an American Indian whom she loves and with whom she will have children. She is granted "the gift of her life to live as she wants it to be."[162] Furthermore, Mann does not sustain this perspective in other films: in *Winchester '73* (1950), the hero gives the white heroine a gun with the understanding that she should use the last bullet on herself to prevent being violated if captured.

Aleiss notes that while the Production Code strictly forbade representation of miscegenation between Black and white partners, it made no specific reference to other races.[163] Therefore, ambiguity remained with regard to miscegenation between whites and Indians. Such alliances tended to be presented with more overt eroticism than intraracial relationships and therefore could be held to infringe the Code's stipulation that sex scenes should not be portrayed in ways that could arouse passion or morbid curiosity. While most states with anti-miscegenation legislation prohibited marriage, adultery, and "fornication" between "Negroes" and those deemed to have Caucasian blood, such laws in thirteen states originally applied to American Indians as well, and the prohibition was retained in nine states into the 1950s.[164] Any parties to such marriages were subject to criminal penalties, and any children that resulted were held to be illegitimate. Jeffords's marriage would have been illegal in the nineteenth century, but permissible when the film *Broken Arrow* was made, as, although Arizona did not repeal all anti-miscegenation statutes until 1962, such laws did not apply to American Indians after 1942. The Supreme Court did not rule on the constitutional position of interracial marriages until 1967, when they were still banned in sixteen states. While *Loving v. Virginia*[165] held that state anti-miscegenation laws violated the constitution's Fourteenth Amendment, mixed-race marriages were still controversial. In 1967, the daughter of Secretary of State Dean Rusk married a Black university classmate, and Rusk offered to resign to avoid controversy. Although President Lyndon Johnson did not accept his resignation, several members of Rusk's family, including a brother, did not attend the wedding.

While Philip French acknowledges that *Broken Arrow* and *White Feather* made serious attempts to present the Indians with sympathy and authenticity, he argues that Indians were used as political symbols by filmmakers.[166] He suggests that, particularly during the anticommunist purge of "subversives" in the early 1950s, the Western provided a safety valve through which studios could examine issues of contemporary relevance behind the "cloak of respectability" of a traditional genre. A 1944 edition of *Variety* reports on the formation of a committee to frame a code for the entertainment industry to eliminate discrimination and "caricatures of Negroes." However, in the same edition, there is a report on a practice in southern states whereby censors "will not countenance any scenes showing the Negro on a basis of social equality with the Whites" and that such scenes will be cut from films or newsreels, irrespective of the impact on continuity or quality.[167] In fact, during the 1950s, American Indians were used as a "stand-in for African Americans" in Hollywood's examination of racism. Daves addressed this aspect of racism directly in *Kings Go Forth*, but he recognized the potential

"You show me a white man jury in this land that'd hang four white men for killing an Indian squaw and two Comanche boys." *The Last Wagon*. Richard Widmark. ScreenProd / Photononstop / Alamy Stock Photo.

for using Indians "to present liberal ideas on race that were unacceptable in parts of the country."[168] He referred to his correspondence from South Africa, which testified to the perceived relevance of *Broken Arrow* to issues of prejudice and discrimination under the apartheid regime.[169]

Daves's depiction of American Indians as a representation of contemporary issues relating to the struggle for Black civil rights is indicated in *The Last Wagon*. Comanche Todd's plea in the penultimate scene in court may be viewed as a comment on justice that had been exercised in some American states with regard to defendants of color: "You show me a white man jury in this land that'd hang four white men for killing an Indian squaw and two Comanche boys." Similarly, on the thought of hanging a white man for killing an Indian, Cochise reflects, "that will be something for Cochise to see." The rapists of Annette Butler and the murderers of Black activists Lamar Smith and George Lee as well as Emmett Till, who were found not guilty by white juries in the 1950s or not even put on trial, are just a few examples given by White of many such cases,[170] and the experience of different standards of justice remains an issue in more recent times. Similarly, Cochise's warning to Jeffords and Sonseeahray mirrors the advice that mid-twentieth-century parents might have given their children who were contemplating a mixed-race marriage: "It will not be easy for you . . . There will always be Apaches who have suffered from white men who will hate you for it . . . There will always be whites who will hate your wife because of the color of her skin."

ISSUES OF RACE IN AMERICAN HISTORY

In his interpretative synthesis of the historiography of the West, Gerald Nash notes that from the late 1950s, some historians began to criticize Frederick Jackson Turner's work for its basis in "old and no longer reputable racial assumptions,"[171] but overall Nash concludes that it was historians after 1960 who focused seriously on the inequalities and injustices of the hitherto "forgotten people" of the frontier. Furthermore, John Higham suggests that, apart from within the confines of universities, traditional images remained firmly entrenched, particularly in popular culture, with few films questioning these conventions.[172] Therefore, as an example of Hollywood showing a genuine interest in another culture, *Broken Arrow* may be regarded as a forerunner of "New Western" history, which presents a more inclusive interpretation of the West as a convergence of diverse peoples. Patricia Nelson Limerick, for example, views its history as a shameful legacy of suppression and exploitation of African Americans, American Indians, Hispanics, and women, as well as a reckless spoiling of the natural environment.[173] In so doing, she argues that too much respect has been given to Turner's analysis of American history.[174]

The implication that some films anticipated developments in American intellectual history and that the historian has a role as a moral critic is valid. *Cheyenne Autumn* (1964) recounts the plight of the Cheyenne as victims of government deception. However, made at the height of the civil rights campaigns and fourteen years after *Broken Arrow*, Ford's film does not seem radical. In terms of chronology, Stephen Handzo is more justified in referring to *Devil's Doorway* in this context.[175] However, his claim that the latter film is unique in examining the reality of Manifest Destiny ignores the significance of *Broken Arrow*, particularly as *Devil's Doorway* was released only after the critical and commercial success of Daves's film. Worland and Countryman suggest that *Broken Arrow* is part of a cycle of Westerns that adopted a commendable pro-Indian stance, but which proved to be short-lived and soon forgotten.[176] In fact, the film's theme was not just a temporary phenomenon: many pro-Indian films followed, their quantity diminishing only when the popularity of the Western genre declined from the mid-1960s. In paving the way for a continued examination of attitudes to and treatment of American Indians, Daves's Westerns go further than defying specific details of the

Hollywood Production Code. They pose questions about the cultural and intellectual foundation for the interpretation of American history to which conventional Hollywood Westerns have conformed.

Manchel correctly identifies the conflicting interpretations of themes in *Broken Arrow* as that of acknowledgment of cultural diversity, with American Indians recognized for their cultural heritage, versus assimilation and a belief that minority ethnic groups should be integrated into white society.[177] He argues that, although *Broken Arrow* is well intentioned and a significant step forward, Daves celebrates Anglo values over ethnic heritage, and that the film reflects the policy of "termination" toward the Indian tribes enacted by Congress in the 1950s. The late 1940s and early 1950s brought a reversal in federal Indian policy that constituted a conservative reaction to the prewar policies of John Collier. As commissioner of Indian affairs, his aim had been to reassert Indian sovereignty and cultural autonomy. Kenneth Philp contends that Collier's Indian Reorganization Act (1934) was intended to encourage substantial self-government, collective land management, and cooperative economic enterprises as well as to foster traditional cultural and religious freedom and community values.[178] In seeking to end government expenditure and reduce state intervention, the postwar policy of "termination" was directed toward dissolving the tribe as a legal entity. It encouraged Indians to become ordinary citizens and achieve economic development by becoming small-holding farmers or moving to urban areas to be industrial workers. The policy rejected the concept of special constitutional status for Indians on practical and ideological grounds and was antithetical to the communal culture of many Indian peoples.

Buscombe acknowledges that *Broken Arrow* does not endorse the finality of "termination," but he argues that the film's liberalism, while humane and empathetic, nevertheless reflects a benevolent paternalism inherent in the concept of assimilation.[179] Aleiss acknowledges that an awareness of cultural distinctiveness is recognized in *Broken Arrow*.[180] However, she focuses on differences in views about the aims of Indian policies, specifically the conflict between the preservation of traditional tribal sovereignty and the principle of assimilation. The former encompassed the ideal of communal rather than individual ownership of property and was suspected of being collectivist and therefore "un-American," while the latter envisaged the gradual assimilation of Indians into the wider population, thus weakening the distinctive features of tribal cultures. In this regard, David Murray notes that many Indians continued to stress their uniqueness and cultural differences, resisting efforts toward integration and preferring isolation from policies that might constitute a "de-Indianizing" force.[181]

Many of the pro-Indian films that followed *Broken Arrow* adopted an assimilationist stance as a solution to racial problems and presumed a consequent loss of racial identity. In *Walk the Proud Land* (1956), the Indian agent hero is respectful of the Apaches and their history and traditions, telling a young Apache boy, "You'll have to remember that you're Apache and be proud." However, he emphasizes that the boy "must learn much of the ways of the white man. It's his world now and you must learn to live in it." His overall aim is to "make useful citizens of them." The hero in *Ride Out for Revenge* rejects the racism of the army captain who sanctions the murder of Indians but emphasizes that the Indians should accept that it is not possible to retain their lands or their traditional ways. Aleiss compares Daves's work unfavorably with Ford's in this regard. She argues that Daves accepts that "mutual coexistence demanded a sacrifice of Indian identity,"[182] while Ford's characters retain a distinct identity and culture, even though she then admits that his representation is seldom accurate. Elements of *Broken Arrow* and *Drum Beat* do appear to reflect an assimilationist stance, seemingly emphasizing a divide between Indians who deserve sympathy because they are willing to adapt and those who oppose compromise. The Apaches are expected to adapt to farming rather than hunting, which in turn reduces the amount of land needed for Indians and therefore makes more available for white settlement. Those such as Geronimo who don't accept such change must be condemned, just as in *Drum Beat* the hostile Indians must be defeated.

However, it is difficult to reconcile the assumptions that underlie such an interpretation with the values evinced in Daves's films. In *Broken Arrow*, the Apaches are required to stop raiding and killing, while preserving their cultural traditions, which Daves has presented sympathetically and in detail. Indeed, Terry Mort points out that Cochise made peace primarily on his terms, making concessions with regard to territory while surrendering nothing of his culture and way of life.[183] It is significant, therefore, that in *Broken Arrow* Jeffords does not question or wish to reject any aspect of Apache culture. He emphasizes that each race must examine its assumptions and conduct to accommodate the other. Besides earning a Golden Globe for its "Promotion of International Understanding," the film was given a special award by the Association on American Indian Affairs, a nonprofit organization dedicated to the principle of self-determination and the preservation of the heritage and traditions of Indian peoples. The secretary of the association's Film Committee, Howard Mantell, cited the film as the "first harbinger of change" in attempting a serious portrayal of the Indian side of American history, in which "[s]tereotypes are discarded and Indians and whites emerge as human beings: cruel, frightened, courageous, kindly."[184]

In *Drum Beat*, Captain Jack's obsession with wearing an army officer's coat represents a small victory over the threat to his tribe and way of life. In *Taza, Son of Cochise* (1954), Douglas Sirk's "sequel" to *Broken Arrow*, Taza (Rock Hudson) wears an army coat and rides an army horse. Tom Ryan feels that this film provides evidence of progress in that Taza is the main protagonist, central to the action rather than secondary to a white hero.[185] However, his willingness to take orders from and salute an army captain and live at the fort indicates his readiness to be assimilated into the rules and norms of white society. Aleiss makes a similar point about the ending of *White Feather*. As Tanner and Appearing Day ride away together, the audience is informed that "Broken Hand lived to see his grandson enter the Military Academy at West Point." Walker points to the irony of the grandson joining the forces that oppressed his mother's people,[186] and although the couple marry, Aleiss feels that underlying this "message of tolerance was an attempt to erase Indian identity."[187] She highlights this scene as evidence of Daves's advocacy of assimilation, with peaceful coexistence requiring the absorption of Indian culture.

However, after writing the screenplay for *White Feather*, Daves left the studio, and his papers indicate that this ending does not represent his intentions. Neither his screen treatment or notes, nor his first or final draft screenplays, include any reference to attendance at West Point,[188] which in any event is unlikely, as, in real life, Josh Tanner was English, and the couple left America to live in Kent. Daves has Tanner clean and straighten the twisted body of his dead Cheyenne friend before walking away, hand in hand, with Appearing Day: "I think we're going to be able to find a pretty good life together." It is possible that script additions were made after Daves had left the project, perhaps to make the marriage seem more "acceptable." Daves's 1951 treatment of a Western story that was not filmed presents a clear vision in this regard. Karmi, a young white girl, has been saved from a fire and is raised by Blackfeet Indians. Much later, she is traced by her natural parents, who recognize that "she seemed much loved" and observe the "sense of tranquility" at the Indian village. The council of tribal elders decide that she should return with her natural parents, but adjustment proves difficult despite the love and help she receives from her birth family. She experiences "instruments" of assimilation, those of Christianity and education, which are provided sympathetically. However, she finally chooses to return to the Indian village to marry: "Side by side their jubilant voices surmount the drums. Karmi has come home."[189]

Contemporary observer Edward Freeman had noted that Indian children "take kindly to the civilised and Christian teaching which is set before them."[190] While the logic of assimilation seemed obvious, to be effective, "suitable" education was essential, and this has been reflected in films that adopted an assimilationist position. The protagonists in *Indian Uprising* emphasize that education is required to ensure that Indians repress their warlike nature to enable them to play a proper role in civilized society. The predominant aim of Indian education was to "civilize," by making Indians culturally indistinguishable from whites. Therefore, from the late nineteenth century to the 1960s, hundreds of thousands of Indian children were removed, sometimes forcibly, from their reservations. They attended boarding schools, usually located far from their reservations and the influence of family and tribe. They had to abandon traditional tribal ways and adopt American customs through immersion in the language, religion, values, and knowledge of the dominant society. They were given American names and wore different clothes and hairstyles, and any resistance could be met with physical or mental abuse.

After interviewing such pupils, Muscogee Creek academic K. Tsianina Lomawaima suggested that the unintended outcome of their experiences was a common need for survival and resistance, developing into a pupil culture that reaffirmed tribal identity.[191] In Daves's films, there is no such pressure for Indians to change their ways: it is the white people who experience "an education." In *Drum Beat*, Indian fighter MacKay learns a new tolerance for and accommodation with a different culture. Walker suggests that for the young people in *The Last Wagon*, their pursuit of survival becomes a moral journey in which the hazards they experience provide a test for their social and ethical development.[192] In *Broken Arrow*, Jeffords yearns to fully understand the Apache way of life: "I wanna learn about Apache spirits. I wanna learn about Apache ways." The fact that he needs only a "moon" (presumably a month) to achieve this requires a degree of suspension of disbelief, but as he places his hand on his heart to indicate his wish to be "Apache in here," his sincerity is not in doubt. In this sense, Daves's work prefigures films such as *Dances with Wolves* and *Avatar* (2009) in which the hero learns the ways of another culture and is willing to live according to its traditions. In *Avatar* as in *Broken Arrow*, the hero learns how to use a bow and arrow, but with greater success than Jeffords. Technology allows the white protagonist to inhabit an alien form, initially in order to persuade the Na'vi, natives of another world, to move away from their homeland to permit Earthmen to mine a valuable mineral needed as a source of energy, just as nineteenth-century pioneers and prospectors wished to appropriate Indian lands to mine gold and later drill for oil. He comes to despise the way his race views the Na'vi as savages and in time helps them defeat the interlopers.

That whites should learn from other cultures is a key tenet of Dave's films, with meritorious ideas demonstrated by indigenous peoples in *Bird of Paradise* and *Treasure of the Golden Condor*. Jack Weatherford has examined the contributions made by the different Indian tribes to modern medicine, agriculture, textiles, architecture, and ecology.[193] While Higham recognizes the importance of "the trauma of race"[194] in the shaping of American history, he still refers to that history as "spanning a mere three and half centuries."[195] It fell to later historians to explore Higham's own contention that the origins of American democratic values lay "above all [in] the unfolding of an inheritance rather than the flowering of an environment."[196] Weatherford proposes that America's "unique" democratic system of government with its federal structure incorporated, at the instigation of Benjamin Franklin, many of the features of government of the Iroquois. More specifically, he suggests that the first person to propose a federal model for a union of all the colonies with elected delegates was Canassatego, the Iroquois chief, in 1744. In *Bird of Paradise*, Tenga has been educated at an American university and therefore can be successfully assimilated into Western society. Yet he retains great pride in his own culture, despite its lack of Western sophistication, and prefers to return home. In *The Last Wagon*, Jolie regains pride and self-esteem, and while Todd has redeemed himself in the eyes of white society, he rides away from that society, thus adhering to his values and way of life.

Nevertheless, Daves's characters are realists, and his stories accept the logic and reality of history. Cochise is intelligent enough to acknowledge the limits of his ability in the face of destructive new technology. He knows that "the clock cannot be turned back" and that the Apaches cannot have unchecked authority over the whole Southwest: "Why should not the Apache be able to learn new ways? It is not easy to change but sometimes it is required." Just as Tenga advises caution when André and Kalua express their wish to marry in *Bird of Paradise*, Cochise recognizes the difficulties with such relationships. Daves also reflects the historical fact that agreements for peace have worked against the interests of the Indians. In *White Feather*, Tanner appreciates the misery and precarious existence that await the Cheyenne as they accept the fact of removal. As the exodus to their "promised land" begins, he wonders "how long they'll be able to live on promises." Little Dog's hostility to this fate is viewed sympathetically because of the relationship of mutual respect he has established with Tanner.

Daves's narratives recognize that for much of the second half of the nineteenth century, assimilation was the fundamental aim of Indian policy. The reservation system was intended to protect Indians from outside influences until they could be properly integrated into white society, which by definition involved acceptance of that society's beliefs and social and cultural values. However, not only does Daves question assimilation, but he suggests that it may not be entirely feasible. At the conclusion of Jeffords's period of learning, his teacher makes clear: "You've learned to speak our language good: [but] you do not yet think like an Apache." Daves's script for *Bird of Paradise* is more explicit. Tenga warns André that he can "never become one of us," nor, despite Tenga's Western education, "can I become one of your civilized world." André must appreciate that however utopian the island society may seem, there are aspects of the culture he may not understand, such as acceptance of polygamy to mitigate the despair of childlessness. André does not accept these customs but nevertheless respects cultural differences in the sense that he does not seek to change or "civilize": he leaves the island having benefited from evaluating his own assumptions through the experience of another culture.

While Daves recognizes the reality of the political and cultural forces that have impacted the lives of American Indians, at the heart of his films remains a celebration of the distinctiveness and validity of different cultures and an advocacy for their preservation. Thus, rather than reflecting a wish to extirpate Indian identity, Daves's convictions are more in line with the values of Collier's "New Deal," which for Philp represented a rejection of policies of assimilation and Americanization of Indians in favor of one of cultural pluralism.[197] Philp notes that central to Collier's reforms was the reawakening of Indian consciousness and pride.[198] He also emphasizes Collier's belief that the survival of Indian culture not only represented justice for Indians but also offered benefit to whites, in that aspects of tribal communal and cooperative life exemplified ways of living in a fragmented, modern industrialized society.[199]

Gabriella Treglia notes that from 1880 to 1933, federal policies were directed toward discouraging or even banning American Indian religio-cultural ceremonies as incompatible with the responsibilities of citizenship, as well as criminalizing dances considered to be immoral.[200] One of the examples given by Treglia is the Hopi Snake Dance, which federal officials did not accept as religious and claimed was one of many ceremonies that were detrimental to the civilization of Indians.[201] Yet Daves testifies to the pleasure with which he viewed this dance, recalling that he felt privileged to witness the ceremony and that it had a lasting impact on him.[202] Similarly, Catawba Indian author Trudy Griffin-Pierce commends *Broken Arrow* for its portrayal of the girl's puberty ceremony, which she maintains is central to Chiricahua Apache culture.[203] She notes the determination of the tribe to preserve its

"You are my people... I'll always remember the moments of these days." *Broken Arrow*. James Stewart, Debra Paget. AF archive / Alamy Stock Photo.

culture, including the hide paintings of Naiche, Cochise's son, which were intended to "educate" non-Indians, and she feels that such efforts were "an act of resistance" to assimilation.[204] Thus the film's depiction can be seen in the same light, particularly as she emphasizes that the ceremony continues to be conducted. Increasingly, Jeffords accepts and admires the logic and moral principles of Apache customs and values. He explicitly rejects the narrow and prejudiced moral vision demonstrated by the white townspeople and wishes to live with the Apaches. He prefers to be married according to Apache traditions, assuring Sonseeahray: "You are my people." Similarly, in *Bird of Paradise*, André comes to respect Polynesian tradition and wishes to marry according to its customs, whereas in the earlier (1932) version of the film, the white hero wishes to take the native woman away from the island. Therefore, rather than a drive toward assimilation, Daves's portrayal of native cultures anticipated reforms yet to be enacted. Actions taken by Presidents Richard Nixon and Ronald Reagan were directed toward sustaining rather than obliterating tribal cultures, returning tribal lands with compensation, rejecting assimilationist policies, and strengthening tribal governments. The American Indian Religious Freedom Act (1978) was enacted to protect the traditional cultural and religious rights and practices of Indians including the use of traditional sites, ceremonies, and sacred objects.[205]

CRITIQUE OF AMERICAN EXCEPTIONALISM

Clayton Koppes argues that policies enacted for American Indians reveal as much about the nation's image of itself as about the realities of Indians' lives.[206] Just as Daves's work does not conform to the substance of policies of assimilation or termination, nor to their typical representation by Hollywood, his films do reflect the view of James Olson and Raymond Wilson, who conclude that such policies became unacceptable reminders of cultural imperialism.[207] The belief that white Americans had the right and even the duty to establish Christianity and American values throughout the continent was expressed in 1845 by newspaper editor John O'Sullivan, who proclaimed Anglo-Americans' "manifest destiny to overspread and possess the whole of the Continent which Providence has given us." An obvious consequence, observed by contemporary historian Francis Parkman, was that Indians "were destined to melt and vanish before the advancing waves of Anglo-American power, which rolled westward."[208] In *Broken Arrow*, during an argument with townspeople, Jeffords refers to massacres of Indian families, including the death of Cochise's brother: "At Big Crick we murdered Indian women and kids." In advocating peaceful coexistence and respect between the races, with Jeffords exclaiming "I'm sick and tired of killing," *Broken Arrow* recognizes the realities of Manifest Destiny as the annexation of Indian lands by force, or by treaties of uncertain legality followed by the breaking of such agreements. Thus, Daves challenges the morality of annexation and predates Limerick's description of the 1830 Indian Removal Act, which forced tribes such as the Choctaw and the Chickasaw to abandon their lands and move west, as the Cheyenne must resettle in *White Feather*, as one of the greatest official acts of inhumanity and cruelty in American history.[209]

Harry Benshoff and Sean Griffin maintain that Manifest Destiny provided the ideological framework for justifying further US expansion after the closing of the frontier.[210] Theodore Roosevelt's Corollary to the Monroe Doctrine envisaged America as an international police power and justified intervention in countries that did not "realize that the right of such independence cannot be separated from the responsibility of making good use of it." On these grounds, the United States annexed Guam, Puerto Rico, and the Philippines, and its "liberation" of Cuba established the island as a US protectorate. Between 1909 and 1925, there were similar interventions in Nicaragua, Honduras, Haiti, and the Dominican Republic. At the core of such actions was a belief in "American exceptionalism," which celebrated the uniqueness of the country's values and its mission to transform the world. US Cold War foreign policy sought to contain communism on the same basis, encapsulated in James Burnham's statement that "the responsibility for the future of civilization falls unavoidably, today, on the United States."[211] This was reflected in films that advocated the need to defeat rather than "appease" an enemy, including intervention on foreign soil. In Ford's *Rio Grande* (1950), an army colonel (played by John Wayne) is ordered to cross the Mexican border to pursue the Apaches, thus ignoring the conventions of diplomacy and sovereignty. US involvement in Vietnam to secure "freedom" for the South exemplified the same doctrine. Bruce Jentleson concludes that the media adopted a largely uncritical "cheerleader" role to American policies throughout the first few decades of the Cold War, only adopting a more censorious stance as opposition to the Vietnam War increased.[212]

The greater rigor demonstrated by the media in its reporting of details of the Vietnam War began to expose differences between official accounts and the reality on the ground, and this began to be reflected in feature films. *Soldier Blue* re-creates the savagery of the Sand Creek massacre of 1864 in which US soldiers annihilated a Cheyenne village. *Little Big Man* depicts the Washita River massacre of 1868, using the word "genocide" to describe the attacks. Both films are allegorical expressions of outrage at contemporary American actions such as the My Lai massacre in Vietnam. Thus, they provide a response to John Wayne's *The Green Berets* (1968) and question the consensual status of American expansion and exceptionalism. Yet more than twenty years earlier in *Broken Arrow*, the Apaches are shown as people who can engage in purposeful dialogue as equals, and Jeffords explicitly and profoundly challenges the principle of Manifest Destiny and the rights of whites to do as they wish in Apache territory. In response to a whiskey trader's claim that "we're bringing civilization, aren't we?," he angrily retorts, "Who asked us out here in the first place?" Furthermore, "civilization" is exemplified by reference to "clothes, carpets, hats, boots, and medicine" rather than decent behavior or a moral code. Jeffords's question to those who later try to lynch him because of his relationship with Cochise is pertinent to an evaluation of America's postwar foreign policy. Interestingly, Frank Krutnik and colleagues note that as part of the dissent within the military against the Vietnam War, GIs produced as many as three hundred antiwar underground newspapers, one of which was entitled *Broken Arrow*, which was circulated at Selfridge Air Force Base in Harrison Township, Michigan.[213]

The concept of American exceptionalism can be viewed as inherently racist, just as Turner's thesis has been described as "a prose-poem that hymned Westering whites."[214] America's "mission" was the "improvement" of "nonwhite" inhabitants of other nations. Justifying the annexation of the Philippines, President William McKinley stated: "We could not leave them to themselves—they were unfit for self-government," adding that there was a need to "uplift and civilize and Christianize them."[215] In fact, John Nickel's examination of postwar films focused on social problems identifies a new paternalistic stereotype.[216] He argues that despite noble intentions, people of color were invariably presented as in need of help or with some form of disability, and that such figures reassured white audiences that, while dignified and courageous, they did not present any physical or sexual threat if allowed greater freedoms. Thus, "color" was presented as a difficulty to be coped with or overcome, which could not be done without the support of white Americans. An obvious example is the help the psychiatrist and others give to the paralyzed Black soldier in *Home of the Brave* to overcome his physical and psychological difficulties. In *A Man Called Horse* (1970), it becomes the responsibility of a British aristocrat to teach the Sioux to defend themselves against other tribes; John Tuska agrees that the film "is really about a white nobleman proving his superiority in the wilds."[217] In *Avatar*, it seems that only when the white man becomes the leader are the indigenous inhabitants able to resist those who threaten their community.

In *Son of Fury*, the hero relinquishes his property in England and returns to the Polynesian island where he had earlier begun to establish himself. However, he adopts what seems to be a natural position of leadership over the indigenous population as if it is axiomatic that a white man should do so, and it is the native woman who must adapt to his ways. She must learn his language and customs: she arranges their cabin with Western-style furniture, decorations, and utensils. The film shows nothing of the local culture or customs, and any dancing emphasizes sensual rather than cultural aspects. In Daves's remake, *Treasure of the Golden Condor*, it is the hero who becomes integrated into and learns from the values and customs of a different culture. More generally, characters of color in Daves's films tend to be more assertive and willing to initiate action. In *Kings Go Forth*, it is clear that after he was raised in poverty in Georgia, Monique's father has realized his ambitions and potential through his own determination, strength, and ability: "It hadn't mattered what people thought: we walked the streets of Philadelphia proud, defiant." In *The Badlanders*, it is the Mexican Americans who achieve symbolic victory in a reenactment of the Battle of the Alamo, as part of their fiesta celebrations, and they initiate decisive action that unites their community in overcoming those who have exploited and abused them.

Jaskulski feels that Daves makes the assumption that American Indians cannot speak for themselves and require white advocacy to make their case.[218] This may be true in *Drum Beat*. However, in *Broken Arrow*, while the initiative of Tom Jeffords is invaluable, Cochise is presented as his equal in terms of courage and intelligence, and it is clear that Jeffords has much to learn from him. He is articulate, decisive, and authoritative in negotiations. Griffin-Pierce writes that when she was growing up, the dignity and integrity of Cochise as portrayed in *Broken Arrow* provided a positive role model at a time when other children drew attention to her physical differences.[219] Andrew Nelson writes that Daves's later films feature regressive portrayals of Indians, giving Captain Jack as an example.[220] Similarly, Jaskulski argues that the presentation of Jack is "routinely one-dimensional": he is "an inarticulate savage," and his actions are "childishly stubborn."[221] Yet in his papers, Daves wrote: "He is not an unadulterated savage. . . . The moral obliquity of Jack makes it difficult to heroize him, notwithstanding I recognize something grand in his desperate obstinacy."[222] Jack is shown to be a natural and forceful leader, as emphasized by Daves's close-ups, and one who is proud of his race and culture. The film also shows Jack's tactical skill in resisting the army's attack on his stronghold, to which General Howard refers in his record with respect to the actual events.[223] He does not regret the actions he takes on behalf of his people, and at the end of the film, he shows courage as he prepares for his execution. He exhibits sophisticated humor and, as Jaskulski notes, capacity for self-reflection,[224] and in his final conversation with MacKay, the pair express genuine hope for real integration. It is fitting that the white hero and adversary is willing to shake his hand.

In an interview, Daves refers to his respect for other peoples' beliefs and his own efforts to understand their importance and meaning for those peoples.[225] Significantly, in *Spencer's Mountain*, the church service is conducted by a minister of "the Church of God," which is potentially more inclusive than the Baptist church in Earl Hamner's original novel. Writing in 1953, Herbert Jacobson associates the transformation of America into a military and economic world power with the spirit perpetuated by the myths of Western heroes and pioneers and with the progress of Christian civilization.[226] However, he also raises the possibility that the images of Indians in new films such as *Broken Arrow* and *Devil's Doorway* might herald a "genuine reflection of a greater respect for the different point of view of the rest of the world, of whom so many peoples are colored." Indeed, as warfare intensified in Korea, for a reviewer in a religious journal, *Broken Arrow* presented "a persuasive argument for sanity in time of hostilities."[227] General Howard displays none of the missionary/imperialist zeal of many clergy and Indian agents who sought to convert and "civilize" non-Christians, rather than respect their culture or defend their rights. He emphasizes that "the Bible I read, preaches brotherhood for all God's children," and in response to Jeffords's question, "Suppose their skins aren't white. Are they still God's children?," he replies,

"The Bible says nothing about the pigmentation of the skin." Thus, the film attests to the values of mutual tolerance and peace rather than the significance of Christianity in the subjugation of "heathens."

Daves's focus on Jeffords's determination to learn, on his appreciation of Apache language and customs, represents his belief in the importance of learning more about other cultures to enhance mutual respect and peace. The high school teacher in *Spencer's Mountain* reminds her audience of the importance of knowledge of the world outside, while *Pride of the Marines* points out the dangers inherent in American isolationism and complacency, as indicated by the characters' lack of geographical knowledge. Critics have tended to interpret Sonseeahray's statement in *Broken Arrow*, that "[t]he world is so big and I know so little," as an admission of racial inferiority.[228] However, it could equally represent an open-mindedness to other customs and ideas. Daves's Westerns are significant in that they do not sustain the cultural certainty of an American exceptionalism that overlooks any racial transgressions incurred while pursuing that ideal.

For Joyce Appleby, American exceptionalism has achieved a sense of national identity through celebrating the nation's innovative institutions of governance and its dedication to liberty and equality as embodied in the constitution. However, she emphasizes that "exceptionalism raised formidable obstacles to appreciating America's original and authentic diversity."[229] For an example, she suggests that to recognize the culture of African or Native Americans would subvert the American story of progress.[230] Daves's films evince detailed and positive interest in American Indian culture and direct the viewer to an appreciation of Indian experiences and perspectives. Thus, his films anticipate the approach of "New Western" historians who in the 1980s attempted, in Appleby's words, "to recover the diversity of the American past" and give voice to "those men and women who had been muffled by the celebration of American exceptionalism."[231]

Chapter Four

Gender in the Films of Delmer Daves

CARL BOGGS AND TOM POLLARD MAINTAIN THAT NO DISCUSSION OF AMERIcan cinema is complete without a consideration of issues relating to gender, sexuality, and family relations, with the plots of most films relating in some way to these themes.[1] Kate Weigand accepts that the post–World War II years were marked by deepening political conservatism in America and highlights the resurgence of the belief in the preeminence of women's domestic role as central to an understanding of this period.[2] Postwar demobilization of over eleven million men led to massive layoffs of women from their wartime employment. As the postwar birth rate rose in conjunction with an increasing marriage rate, a social life or career for women outside the home was regarded as secondary to motherhood, as reflected in the publications of pediatrician Benjamin Spock, who emphasized a mother's responsibilities for attending to a child's emotional and physical needs. Furthermore, historian Ferdinand Lundberg and psychiatrist Marynia Farnham identified feminism as a disruptive force in society, alongside socialism, communism, and anarchism.[3] Such attitudes were reflected in Hollywood films. Marjorie Rosen concludes that by the 1950s, filmmakers were "reaffirming male dominance and female subservience."[4] While wartime films portrayed women's experiences in combat situations and in varied occupations at home, Rosen shows that during the 1950s films tended to avoid controversial or timely stories and reemphasized traditional prewar family roles, with images of an "ideal wife." *Every Girl Should Be Married* (1948) is an obvious example. Similarly, Laura Mulvey argues that in most Hollywood films, audiences were expected to identify with male characters, who were active and "doing," as opposed to females, who were "looked at" and passive.[5]

However, Daves's films evince a more progressive attitude to women's employment. Daves's heroines, even if young and inexperienced, are shown to be confident, independent, and aspirational, with qualities and capabilities that enable them to fulfill more than conventional caring and nurturing roles. Daves's portrayal of women, and of family and sexual relationships, is more sophisticated and multilayered than that invariably seen in mainstream Hollywood's vision of the roles and behaviors expected of women, which is encapsulated in Rosen's view that "[m]ovies glorified women who were young, beautiful, highly moral and ready to drop job and glitter for a good man."[6] The ideas and values inherent in Daves's films are in line with contemporary sociological analysis and empirical research in this area of human experience, at a time when Betty Friedan found that "something is very wrong with the way American women are trying to live their lives today," when it was no longer possible to "dismiss the desperation of American women."[7] In addition, I am considering the characteristics of Daves's heroes in the context of the 1950s and early 1960s, a time when, according to Arthur Schlesinger, "something has gone badly wrong with the American male's conception of himself."[8]

GENDER IN HOLLYWOOD FILMS

Even when she has successfully auditioned for a role on Broadway, a young actress (played by Debbie Reynolds) makes clear in *The Tender Trap* (1955) that a "career is just fine but it's no substitute for marriage," and adds, "a woman isn't really a woman at all until she's been married." Moreover, Hollywood seemed to indicate that other, nontraditional life choices were "unnatural." In the musical comedy *Lady in the Dark* (1944), a female editor (Ginger Rogers) initially dresses rather awkwardly in trousers, and her bad temper and indecisiveness suggest her unsuitability for this role. Her male assistant levels an accusation: "You have magazines instead of babies." Her psychiatrist hopes that "perhaps some man will dominate you," and she agrees to give up her career: "I'm going to live my life as a woman." Such a scenario is consistent with Lundberg and Farnham's belief that women in "unsuitable" roles can develop characteristics of aggression, dominance, and independence, which are a distortion of natural femininity and can only lead to anxiety, unhappiness, and an inability to cope with life.[9] Such views are clearly implied in *The Snake Pit* (1948), which was commended for drawing attention to degrading and inhumane conditions in American mental institutions. Shortly after marriage, the writer-heroine suffers a breakdown and is institutionalized. It is only when she is ready to accept the primacy of her role as a wife and recognize a desire for motherhood that she is "cured" and ready to leave the institution. Leslie Fishbein argues that, unwittingly, the film suggests that intellectual activity is secondary to women's fundamental femininity and therefore equates mental health with domesticity, almost as if feminine aspiration is diseased.[10]

As well as being portrayed as "unnatural," an insufficiently conservative stance tended to be regarded almost as unpatriotic. The culture of the Cold War and perceptions of gender seemed inextricably linked in character and direction. Wini Breines refers to the emphasis on women's domestic responsibilities as "a policy of containment,"[11] suggesting that this "containment" in a subordinate role is an adjunct to the "containment" of communism. Family stability and traditional gender roles were seen as key to the nation's security at a time of crisis, thus discouraging dissent and reform and strengthening the status quo. In *I Married a Communist* (1949), a new wife remains loyal to her husband, a "reformed" communist, and helps to defeat the attempts of a femme fatale figure to lure the husband and others to work for the party. Political activism was almost analogous with subversion, to the extent that Lundberg and Farnham raised the possibility that disruptive theories of feminism were inflamed by agents of the Kremlin,[12] and Susan Hartmann gives examples of feminists and women activists who were discredited or smeared with charges of radicalism or association with communists.[13] A feature of anti-Russian propaganda emphasized that Russian women could achieve high positions in traditional male careers; June Whitney, for instance, claimed: "A woman in Russia has a chance to be almost everything—except a woman."[14] Emily Rosenberg maintains that this connection between national/international and gender politics is reflected in Hollywood films, focusing on *The Man in the Gray Flannel Suit* (1957) as an example.[15] While the wife must show selflessness and forbearance in maintaining the family and agreeing that her husband's wartime Italian lover and child should receive financial support, America must be prepared to make sacrifices to protect American political and economic interests abroad.

Gavin Lambert casts doubt on the prewar image of strong-willed figures such as Greta Garbo, Marlene Dietrich, Katharine Hepburn, and Rosalind Russell. He suggests that, in many instances, their characters tended to "exploit traditional female wiles and gambits rather than assert themselves as independent beings" and ultimately would sacrifice their careers for a man.[16] Some mainstream films did portray capable and independent women. In *Johnny Guitar* (1954) and *Rancho Notorious* (1952), Joan Crawford and Marlene Dietrich, respectively, play authoritative, successful businesswomen, with the latter film emphasizing the seriousness of the crimes of rape and violence against women and the lack of action by authorities to counter them. Blake Lucas describes the heroine in *Devil's Doorway* as a frontier lawyer of intelligence, insight, and courage as well as adult passion.[17] In John Ford's final film, *Seven Women* (1966), a female doctor (Anne Bancroft) is indifferent to disapproval of her lifestyle, language, and past. She has endured discrimination in a male-dominated profession, but, as David Meuel emphasizes, she is a dedicated practitioner who courageously makes the ultimate sacrifice to fulfill her oath to preserve human life.[18] In fact, Meuel argues that most of Ford's films feature women who are strong, assertive, and independent.[19] Examples range from the indomitable spirit of Ma Joad in *The Grapes of Wrath* and the mature pioneer wives in his cavalry films to the sexually provocative playgirl in *Mogambo* (1953). More generally, however, their aspirations do not extend beyond the family or securing a lasting relationship. Meuel feels that in *The Quiet Man* (1952), Mary Kate's insistence on reclaiming her fortune from her brother symbolizes her independence and determination not to be "absorbed" by her husband.[20] Yet she burns her money and presumably must be supported by him.

Howard Hawks has been noted for his portrayal of confident and resourceful women in his Westerns and screwball comedies, with stars such as Barbara Stanwyck. However, Hawks denied that he advocated a feminist position, saying that he merely portrayed the types of women he found attractive.[21] In *Rio Bravo*, gambler and entertainer Feathers (Angie Dickinson) is intelligent and independent and takes the initiative in her relationship with John Wayne's character with confidence and humor. In earlier films, this character would be attractive to the hero but invariably would die, allowing him to have a more suitable marriage. Dietrich's character in *Destry Rides Again* (1939) is one such example. However, Feathers indicates that she will give up her employment to secure this relationship, and in the final act of the film she discards an item of clothing of which he disapproves. This tendency toward a conventional ending is evident in many Hollywood films of the period. In *The Bride Walks Out* (1936), an independent woman (Stanwyck) had enjoyed her own income before marriage. She resists her husband's objections to her working, even when facing hardship. On the point of divorce, she agrees that she should not work and that her place is in the home. While some of Daves's films also end conventionally, in the main his characters make their decisions by free choice and informed by experience, rather than because of what might be expected of them.

ISSUES OF GENDER IN THE FILMS OF DELMER DAVES

While Daves worked with many renowned Hollywood actors, apart from Lauren Bacall in *Dark Passage*, his films did not feature major female stars. Claudette Colbert, Mary Astor, and Maureen O'Hara were approaching or had reached the end of their years in films, while relatively early in their careers, actresses such as Anne Bancroft and Susan Hayward had yet to attain their Oscar-winning star status. Other than Natalie Wood, who had already been nominated for a Best Supporting Actress award when she appeared in *Kings Go Forth*,[22] perhaps his most notable female star was Gene Tierney, albeit in one of his weakest films. Her acting was generally underrated because of her beauty, with one review of *Never Let Me Go* criticizing her acting and her attempt at a Russian accent.[23] However, her performance is sensitive and heartfelt and is convincing to the extent that François Truffaut remarked that she "makes us want to look for our future wives on Russian soil."[24] The acting of Suzanne Pleshette, Felicia Farr, Eleanor Parker, and Leora Dana is intensely sympathetic and compelling in their respective films for Daves and was indispensable in realizing his intentions. Also, Daves worked with well-respected actresses such as Judith Anderson and Maria Schell; Wendell Mayes, coscreenwriter of *The Hanging Tree*, described Schell's acting as marvelous.[25] Her performance is understated yet powerful and expressive and conveys great warmth and tenderness as well as strength of character and determination.

Daves consistently endows his female characters with dignity and inner as well as physical strength, sometimes momentarily, as in *Kings Go Forth*, with the expression of an elderly woman offering wine to liberating troops, encapsulating the joy that follows the pain of occupation, or sometimes in reference to events occurring outside the incidents of the narrative. While *The Very Thought of You* is set during World War II, the heroine's father makes passing reference to his sense of failure after being forced to accept a menial occupation during the Depression and to his daughter's strength during that time: "You're a scrapper. You held this family up when I went to pot." In *Demetrius and the Gladiators*, Messalina is scheming and amoral, but she is highly confident and intelligent and easily matches in skill and guile the efforts of men to temper the excesses of Caligula. Jean-Pierre Coursodon recognizes that of the Bogart/Bacall films, *To Have and Have Not* (1944) and *The Big Sleep* (1946) are better known than *Dark Passage* and that the latter does not include the sardonic, verbal sparring associated with these stars.[26] However, he maintains that Daves's dialogue evokes the awakening of mutual feelings more convincingly and better creates a sense of intimacy. Terence Pettigrew notes that in the earlier films, it is the Bogart characters who dominate the terms of the relationships. However, in *Dark Passage* it is more of a relationship of equals.[27] Bacall's character does display nurturing characteristics, but she is also shown to be independent, decisive, and resilient, and at times Bogart's character is content to be dependent on her initiative.

Kevin Gough-Yates argues that conventionally, the film heroine was judged on the extent to which she conformed to certain standards of behavior and that little changed over the years in this regard. These "obligations" are centered on her sexual role, but also there was an expectation that a woman should exhibit a readiness for self-sacrifice for the love of a man or family and "should not attempt to compete with men on their territory."[28] However, in his early stories and screenplays, Daves was willing to consider different viewpoints. While *Flirtation Walk* celebrates the values and traditions of West Point, army officers perform a musical play in which it is a woman who commands the army and who behaves honorably and decisively in that role. Also, the screenplay makes fun of the phrase "a woman's place is in the home." *Miss Pacific Fleet*, to which Daves contributed to the script, satirizes female beauty pageants and emphasizes the cynical profit motive behind such events. In *It All Came True*, the heroine is assertive and not content with a humdrum "female" job, to the extent that her mother fears that she does not behave as a "good girl" should. Her reply, "I act and talk and dress as I please," indicates her confidence and independence. She is caring and supportive, but she is also organized and decisive and more effective than males in outwitting a gangster in hiding (played by Bogart).

In his screenplay for *Stranded*, Daves portrays the protagonists as mutually attracted because they recognize in each other their strength of character and personality and their ability to challenge each other's ideas with affection and humor. Yet in reflecting traditional ideas of women in marriage, Mack belittles Lynn's work as a "useless mad-house job" and feels that she is wasting her time. He takes pride in constructing the Golden Gate Bridge but does not appreciate that she, too, finds her work to be important and fulfilling: "Are you really fond of this job of yours?" he asks in disbelief, as marriage would ensure that "you'll have everything you need or want." He insists: "You're going to give up that job of yours today.... I want you to put us first" and that "[f]rom now on you're just the wife of a construction engineer." A contemporary review agreed that Lynn took her job too seriously and implied that it should be secondary to a domestic role.[29] Significantly, Leyland Axelson, writing in 1963, found evidence that this attitude prevailed even thirty years later. His research concluded that "[t]he working wife continues to be perceived as a real threat by the male in our society" and that, as well as causing damage to children, men felt that any increase in independence for a wife would threaten their own culturally defined dominance.[30] However, despite this disagreement, Lynn is deeply devoted to Mack and anxious for marriage—"Whatever you are I like you"—but she refuses to commit to him on this basis: "You just can't understand." While love and marriage would provide greater contentment and completeness in her life, she feels a need for fulfillment and respect as an individual: "I like my job. It's part of me." She is unwilling to sacrifice her individuality and argues for a relationship of equals: "I want you on a self-respecting 50/50 basis. One that's fair to both of us."

A similar view is adopted by Jeanne (Suzanne Pleshette) in *Youngblood Hawke*, which was filmed at the same time that Axelson's research was conducted. Jeanne is able to separate her personal concerns from her employment as a literary editor. She continues to maintain the highest standards of integrity and efficiency in her work and refuses to be at the beck and call of the protagonist, author Arthur "Youngblood" Hawke, whom she loves. When they are introduced, Hawke is taken aback by her youth and beauty—"You're awfully young aren't you"—but her reply, "Well so are you," indicates her view that men and women should be judged according to the same criteria. Also, through the words of her publisher-employer, Daves's script goes on to emphasize her gifts, which Hawke comes to recognize and value, as well as her impressive academic qualifications and her ability to recognize and nurture a new talent. Herman Wouk, who wrote the original novel, was critical of this element of Daves's screenplay, stating that it was unrealistic that Jeanne would "wait" for Hawke, as his "heedless adultery" would "drive the spirited Jeanne out of his reach into another man's arms,"[31] as occurred in Wouk's novel. However, while Jeanne would welcome a loving relationship, it must not be at any cost to her standards or expectations. Daves's character does not depend on a relationship to be happy. She rejects a sincere suitor because she doesn't love him, and she finds independence and contentment in a challenging and fulfilling career conducted with integrity: "My life is my own." In contrast, Hawke's married lover leads a wealthy but cynical and amoral existence as manifested in a willingness to indulge in meaningless, short-term affairs. When she is with her children, she shows sensitivity and humanity, and when her son dies, her grief is deeply felt, but her life is aimless and unfulfilled, without purposeful activity.

It is significant, therefore, that in *Stranded*, it is Mack who revises his attitudes to Lynn's work. He recognizes the value of her work and that she has an important contribution to make: "I know what you mean now.... You've cracked my heart and my eyes wide open." This is a thought-provoking sentiment with which to conclude the film, at a time when married women were discouraged by politicians and unions from working outside the home in order to "preserve" scarce jobs for men during the Depression. Section 213 of the Federal Economy Act (1932) stipulated that when the government made cuts in personnel, those workers with spouses should be discharged first. This provision was gender neutral, but Robert Griswold shows that the intent and result was that wives rather than husbands were dismissed,[32] and even when Section 213 was repealed in 1937, employers continued to discriminate against women. Almost 80 percent of school districts dismissed or refused to hire married women, and in 1939, twenty-six states actively considered legislation to implement such restrictions.

In considering the extent to which *Stranded* reflects the outlook of director Frank Borzage or of Daves as screenwriter, commentators have referenced the metaphysical dimension to love in Borzage's films and the characters' ability to transcend their immediate surroundings. In contrast, Daves's view of male and female sexual attraction is more temporal and explores social issues that provide a backdrop to a relationship. Lynn makes clear that she "see[s] life in terms of human beings," and the film shows the different aspects of her job that bring her into contact with immigrants, unwed mothers, the poor, and the unemployed. Also, it is noteworthy that in Borzage's *Living on Velvet* (1935), made immediately prior to *Stranded*, with the same stars but with another writer, the heroine promises her husband: "I'll be what you want me to be. I'll do what you want me to do." Her desire to make her husband happy overrides all other considerations: "I'll feel that I've got out of life everything I want.... I don't want to be free."

Daves's female characters display the strength to uphold their convictions. In *To the Victor*, Taggart (Dennis Morgan) and Christine (Viveca Lindfors) face the same dilemma as Rick and Ilsa in *Casablanca*: they must choose between "escaping" for personal happiness together or taking actions that, while courageous and moral, will threaten their safety and love. Ilsa leaves the decision entirely to Rick: "I don't know what's right any longer. You'll have to think for both of us." Christine faces the same emotional turmoil and initially is uncertain: "What do you want me to do?... tell me." However, she has the courage to acknowledge her guilt and testify before an international court, willing to face any consequences: "That's a decision you've got to make for yourself, either way I love you.... What's right for me may be wrong for you." She has the confidence to make the final inspirational speech expressing the importance of a commitment to freedom and liberty, during which the cynical journalist and other like-minded American expatriates seem more hopeful and ready to believe in such ideals. While Bosley Crowther feels that this theme is false and contrived,[33] these scenes are enriched and humanized by Lindfors's subtle and nuanced performance, which contrasts with the more stolid acting of Morgan. She gives Christine an intense yet dignified passion that provides the film's emotional energy as she declares her love, allowing moral certainty to emerge from confusion.

Even in the musical comedy *You Were Never Lovelier*, Daves touches upon the issue of society's expectations for women in his screenplay, albeit in a lighthearted and limited manner. The film is a conventional Fred Astaire musical with regular opportunities to showcase his dancing and with particularly memorable music composed by Jerome Kern and witty lyrics from Johnny Mercer. Although slight, the story focuses on the attempts of the family of Maria (Rita Hayworth) to ensure that she marries an appropriate suitor. In their eyes, her independent thinking and reluctance to commit mean that "[t]here's something terribly wrong with Maria." Although at heart she is highly romantic and responds positively to old-fashioned romantic behavior, she eschews any idea of marriage for wealth or position and instinctively disapproves of the values of her social circle, finally falling in love with an out-of-work dancer (Astaire), against the initial wishes of her father (Adolphe Menjou). However, she insists on honesty and retaining her individuality, for example refusing to follow her sisters' advice, such as: "Don't frighten him with your intelligence. Just act simple."

In his screenplays and films as director, Daves's view of society not only incorporates opportunities for women in work but also recognizes that women are entitled to fulfill wider ambitions and dreams. His first screenplay, *So This Is College* (1929), warns that marriage too early may deprive young men of important experience, in this case a full and rich time in college, "the finest thing in the world and we almost lost it." In Daves's penultimate appearance as an actor, his character cautions the two leads about their jealous feuding over a female student: "Hey! Cool off you two . . . you take things too seriously." That Daves felt that young women should also, if they wish, have opportunities for wider experiences is made explicit in *Rome Adventure*, in which Prudence (Suzanne Pleshette) acts on her belief that "a girl has every right a man has, especially the right to be free." In Daves's screenplay for *The Petrified Forest*, Mrs. Chisholm remains bitter because she believes that she has sacrificed her individuality and self-respect. She encourages Gaby, a young waitress (Bette Davis), not to limit her ambitions: "I do know what it means to repress yourself and starve yourself to what you conceive to be your duty to others." In fact, Gaby believes that "there's something in me that wants something different . . . [but] the American in me speaks up and spoils everything." However, Squier appreciates her imagination and potential: "She's the future; she's the renewal of vitality, of courage and aspiration. . . .

She's essential to me and the whole God-forsaken country." He encourages her to leave to fulfill her dreams and finally sacrifices his life to ensure that she has the means to begin her journey: "She has heroic stuff in her. I want to show her that I believe in her." In *Spencer's Mountain*, while still hoping for marriage, the young woman (Claris, Clay-Boy's girlfriend) also contemplates new horizons: "I've always wanted to go somewhere where nobody's been." As Joseph Pomp points out, it is she who has drive and ambition and wants to be an archaeologist, while in Earl Hamner's novel, Claris is content to fit into Clay-Boy's plans to enter that profession.[34] Despite references to the drudgery of domestic duties, with no break, holiday, or even honeymoon, she believes that Clay-Boy's mother, who has had nine children, is the most fulfilled woman she has ever known.

None of the young women to whom the hero in *Parrish* is attracted display the wholesome "girl-next-door" characteristics conventionally represented by Hollywood as ideal for marriage and family life. Lucy is more experienced than Parrish and is pregnant with an illegitimate child, and Alison misuses wealth and lives a discontented and aimless life. Parrish finally decides that he loves Paige (Sharon Hugueny), his business rival's daughter. She is the youngest of the romantic prospects and, with no reference to past relationships, may seem best suited for marriage with the hero. In fact, Parrish is not prejudiced in this regard: he makes no adverse judgments about Lucy's pregnancy and is proud to accompany her in public while others shun her. However, while it is significant that any relationship with Lucy or Alison would have been conventional in maintaining a clear separation of male and female roles within the family, this is less likely with Paige. She is more independent and strong-minded: unlike her weak and incompetent brothers, she is able to stand up to their overbearing and bullying father. She has lived away from home, attending agricultural college as the only female in her course of study. She has clear thoughts on business practices, rejecting the methods of her father, who "does all his farming over the telephone," and advocating a more hands-on, cooperative style of management. She is more knowledgeable about the tobacco industry than Parrish, and, just as in *Stranded*, in which Lynn is instrumental in preventing a corruptly organized walkout that would have damaged the construction of the Golden Gate Bridge, Paige takes the initiative in recruiting workers who are willing to defy the blacklists and boycotts threatened by her father. Thus, her relationship with Parrish is very likely to be one of a partnership of equals.

One of the most popular postwar female stars was Doris Day, who, for many, personified a wholesome "girl next door" who is able to fend off the advances of sexually aggressive males before giving herself to the man she loves in a conventional marriage. However, this image of Day has been questioned by some critics.[35] Particularly in her later films, they suggest that her characters are independent and capable and more than able to equal men in terms of efficiency, competence, and wit. Molly Haskell emphasizes that Day's characters do not seek a man "to lean on" and actually have to work for a living.[36] In *Pillow Talk* (1959) she is an interior decorator, and in *Lover Come Back* (1961) she is an advertising executive. Kathrina Glitre argues that, while Day's characters are hoping for marriage, they are unwilling to lower their standards or expectations of a partner.[37] Yet a decade earlier, the character played by Jane Wyman in *A Kiss in the Dark* displays many of the same character traits and motivations. One contemporary review criticized the film as "an unusually trite comedy."[38] To the modern viewer, the pacing seems uneven, with the action or dialogue either unduly frantic or sluggish and verbose. The comedy is forced, and the episodes of visual humor are predictable. The acting ranges from the extravagant overacting of Broderick Crawford to the rather stilted playing of other supporting players, and the performance of David Niven lacks subtlety. Only the acting and the character of Wyman (Polly) stand out as spontaneous and engaging. Polly values her career and independence and enjoys living alone. She is witty and good humored, confident in her own abilities, and while aware of her sexual attractiveness, her manner is natural and unselfconscious. Her suggestion that in order to "persuade" an unpleasant tenant to leave, one should make enough noise to cause sleep deprivation, seems unpleasant. Strangely, it is the one sequence in the film that Richard Whitehall feels is funny,[39] but it does show that she has a harder aspect to her character. Otherwise, she is considerate toward others, she demonstrates intelligence and the ability to organize when she takes the lead in arranging tasks and duties among tenants and craftsmen for improvements to their apartment building, and she is decisive in building an active community ethos.

In their reappraisal of the Doris Day persona, Jane Clarke and Diana Simmonds feel that her independence is important and that her willingness to enter into a sexual relationship only on equal terms necessitates the males to modify their expectations and behavior, often requiring them to show a softer side of their nature.[40] This interpretation could apply to *A Kiss in the Dark*. Polly's absentee landlord (Niven) is a wealthy pianist for whom the apartment building is just one of many investments in which he takes no active interest, in either the condition of the building or the welfare of the tenants. At the outset he is seen to be temperamental, self-centered, and set in his ways. His lack of perspective is suggested by his physical unsteadiness and the fact that he often falls or is easily pushed over. Frequently, Polly helps him back onto his feet and supports and guides him, physically and metaphorically, in the right direction. Because of her influence, he appreciates the shallowness of his life and develops a more thoughtful insight and sense of purpose: he becomes involved in the improvements to the building and begins to relate positively to people he would hitherto have regarded as inferior. As a result, he is more ready for marriage with Polly.

GENDER AND FAMILY ISSUES IN *A SUMMER PLACE* AND DAVES'S LATER FILMS

Glitre argues that the Doris Day persona can be defined by her success in her on-screen careers.[41] Notwithstanding the proposition that Wyman's character in Daves's film predates the image of Doris Day as a modern and independent woman, this interpretation of Day's image may be challenged. Benshoff and Griffin note that when Julia Roberts is first seen in *Pretty Woman* (1990), the camera focuses on parts of her body as she dresses.[42] They suggest that such breaking down of the female form into individual parts is indicative of recognition of women not as "complete" human beings but rather as composites of body parts that appeal to the sexual desires of men. They note also that the opening shots of *Pillow Talk* begin in a similar way, with the camera focusing on Day's legs as she puts on her stockings. Such scenes exemplify Laura Mulvey's focus on the centrality, in film analysis, of the concept of the controlling "male gaze," which views "woman as icon, displayed for the gaze and enjoyment of men."[43] Thus, the passivity of the female is symptomatic of a patriarchal order in which the observer is superior to the observed and relegates women to the status of objects, exemplified as Day is carried away over a man's shoulder at the end of the film. Proposing that Day's character in *Pillow Talk* will continue to work after marriage, Glitre cites her role as a working mother in *The Thrill of It All* (1963). However, the resolutions of the questions raised in this film do not justify this assumption. Married to a doctor, Day is an upper middle-class housewife who wants to take up an offer of lucrative employment despite promising that she would never consciously look for a job. Her husband (James Garner) points out that there is no such need: they have a healthy bank balance, and the children would suffer. While she feels in need of greater fulfillment, she has to promise not to "let anything interfere with my wifely duties." Attending a dinner party, she is asked who she is, and her husband replies, "She's with me," which suggests that she lacks any identity independent of her husband. Ultimately, she accepts that his work is more important than her aspirations and that being a doctor's wife is fulfillment enough: the final scene implies that they will have another baby, which will ensure that she remains in the home.

Typical review comments praised the film's "excellent script."[44] Albeit with growing challenge, Hollywood's popular image of marriage shows Doris Day and her screen husband sleeping in separate single beds and emphasizes her willing acceptance of the primacy of her family responsibilities. In *A Summer Place*, Daves presents a more penetrating and, for its time, controversial picture of relationships and morality in contemporary America. Sloan Wilson, author of the original novel, wrote of Daves's screenplay: "I think this is a great job. It's certainly miles ahead of anything we've had yet and I believe it can be made into a fine movie." However, he added that the dialogue contains "patches of bad taste."[45] Jympson Harman's review claimed that the film was "sex-obsessed with dialogue not usually heard in decent homes" and advocated more rigorous censorship to protect teenage audiences.[46] Correspondence from the PCA concluded that "[t]he film does little or nothing in pointing up right moral standards" and required significant script changes.[47] These included excision of references to abortion, a noncondemnatory reference to divorce, nude swimming, and overly revealing clothing, as well as "questionable" dialogue.[48] Nevertheless, the fact that some explicit dialogue is retained may indicate the waning influence of the Production Code. The film was given a Category B Seal of Approval from the Legion of Decency, indicating that it was considered to be morally objectionable in part for all audiences.

The narrative focuses on the reawakening of adult passion set alongside the innocence and tenderness, and as well as the frustration and confusion, of young lovers. Two unhappily married couples, Ken and Helen (Richard Egan and Constance Ford), with a teenage daughter, and Sylvia and Bart (Dorothy McGuire and Arthur Kennedy), with a teenage son, meet again after twenty years. Before their respective marriages, Ken and Sylvia had been lovers, but their relationship had ended because her rich family objected to Ken, as he was a mere lifeguard. Ken and Sylvia agree that their mistakes have resulted in frustration and emptiness in their lives and unhappiness for their spouses. Ken and Sylvia rekindle their love and commit adultery, and they marry after the resulting divorces. Drawn closer together because of the scandal over the failure of their respective parents' marriages, the son and daughter, Johnny and Molly (Troy Donahue and Sandra Dee), begin a romantic relationship that results in pregnancy.

The film centers on females who display strength of character and resolution. After being sent to boarding school and separated from Johnny, Molly exhibits quiet determination in defying her domineering mother and resuming contact, which leads to renewed happiness for the young couple, just as Sylvia and Ken gain a contentment that they had not known during most of their adult years. With Bart's decline into alcoholism and his reckless behavior, it is Sylvia who shows business acumen and competence in successfully taking responsibility for the management of their hotel. Initially, Sylvia's aunt Emily seems rather shallow and insipid, but she is the first to appreciate that Ken and Sylvia have renewed their relationship. Her bluntness—"I believe in facing facts.... Have you ever considered divorce?"—helps Sylvia realize that she cannot remain with Bart and that "an affair of sorts ... a few lies here and there, invented excuses ... the quick clinches in the night" would not bring happiness. Although from an earlier generation, Emily is certain that Sylvia must defy convention and leave Bart. Interestingly, nearly two decades earlier, a character in *The Very Thought of You* played by the same actress (Beulah Bondi) expresses a similar sentiment. As this film begins, there is a celebration dinner for her wedding anniversary, but these early scenes reveal bickering parents and siblings, and it is clear that she regrets missed opportunities resulting from an early marriage that has confined her to domesticity. Therefore, she does not want her daughters to make similar decisions: "I wanted them to profit from my mistake."

A Summer Place is overlong and, other than that of Arthur Kennedy, the acting is not exceptional; in places, Daves's script is too literary, with characters making carefully composed and excessively articulate speeches. Although financially very successful, the film received mixed notices, viewed almost as a commercial for illicit love and adultery by some critics.[49] Certainly the film departs from a conventional idealized picture of an American nuclear family as a pillar of social stability. It focuses on teenage pregnancy and also portrays adultery empathetically as well as the acceptability of divorce and remarriage, at a time when (three years later, in 1962), Georgia congresswoman Iris Blitch asked Attorney General Robert Kennedy to consider whether Richard Burton and Elizabeth Taylor, who had conducted a well-publicized extramarital affair, should be allowed to reenter the United States. Boggs and Pollard acknowledge that "family values" had long been a cherished staple of American culture and that Hollywood venerated the family as the basic unit of American society. With a patriarchal father and happily domesticated mother central to strengthening these values, they feel also that this bred a sense of failure if this ideal was not achieved.[50] Daves does not belittle this image: the gunman in *3:10 to Yuma* is envious of the homesteader's domestic life. In *Destination Tokyo*, as the submarine returns to San Francisco, the captain sees his wife and children and says to himself, "I couldn't be that lucky ... but I am." *Love Affair* and *An Affair to Remember* celebrate the power of unconditional love and its capacity for enhancing the best in character and personality. However, Daves recognized the reality of the difficulties and challenges that families may experience, and he advocated tolerance and understanding toward those in different domestic situations.

Boggs and Pollard maintain that postmodern cinema, which offers a more jaundiced view of family values, began in the late 1970s,[51] and thus Daves's later films anticipate this questioning of established social conventions. *A Summer Place* provides a critique of American life emphasizing that class prejudice had obstructed what might have been a loving and fulfilling relationship and that economic success had not brought happiness. Generally, the film was criticized for having "a preoccupation with sex"[52] or dismissed as a glossy "soap opera" that was unrelated to contemporary issues because of the wealth of the main characters, exemplified by the fact that a New England home featured in the plot was built by Frank Lloyd Wright. Yet it is this same background of characters who live in homes cluttered with signs of affluence and material success that provides the setting for the later American melodramas of Douglas Sirk, which have in more recent times attracted critical praise. Tom Ryan notes that Sirk was regarded as just a "director of glossy melodramas and other genre films" but now is "entrenched as an esteemed Hollywood *auteur*," with *Imitation of Life* (1959) regarded as "an American masterpiece."[53] He emphasizes Sirk's understanding and empathy for his characters, which acknowledge their humanity, but also that he maintains an ironic distance that offers critiques of their ideologies.[54] Michael Stern accepts that Sirk utilized domestic melodrama as a metaphor for a decaying social order and thus exposed cracks in the fabric of society, presenting a view of the complacency and repression of the Eisenhower period.[55] However, in creating this intellectual distance, there is a sense that Sirk may dislike his characters.

In Daves's late melodramas, there is no such distancing. In *A Summer Place* he conveys real warmth for his characters and sincere empathy for their experiences. He evokes genuine hope for a new tolerance and maturity in attitudes to sexual relations, and in so doing, the film heralds a major change in the ways that sex was presented in American films. In treating his material with overt seriousness and his characters with great respect, Daves presents a view of America at the onset of significant change in sexual mores that is meaningful and likely to engage the imagination and empathy of a mass audience, irrespective of class, educational background, or gender. One review accepted that the film was expertly written, directed, and produced but concluded that "Daves's taste is not equal to his technique."[56] He is accused of lacking social responsibility and encouraging immoral behavior through imitation. However, with its frank consideration of issues of divorce, sex outside marriage, pregnancy, and virginity, the film presents a more thoughtful examination of social issues of concern to adolescents and parents than that recognized in Howard Thompson's review, which advised young people of the importance of obeying their parents.[57] The film emphasizes that it should be possible to discuss issues of sexuality openly at a time when Janice Irvine reports that there was strong conservative opposition to sex education in schools.[58] As such, the film anticipates Hollywood's treatment of more adult themes that accompanied the changes in sexual attitudes and behavior during the 1960s.

In this regard, one review reprimanded *A Summer Place* because it lacked moral and social responsibility and "treats adultery as if there were nothing at all holy about matrimony."[59] Despite being married, Sylvia promises Ken: "I will come to you every time you desire." However, the adulterous couple find peace of mind, and Daves is sympathetic to their emotional and sexual feelings and their need to be together: hitherto, their lives had been "never really fulfilling, never being fulfilled. I'm hungry for everything it hasn't been." There is no overt condemnation of the severing of an unhappy union or of sex outside marriage. Ira Lurvey and Selise Eiseman write that Hollywood had effectively suppressed films that featured divorce unless they emphasized reconciliation,[60] ranging from, for example, *The Awful Truth* (1937) and *The Philadelphia Story* (1940) to *The Parent Trap* (1961). Even as the Code's influence diminished, *Divorce American Style* (1967) focused on the difficulties of divorce and the benefits of remaining married. Such films emphasized that "unhappiness in marriage may be a staple of modern life, but divorce is worse,"[61] particularly if, as in the latter film, women are shown to be avaricious in terms of a divorce settlement. Films of the 1950s that were considered radical in fact advocated conservative answers to social issues, such as the reassertion of a father's authority in *Rebel without a Cause* (1955) and acceptance of traditional discipline and order in *The Wild One* (1953). *From Here to Eternity* (1953) is perhaps the most famous film from this time that portrayed the adultery of the principal characters. Despite her intolerable marriage, a woman leaves Hawaii with her husband rather than begin divorce proceedings to be with her lover, and unlike James Jones's novel on which it is based, the film suggests that her unhappiness is due primarily to the absence of the opportunity for motherhood. Historian Roderick Phillips notes that it was not until the 1970s and 1980s, with films such as *Kramer vs. Kramer* (1979) and television series such as *The Golden Girls* (1985–1992), that popular culture focused directly on the personal and social aspects of divorce.[62]

Therefore, *A Summer Place* made an early and important contribution toward a more open and balanced and less judgmental treatment of marital discord. The reaction of the small New England community to the scandal of their neighbors' adultery and divorce is predictable. However, Daves's portrayal of Ken and Sylvia's relationship epitomizes an increasingly liberal attitude to divorce, and the prominence of glass windows in the design of their new home is indicative of their openness. The film anticipates psychologist George Levinger's analysis of the reasons for the increasing divorce rate in the 1960s.[63] Levinger identifies verbal abuse, neglect, financial problems, mental cruelty, and excessive drinking as reasons for divorce applications, and clearly Sylvia experienced such difficulties with Bart. Levinger also highlights sexual incompatibility as an important factor in marital breakdown, and this a fundamental cause of Ken's unhappiness. The relationships in the film reflect another significant reason for increasing marital discord in the postwar period. Phillips maintains that the issue of family finance was proving to be less of a deterrent to divorce.[64] Women's increasing role in the workforce, with for example Sylvia proving her competence in running a business, was an enabling factor for women in rising expectations of marriage. Phillips also emphasizes the increasing importance of communication and the wish to derive emotional as well as physical fulfillment as determining factors in the duration of a marriage. Couples increasingly contemplated the need for companionship and an understanding of each other's needs: Sylvia says of Ken, "He's given me back a hope I thought had gone ... for happiness, being loved." It is a sentiment that matches the view, later expressed by Levinger, that the success of a marriage was increasingly being judged not in terms of its duration but more by its enhancement of both partners' personal potential.[65]

Initially, Molly and Johnny shun their parents because of the scandal of their adultery and divorce. However, their own experiences bring a more mature understanding, with Molly rejecting the intolerance of her mother's irrationality. Therefore, at a time when Hollywood did not present divorce as a possible solution to difficulties, Daves's film reflects an increasing body of academic literature that examined the premise that divorce may offer "the chance of a new lifetime."[66] Based on their interviews with divorcées in Boston, Carol Brown and colleagues acknowledge the potential difficulties of greater financial, family, and household responsibilities as well as the possibility of facing social stigma.[67] However, they report also that many divorcées felt happier or at least relieved despite such difficulties: they no longer felt compelled to subordinate their wishes or opinions to those of a spouse and in general enjoyed a greater feeling of independence, personal autonomy, and competence. Many experienced a more satisfying sex life. This applied to those who entered more fulfilling relationships, as did Sylvia and Ken, and also to those who remained single; the latter group made it clear that if they remarried, such a decision would be better informed, and they would do so with clearer expectations with regard to retaining their integrity in a long-term relationship.

In fact, Daves had examined such themes in one of his earliest stories and screenplays, albeit at a time when the Production Code was not yet rigorously enforced. In *Divorce in the Family* (1932), a young boy is affected by the legal and emotional conflict between his divorced parents. The mother, who has custody and has remarried, attempts to prevent access to the child by his father, who then contemplates taking his son abroad. The court prevents both "solutions," emphasizing that it "has no intention to deny [the man's] rights as a father" or "deprive the boy of the influence of his mother," and the father admits: "I've learned an awful lot about what goes on in the heart of youngsters."[68] The Delmer Daves Papers show that this project underwent numerous changes in titles and scenarios, but there is no suggestion of reconciliation or that divorce is undesirable for this family. Instead, it is clear that both parents are happier, and the script emphasizes that a child need not be adversely affected.[69]

Daves's final film, *The Battle of the Villa Fiorita*, might appear to contradict this stance. The life of a hitherto conventional upper middle-class Englishwoman, Moira (Maureen O'Hara), is disrupted when she falls in love with a visiting Italian concert pianist and widower, Lorenzo (Rossano Brazzi) while her diplomat husband (Richard Todd) has been abroad. Having informed him of the affair, she immediately leaves with her lover to start a new life in Italy. Her two children refuse to accept this situation and travel to Italy to persuade her to return. With the help of Lorenzo's daughter, they take steps to disrupt the adults' relationship. After their attempts end in near tragedy, the adults agree that they cannot marry, and Moira returns with her children to England. Most reviews praised the beautiful color photography of settings alongside the River Thames and in the Italian countryside, and there are effective moments such as the wordless shots of the two children when they arrive at the villa and see their mother's shoes next to a pair of a man's shoes outside a bedroom door. The acting of the largely British cast is sincere, but the film's main weakness is the obvious lack of chemistry between the two lovers, which may reflect the poor relationship between the two actors, as O'Hara describes in her autobiography.[70] Their developing love affair is portrayed effectively and with subtlety in long shots as the couple walk along the riverbank and across bridges, and Moira's internal emotional battle is sensitively conveyed in one wordless, slowly rising crane shot as she walks alone along a narrow path lined with trees. However, in the dialogue and in close-up, particularly in Brazzi's performance, there is no passion or intensity of feelings. Their declarations of love are unconvincing, and the premise that this woman is willing to leave her children for this man, without explanation or saying good-bye, and contemplate life without them, lacks credibility, particularly when he is compared with the quiet dignity of her husband.

Nevertheless, the film does examine important social issues. That the mother decides to leave her lover and return home supports Gough-Yates's argument that for a heroine, accepting conventional social expectations and filial duties outweigh the fulfillment of emotional needs.[71] As well exemplifying the social expectations of married women in the 1950s and 1960s, this reflects the realities of contemporary divorce law and the fundamentals of child development theory as understood at that time. Before 1969 and the liberalization of divorce legislation, English law acted punitively against a party, male or female, held to be guilty of a matrimonial offence such as desertion or adultery. Thus, in Daves's narrative, Moira is likely to have lost all rights with regard to her children as well as to any marital assets. Also, she would be subject to social as well as legal censure due to the broad acceptance of conclusions drawn by psychiatrists such as John Bowlby, "that the prolonged deprivation of the young child of maternal care may have grave and far-reaching effects on his character and so on the whole of his future life."[72] Additionally, her behavior would be considered reprehensible, as many would have felt that she had been generously provided with everything she needed and that she should have been content.

Thus, a review of the film concluded: "The story itself is nothing if not strictly moral."[73] The adulterous couple are made to admit to and correct their transgressions, thus implying approval for the actions of the children, as in *The Parent Trap*, which also stars Maureen O'Hara as one of the parents. In Disney's film, the children's attempts to sabotage their father's relationship with another woman are portrayed humorously. These attempts are successful, and the parents are reunited: there is no questioning of the probity of the children's actions, nor is there any doubt about the rectitude of the parental reconciliation. *Demetrius and the Gladiators* seems to take a similar stance. Messalina (Susan Hayward) has been aggressively promiscuous and has openly humiliated her husband, Claudius. However, she repents as increasingly she recognizes his innate dignity and moral strength in subverting the evil of Caligula. "I've mocked my marriage vows.... I've disgraced my husband and myself. That too has ended."

However, Daves's narrative is more nuanced. Messalina's expression of emptiness and loss as Demetrius leaves, and her final words, "I am Caesar's wife and I will act the part," introduce a degree of ambiguity. Similarly, the merit of the children's efforts to reunite their parents in *The Battle of the Villa Fiorita* is uncertain, just as contemporary research suggested that conventional thinking on the impact of family disruption was in need of revision. In his analysis of a sample of students whose parents had divorced during their childhood, sociologist Judson Landis examined the assumption that divorce or separation almost always results in great unhappiness for children and concluded that it is a mistake to view such children as a homogeneous set.[74] He accepts that for some, the experience of a separation may be extremely traumatic, but suggests that the degree of trauma is dependent on children's perceptions of family relationships, with children who saw their homes as happy experiencing greater difficulties in adjustment, and those for whom the preseparation home was not happy experiencing fewer.

In *The Battle of the Villa Fiorita*, the lovers decide to part, and the children are triumphant: "We won, you clot." However, the film ends with an intense feeling of foreboding, reinforced by the son's final thoughts. After initial triumph, he is more pensive: "Was it right . . . were we right?" Child psychologist Åse Skard argues that children develop more contentedly when the mother herself is happy,[75] and with Moira's final anguished expression and her desperate plea to her young daughter, "Help me Debbie; help me," Daves leaves the viewer with a sense that the reconciliation will not be happy and that this may impact the children. Writing at a time when color was yet to fully replace monochrome as the norm for cinematography, William Johnson discusses the use of color by directors and notes that in this film, Daves uses a clash of severe light and dark colors in the clothes worn by the married couple as a comment on their relationship.[76] In contrast, when the lovers are together, the colors of their clothes are more visually harmonious.

Sociologist Francis Ivan Nye's investigation of this social issue concludes that many children feel more secure after separation and show significantly better adjustment than those from unbroken but unhappy families as measured in terms of parent-child relationships, incidents of delinquent behavior, and psychosomatic illnesses.[77] Therefore, Daves is ensuring that the viewer questions the advisability of this reconciliation, particularly with the probability of the mother's unhappiness. In presenting sympathetically the dilemma of a mother who is willing to take the extreme action of leaving her children, Daves is implying that she is right to expect more in a relationship, which is consistent with the increasingly disseminated view as expressed by Skard that "[a] woman is more than just a milieu for her child or her children—she has her own value as a human being."[78] Unusually for this time, Skard goes on to emphasize the stress that may be caused by paternal deprivation.[79] Although Moira, as the "wrongful party" in this story, would have few rights over the children, her husband rejects the advice of his solicitor to exert his full legal rights and insists that the children should maintain contact with their mother. This recognition that both parents are important for the security and well-being of children was only explicitly established in English law with the Children and Families Act in 2014, when courts were required to take account of the principle that both parents should continue to be involved in children's lives.

PORTRAYAL OF WOMEN IN DAVES'S WESTERNS

Jim Kitses argues that "the feminine in the genre exists only to validate masculinity as the dominant norm,"[80] and Jacqueline Levitin accepts this analysis. She recalls that when young, she enjoyed Westerns but felt that she had to identify with male heroes because female characters were not as exciting as their male counterparts and therefore not satisfying as role models.[81] She recognizes that films such as *Johnny Guitar* (1954) and *Comes a Horseman* (1978) have been identified as presenting women as more active. However, overall, she doubts that the genre has provided opportunities for female characters to behave outside a rigidly defined range of emotions, attitudes, and actions and concludes that an essential premise of the genre is encapsulated in her characterization of the relationship between Dallas and Ringo in *Stagecoach*: "She waits while he acts. She will prepare the home while he challenges society."[82] Westerns in which women matched or outshone men in ability to use a gun or rope tended to be lighthearted, such as the musical comedies *Annie Get Your Gun* (1950) and *Calamity Jane* (1953). However, they had to learn that to attract a man, they had to "feminize" their clothes and behavior.

The portrayal of women in *The Badlanders* presents a riposte to Levitin's conclusion that "[t]he Western held little inspiration for young feminists,"[83] particularly when the film is examined alongside *The Asphalt Jungle* (1950) and *Cool Breeze* (1972), the latter a remake of Huston's film made with a mainly Black cast. Because *The Badlanders* was a remake, it received little critical attention. However, segments of the film such as the plotting and execution of the robbery are acutely taut and engrossing, and the female characters are sharply delineated. In Huston's film, the women are presented as weak stereotypes, without initiative or independence. The wife of the corrupt lawyer has little pride and is constantly trying to make herself more presentable when it is clear that all love and respect have dissipated from the marriage. Angela, the lawyer's "kept" mistress (Marilyn Monroe), displays an innocent and carefree sexuality that is both wholesome and erotic, and irresistible to the lawyer and other male characters. However, it is unlikely that she would be able to survive independently in a harsh, "real" world. When the lawyer is confronted by the police and her first thought is that their planned "escape" to Cuba would not take place, he remarks wistfully, "Don't worry baby. You'll have plenty of trips": there is a sense that she will soon be in another sugar-daddy relationship.

Ada (Claire Kelly) is the equivalent character in *The Badlanders* and seems more exploited than Angela, as she is locked in a hotel room for long periods in her "keeper's" absence. However, while Kelly did not have the same memorable on-screen impact as Monroe, her character is more worldly and self-aware, displaying an acute sense of irony as she explains her situation: "If a gentleman does you the honor to become your gentleman friend, don't you think you should do what he asks you to do? That is if you are a lady." Ada knows that she is treated as a possession but makes no secret of her lifestyle: "I as much as told you what I am. I hate false pretenses." She is intelligent, confident, and in control of her life, almost as if she were using men rather than being used, and she is content to continue while it suits her. She makes an independent decision to give up that existence, although there is an implication that a relationship with Van Hoek (Alan Ladd) will develop. Significantly in this context, Van Hoek is not only attracted to Ada, he is also not repelled by her lifestyle.

The character of Anita (Katy Jurado) is the parallel figure to the appropriately named Doll (Jean Hagen), perhaps the most pathetic character in *The Asphalt Jungle*. Doll has no pride or initiative: she is content to attach herself to a criminal rather than stand alone, and the scenes in which she is desperate to please and ingratiate herself with a man are embarrassing to a modern audience. In contrast, Anita is a leader in the struggle against the exploitation and poverty of the Mexicans amid the gold-rich wealth of white society, and through her, McBain learns of the suffering of her people, with references made to starvation and infant mortality. After McBain and Anita spend the night together, he learns that she has slept with men for money. Conventionally this would mean that the character does not "deserve" happiness, but McBain looks beyond this: "I see inside, what I see is good," and their relationship is portrayed with obvious warmth. Anita demonstrates strength of character and determination to survive and help her people cope with hardship and discrimination. It is her initiative that mobilizes the united action against the corrupt officials and businessmen, and it is the efforts of her community, rather than that of the white heroes, that is decisive. In *Cool Breeze*, the demise of the Production Code is indicated by the fact that the leader of the heist and the corrupt police officer escape retribution. However, women demonstrate stereotypical "hip" behavior and language. The Hagen equivalent character is less pathetic, but Monroe's equivalent is more childlike despite her explicit language. In general, the female characters do little more than provide sexual satisfaction for the males, whether for love, lust, or payment.

A notable image of women in Hollywood films is that of the sexually provocative female, often portrayed as a disruptive force, particularly in films noir and Westerns. Daves's representation of this convention is more nuanced, and this is recognized in Matthew Carter's focus on the female characters in *Jubal*.[84] Examining the film in the context of post–World War II film noir in which women are not kept passively in the background, he shows that *Jubal* presents a challenge to a patriarchal order. He focuses on the figure of the femme fatale as embodied in Mae (Valerie French), who is adulterous and deceitful and exploits her sexuality to manipulate men. As Carter explains, it is such female sexuality, as a symbol of independence, that constitutes a threat to the patriarchal order and therefore should be repressed. Conventionally such characters are exposed and "punished" in order to allow a man to escape entanglement, and indeed Mae is brutally murdered. However, Carter notes Daves's sympathy for her unhappiness with her life of "10,000 acres of lonesomeness." She is active, intelligent, and resourceful and resents being relegated to a passive, domestic role. Thus, she can be viewed as a victim of male power as represented by Pinky's aggressiveness as well as her husband's attitudes and expectations, which have led to her frustration and the repression of her talents and her femininity. Just as Frenchy feels a sense of ownership and entitlement after saving Elizabeth in *The Hanging Tree*, Shep treats Mae as a possession for serving his needs. When asked why she doesn't leave, Mae's answer, "and go where," exposes the vulnerability of many women in an unhappy and passionless marriage, a reality of that era that persisted well into the twentieth century. Mae is killed by a jealous Pinky (Rod Steiger), "punished" not because of her sexual precociousness but more because of her deliberate lies that result in the tragic death of her husband, which she almost welcomes, as she had married him for his wealth.

Despite his attraction to Mae, who is obviously seductive and confident, Jubal prefers the more virginal Naomi (Felicia Farr), who seems to be a more conventional choice. She fulfills an obvious caring role, tending his physical wounds after he has been shot. She also helps to restore his emotional health as she listens and responds supportively as he recounts the traumas of his childhood. The importance of such qualities are highlighted by their absence in the character of Mae. However, her expression of longing and her willingness to take the first step—"I've not been kissed. I'd like it always to remember you were the first"—suggests a more refined eroticism, to which Jubal readily responds. From a sheltered and disciplined background—"I never had no choosing to do"—she nevertheless is able to assert herself and defy expectations of her behavior ("I'm not doing nothing wrong"), and in the final scene, it is Naomi who leads Jubal across the river toward their "Promised Land." The scenes between Naomi and Jubal are understated and both tender and sensual, as are many of the love scenes in Daves's films, with no disgrace or dishonor felt at such openness with regard to sexual feelings.

Both *Drum Beat* and *White Feather* might be viewed as confirming stereotypical images of women who "deserve" or "don't deserve" happiness and the love of the hero, with those of color displaying greater sexual license than conventional heroines. In *Drum Beat*, the young Modoc woman offers herself to MacKay: "Take me for your woman tonight,... I would do all those things that you would wish me to do." Similarly, in *White Feather*, Appearing Day is naked, but covered, as she waits in bed for Tanner. Later, Toby is killed, but it is clear that she acts out of genuine feeling for MacKay—"I have much love for you; very much"—as does Appearing Day, who will eventually marry Tanner. Furthermore, in *Drum Beat*, it is Daves's white heroine who takes the initiative in a love scene. Her kisses are interspersed with suggestive murmurings about the need to "know how to plough ... plant seeds ... and harvest," and Michael Walker feels that this foreshadows the love scenes in *The Last Wagon* and *3:10 to Yuma*.[85] In these films, as in his later dramas, the young women have the confidence to take sexual initiatives without any loss of self-respect. The saloon girl in *3:10 to Yuma* is unashamedly open about her needs and certainly has no regrets: "I've got something to remember." Her brief liaison is life enhancing: it evokes lingering memories of a more exciting past and opens her mind to the possibility of other opportunities and wider horizons.

Blake Lucas rejects the view of the Western as a genre in which women have only a marginal role and seeks to expose the myth of the conventional Western heroine as a passive figure. Rather than a masculine genre, he argues that it is more balanced in gender terms and has provided opportunities for the portrayal of satisfying and fully rounded women characters. He concludes that "it is the rule rather than the exception that the strongest Westerns tend to be those in which women are most realized and vital to the whole."[86] He emphasizes that it is a mistake to assume that such women must be shown to be able to behave, or "shoot it out," like men. Thus, he rejects Levitin's assertion that wearing trousers and having the ability to shoot are evidence of a Western's intention to give women prominence.[87] Of the women in Daves's Westerns, only Jenny in *The Last Wagon* wears trousers, and none take action with guns. His heroines do tend to exhibit the calmness and gentleness that are usual for women in this genre. However, these characteristics should not be confused with passivity or weakness, particularly as the more reflective aspects of Daves's Westerns are at least as important as the intense and active.

Lucas lists his personal selection of the best examples of Westerns in which the feelings and experiences of women have been represented with caring and sensitive expression, and he includes the barmaid Emmy and the rancher's wife Alice from *3:10 to Yuma*.[88] In one sense, they are both conventional female characters, but they are portrayed as women who exhibit resilience and loyalty alongside grace and dignity as well as natural eroticism and independence. In the same film, Daves conveys with great sensitivity the dreams and sexual longings of youth but also the fulfillment and difficulties of mature love and marriage. In *The Last Wagon*, Jenny has no intention of subverting conventional propriety. She intends to marry a man who is willing to "take care" of her brother and herself, but one whom she does not love. The early scenes emphasize her nurturing role. Not only is she responsible for her younger brother, but her initial contact with Todd is to care for him, insisting that he have food and water. At first, she is taken aback by Todd's explicit sexual references. However, she does not deny the intensity of her feelings and is willing to defy convention with regard to premarital sex and miscegenation. Furthermore, it is her courtroom intervention that is instrumental in ensuring that the "Christian General" adopts a less rigid position with regard to the law.

The women in Daves's films tend to have conventional upbringings, but because of the circumstances they face, they are able to adapt with sufficient determination and strength and show independence and a readiness to deviate from society's expectations. Emmy shows no guilt or regret about her brief liaison with the gunman in *3:10 to Yuma*: in opening the stagecoach door for the handcuffed gunman, she openly acknowledges her feelings and actions in defiance of the town's sense of respectability. In *The Very Thought of You*, Janet fulfills the role of supportive and faithful wife, but she is active in essential war work in a factory and also is the de facto head of a household that includes men who are not in the forces. Daves eschews a conventional Hollywood portrayal of women in which it is passive females who tend to succeed or win the hero's love rather than those who exhibit more forceful characteristics. However, he does not denigrate a traditional caring and nurturing female role. The wrongly convicted murderer in *Dark*

Passage is helpless without the aid and then love of a woman. Schmid's nurse and his wife in *Pride of the Marines* provide the support he needs to accept and deal with his blindness. However, it is often robust and uncompromising support that refuses to accede to Schmid's anger and self-pity: "I like the way you stand up to me."

In *Return of the Texan*, Anne (Joanne Dru) is attracted to Sam, a widower (Dale Robertson) with two young boys who has returned to his hometown. Her nurturing capabilities are obvious: she establishes an immediate rapport with the boys and gives comfort at times of crisis when their father seems more aloof. However, she is also more skilled at the "masculine" pursuit of fishing and shows that she is calm and decisive in an emergency when Grandpa (Walter Brennan) has a stroke. She resists the wishes of her family for a more suitable marriage with a doctor from a wealthy family and is willing to take the initiative in her relationship with Sam. She is socially assured, and she demonstrates her confident sense of humor when she catches her hair in the hero's trouser belt in the darkness of a cinema. This contrasts with her older sister, who plays no part in the management of the ranch inherited from their father. Murray (Richard Boone), the sister's husband, has assumed this responsibility: "I own this place."

In *The Hanging Tree*, Elizabeth has been temporarily blinded after lying in the sun for several days after a stagecoach holdup in which her father is killed. While it is Dr. Frail who nurses her back to health, he seeks to exert complete control over her, forcing her to ask, "Am I a prisoner?," and for Rune to accuse him: "You don't own her, Doc." Initially, Elizabeth feels vulnerable and dependent—"Don't send me away"—but she gains in authority and confidence, resisting Frail's demands that she leave the mining community: "You will not again tell me what to do ... I came to make this my home and I will do it." She asserts her independence ("We're going to dig for gold") and takes the initiative in staking a claim, albeit with Frail's secret financial support. Just as in *A Summer Place*, in which Sylvia manages a successful business, Elizabeth organizes the mining enterprise, keeps spirits up when progress is slow, makes confident decisions in determining contractual conditions, and also begins to teach reading to local miners. She undertakes heavy, physical labor, rejecting offers to sit in the shade: "I will do my share of the work." While it is Frail who treats her physical injuries, it is her courage and determination to save his life that helps Frail overcome his mental wounds and finally embrace her. In his discussion of film adaptations of Dorothy Johnson's stories, Walter Metz notes that while *The Man Who Shot Liberty Valance* has been highly regarded, *The Hanging Tree* has been largely ignored.[89] He suggests that this is in part because Ford's film reinforces the status quo, while Daves challenges the gender politics of the Cold War period. Ford's heroine is a passive figure, essentially a prize for whom the two main male characters compete, but Daves's Elizabeth is more independent. At the end of the film, she saves Frail's life, rather like a last-minute charge of an all-male cavalry.

REPRESENTATION OF THE SEXUAL AND MORAL BEHAVIOR OF YOUNG PEOPLE

After the opening credits of *Blackboard Jungle* (1955), an on-screen paragraph states: "We are concerned with juvenile delinquency." Anxiety over lack of respect for authority and threats to property and public order was reflected in films such as *Rebel without a Cause*, which focused on the importance of families, teachers, and social workers in alleviating these threats. However, Hollywood's portrayal of sexual relationships changed little while the Production Code was enforced, with censorious attitudes to premarital sexual activity continuing even when there was evidence of greater sexual license. Social workers, public health professionals, and the popular media increasingly believed that calls for restraint before marriage would be futile, and they tended to advocate that the best way to "contain" immoral sexual activity was through early marriage. By the early 1960s, 40 percent of American brides were teenagers, and 50 percent of all young women were married by the time they were twenty years old,[90] which is reflected in popular Hollywood films. An obvious example is *Father of the Bride* (1950), followed by *Father's Little Dividend* (1951), in which there is an early pregnancy for the young couple.

This advice ignored increasing evidence that couples who married with one or both partners in their teens were much more likely to be separated or divorced within a few years.[91] More specifically, the divorce rate for women under nineteen years was nearly twice that for women of nineteen to twenty-four years, itself nearly twice that for those of twenty-four to twenty-nine years. However, just as *So This Is College* warned young men against unnecessarily early romantic commitments, in *Rome Adventure*, a young woman is anxious for wider experience before making any final commitment: "I've got a lot of love bottled up in me. Unhappily it's a natural resource that's never been fully explored." While Daves was criticized for condoning promiscuity, his films recognize the reality of adolescents' sexual desires and conduct and reflect the conclusions of social psychologist Thomas Poffenberger, whose 1960 study recognized that "the old code of premarital sex behavior ... has become progressively less effective.... [A] large percentage of young people violate the code," and that "premarital coitus seldom has devastating results."[92] In *Parrish*, as the protagonist's early relationship with Lucy deepens, his mother (Claudette Colbert) asks, "How far's this thing gone?" Her expression of acceptance indicates that she had no illusions about the nature of relationships between young people. Lucy is able to enjoy sex without feeling the need to commit to a permanent relationship or marriage, making clear to Parrish: "I am yours whenever you want." This contrasts with Hollywood's conventional representation of youth as exemplified in *Looking for Love* (1964), in which the central character declares, "Now I can concentrate on my big ambition in life, to get married and have babies." Lucy gives birth to an illegitimate child but accepts the resulting responsibilities. Considered by several of the characters to be of loose morals, she is natural and spontaneous and not constrained by narrow-minded conventions. She is honest and good humored and ultimately shows that she is trustworthy and loyal and will be a responsible single parent.

In fact, Eugene Gilbert finds evidence of some concern that adolescents may be *too* conventional, arguing that young adults should embark on more adventurous pursuits before taking a steady job, and that young women should have more varied experiences before settling down,[93] as does Prudence in *Rome Adventure*. Daves's own experience illustrates this attitude to life. After leaving university, he traveled extensively and enjoyed the life of a bachelor in Hollywood before marrying relatively later in life, aged thirty-four years, a marriage that lasted until his death in 1977. It is an attitude that celebrates the initiative and independence of the young, and this is reflected in his films. In *Spencer's Mountain*, a young woman is willing to discuss the realities of reproduction and pregnancy, whereas the older woman exclaims, "We don't talk about such things in this house." As early as *Dames*, Daves's screenplay emphasizes the foolishness of the rich and powerful in attempting to effect "the elevation of American morals" and impose their views on others. In *The Red House*, the farmer's sister has repressed her knowledge and feelings to maintain a tenuous family harmony. It is the young people who are willing to ignore expectations of their behavior, and they ultimately expose evil and reveal the truth of past events. Walker suggests that in *The Last Wagon*, the Apaches may embody the young travelers' collective id, with the massacre of their families representing their unconscious wish to be free from society's conventions and restraints.[94] What is certain is that the young people show a willingness to indulge in behavior of which their families would disapprove, as indicated by the enthusiasm with which they arrange to go skinny-dipping. Any form of improper behavior, particularly by females, was invariably "punished" in keeping with the requirements of the Production Code. A notable example as late as 1975 is in the opening scene of Steven Spielberg's *Jaws*. Therefore, it is significant that in *The Last Wagon*, it is the youngsters' willingness to defy convention and take risks that saves their lives and ensures that they will take advantage of opportunities for maturation and growth.

In 1952, Robert Blood argued that premarital chastity permitted the development of the mutual respect and love necessary to secure a relationship with "a status above the animal level." His conclusion that "premarital sexual relationships and romantic attitudes are mutually incompatible"[95] is consistent with the tenet conventionally promoted by Hollywood, that "nice girls" do not indulge in sexual activity outside marriage. In this regard, Georganne Scheiner comments on the famous refrain in *Grease* (1978) in which Sandra Dee is remembered as "lousy with virginity," who "won't go to bed 'til I'm legally wed."[96] Scheiner points out that Dee's troubled private life was far removed from this representation, and although some of her characters, such as those in the *Gidget* and *Tammy* films, did correspond with such an image, in the main her film roles portrayed a young woman conflicted about her developing sexuality, as in *A Summer Place*. Daves's script may be overly verbose in places, but it does reflect the uncertainty and confusion of adolescents as their feelings seemed to conflict with the behavior expected of them. References to sexual behavior and appearance are unusually explicit. Molly confesses to times when she "felt naughty" and experienced "naughty dreams," complaining that her mother is "anti-sex" and makes her "feel ashamed of having a body." She tells her father that she had undressed in front of her bedroom window in order to be seen by the boy next door.

Although Molly sometimes dictates that "we've got to be good," it is she who initiates intercourse with Johnny, just as, Pomp notes in *Spencer's Mountain*, Claris exhibits sexual confidence,[97] asking: "Do we have to wait four years? . . . Can't we start practicing now?" Similarly, as she embarks on her first love affair, the young heroine in *Susan Slade* remarks: "I haven't had enough practice." Daves's later films recognize the reality of changing attitudes, and in *A Summer Place*, Helen's feeble attempts to flatten and hide Molly's developing figure symbolize the absurdity of denying reality, as evidenced in later research. In his study of sexual attitudes and behavior, journalist and social critic Vance Packard notes variance in regions and levels of education but concludes that by 1950, half of American brides were non-virgins.[98] He found that many of those brides who had consented to premarital sexual experiences did so with their future husband only; in *Susan Slade*, Susan consents to intercourse only when she has become engaged, albeit secretly. However, surveys of female college students in

1958 and 1968, at the same university, found that that the percentage of the sample having had premarital intercourse had doubled during the intervening decade.[99] The researchers concluded that the need to be engaged had become far less of a prerequisite for agreeing to intercourse, and also that the guilt the students felt for "going too far" had diminished and that more were willing to have more than one partner.

Therefore, *A Summer Place* can be regarded as groundbreaking in the way that Daves exposes the widening gulf between Hollywood's conventional expectations of behavior and the reality of the sexual feelings and conduct of young adults. He does not advocate promiscuity but, unusually for a mainstream Hollywood production, he does not ignore the reality of changing attitudes with regard to sexual ethics. The film is honest about the importance of sexual desire in the minds of adolescents, and in the sense that there was no need to feel shame in such feelings. It is honest about adolescents' growing sexual awareness and that sexual behavior was to be expected.

Thus, Daves's views are compatible with those of eminent behavioral psychologist Albert Ellis. Although Ellis acknowledged that many individuals voluntarily choose to have premarital sex and that such behavior may be disadvantageous for some, it is not in itself intrinsically wicked.[100] Similarly, psychiatrist and pioneer in the field of family planning Walter Stokes regarded as irrational the restriction of the sexuality of young adults to "an unreal, romantic, de-sexualized idealism that ignores the erotic emotions and physical realities of sex."[101] This position is reflected in *Rome Adventure*, in which Prudence (Suzanne Pleshette) is disciplined by the school board for introducing material considered to be "too adult" for young women. It had been her intention to counter the view that "had made intimate relations between men and women so ugly," as well as to discuss perceptions of "womanhood and fulfillment." She travels alone to Italy to benefit from new experiences, showing herself to be open to ideas from a different culture, and she is keen to learn a foreign language. She responds to suitors who are nervous and gauche as well as suave and very experienced, before her love for Don (Troy Donahue), a graduate student, grows.

Although too much of the film is devoted to viewing the sights of Italy alongside the perorations of tour guides, their relationship develops almost wordlessly, in gestures, expressions, and reactions, particularly by Pleshette, which convey sensitively their increasing pleasure in being together. This is the most convincing of the relationships involving Donahue in Daves's films, largely because of the presence of Pleshette in her first starring role. Her visual expressions suggest an understated but obvious sensual and passionate nature, and her verbal expression shows tenderness and honesty as well as provocativeness. These emotions are conveyed in one memorably sensitive yet erotic close-up scene in which Don tickles Prudence's face and neck with a sheaf of grass. She whispers, "Every place you pick, tickles," but adds: "I tickle other places too." As his lips get closer to hers, the movement of her eyes and mouth suggest both devotion and physical longing as she whispers, "Oh yes. Now!," as does her expression in a later scene when he whispers, "[Do] you think we'll sleep tonight?," followed by moments of quiet contentment at breakfast. A contemporary review felt that the dialogue was overly suggestive, distasteful, and nasty.[102] However, in such sequences, Daves portrays the urgency of physical longing and the pleasure of fulfillment that can be shared equally without guilt by young women as well as men. Although the film ends conventionally with the implication of a lasting relationship, the attitudes and behavior of Prudence are not those traditionally shown by a typical young Hollywood heroine of this era.

Daves also shows empathy toward his characters whose experiences conventionally have brought censure, as indicated in his response to the comments he received about *A Summer Place*. Replying to a letter from a member of the public, he wrote of the need for "compassion as against punishment in the conclusion of the film. This world is quick to punish and slow to forgive."[103] In her study of post–World War II attitudes and public policy, Rickie Solinger finds that unmarried pregnancy was perceived as an issue of maladjustment and that an individual need not be defined by her "error." She could transcend her maladjustment by preparing herself for marriage, but this could involve a trade-off: "In exchange for their babies, they could reenter normal life."[104] Before the early 1960s, unmarried mothers, however sympathetically portrayed in films, conventionally suffered for their "misdeed" by the loss of their child or the man they love, unless they were fortunate in having a forgiving man willing to offer marriage and respectability. Films of this period such as *Mildred Pierce* (1945) and *Letter from an Unknown Woman* (1948) tended to show the difficulties encountered by women who were raising a child without a paternal figure. *Love with the Proper Stranger* (1963) was recognized as groundbreaking in showing a more progressive attitude to premarital pregnancy, but released four years earlier, *A Summer Place* represents a significant departure in the depiction of sexual behavior and attitudes. Ken and Johnny are caring and compassionate. Extramarital sex is not condemned, and Molly's pregnancy is not a detriment to a caring, committed, and passionate relationship. In *Susan Slade*, the young rancher's love for Susan remains constant despite her previous affair, and he certainly wants more from the relationship than offering the opportunity for respectability for the unmarried mother.

Ellis claims that those who believe that no female should ever have non-marital sex, even with no harm to herself or others, are male supremacists who are degrading to women.[105] This raises the hypocrisy of the double standard of premarital intercourse, which sociologist Ira Reiss maintains had been neglected in academic literature.[106] Reiss focuses on the convention that a woman who has sexual intercourse outside marriage is morally suspect, while such experience is excusable, if not desirable, for men and therefore need not warrant the same reproach.[107] Robert Bell adds that, rather than social criticism, a male may gain some prestige in the eyes of his peers for such behavior,[108] whereas there would be a loss of respect for a young woman who is persuaded to have sex. Hollywood films tended to conform to this moral stance, with traditional standards rewarded and deviance "punished." Oscar-winning romantic adventure *Anthony Adverse* (1936) narrates the story of a French couple who are separated for several years. The hero is an Atlantic slave trader, and the film implies that he is intimate with African and Cuban women; his wife, meanwhile, believing him to be dead, begins a new relationship. After the couple has been reunited, he learns of this relationship and, as a consequence, leaves his wife, taking their son and setting out for a new life in America. What is perhaps more surprising to a modern audience is that his wife accepts that this is just, believing that she has been an unfit mother. Similarly, the heroine in *Waterloo Bridge* (1940) commits suicide because she believes that her "past" disqualifies her from marrying into a respectable family.

It is an issue that Daves considers. Conn, Susan's first love in *Susan Slade*, is a mountaineer, and his use of related imagery is unambiguous: "Give one of us a virgin peak and we dream about her and get jealous of the men who beat us to it." He adds that "we keep looking for new peaks to conquer," and after Susan has "given in," he makes no attempt to contact her despite his promises. Similarly, a later fiancé ends their relationship on learning of Susan's past. However, it is a moral position that Daves explicitly rejects. Rather than the woman who agrees to make love outside marriage, in this film it is the man whose behavior is "punished": Conn dies on a mountain climb, while eventually Susan finds happiness. In this sense, Daves anticipates the conclusions of Michael Schofield's research, which found evidence of changing attitudes to premarital sex.[109] His study found that only a small minority of young people agreed that such experience was more acceptable for males than for females or that to marry a virgin was essential. A far greater proportion disagreed with the view that premarital sex gave a young woman a bad reputation. When Johnny asks, "Who taught you to kiss so perfectly?," he is surprised at Molly's response, but this does not alter his feelings: "I knew it would be like this." The fact that in *Parrish*, Lucy has an illegitimate child, does not affect Parrish's genuine feelings toward her. Daves's sympathetic and noncondemnatory portrayal of Lucy does not ignore the difficulties that premarital sex may bring, but it recognizes that this is a reality. When the truth of Susan's illegitimate child eventually becomes public in *Susan Slade*, her mother is able, eventually, to show and express in public her pride in her daughter, and Susan at last realizes her love for a local rancher (Donahue) who has remained devoted to her and for whom the "scandal" makes no difference.

Poffenberger found evidence that young women were less willing to accept double standards with regard to premarital sex and more likely to expect the same sexual pleasure as the male or to apply to him the same restrictions.[110] At a time when, in 1962, the president of Vassar, Sarah Blanding, warned students that those who wished to indulge in premarital sex should withdraw from college,[111] a key feature of Daves's films is the tenderness with which he portrays experiences of love, recognizing the impulses of the young and showing compassion for their frustrations. The young woman in *The Red House* who boasts "I'm good at things they don't teach at school" shows a healthy, nonprudish attitude, in contrast to the suppression of feelings by older characters, which has led to their frustration, possessiveness, and obsession. Similarly, in *Spencer's Mountain*, the youth who underlines all the "rude" words in a dictionary is treated with sympathetic affection, and so is, Pomp points out, the young woman who entices Spencer's son: "You and me could have some fun. . . . Whenever you get the urge to, I'll come running."[112] Susan Slade is not condemned because of her premarital sex: her mistake is to give in to her parents' initial wish to hide her illegitimate child. In *A Summer Place*, Ken's calm and considered response to Molly's growing sexual awareness is supportive of her relationship with Johnny: "There's one great reason for living; to love and be loved." He throws away the clothes selected by Helen to flatten Molly's figure and reproaches her for trying to "suffocate every natural instinct in our daughter" and for teaching her that "sex itself is a filthy word."

The shallowness of Helen's obsession with social appearance and the affectation in her manner and language that have alienated her family are manifested in the small and obviously artificial Christmas tree that so easily topples over. In Hollywood films, a large, real, and extravagantly decorated tree is invariably a symbol around which a family comes together. Contemporary literature focused on the crucial importance of parental attitudes. Sociologist Lester Kirkendall did not endorse unfettered premarital sexual liberality. However, he recognized that the authoritarian emphasis on the dire consequences of pregnancy and the social stigma that were used to discourage such behavior and were invariably expressed in a manner largely irrelevant to the young had been unsuccessful.[113] Helen's advice to Molly is expressed in such terms. Robert Bell and Jack Buerkle show that the attitudes of young women to the importance of virginity at the time of marriage were considerably more liberal than those of their mothers, irrespective of age, religion, and educational background, and they conclude that "premarital sexual behavior provides one of the greatest potential areas of mother-daughter conflict."[114] In *The Very Thought of You*, Janet is slapped by her mother after spending several hours in a motel room with the soldier she loves: "It's not enough for you to cheapen yourself. I brought you up decent."

In *A Summer Place*, this is reflected in relations between Helen and Molly, an early attempt by Hollywood to examine such a relationship. Helen's view that "[l]ove should be more than animal attraction" is valid in itself, but her thoughts are expressed with insensitivity and callousness and evoke a view of a relationship that is unnatural and calculating: "You have to make him want you and never betray that you want him." She had refused to live near Catholics, Italians, and Jews, while "Negroes have to be avoided at all costs," and it is she who expounds conservative and traditional values about what behavior should be expected from respectable young women and what they must or must not do on dates. However, it is a lesson that is devalued by her irrational and hysterical manner. In propounding the "evils" of sex, she personifies the dangers of the unnatural repression of sexual feelings and is unable to offer the support and guidance needed by a young woman from her mother. After capsizing and wrecking a yacht, Johnny and Molly are forced to spend a night on an island. Helen seems less concerned with Molly's safety than with her "honor": she accuses Molly of immoral behavior and forces her daughter, despite her hysterical state, to undergo a humiliating gynecological examination to check that she is still a virgin. Immediately thinking the worst of her daughter, she shows no trust: "I'm not asking for the truth because I know you'd lie." Similarly, Bart's comment that Molly and Johnny are too young for such a commitment is not without value. However, it is given in a spirit of drunken bitterness and misogynistic cynicism and encapsulated in his view of women that "they're all alike in the dark."

Molly expects a condemnatory reaction to news of her pregnancy: "I thought you were going to tell me it was all my fault," and so appreciates the understanding she receives. Ken's initial instinct is anger when he realizes that Johnny has been intimate with his daughter, but he and Sylvia refrain from making moral judgments about the behavior of their respective children, particularly in the light of their own affair: "We didn't settle for a walk on the beach." While films that focused on teenage anxieties were becoming more common, *A Summer Place* is unusual in its presentation of parents who recognize that simplistic moralizing is insufficient guidance for adolescents, particularly as they recognize and act upon their own sexual feelings. It is this principle that Ken and Sylvia and Susan's parents adopt, albeit with initial uncertainty and awkwardness, and it is an approach that is sensitive to the sexual feelings and behavior of young people. They realize that they need to offer support and understanding: "We're not throwing any stones." They are also realistic: "If they experiment they must always remember what the cost can be." A young couple in such circumstances may face difficulties: "You've got a fight ahead of you, kid, but you've got the beauty and strength of love on your side." The scene in which Ken and Sylvia consider what they can say to the young couple is intense and heartfelt, but honest and restrained in its portrayal of the difficulties that parents may face: "I've got to talk to her. What can I say? What advice can I give her? . . . I can't tell her to be half good." However, it is such efforts, made despite a conflict of emotions, that Johnny and Molly value, as does Susan in *Susan Slade*. Her parents offer supportive comfort and advice as she is growing up and ultimately trust her and allow her to make her own decisions. When Susan finds that she is pregnant and worries that with "one mistake, you have to pay for it the rest of your life," her mother is supportive and realistic: "You think all girls who marry are virginal?"

A Summer Place condemns the insensitivity of many adults, which can add a sense of guilt or shame to the uncertainty and confusion that many adolescents experience. At a time when the Hollywood blacklist still operated, Alfred Hitchcock's *Rear Window* (1954) seems to approve of a character's comment that "[w]e've become a race of Peeping Toms" as a murderer is exposed. In Daves's film, the direction of the narrative is determined by characters watching or being watched secretly, but this is shown to be spiteful and hypocritical voyeurism. As in the first shots of the film, Bart is regularly spying on guests or his family, and Helen intercepts Molly's mail. With Molly remarking on a "funny feeling being looked at without knowing," Johnny and Molly often sense that they are being watched, and Helen spies on the couple when they kiss in the garden, as does a classmate of Molly's and her parents, who spread gossip when they see the young couple together. A handyman observes a secret meeting between Ken and Sylvia and gossips to Helen, which results in a public scandal. Such voyeurism is consistent with Mulvey's identification of the "male gaze," with a woman appearing as an erotic object for viewing by male characters or a male audience. Scheiner writes that "Molly is eroticized by the male gaze."[115] This may represent an aspect of Mulvey's thesis in that a woman who welcomes such a gaze is seeing herself through the "eyes of men" and so complies with their expectations or fantasies. However, while Mulvey emphasizes the male as a controlling figure with whom the audience may identify,[116] Molly's actions may be seen as a form of exerting her control in the context of the conflict between her growing sexual awareness and preconceptions of proper behavior. Her embrace with Johnny in public, at the end of the film, can be seen as further exercise of control and is reflected in Scheiner's reference to a female colleague who, as a teenager, claimed that the film gave her "permission to be sexual."[117] Furthermore, while Johnny's first sight of Molly is through binoculars, Molly also "gazes" at him in the same way.

In *The Hanging Tree*, when Frenchy (Karl Malden) finds Elizabeth, he exemplifies the male gaze in the extreme when remarking, "ain't much left from the neck up but she sure is all woman from there down." However, his words are met with disapproving silence from the rest of the male search party, just as there is approval later when she reprimands him, "Find something to do with your hands besides putting them on me." She is not objectified sexually by the male protagonist: she gains in strength and confidence, relying less on male support or direction and becoming independent and self-driven, providing more than mere support for the leading male character. Therefore, she does not function just as an erotic object, and it is perhaps for this reason that coscreenwriter Wendell Mayes refers to the film as the only Western he had seen that was a woman's film rather than a man's.[118] In 1961, Daves prepared an adaptation of Evan Hunter's novel *Mothers and Daughters*, which was never filmed.[119] Daves's treatment focuses mainly on the lives of two young women who meet at college. One chooses to prioritize family rather than a career and, despite some moments when she contemplates missed opportunities, she is very happy. However, she makes this choice freely: she graduates from college despite her mother's attempts to rush her into marriage. The other woman pursues a career, believing, "I really think I made an excellent case for the emancipation of the American female." She has a series of unhappy relationships before meeting again her "first love," at a time of maturity and with the benefit of experience. Daves's feelings in this regard are perhaps encapsulated in *The Very Thought of You* as Janet's father advises her, "Think it out; make your own decisions. Maybe they'll be wrong, maybe they'll be right, but that's the way to learn. Nobody can do it for you." Gough-Yates points out that if a woman character adopts a more masculine role out of necessity, it was expected that she should revert to her feminine way of life when possible, or be made to recognize her error.[120] In *A Ticket to Tomahawk* (1950), when temporarily fulfilling the role of sheriff, the heroine shows greater concern for justice and proves to be more skilled with a gun and knife than the male characters. Yet by the end of the film, she willingly relinquishes the position for marriage and family: "I'm giving up gun-slinging.... I'm not a he, I'm a she."

However, Daves's portrayal of women is more consistent with Betty Friedan's vision of the importance of the qualities and strengths that women may bring to society. Friedan does not denigrate women's domestic activities: she encourages marriage and femininity, but emphasizes that women need not live solely through their husbands and children.[121] Daves's heroines clearly demonstrate capacity for caring and nurturing, and while they seek fulfillment in a relationship, they adhere to their own expectations and standards and are unwilling to renounce their individuality in that relationship. They demonstrate intelligence, insight, and determination, and while in some cases they are inexperienced, they are at ease with their feelings and their sexuality. Daves's heroines exert a crucial influence on the ways in which the films' narratives develop and themes are explored. Even if a woman has a small role, Daves ensures that there are moments in which her expression, a look or gesture, reveals strength, intensity of feeling, and capacity for personal growth. Tavernier writes that such women educate, influence, and challenge Daves's heroes;[122] Lucas emphasizes that "the ability to listen to a man does not make a woman a passive vessel."[123] As well as taking initiatives to ensure that men acknowledge their feelings and helping men to achieve their potential, they also ensure that their own destiny is realized.

IMAGES OF MASCULINITY IN POST-WORLD WAR II HOLLYWOOD

J. Ronald Oakley refers to the 1950s as "a time of unprecedented sentimentalization of marriage and family life."[124] It was a period in which the role and conduct of men was an issue of debate to the extent that Steven Cohan identifies a cultural "redefinition of manliness to include characteristics traditionally associated with femininity such as the maintenance of family life."[125] Therefore, just as for young women, marriage was the most appropriate and responsible choice of lifestyle for men, and scenarios where confirmed bachelors are finally married were typical in films. However, Cohan notes also that contemporary writer Louis Lyndon had warned readers that, with the increasing emancipation of women, this domestic role "is built upon the repression of 'certain deep and perfectly normal masculine drives' ... [the inhibition of which] threatens married men with emasculation."[126] In 1957, sociologist Helen Mayer Hacker's research found that men were expected to bring sensitivity and understanding to their relationships and that this conflicted with men's position as breadwinner and head of the household. She concluded that as a result, "all is not well with men."[127] It is an image of American masculinity that is reinforced in *Rebel without a Cause* in which the discontent and antisocial behavior of Jim (James Dean) is in part due to his lack of respect for his father as a role model. He is shown to be kind and thoughtful but indecisive and henpecked—"She eats him alive and he takes it"—and his "weakness" is emphasized by his wearing of an apron.

Arthur Schlesinger identified an "overpowering conspiracy of blandness" and emphasized that the crisis of American masculinity was of more profound significance than merely a consequence of the emerging emancipation of American women.[128] In relating his argument to the national and international arena, he likened the crisis of masculinity to the rise of communism, which "perverts politics into something secret, sweaty and furtive like nothing so much...as homosexuality in a boys' school."[129] The threat of communism is portrayed in terms of assertion of masculine sexual potency: "these half concealed exercises in penetration and manipulation";[130] he fears that Russia "will have a superiority in the thrust of its missiles and in the penetration of outer space."[131] He compares the political failure of leadership to deal with this threat to "the weakness of impotence," and the "result was to emasculate the political energies of the ruling classes."[132] He argued that, in practice, democracy demanded strong leadership and that "[a] free society cannot get along without heroes," going on to submit that a revival of heroic leadership is essential to save freedom.[133] Just as the "containment" of women can be linked with the containment of communism, the assertion of masculinity can be seen to reflect the will to defeat communism. K.A. Cuordileone is very clear that the image of a secure and restored American masculinity was reflected in Cold War politics.[134] She notes that for Schlesinger, John F. Kennedy epitomized a virile leader who was an antidote to the nation's crisis in masculinity.[135] Criticizing the Eisenhower years, Kennedy referred to the feminized luxury worship of indulgent consumerism and asserted: "I would rather take my television black and white and have the largest rockets in the world."[136] Robert Dean accepts that Kennedy projected an image of youth, strength, and vigor but points out that this "ideology of masculinity" permeated decision-making that resulted in counterinsurgency strategies, covert warfare, assassination schemes, and the Green Berets as well as escalating involvement in Vietnam.[137]

The assertion of masculinity is central to the tone and language of George Kennan, one-time US ambassador to Yugoslavia and the Soviet Union, whose "Long Telegram"[138] contributed to the formulation of the Cold War policy of containment of perceived threats of Russian expansion. He referred to

Russian "insistent, unceasing pressure for penetration and command of key positions" in other countries and insisted that without a decisive American response, "there will be created a vacuum which will favor Communist-Soviet penetration."[139] Frank Costigliola points out that in his telegram, Kennan repeats the word "penetration" five times.[140] More generally, he uses the language of forceful masculine behavior behind which lies an assumption of male potency and superiority, indicated also in his view that, to "gain respect in Russia we must be prepared to undertake a 'taming of the shrew.'"[141] This attitude is reflected in films such as *Rebel without a Cause*, which asserts the need for clear moral guidance for the young. Jim derides his father's attempts to win his respect and his failure to provide appropriate discipline or authority: "He always wants to be my pal." Just as Kennan's approach to "containing" Russia is for America to retain sufficient force to ensure that "everyone knows we can pack a mean punch,"[142] Jim wants his father to assert his masculine authority, particularly over his domineering mother. He wonders aloud "if he had the guts to knock Mom cold once, then maybe she'd be happy and stop picking on him." His juvenile crime officer seems to be progressive and supportive, but he does not challenge Jim's remark. Suggestions of aggressiveness toward women as an indicator of masculinity did not seem to be a concern. In a sense, therefore, it was Hollywood that provided this heroic leadership, such as in films in which courageous individuals countered fascist or communist threats to the American way of life, just as Westerns still celebrated the qualities that Theodore Roosevelt referred to as "the stern manly qualities that are invaluable to a nation."[143] While *The Man in the Gray Flannel Suit* emphasizes the importance of stability at home, symbolized by a husband's eventual prioritizing of his family, the film is careful not to condemn ambition for career and corporate success, as such determination and dedication may be necessary for American prosperity and the preservation of American values.

CHARACTERISTICS OF DAVES'S HEROES

To exemplify her discussion of the "burdens of masculinity" in the 1950s, Hacker quotes the testimony of a skilled car mechanic who feared that listening to his Caruso records would cast doubt on his manhood.[144] In the same year, Daves was filming *Cowboy*, in which the tough cattle-trail boss, skilled in using guns and fists, enquires about opera performances as soon as he arrives in Chicago: "You call yourself civilized and you don't know anything about the opera season?" Furthermore, he is able to sing a Donizetti operatic melody, albeit drunkenly. Similarly, in *Destination Tokyo*, after declaring that "I'm no highbrow," an ordinary seaman openly states: "When I come home from a patrol, if there's any grand opera playing, the whole Connors family goes." Particularly as Daves worked with many of the top male box-office stars of his day, it may not be surprising that Serge Chauvin begins his discussion of his Westerns by stating that the issue of what it means to be a man resonates in many of his films.[145] In his first Western, Daves raises the issue of what might constitute recognizable masculine behavior. In *Broken Arrow*, Jeffords rejects the army's violent solution to the problem of Cochise, which proves unsuccessful, preferring empathetic dialogue to achieve peace and security. Also, rather than kill an injured Indian youth, Jeffords tends his wounds: "It is not my way to fight," to which an Apache replies, "You are a woman maybe." Thus, Daves examines an issue that illustrates Wendy Peek's thesis that American culture was redefining masculinity, with aspects of feminine behavior embraced into masculinity.[146] Jeffords shows courage in seeking out Cochise and facing the anger of settlers in order to achieve peace through dialogue and understanding rather than conquest. Therefore, just as does Peek, Daves raises the question whether strength and physicality are the only measures of masculinity and if peacefulness must equate only with femininity.

In developing her argument, Peek focuses on the main characters in Ford's *Fort Apache*. However, clear exemplification of her reasoning is provided in *Cowboy*, which exposes the mythology of the romance of the life of the cowboy on the open plains. In this film, Reece (Glenn Ford) is an archetypal tough boss of a cattle drive. He is a man of action and is very decisive on the trail and in business negotiations. He feels no responsibility for his crew and shows little emotion when a trail hand suffers a fatal snakebite. "In the long run I don't think it would have made any difference." However, Harris (Jack Lemmon) is deeply upset, particularly because the snakebite resulted from irresponsible behavior. Harris is a hotel desk clerk who writes love poetry, and in order to impress a woman, he buys into the cattle drive after Reece lost money at poker and needs investors. He is naïve and has an overly idealistic image of the cattle business: he has no idea of the difficulties or hardships of working on a cattle drive and is taken aback by the self-seeking and insensitive behavior of the cowboys. At the outset, the two men dislike and distrust each other, but enforced living and working together leads them to recognize each other's strengths and frailties and gradually achieve a level of mutual respect and equality. Reece becomes less callous and single-minded and more considerate of others. He is genuinely troubled when Doc Bender (Brian Donlevy) commits suicide, and he is willing to lose some cattle and sacrifice profit to come to aid of a fellow cowboy: "Maybe I changed my mind. Maybe watching you made me change it." Harris becomes more resilient and shows qualities of leadership when Reece is wounded. They learn from each other and find that working together ensures a safer and more successful cattle drive.

Traditional masculinity as symbolized by the possession and use of a gun is embodied in the character of Grandpa in *Return of the Texan*. He refuses to stop trespassing and poaching and objects to fences designed to restrict his freedom, shooting at Sam's brother-in-law even though he is on his own property: "In the old days he would've got plugged right between the eyes." The loss of his gun means he must "stay home like an old woman," as "a man ain't got much left without his pride and self-respect." At the end of the film, he sits down in the forest, and, holding his great-grandson's hand, he waits to die. It is a scene that is as moving as the funeral of Tom Doniphon, whose death symbolizes the passing of the "Old West" in *The Man Who Shot Liberty Valance* (1962). It is poignant because the achievements of earlier generations are valued: "Who do you reckon made it safe for a man like Murray to own a piece of land." However, he finally appreciates that "we gotta learn to let go" and that resistance to changing values is like "letting the dead stand in the way of the living."

In *Cowboy*, Doc Bender reflects, "A man has to have something besides a gun and a saddle," and significantly Sam never wears a gun. Thus, Grandpa's death represents the rejection of a view of masculinity that is embodied in the objections to restrictions on possession of guns. Walker refers to scenes in which an older mentor-hero teaches his charge how to shoot and defend himself as a familiar Western convention.[147] However, while this occurs in Dorothy Johnson's story, in Daves's *The Hanging Tree*, Rune learns how to care for others and develops a sense of community responsibility. Similarly, after the murder of his companion in *3:10 to Yuma*, Evans seems to be subordinating his own instinct for safety to that of a wider civic responsibility in persisting with his objective when he has been absolved of this responsibility: "Do you think I can do less?" This differs from director James Mangold's remake (2007), in which Evans negotiates an increase in payment and secures water rights, which Stephen Mexal equates with the financial and property acquisitiveness of post–Cold War politics, encapsulated in Wade's declaration that "[i]t's man's nature to take what he wants."[148]

The need for community is a distinguishing characteristic of Daves's heroes. In *Cowboy*, Doc Bender advises the tough trail boss, "You just can't make it all by yourself," and in *Jubal*, the hero relies on the community for help and protection. For John White, this questions the individualistic ideology inherent in free-market capitalism as "insufficient for real human beings living in the real world."[149] Similarly, Shep's advice to Jubal, that "[n]obody learns without help," echoes Schmid's nurse in *Pride of the Marines* who emphasizes the importance of communication and support. This represents a challenge to the myth of the "American Adam," which is raised explicitly in Jeffords's reference to the story of Adam and Eve as he sits with Sonseeahray by the river. He goes on to admit that he has always lived alone and that he's "wanted it that way," but the community spirit of the Apaches engenders dissatisfaction with that existence and enhances his absorption into the indigenous culture. With a similar experience for the protagonist in *White Feather*, Daves's heroes contradict the image of the strong, silent Westerner, a figure that R. W. B. Lewis depicts as "an individual standing alone, self-reliant and self-propelling, ready to confront whatever awaited him with the aid of his own unique and inherent resources."[150]

As Jonathan Mitchell states, it would be difficult not to visualize such an image in the figure of the pioneer or frontiersman hero as a protector of American civilization.[151] Furthermore, he points to the inferable image of American uniqueness as a utopian nation and Garden of Eden, but also American identity as white, male, and Christian with a means of excluding or subjugating those outside that idealized identity.[152] However, in *Broken Arrow* it is the Apache world that represents Eden, where there is a willingness to learn, cooperate, and mutually respect and love. It is white racism that represents "the Fall" and destroys Jeffords's contentment. Additionally, Daves's heroes contest a corollary to the image of the "American Adam" that envisages women as Eve and as secondary to man. As Mitchell emphasizes, this constitutes "a masculine privileging paradigm" whereby "[t]he ultimate sin in America is to be ... deemed feminine where one should not be." Femininity has its place in the home and bedroom, "in subservience to men, but never in men themselves or in 'manly pursuits,' the most manly of which is being *American*."[153] Daves's characters are more consistent with Peek's conclusion that a hero is one who is able to show competence and achieve success, and in order to do so, he displays a broad range of characteristics that fall within the range of masculine and feminine behavior.[154]

Just as Schmid in *Pride of the Marines* boasts, "You got to be real rugged to get into the Marines" and "I like to live life independent," so the strong, silent, self-reliant Western frontiersman hero has represented a particular image of masculinity. Hacker discusses aspects of this traditional image, which by definition proscribed the expression of psychological problems or insecurities, lest such signs of "weakness" be taken for effeminacy.[155] A protagonist who is searching for emotional security and who is willing to reveal his uncertainties

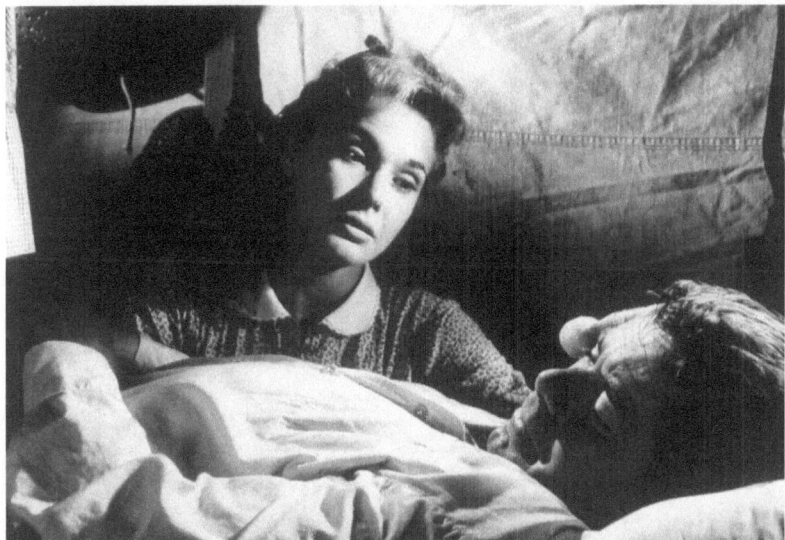

"Stop grieving so deep... You mustn't be ashamed needing somebody." *Jubal*. Felicia Farr, Glenn Ford. Photo 12 / Alamy Stock Photo.

and insecurities to a young woman would appear to be incompatible with the conventional image of the Western hero who must demonstrate the unambiguous qualities of strength and confidence. Yet this is exactly how Jubal behaves in sharing his worries and insecurities with Naomi. Although he recovers his physical strength after being "saved" by Shep, it is clear that his life has been lonely and troubled: "Maybe I am running from something." He is haunted by memories of rejection, his illegitimacy, his mother's hatred, her willingness to let him drown, and her accusations of blame for his father's death when saving him. Hacker states that the conventional male figure may be permitted moments of weakness when he may need female support.[156] However, she emphasizes that such support is in the nature of encouragement and "ego-building" rather than the direct participation and counsel of "equals," and therefore not as Jubal confides in Naomi. She encourages Jubal to talk, after which he admits, "I never talked like this to anybody in my life." For Naomi, this does not diminish his masculinity or attractiveness: "You mustn't be ashamed needing somebody. Everybody does."

Carol MacCurdy states that the raison d'être of the Western has been to examine "manhood," a topic on which *3:10 to Yuma* makes profound statements.[157] In this film, Dan Evans (Van Heflin), an instinctively passive rancher, does not wear a gun and is very reluctant to involve himself in apprehending a murderer: "If I didn't have to do it, I wouldn't." In fact, Mangold equates the character's hesitancy and nervousness in Daves's film with cowardice

"If I ever said anything that made you think I was complaining... I love everything, every minute." *3.10 to Yuma*. Leora Dana, Van Heflin. Photo 12 / Alamy Stock Photo.

and makes clear that he was anxious to ensure that Evans was not seen in the same way in his version of the film.[158] Similarly, it is generally accepted that Howard Hawks made *Rio Bravo* as a response to *High Noon* (1952) and *3:10 to Yuma*, in which he maintained that the protagonists were consumed and almost defeated by self-doubt and mental turmoil in dealing with the villains.[159] Mistakenly referring to Evans as the marshal, Hawks saw his worry and indecision as Wade (Glenn Ford) taunts him as weakness; Hawks was in no doubt that to fulfill his duty, Evans should make clear his willingness to shoot Wade, as in Elmore Leonard's short story on which the film is based and in which the character declares, "I'm going to pull both triggers at once—without first asking questions."[160]

In Daves's film, Evans makes such threats but without conviction and naïvely almost allows Wade to overpower him. Furthermore, he is unable to take any practical steps to prevent the stagecoach holdup, and his helplessness is compounded as he fails to respond to his sons' expectation for him to take action: "Aren't you gonna do something?" His humiliation deepens at home with the reaction of Alice, his wife: "What did you do?... It seems terrible that something bad can happen and all anybody can do is stand by and watch." His response is defensive and seems inadequate: "What could I do.... What and get myself shot, too?" In the context of Schlesinger's emphasis on a need for liberal activism to be virile and forceful, Evans has failed as a father and husband, with his ranch increasingly unproductive. He has failed to live up to traditional expectations of providing emotional, physical, and financial security, attributes that Hacker suggests impact sexual attractiveness and confidence with women.[161] Daves's visual emphasis on the parched, cracked earth may be seen as a metaphor for the state of their relationship as Evans longs for an end to the drought and hopes, "Maybe you and I won't be so tired any more." His sense of inadequacy is heightened as Wade's taunts draw attention to his "failings": "I wouldn't make her work so hard.... I'll bet she was a real beautiful girl before she met you."

Therefore, as several critics have noted, on one level the film is about Evans's attempt to reassert a traditional form of masculinity.[162] Desperate for the $200 reward offered by the stagecoach owner, he agrees to take Wade to Contention City and then by train to the authorities in Yuma, rejecting the opportunity to back out even when payment is guaranteed. As a result, his wife assures him, "[t]he boys are so proud.... I'm proud too." In the remainder of the film, there is a psychological battle of wits between the two men as they wait in a hotel room and as Wade alternately tries to charm, bribe, and threaten Evans while his gang seeks to free him. MacCurdy suggests that Alice stands by their marriage and family because her husband has rediscovered his manhood.[163] The fact that Evans's participation is reluctant and that he is anxious to return to normal life does not detract from the fine qualities that he demonstrates and that, in the end, are valued by his wife, with Simon Petch viewing her words as a validation of their marriage:[164] "Please forgive me.... If I ever said anything that made you think I was complaining... it just isn't true.... I love everything, every minute." Regretting that she provoked him, she appreciates his qualities, and in the final scene the coming of rain, which will replenish the parched soil, suggests that the anxieties in their marriage will be resolved. Evans shows that he is able to make decisions and take decisive action, but his wife's change of heart represents a recognition of qualities to be valued in men other than a capacity for tough and virile action. Evans is able to show courage and take a determined moral stance against overwhelming odds. However, he succeeds only because Wade protects him and then jumps with him onto the train. Without this action, Evans would certainly have been killed. When Alice "repents," she is accepting that particular behaviors are alien to his nature—"You just seem to expect something from me that I'm not"—just as she recognizes that other qualities and values are important. Dan is steadfast, reliable, and considerate of others, and his apparent inaction can be seen as sensible and careful thoughtfulness.

Daves's male characters show the capacity to revise their attitudes and behavior in this regard. In *To the Victor*, Taggart has pursued amoral and selfish relationships. When asked, "Did you care who the woman was?," he makes clear: "I don't want to look more involved than I am." He initially agrees to help Christine only because she is attractive but comes to revise his feelings and attitudes to others. In *Pride of the Marines*, manual laborer Al Schmid works and plays hard while "girls are great for laughs." He enjoys asserting male superiority and takes pleasure in showing his prowess at hunting and sports, but after he is blinded, he cannot fulfill a traditional male role: "I'll never earn enough money to keep her." He must adopt a different form of manliness and learn that there are other ways to show courage and determination. In *3:10 to Yuma*, Evans's sense of inadequacy is only heightened by the charisma and sexual magnetism of Wade, which is obvious, not only with his seduction of the barmaid but also in the way he charms Alice when the posse stops at Evans's home. Ironically, therefore, Wade gains respect for the character and determination of Evans and assesses his own life accordingly. Initially he taunts Evans about his inability to provide for his wife. However, observing Evans's relationship with his family, his remark about "[a] woman like that to come home to every night. Real close" adopts a more wistful tone, hinting at a realization of missed opportunities and wasted potential.

It is this premise that helps to explain the film's surprising ending, which different critics have found to be inconsistent and unconvincing.[165] Slavoj Žižek's suggestion that Wade is willing to sacrifice his freedom because he has been won over by Evans's integrity is too literal.[166] Gough-Yates seeks to explain this by suggesting that Evans actually dies, with the final minutes of the film presenting the wish fulfillments of a dying man.[167] This occurs in the Oscar-winning short film *Occurrence at Owl Creek Bridge* (1961), but the final seconds of Roberto Enrico's film show clearly that the action has been a vision at the moment of death. There is no such explanation in Daves's film. In fact, Wade's actions are akin to those of the gunfighter in *Shane*, who leaves the valley and those he has come to love because he realizes that his way of life is becoming irrelevant in a changing world. Wade accepts that there is no place for the way he has lived and that the future lies in the hands of men like Evans. Thus, Daves anticipates later Westerns such as *Warlock* (1959), in which the skilled mercenary leaves town, giving way to the less confident deputy; and more significantly *The Man Who Shot Liberty Valance*. In Ford's film, Tom Doniphon (John Wayne), who has represented the independence and freedom of the conventional Western hero, shoots Liberty Valance secretly, thus saving the life of his more passive rival (James Stewart), to whom he thereby cedes his authority in the community and also the woman he loves.

While William Savage writes that "the cowboy is the embodiment of masculinity," he adds: "For any practical purpose masculinity is a cultural rather than a biological characteristic."[168] Daves's heroes may display traditional masculine heroic qualities of courage, decisiveness, and leadership but they also reflect Friedan's belief that men should not need the weaknesses of others to prove their masculinity.[169] They are also caring and display concern for family, and the fact that they show uncertainty and worry does not detract from their status as hero. In *Jubal*, Daves highlights an issue that has grown in significance in more recent times. Despite his many fine qualities, Shep's behavior toward Mae might be regarded as misogynistic. He is embarrassingly naïve and socially inept, touching Mae playfully but inappropriately in front of others and routinely smacking her behind: "I always do that." His response to Jubal's question, "Do you think she likes being swatted?," is: "Don't all women?" His labels for different women are "a nice piece of gingham" and "the liveliest filly I ever rode," and he refers to his wife as his "Canadian heifer." He believes that such behaviors are demonstrations of love, but Jubal points out that "[t]here are other ways you know, Shep," and advises him that "there's a lot of things a man does that bother a woman ... slurping coffee out of a saucer, spitting, scratching, whacking her on the behind when she isn't looking." Thus, Daves draws attention to attitudes and behaviors that might have been considered acceptable in a traditionally male-dominated environment, but that may cause distress to women who may feel vulnerable in that environment.

In Daves's screenplay for *Mothers and Daughters*, a prominent male character is an ambitious, successful lawyer, but family matters are just as important, and he is equally anxious that his wife should fulfill her ambitions. For Joan Mellen, Cary Grant's character in *Destination Tokyo* "periodically offers lessons in manliness."[170] He is suave, brave, calm, and decisive under pressure, and above all inspirational to his crew. Yet he also shows tenderness and sensitivity as an anesthetic is administered to a young sailor, listening to the man's prayers and carefully holding the sailor's head as he wakes up after the operation. More generally, Daves's characters exemplify what Peek envisages as "new men" within a concept of masculinity that is dynamic rather than static and that incorporates diverse gendered behaviors.[171] Susan's mother in *Susan Slade* condemns young men who, "to prove themselves ... have to make a conquest of every girl they meet ... merely satisfying an urge." Conversely, the characters played by Troy Donahue in this film and in *A Summer Place* and *Parrish* reflect David Riesman's contention that, for young men, the value of love is of increasing importance—they seek relationships for more sincere and profound reasons than male vanity.[172]

Conclusion

IN HER ANALYSIS OF THE AMERICAN CHARACTER DURING WORLD WAR II, anthropologist Margaret Mead wrote that "we must feel we are on the side of the Right" and that we "are fighting for a new and better world, not for the perpetuation of an old, indifferent one."[1] In *Pride of the Marines*, Daves shows no doubt about the morality of American action at Guadalcanal in the way that Terrence Malick interprets the same campaign in *The Thin Red Line* (1998). Malick emphasized that "if you die, it's gonna be for nothing" and that "[w]ar does not ennoble men, it turns them into dogs." For Daves, the nobility of America's cause is certain, and this is encapsulated in one shot near the end of *Task Force* in which the distant Statue of Liberty is framed by the twisted and contorted structure of a damaged aircraft carrier as it returns to America after the Battle of Midway. Daves did not disparage American traditions or ideals. Invited to contribute to Stanford University's seventieth anniversary publication in 1962, he emphasized the importance of the achievement that "lies with those who have gone before."[2] He expressed pride that his own ancestors were part of America's pioneer heritage[3] and in being able to retrace the routes taken by his grandfather when he worked as a wagon train leader and Pony Express rider: "I was inspired by it because I got a great sense of belonging to this country."[4]

Opening with bars of a typically lush Max Steiner score, which incorporated the chords of "America the Beautiful," *Spencer's Mountain* was interpreted as a celebration of traditional American family values. In one wordless sequence, an old man walks slowly into the family graveyard. He kneels down and, after tenderly dusting a grave and pulling out some weeds, touches the gravestone in silent remembrance of his parents, who had settled in the valley. Although brief, the scene is as poignant as Ford's graveyard scenes, particularly so as the actor is Donald Crisp, a member of the "John Ford Stock Company." However, in *The Red House*, the farmer's secrecy and repression of his niece's natural development is a metaphor for fear of change: "We've been content with the way things were.... Why are you suddenly questioning things?" His obsession with the status quo develops into madness, which the young people must overcome for the community to grow with openness and honesty. In his Stanford interview, Daves claimed that "[w]e're afraid of the strange and different" and that "[t]he motto of everybody on earth should be 'there is a better way.'"[5] While Daves did not doubt the importance of American traditions, he continued to act as a "critical friend" in examining political and social issues that provoked debate, and his hypotheses accorded with progressive analyses of developing priorities in social attitudes and policy. His work conveys his vision of a better world and his instinct for and sense of fairness, tolerance, and openness to diversity.

Daves expressed his belief that "to understand is to love,"[6] and such understanding represents the core of many of his films in which a hero is one who learns about and from those of another background, race, or culture, or one who is able to "treat" the intolerance and prejudice of others. A belief in the importance of gaining knowledge and understanding is maintained in his films. Daves's first screenplay for *So This Is College* emphasizes that students should take full advantage of opportunities at college. This principle continued in later films at a time when, during the period of McCarthyist witch hunts, films such as *My Son John* accused college tutors of poisoning the minds of American youth. *Spencer's Mountain* focuses on a father's efforts to ensure that his son gets a college education. His son is the first in his extended family to attend college, and in 1963, the year of the film's release, this was an experience shared by many American families, particularly those from less advantaged backgrounds, with the provisions of the GI Bill. In *Bird of Paradise*, Tenga has benefited from attendance at an American college at a time when segregation in schools and colleges was still prevalent in some states and was soon to become a major political issue. Tenga's experience is positive but does not devalue the culture and traditions of his community, which, as in Daves's other films, are presented with respect. The teacher in *Spencer's Mountain* celebrates "the beauty and wisdom [students] can find in books." However, her emphasis on the value of an enquiring mind and the wider opportunities for learning mirrors Daves's Stanford reminiscences in stressing the importance of education in its broadest sense and his conviction that "much of Stanford's greatness lies outside the classrooms."[7]

Jonathan Kirshner identifies 1967–1976 as a particularly distinctive time for Hollywood, when new films were notably different from their predecessors. He concludes that, apart from some notable exceptions, films made before the collapse of the Production Code are characterized by their timidity, conformity to a predominantly uncritical vision of America, and adherence to the Code's moral certainty.[8] He suggests that *Point Blank* (1967) is an early exemplification of this "new American cinema," with a protagonist who is a violent criminal but who still "has the audience rooting for him." Yet the criminal's status as one who is "trying to find his humanity" could justifiably be applied to the outlaw in *3:10 to Yuma*, who attracts audience empathy even though he is a cold-blooded killer. The classic Hollywood theme of opposition of good and evil is of less interest to Daves. His films maintain a level of moral ambiguity in that the protagonists are not of wholly good or bad character: they are imperfect people who are faced with situations in which they must make difficult personal or morally complex choices and who need not be "punished" if they take a questionable course of action. Daves judges his characters in relation to the social circumstances in which they act, and explanations for their conduct are recognized. That said, this does not prevent his films from attacking the evils of intolerance and racism that he despises.

Kirshner claims that *The Graduate* (1967) also crystallizes elements of the "new Hollywood."[9] Because her daughter has just been married when Benjamin attempts to "rescue" her, Mrs. Robinson exclaims triumphantly, "It's too late!" However, the daughter's reply is, "Not for me." Yet nearly a decade earlier, the principle that an unhappy or loveless relationship need not be endured, together with confidence in the ability of young people to show independence, were evident in *A Summer Place*. The characteristics and themes that Kirshner attributes to more revisionist American cinema and that demonstrate "the ability to traffic in that which was previously forbidden"[10] were already apparent in Daves's work, released when the Code's precepts were more rigorously applied. His films present "explorations of complex episodes that challenged the received normative structure of society,"[11] notably in recognizing and commenting on fundamental issues of inequality and discrimination inherent in the struggle for civil rights and women's equality, and against the injustice of political intolerance.

Daves's films challenged the conventions of postwar Hollywood filmmaking, as in his advocacy of tolerance and understanding in personal relationships. His characters are open-minded and willing to question long-held beliefs and expectations. Philip Deloria contends that, after wartime experiences that had brought "a glimpse of freedom and opportunity" to people of color, Americans of all classes and colors were more conscious of issues of racial diversity and oppression.[12] Daves's early focus on Indian issues and customs precedes later campaigns to secure Indian self-determination and preserve Indian culture, and present a vision more of multiculturalism than of assimilation. His films expose the prejudice and racism of the white settlers in *Broken Arrow* and the trader in *Bird of Paradise*, and the dangers faced by the young people in *The Last Wagon* force them to assess their assumptions and values. Just as *Pride of the Marines* deals with a soldier's adjustment to his blindness and, in *The Hanging Tree*, the treatment of a robbery victim's blindness helps a doctor overcome the demons of his past, Daves's films condemn the "blindness" of prejudicial stereotypes and intolerance. Max Tessier writes that *Pride of the Marines* reflects the "left-wing Hollywood" that was decimated by the witch hunts and blacklisting of the McCarthy period.[13] Certainly Daves repudiated the political extremes of this period, and his Republicanism was enlightened by an optimistic advocacy of justice, tolerance, and equality. In *Broken Arrow*, Jeffords persuades Cochise that allowing the mail to pass unhindered through Apache land is an important step in demonstrating that peoples may "live together like brothers," continuing: "It is a good step. The seed is small, maybe the tree will grow big." In the same way, the films of Delmer Daves represent significant progress in recognizing that in America's past there have been episodes of injustice, discrimination, and exploitation as well as heroism, and therefore they presage an important shift in direction in the interpretation of American history.

NOTES

INTRODUCTION

1. Jacqueline Nacache, "Au long des passages obscurs: sur *Dark Passage*, 1947," in *Delmer Daves: La Morale des pionniers*, ed. Jean-Pierre Garcia and Dominique Païni (Amiens: Éditions Vol de Nuit, 1999), 73.

2. Delmer Daves Papers, Department of Special Collections, Stanford University Libraries, Stanford, California (hereafter cited as Delmer Daves Papers), Box 8, Folder 3 (December 13, 1938). Story credited to Leo McCarey and Mildred Cram; screenplay credited to Delmer Daves and Donald O. Stewart.

3. Daves received this nomination for *Cowboy* (1958).

4. Ian Cameron, "Films, Directors and Critics," *Movie* 2 (September 1962): 4–7.

5. Cameron, "Films, Directors and Critics," 6.

6. Jim Kitses, *Horizons West: Directing the Western from John Ford to Clint Eastwood* (London: British Film Institute, 2004), 16.

7. Martin Scorsese and Michael H. Wilson, *A Personal Journey with Martin Scorsese through American Movies* (London: Faber and Faber, 1997), 14–16.

8. *The New York Times Film Reviews 1913–1968*, vol. 3, *1939–1948* (New York: New York Times and Arno Press, 1970), 2040, 2097.

9. Under the National Film Preservation Act (1988), the National Film Registry selects films in order to preserve US film heritage.

10. The four films are *Broken Arrow*, *3:10 to Yuma*, *The Last Wagon*, and *The Hanging Tree*. John G. Cawelti, *The Six-Gun Mystique* (Bowling Green, OH: Bowling Green State University Popular Press, 1975), 119–22.

11. Nick James, ed., "The Greatest Films of All Time," *Sight and Sound* 22, no. 9 (September 2012): 52.

12. Slavoj Žižek, "Guilty Pleasures," *Film Comment* 42, no. 1 (January–February 2006): 13.

13. Memorandum from Darryl F. Zanuck, Delmer Daves Papers, Box 29, Folder 15 (June 15, 1950).

14. Richard Whitehall, "The Heroes Are Tired," *Film Quarterly* 20, no. 2 (Winter 1966–1967): 21.

15. Homer Dickens, *The Films of Gary Cooper* (New York: Citadel, 1970), 268.

16. Gérard Legrand, quoted in Adrian Wootton and Paul Taylor, eds., *David Goodis/Pulps Pictured: For Goodis' Sake!* (London: British Film Institute, 1989), 17.

17. Edward Buscombe, *100 Westerns* (London: British Film Institute, 2006), xii.

18. Charles Burnett, "Anger Management," *Sight and Sound* 21, no. 4 (April 2011): 11; and Richard Whitehall, "On the 3:10 to Yuma," *Films and Filming* 9, no. 7 (April 1963): 53.

19. Robert Nott, *He Ran All the Way: The Life of John Garfield* (New York: Limelight Editions, 2003), 168–70; and George Morris, *John Garfield* (New York: Jove, 1977), 98–105.

20. Dominique Rabourdin, "Delmer Daves ou le secret perdu," *Cinéma* 72, no. 226 (October 1977): 53.

21. Wheeler Winston Dixon, *The Early Film Criticism of François Truffaut* (Bloomington: Indiana University Press, 1993), 148.

22. Bertrand Tavernier, "The Ethical Romantic," *Film Comment* 39, no. 1 (January–February 2003): 42.

23. Haden Guest, "Festival Report: Cinema Ritrovato 2010," *Cinema Journal* 50, no. 3 (Spring 2011): 97, 100.

24. Jean-Pierre Garcia and Dominique Païni, eds., *Delmer Daves: La Morale des pionniers* (Amiens: Éditions Vol de Nuit, 1999).

25. Michael Walker, "The Westerns of Delmer Daves," in *The Movie Book of the Western*, ed. Ian Cameron and Douglas Pye (London: Studio Vista, 1996), 123–60.

26. Joachim Kreck, *Delmer Daves* (Oberhausen, Germany: Will Wehling, 1972).

27. Matthew Carter and Andrew Nelson, eds., *ReFocus: The Films of Delmer Daves* (Edinburgh: Edinburgh University Press, 2016).

28. Fran Pheasant-Kelly, "Delmer Daves' *3:10 to Yuma*: Aesthetics, Reception, and Cultural Significance," in *ReFocus: The Films of Delmer Daves*, ed. Matthew Carter and Andrew Nelson (Edinburgh: Edinburgh University Press, 2016), 149–65.

29. Fernando G. Berns, "Changing Societies: *The Red House*, *The Hanging Tree*, *Spencer's Mountain*, and Post-War America," in *ReFocus: The Films of Delmer Daves*, ed. Matthew Carter and Andrew Nelson (Edinburgh: Edinburgh University Press, 2016), 166–83.

30. John White, "Trying to Ameliorate the System from Within: Delmer Daves' Westerns from the 1950s," in *ReFocus: The Films of Delmer Daves*, ed. Matthew Carter and Andrew Nelson (Edinburgh: Edinburgh University Press, 2016), 63–79.

31. David Thomson, *The New Biographical Dictionary of Film*, 5th ed. (London: Little, Brown, 2010), 233.

32. Pheasant-Kelly, "Delmer Daves' *3:10 to Yuma*," 152, 157–58.

33. Joseph Pomp, "Home on the Range: *Spencer's Mountain* as Revisionist Family Melodrama," in *ReFocus: The Films of Delmer Daves*, ed. Matthew Carter and Andrew Nelson (Edinburgh: Edinburgh University Press, 2016), 135–48.

34. Robert Hatch, review of *Broken Arrow*, *New Republic*, July 31, 1950, 23.

35. Peter Wollen, *Signs and Meaning in the Cinema* (1972; London: British Film Institute, 1998), 71.

36. Luc Moullet, "Sam Fuller: Sur les brisées de Marlowe," *Cahiers du Cinéma*, no. 93 (March 1959): 14.

37. Christopher Wicking, "Interview with Delmer Daves," *Screen* 10, nos. 4–5 (October 1969): 55.

38. Jean-Pierre Coursodon, "Delmer Daves," in *American Directors*, vol. 1, ed. Jean-Pierre Coursodon with Pierre Sauvage (New York: McGraw Hill, 1983), 87.

39. Coursodon, "Delmer Daves," 82.

40. Delmer Daves Papers, M0192.

41. Albert Maltz Papers, 1910–1985, Collection 02675, American Heritage Center, University of Wyoming (hereafter cited as Albert Maltz Papers).

42. Delmer Daves, *Reminiscences of Delmer Lawrence Daves*, transcript of a tape recording, Oral History Program at Columbia University, New York, Series 3, vol. 7, no. 322 (June 1959) (hereafter cited as Delmer Daves, Columbia Oral History Program).

43. Andrew Sarris, "Notes on the Auteur Theory in 1962," *Film Culture*, no. 27 (Winter 1962–1963): 6–8.

44. John Belton, *American Cinema/American Culture*, 2nd ed. (New York, McGraw Hill, 2005), 349–50.

45. Belton, *American Cinema/American Culture*, 350.

46. Bernard F. Dick, review of *ReFocus: The Films of Delmer Daves*, ed. Matthew Carter and Andrew Nelson, *Film and History* 48, no. 1 (Summer 2018): 70–71.

47. Andrew Sarris, *The American Cinema: Directors and Directions, 1929–1968* (New York: Dutton, 1968), 27.

48. Matthew Carter and Andrew Nelson, "Introduction: No One Would Know It Was Mine; Delmer Daves, Modest Auteur," in *ReFocus: The Films of Delmer Daves*, ed. Matthew Carter and Andrew Nelson (Edinburgh: Edinburgh University Press, 2016), 8.

49. Edward Hallet Carr, *What Is History?* (London: Macmillan, 1961), 15.

50. Carter and Nelson, "Introduction," 23–26.

51. Cited in Murray Pomerance, "Movies and the Specter of Rebellion," in *American Cinema of the 1960s: Themes and Variations*, ed. Barry Keith Grant (New Brunswick, NJ: Rutgers University Press, 2009), 92.

52. Matthew Carter, "'This Is Where He Brought Me: 10,000 Acres of Nothing!' The Femme Fatale and Other Film Noir Tropes in Delmer Daves' *Jubal*," in *ReFocus: The Films of Delmer Daves*, ed. Matthew Carter and Andrew Nelson (Edinburgh: Edinburgh University Press, 2016), 199–221.

53. Carter and Nelson, "Introduction," 27–28.

54. Robin Wood, "Ideology, Genre, Auteur," *Film Comment* 13, no. 1 (January–February 1997): 46–47.

55. Judith H. Wright, "Genre Films and the Status Quo," in *Film Genre Reader II*, ed. Barry Keith Grant (Austin: University of Texas Press, 1995), 41–49.

56. Jean-Loup Bourget, "Social Implications in the Hollywood Genres," in *Film Genre Reader II*, ed. Barry Keith Grant (Austin: University of Texas Press, 1995), 50–58.

CHAPTER ONE

1. Roger Huss, "Critics' Choice," *Cinema* (UK), no. 4 (October 1969): 2–5.

2. Blake Lucas, "Saloon Girls and the Ranchers' Daughters: The Women in the Western," in *The Western Reader*, ed. Jim Kitses and Gregg Rickman (New York: Limelight Editions, 1998), 317.

3. Howard Barnes, review in the *New York Herald Tribune*, reprinted in Joe Morella, Edward Z. Epstein, and John Griggs, *The Films of World War II* (Secaucus, NJ: Citadel Press, 1973), 228.

4. Tavernier, "The Ethical Romantic," 42.

5. David Quinlan, *Quinlan's Film Directors: The Ultimate Guide to the Directors of the Big Screen*, 2nd ed. (London, B. T. Batsford, 1999), 79–80.

6. *Monthly Film Bulletin*, review of *To the Victor*, vol. 15, no. 178 (October 1948): 143.

7. Allen Eyles, "Suzanne Pleshette: Filmography," *Focus on Film*, no. 3 (May–August 1970): 58.

8. Allen Eyles, review of *Youngblood Hawke*, *Films and Filming* 11, no. 2 (November 1964): 29–30.

9. E.g., Tom Milne, review of *Youngblood Hawke*, *Monthly Film Bulletin* 31, no. 371 (November 1964): 162.

10. Eyles, review of *Youngblood Hawke*, 30.

11. Quinlan, *Quinlan's Film Directors*, 79–80.

12. In a BFI poll in *Sight and Sound* (September 2012, 40–71), Coppola ranks in the "Top Ten Directors." The three films are *The Godfather* (1972), *The Godfather Part II* (1974), and *Apocalypse Now* (1979).

13. Tavernier, "The Ethical Romantic," 42.

14. The review was published in the *Observer*, quoted in Graham Lord, *Niv: The Authorised Biography of David Niven* (London: Orion, 2003), 154.

15. Sarris, *The American Cinema*, 35.

16. William R. Meyer, *Warner Brothers Directors: The Hard-Boiled, the Comic, and the Weepies* (New Rochelle, NY: Arlington House, 1978), 112.

17. Rabourdin, "Delmer Daves ou le secret perdu," 53.

18. Peter Bogdanovich, *Picture Shows: Peter Bogdanovich on the Movies* (London: George Allen and Unwin, 1975), 11.

19. Bruce Beresford, "John Ford: Decline of a Master," *Film* 56 (Autumn 1969): 7.

20. Thomson, *The New Biographical Dictionary of Film*, 233.

21. Memorandum from Darryl F. Zanuck, Delmer Daves Papers, Box 29, Folder 15 (June 25, 1949; June 15, 1950).

22. Memorandum from Darryl F. Zanuck, Delmer Daves Papers, Box 29, Folder 15 (October 6, 1949).

23. Thomson, *The New Biographical Dictionary of Film*, 233.

24. David Thomson, *"Have You Seen . . . ?" A Personal Introduction to 1,000 Films* (London: Allen Lane, 2008), 888.

25. Tavernier, "The Ethical Romantic," 42.

26. Coursodon, "Delmer Daves," 87.

27. Henry Fonda and Howard Teichmann, *Fonda: My Life as Told to Howard Teichmann* (London: Book Club Associates, 1982), 283.

28. *Monthly Film Bulletin*, review of *Spencer's Mountain*, vol. 30, no. 348 (January 1963): 121.

29. Eyles, review of *Youngblood Hawke*, 29.

30. *Monthly Film Bulletin*, review of *Lovers Must Learn*, vol. 29, no. 341 (June 1962): 82.

31. Robin Bean, review of *Lovers Must Learn*, *Films and Filming* 8, no. 10 (July 1962): 37.

32. Philip Strick, review of *Susan Slade*, *Films and Filming* 8, no. 7 (April 1962): 32–33.

33. Bertrand Tavernier, "Chronique hollywoodienne: Extraits d'une correspondence avec Delmer Daves," in *Amis Américains: Entretiens avec les grands auteurs d'Hollywood*, by Bertrand Tavernier (Lyon: Institut Lumière; Arles: Actes Sud, 1993), 243.

34. Delmer Daves, "Responses d'amérique," *Cahiers du Cinéma*, nos. 150–151 (December 1963–January 1964): 39.

35. *Monthly Film Bulletin*, review of *Parrish*, vol. 28, no. 330 (July 1961): 93–94.

36. Robin Bean, review of *Parrish*, *Films and Filming* 7, no. 12 (September 1961): 30.

37. Tavernier, "The Ethical Romantic," 42.

38. Lawrence J. Quirk, *Claudette Colbert: An Illustrated Biography* (New York: Crown, 1985), 179–80.

39. *Monthly Film Bulletin*, review of *The Battle of the Villa Fiorita*, vol. 32, no. 380 (November 1965): 130–31.

40. *New York Times*, review of *The Battle of the Villa Fiorita*, May 27, 1965, 27–28.

41. Letter from Rumer Godden to Delmer Daves, Delmer Daves Papers, Box 72, Folder 2 (April 14, 1964).

42. Maureen O'Hara with John Nicoletti, *'Tis Herself: An Autobiography* (New York: Simon and Schuster, 2005), 291–93.

43. Cedric Hardwicke, *A Victorian in Orbit: The Irreverent Memoirs of Sir Cedric Hardwicke* (Gateshead, Tyne and Wear, England: Northumberland Press, 1961), 215, 182.

44. Hortense Powdermaker, *Hollywood, the Dream Factory: An Anthropologist Looks at the Movie-Makers* (London: Secker and Warburg, 1951), 316, 315.

45. Frank Capra, quoted in Lindsay Anderson, "The Director's Cinema?," *Sequence*, no. 12 (Autumn 1950): 10.

46. Memorandum from Darryl F. Zanuck, Delmer Daves Papers, Box 29, Folder 15 (June 15, 1950).

47. As noted in Karen McNally, *When Frankie Went to Hollywood: Frank Sinatra and American Male Identity* (Urbana: University of Illinois Press, 2008), 88.

48. Alvah Bessie, *Inquisition in Eden* (1965; Berlin: Seven Seas Books, 1967), 73–75.

49. Tavernier, "Chronique hollywoodienne," 239.

50. Memorandum from Darryl F. Zanuck, Delmer Daves Papers, Box 29, Folder 15 (June 15, 1950).

51. François Truffaut, *Hitchcock* (London: Panther, 1969), 146, 164–69.

52. Heinz-Gerd Rasner, Reinhard Wulf, and Wolf-Eckhart Bühler, "Gespräche mit Delmer Daves," *Filmkritik* 19, no. 217 (January 1975): 7.

53. Tavernier, "Chronique hollywoodienne," 240.

54. Delmer Daves, Columbia Oral History Program, 19.

55. Daves, "Responses d'amérique," 39.

56. Thomas Schatz, *The Genius of the System: Hollywood Film-Making in the Studio Era* (London, Faber and Faber, 1998), xiii.

57. Schatz, *The Genius of the System*, 4–8.

58. Powdermaker, *Hollywood, the Dream Factory*, 39.

59. Powdermaker, *Hollywood, the Dream Factory*, 79.

60. Powdermaker, *Hollywood, the Dream Factory*, 79.

61. Howard Koch, quoted in Anderson, "The Director's Cinema?," 10.

62. Richard Corliss, "Screenwriters Symposium," *Film Comment* 6, no. 4 (Winter 1970–1971): 89.

63. Corliss, "Screenwriters Symposium," 89.

64. Andrew Nelson, "Don't Be Too Quick to Dismiss Them: Authorship and the Westerns of Delmer Daves," in *ReFocus: The Films of Delmer Daves*, ed. Matthew Carter and Andrew Nelson (Edinburgh: Edinburgh University Press, 2016), 62n11; and Delmer Daves Papers, Box 49, Folder 2 (May 7, 1958).

65. Nelson, "Don't Be Too Quick to Dismiss Them"; and Delmer Daves Papers, Box 50, Folder 2 (January 21, 1958).

66. Joseph Taft, "Dialogues with a Director," *Persimmon Hill* 5, no. 2 (1975): 49–51; and Delmer Daves, Columbia Oral History Program, 60–61.

67. Pheasant-Kelly, "Delmer Daves' *3:10 to Yuma*," 156.

68. Delmer Daves Papers, Box 44, Folder 15 (November 21, 1956).

69. Delmer Daves et al., "Can Screen Writers Become Film Authors?," *Screen Writer* 3, no. 1 (June 1947): 34–38.

70. Delmer Daves, Columbia Oral History Program, 15–16, 65.

71. Delmer Daves, Columbia Oral History Program, 52–53, 65.

72. David A. Gerber, "In Search of Al Schmid: War Hero, Blinded Veteran, Everyman," *Journal of American Studies* 29, no. 1 (April 1995): 21–30.

73. Daves's note on the title page of the final script. Delmer Daves Papers, Box 19, Folder 2 (October 24, 1944).

74. Kreck, *Delmer Daves*, 20.

75. Letter from Albert Maltz to Jerry Wald, Delmer Daves Papers, Box 19, Folder 5 (December 2, 1944).

76. Letter from Albert Maltz to Jerry Wald, Delmer Daves Papers, Box 19, Folder 5 (December 2, 1944).

77. Joan Mellen, *Big Bad Wolves: Masculinity in the American Film* (London: Elm Tree Books, 1978), 149.

78. Barbara Zheutlin and David Talbot, "Albert Maltz: Portrait of a Hollywood Dissident," *Cinéaste* 8, no. 3 (Winter 1977–1978): 5.

79. A. J. Reynertson, *The Work of the Film Director* (London: Focal Press, 1970), 14–15.

80. Paul Rotha, *The Film Till Now: A Survey of World Cinema*, 3rd ed. (London: Vision Press, 1960), 20.

81. Tavernier, "Chronique hollywoodienne," 236.

82. C. Courtney Joyner, *The Westerners: Interviews with Actors, Directors, Writers and Producers* (Jefferson, NC: McFarland, 2009), 18.

83. Carter and Nelson, "Introduction," 5–6; and Delmer Daves Papers, Box 44, Folders 15, 16 (November 21, 1956), and Box 45, Folders 3, 5 (n.d.).

84. Peter Ford, *Glenn Ford: A Life* (Madison: University of Wisconsin Press, 2011), 165.

85. Joe McNeill, *Arizona's Little Hollywood: Sedona and Northern Arizona's Forgotten Film History, 1923–1973* (Sedona, AZ: Northedge and Sons, 2010), 546–48.

86. Maximilian Schell, dir., *My Sister Maria*, Rainbow Release, 2002.

87. Sarris, *The American Cinema*, 37.

88. Sarris, *The American Cinema*, 176–77.

89. Schatz, *The Genius of the System*, 5–6.

90. John Wakeman, ed., *World Film Directors*, vol. 1, *1980–1945* (New York: H. W. Wilson, 1987), 199.

91. Memorandum from Walter MacEwen, Delmer Daves Papers, Box 72, Folder 2 (March 31, 1964).

92. *Hollywood Close-Up*, May 21, 1959, quoted in Kreck, *Delmer Daves*, 92.

93. Corliss, "Screenwriters Symposium," 89–90.

94. Wollen, *Signs and Meaning in the Cinema*, 50–51.

95. Rasner, Wulf, and Bühler, "Gespräche mit Delmer Daves," 3.

96. Delmer Daves, Columbia Oral History Program, 38–39.

97. Michael Daves, radio conversation with John Mulholland, *Icons Radio Hour*, July 29, 2007.

98. Douglas McVay, "The Five Worlds of John Ford," *Films and Filming* 8, no. 9 (June 1962): 17.

99. Joyner, *The Westerners*, 19.

100. Delmer Daves, Columbia Oral History Program, 4–6, 49–51.

101. McNeill, *Arizona's Little Hollywood*, 555–58.

102. Tavernier, "The Ethical Romantic," 49.

103. George Duning, "*3:10 to Yuma*," in *Film Music: From Violins to Video*, ed. James L. Limbacher (Metuchen, NJ: Scarecrow Press, 1976), 111–12.

104. Sarris, "Notes on the Auteur Theory," 7.

105. Carol Donelan, "'Too Marvelous for Words': Bogart and Bacall's *Dark Passage* through Myth to the Enlightenment of Modernized Melodrama," *Film Criticism* 42, no. 1 (March 2018): 17.

106. Tavernier, "The Ethical Romantic," 48.

107. Wicking, "Interview with Delmer Daves," 60.

108. Delmer Daves, "Closing the Gap," *Action* 5, no. 2 (January–February 1970): 26; and Taft, "Dialogues with a Director," 50–51.

109. Memoranda from Darryl F. Zanuck to Frank Ross, Delmer Daves Papers, Box 38, Folder 6 (June 10, 1953; June 27, 1953).

110. Barry Salt, *Film Style and Technology: History and Analysis*, 2nd ed. (London: Starword, 1992), 246–47.

111. Rasner, Wulf, and Bühler, "Gespräche mit Delmer Daves," 34–35.

112. Memorandum from Darryl F. Zanuck to Frank Ross, Delmer Daves Papers, Box 38, Folder 6 (June 12, 1953).

113. Revealed by film archivist Tom Vincent in *Epic: A Cast of Thousands*, a BBC production in the *Timeshift* series. Clare Wilmshurst, dir., *Epic: A Cast of Thousands*, BBC, 2011.

114. E.g., *Films and Filming*, review of *Drum Beat*, vol. 1, no. 6 (March 1955): 22; and *Monthly Film Bulletin*, review of *Drum Beat*, vol. 22, no. 253 (February 1955): 19.

115. Nacache, "Au long des passages obscurs," 63–68.

116. Carter and Nelson, "Introduction," 34–36; Delmer Daves Papers, Box 23, Folder 15 (September 9, 1946); and Rasner, Wulf, and Bühler, "Gespräche mit Delmer Daves," 21–22.

117. Delmer Daves Papers, Box 23, Folder 3 (n.d.) and Folder 5 (October 22, 1946).

118. Handwritten comment on typed note, Delmer Daves Papers, Box 23, Folder 15 (September 9, 1946); and Carter and Nelson, "Introduction," 36–37.

119. *Monthly Film Bulletin*, review of *Dark Passage*, vol. 15, no. 171 (March 1948): 32.

120. Bosley Crowther, review of *Dark Passage*, *New York Times*, September 6, 1947, 11.

121. Bernard F. Dick, *Anatomy of Film* (New York: St. Martin's Press, 1978), 67.

122. Salt, *Film Style and Technology*, 230.

123. Pedro Poyato, "An Essay on Subjectivity in Hollywood: *Dark Passage* (Delmer Daves, 1947) and Its Assimilation of Avant-Garde Features," *L'Atalante* 27 (January–June 2019): 91–104.

124. Jean Effel, "Delmer Daves," *Cinéma* 92 (January 1965): 46; and Wicking, "Interview with Delmer Daves," 66.

125. Raymond Durgnat, "This Damned Eternal Triangle: Films, Theatre, Literature Are Just Not Meant to Mix," *Films and Filming* 11, no. 3 (December 1964): 17.

126. Sarris, *The American Cinema*, 176–77.

127. Sarris, *The American Cinema*, 202.

128. Guy Hennebelle, "Daves: Si c'était a refaire?," *Cinéma* 101 (December 1965): 37.

129. Walker, "The Westerns of Delmer Daves," 142.

130. Wicking, "Interview with Delmer Daves," 65–66.

131. Memorandum from Darryl F. Zanuck, Delmer Daves Papers, Box 29, Folder 15 (June 15, 1950).

132. Memorandum from Darryl F. Zanuck, Delmer Daves Papers, Box 33, Folder 7 (December 22, 1951).

133. Tavernier, "The Ethical Romantic," 42.

134. Tavernier, "The Ethical Romantic," 49.

135. Cesare Zavattini, "Some Ideas on the Cinema," *Sight and Sound* 23, no. 2 (October–December 1953): 64.

136. Delmer Daves, Columbia Oral History Program, 59–60.

137. Carter and Nelson, "Introduction," 37.

138. White, "Trying to Ameliorate the System from Within," 63, 65, 69, 77.

139. Albert Maltz, "Five-Year Diary," April 25, 1946, Albert Maltz Papers.

140. Michael Daves, radio conversation with John Mulholland.

141. Joel Gardner, interview with Albert Maltz, August 5, 1976, 17, 41, Text Encoding Initiative, University of California, Los Angeles.

142. *Daily Palo Alto*, May 21, 1925, 1; and May 22, 1925, 1.

143. Vivian C. Sobchack, "Round-Up in Sun Valley," *Journal of Popular Film* 5, no. 2 (1976): 157–65. Sobchack was reporting on the Western Movies: Myths and Images conference in Sun Valley, Idaho, June 29–July 4, 1976.

144. Jean-Louis Rieupeyrout, "Rencontre avec Delmer Daves," *Cinéma* 53 (February 1961): 14.

145. George E. Mowry, *The California Progressives* (1951; Chicago: Quadrangle Books, 1963), 88–89, 92, 101–2.

146. Terry Christensen and Peter J. Haas, *Projecting Politics: Political Messages in American Films* (Armonk, NY: M. E. Sharpe, 2005), 62–64, 110–11.

147. Mellen, *Big Bad Wolves*, 188–89.

148. J. Ronald Oakley, *God's Country: America in the Fifties* (New York: Dembner Books, 1986), 314–15, 434–35.

149. Dwight Eisenhower, in a speech on May 19, 1958, in Little Rock, Arkansas, quoted in Oakley, *God's Country*, 376.

150. Oakley, *God's Country*, 296–97.

151. William H. Chafe, *The Unfinished Journey: America since World War II*, 3rd ed. (New York: Oxford University Press, 1995), 134.

152. Arthur Schlesinger Jr., "The Crisis of American Masculinity," *Esquire* 50, no. 5 (November 1958): 63–65.

153. Chafe, *The Unfinished Journey*, 97–99.

154. Clayton R. Koppes, "From New Deal to Termination: Liberalism and Indian Policy, 1933–1953," *Pacific Historical Review* 46, no. 4 (November 1977): 550.

155. Arthur S. Link and Richard L. McCormick, *Progressivism* (Wheeling, IL: Harlan Davidson, 1983), 118.

156. E.g., Paul Simpson, *The Rough Guide to Westerns* (London: Rough Guides, 2006), 134.

157. Bosley Crowther, review of *3:10 to Yuma*, *New York Times*, April 29, 1957, 22.

158. Bosley Crowther, review of *To the Victor*, *New York Times*, April 17, 1948, 11.

159. M. Elise Marubbio, *Killing the Indian Maiden: Images of Native American Women in Film* (Lexington: University Press of Kentucky, 2006), 65–71.

160. Letter from Albert Maltz to Jerry Wald, Delmer Daves Papers, Box 19, Folder 5 (December 2, 1944).

161. Andrew Howe, "Partial Rehabilitation: *Task Force* and the Case of Billy Mitchell," in *ReFocus: The Films of Delmer Daves*, ed. Matthew Carter and Andrew Nelson (Edinburgh: Edinburgh University Press, 2016), 184–98.

162. Washington and New York interviews, Delmer Daves Papers, Box 20, Folder 6 (n.d.).

163. Mowry, *The California Progressives*, 97–99.

164. Frank Norris, *The Octopus: A Story of California* (New York: Doubleday and Page, 1901), 652.

165. Sarah Pearsall, "Women from the Colonial Era to 1900," in *The Columbia Companion to American History on Film: How Movies Portrayed the American Past*, ed. Peter C. Rollins (New York: Columbia University Press, 2003), 307.

166. Yves Kovacs, "Mythologie du Western," *Études Cinématographiques* 2, nos. 12–13 (Winter 1961): 243–50.

167. Delmer Daves Papers, Box 8, Folder 6f (December 13, 1938).

168. Delmer Daves Papers, Box 43, Folder 7 (January 27, 1956).

169. Crowther, review of *To the Victor*, 11.

170. Adaptation notes, Delmer Daves Papers, Box 51, Folder 10 (October 4, 1958).

CHAPTER TWO

1. Cameron's review appeared in the *New York Daily News* (1945), quoted in Kreck, *Delmer Daves*, 19.

2. E.g., Frank Nugent, review of *Dames*, *New York Times*, August 16, 1934, 20; Frank Nugent, review of *Stranded*, *New York Times*, June 20, 1935, 16; and Frank Nugent, review of *Shipmates Forever*, *New York Times*, October 17, 1935, 29.

3. Bosley Crowther, review of *Return of the Texan*, *New York Times*, February 14, 1952, 23.

4. Bessie, *Inquisition in Eden*, 89–90.

5. *Hollywood Reporter*, review of *The Very Thought of You*, vol. 80, no. 32 (October 16, 1944): 3.

6. From a letter written by a soldier on active service, *News Chronicle* (UK), May 19, 1945, 2.

7. Andre Sennwald, review of *Flirtation Walk*, *New York Times*, November 29, 1934, 33.

8. John Davis, "Notes on Warner Brothers Foreign Policy, 1918–1948," *Velvet Light Trap* 4 (Spring 1972): 25, 30.

9. Tavernier, "Chronique hollywoodienne," 238.

10. Original screenplay by Daves, Delmer Daves Papers, Box 17, Folder 6 (October 15, 1943).

11. Sherrie Tucker, *Dance Floor Democracy: The Social Geography of Memory at the Hollywood Canteen* (Durham, NC: Duke University Press, 2014), 285–86.

12. Tavernier, "Chronique hollywoodienne," 236.

13. Bosley Crowther, review of *Task Force*, *New York Times*, October 1, 1949, 8.

14. Delmer Daves, "John Garfield," *Positif*, no. 120 (October 1970): 3. "Eating by the clock" is meat at the position of noon, potatoes at three o'clock, and vegetables at six o'clock.

15. Dorothy B. Jones, "Communism and the Movies: A Study of Film Content," in *Report on Blacklisting: 1, Movies*, ed. John Cogley (1956; New York: *New York Times* and Arno Press, 1972), 218.

16. Tavernier, "Chronique hollywoodienne," 236.

17. Delmer Daves, Columbia Oral History Program, 24–25.

18. Morella, Epstein, and Griggs, *The Films of World War II*, 164–65.

19. Robert Eberwein, *The Hollywood War Film* (Chichester, W. Susx., England: Wiley-Blackwell, 2010), 81–82.

20. Jeanine Basinger, "The World War II Combat Film," in *The War Film*, edited by Robert Eberwein (New Brunswick, NJ: Rutgers University Press, 2005), 40–41.

21. Frank J. Wetta and Martin A. Novelli, "On Telling the Truth about War: World War II and Hollywood's Moral Fiction, 1945–1956," in *Why We Fought: America's Wars in Film and History*, ed. Peter C. Rollins and John E. O'Connor (Lexington: University Press of Kentucky, 2008), 273.

22. Bosley Crowther, review of *Pride of the Marines*, *New York Times*, August 25, 1945, 7.

23. Bernard F. Dick, *The Star-Spangled Screen: The American World War II Film* (Lexington: University Press of Kentucky, 1985), 230.

24. Thomas M. Prior, review of *The Very Thought of You*, *New York Times*, November 8, 1944, 16.

25. Robert A. Nisbet, "The Coming Problem of Assimilation," *American Journal of Sociology* 50, no. 4 (January 1945): 261, 263, 265.

26. Delmer Daves Papers, Box 4, Folder 7 (n.d.).

27. Peter B. Kyne, *The Go-Getter: A Story That Tells You How to Be One* (1921; New York: Cosimo Classics, 2011), 57.

28. Thomas Doherty, *Projections of War: Hollywood, American Culture, and World War II* (New York: Columbia University Press, 1993), 269.

29. Harold Russell, *Victory in My Hands* (London: John Lehmann, 1950), 115, 95–96.

30. Martin Halliwell, "'No Place to Go, See': Blindness and World War II Demobilization Narratives," *Journal of Literary and Cultural Disability Studies* 3, no. 2 (2009): 163–68.

31. Halliwell, "No Place to Go, See," 167.

32. George K. Pratt, *Soldier to Civilian: Problems of Readjustment* (New York: McGraw Hill, 1944), 130.

33. Halliwell, "No Place to Go, See," 169, 172.

34. Roger Butterfield, *Al Schmid, Marine* (New York: W. W. Norton, 1944).

35. Frances A. Koestler, *The Unseen Minority: A Social History of Blindness in the United States* (New York: David McKay, 1976), 247–51.

36. Halliwell, "No Place to Go, See," 168, 180–81.

37. John Bodnar, *Blue-Collar Hollywood: Liberalism, Democracy, and Working People in American Film* (Baltimore: Johns Hopkins University Press, 2003), 95–99.

38. Sonya Michel, "American Women and the Discourse of the Democratic Family in World War II," in *Behind the Lines: Gender and the Two World Wars*, ed. Margaret Randolph Higonnet, Jane Jenson, Sonya Michel, and Margaret Collins Weitz (New Haven, CT: Yale University Press, 1987), 154, 167.

39. Gerber, "In Search of Al Schmid," 19.

40. Pratt, *Soldier to Civilian*, 132.

41. Halliwell, "No Place to Go, See," 165.

42. Halliwell, "No Place to Go, See," 168.

43. Koestler, *The Unseen Minority*, 258–66.

44. Charles Hurd, *The Veteran's Program: A Complete Guide to Its Benefits, Rights and Options* (New York: McGraw Hill, 1946), 40–41.

45. Quoted in Halliwell, "No Place to Go, See," 169.

46. Delmer Daves Papers, Box 4, Folder 7 (n.d.); Box 11, Folder 21 (February 1, 1940); and Box 11, Folder 24 (February 2, 1940).

47. Paul A. Carter, *Another Part of the Fifties* (New York: Columbia University Press, 1983), 209.

48. Bruce W. Jentleson, *American Foreign Policy: The Dynamics of Choice in the 21st Century*, 2nd ed. (New York: W. W. Norton, 2004), 142.

49. Jentleson, *American Foreign Policy*, 140.

50. Quoted in Nicole Potter, "Tales of the Red Menace," *Films in Review* 47, nos. 5–6 (September–October 1996): 29.

51. Russell E. Shain, "Hollywood's Cold War," *Journal of Popular Film and Television* 3, no. 4 (Fall 1974): 334.

52. Guidance detailed in Karl F. Cohen, *Forbidden Animation: Censored Cartoons and Blacklisted Animators in America* (Jefferson, NC: McFarland, 1997), 169–70.

53. Steven Ross, *Working-Class Hollywood: Silent Film and the Shaping of Class in America* (Princeton, NJ: Princeton University Press, 1999), 241.

54. Shain, "Hollywood's Cold War," 334.

55. This declaration was made by studio heads after a meeting at the Waldorf Astoria Hotel in New York.

56. The "Ten" included Albert Maltz, Alvah Bessie, and Dalton Trumbo; they were known collectively as "the Hollywood Ten Unfriendly Witnesses."

57. This group included Humphrey Bogart, Lauren Bacall, Danny Kaye, Gene Kelly, John Huston, Frank Sinatra, Larry Adler, William Wyler, and Groucho Marx.

58. Larry Ceplair and Steven Englund, *The Inquisition in Hollywood: Politics in the Film Community, 1930–1960* (New York: Anchor/Doubleday, 1980), 387–88.

59. Rasner, Wulf, and Bühler, "Gespräche mit Delmer Daves," 8–9.

60. M. Stanton Evans, *Blacklisted by History: The Untold Story of Senator Joe McCarthy and His Fight against America's Enemies* (New York: Three Rivers Press, 2007), 18–21.

61. Rasner, Wulf, and Bühler, "Gespräche mit Delmer Daves," 9.

62. Robert E. Sherwood, *The Petrified Forest* (New York: Charles Scribner's Sons, 1935).

63. Daves, "John Garfield," 2.

64. Donald Ogden Stewart, *By a Stroke of Luck! An Autobiography* (New York: Paddington Press, 1975), 244.

65. The Screen Writers Guild expected that a contribution of at least one-third of a script should warrant a cowriting credit. Maltz contributed less than one-fifth of the screenplay for *Destination Tokyo*.

66. Rasner, Wulf, and Bühler, "Gespräche mit Delmer Daves," 9.

67. Albert Maltz, "What Shall We Ask of Writers?," *New Masses*, February 12, 1946, 19.

68. Maltz, "What Shall We Ask of Writers?," 19.

69. Bessie, *Inquisition in Eden*, 89.

70. Rasner, Wulf, and Bühler, "Gespräche mit Delmer Daves," 9.

71. Jones, "Communism and the Movies," 196–233.

72. Thom Anderson, "Red Hollywood," in *Literature and the Visual Arts in Contemporary Society*, ed. Suzanne Ferguson and Barbara Groseclose (Columbus: Ohio State University Press, 1985), 156.

73. Anderson, "Red Hollywood," 166.

74. Zheutlin and Talbot, "Albert Maltz: Portrait of a Hollywood Dissident," 9, 14.

75. Józef Jaskulski, "Bent, or Lifted Out by Its Roots: Daves' *Broken Arrow* and *Drum Beat* as Narratives of Conditional Sympathy," in *ReFocus: The Films of Delmer Daves*, ed. Matthew Carter and Andrew Nelson (Edinburgh: Edinburgh University Press, 2016), 99.

76. Albert Maltz, "Five-Year Diary," April 25, 1946, Albert Maltz Papers.

77. Juan Cobos, "Una conversación con Delmer Daves," *Film Ideal* 106 (October 1962): 617.

78. Tucker, *Dance Floor Democracy*, 246–47, 260.

79. Tucker, *Dance Floor Democracy*, 285–86.

80. Tavernier, "Chronique hollywoodienne," 236.

81. FBI file number 100-HQ-138754, "Communist Infiltration of Motion Picture Industry", Part 7 of 15. October 2nd 1947. Page 157.

82. Edendale is now better known as Silver Lake and Echo Park.

83. Daniel Hurewitz, *Bohemian Los Angeles and the Making of Modern Politics* (Berkeley: University of California Press, 2007), 94, 189–228.

84. Daves cowrote *Love Affair* and its remake, *An Affair to Remember*, both of which McCarey directed.

85. Daves's changes to Grant's revised script, Delmer Daves Papers, Box 43, Folder 7, 43–108 (January 27, 1956).

86. Susan Carruthers, "Between Camps: Eastern Bloc 'Escapees' and Cold War Borderlands," *American Quarterly* 57, no. 3 (September 2005): 911–12.

87. Quoted in Dixon, *The Early Film Criticism of François Truffaut*, 149.

88. Tavernier, "Chronique hollywoodienne," 239.

89. Cable from Delmer Daves to Dore Schary, Delmer Daves Papers, Box 34, Folder 15 (May 15, 1952).

90. Detailed in Kenneth More, *More or Less* (London: Hodder and Stoughton, 1978), 151.

91. Lary May, *The Big Tomorrow: Hollywood and the Politics of the American Way* (Chicago: University of Chicago Press, 2000), 206–7, 283.

92. Walker, "The Westerns of Delmer Daves," 129–33.

93. John H. Lenihan, *Showdown: Confronting Modern America in the Western Film* (Urbana: University of Illinois Press, 1985), 40–42.

94. Bob Herzberg, *Savages and Saints: The Changing Image of American Indians in Westerns* (Jefferson, NC: McFarland, 2008), 161.

95. Lenihan, *Showdown*, 43n12.

96. John Tuska, *The American West in Film: Critical Approaches to the Western* (Lincoln: University of Nebraska Press, 1985), 251.

97. Nelson, "Don't Be Too Quick to Dismiss Them," 54–55; detailed in the Delmer Daves Papers, Box 39, Folders 1, 2 (n.d.).

98. Treatment of a Western version of "Bali Story," Delmer Daves Papers, Box 31, Folder 9 (April 9, 1951).

99. Michael Coyne, *The Crowded Prairie: American National Identity in the Hollywood Western* (London: I. B. Tauris, 1998), 3.

100. Adlai E. Stevenson, *Call to Greatness* (London: Rupert Hart-Davis, 1954), 56.

101. Stevenson, *Call to Greatness*, 43, 45.

102. Stanley Corkin, *Cowboys as Cold Warriors: The Western and U.S. History* (Philadelphia: Temple University Press, 2004), 117–20.

103. White, "Trying to Ameliorate the System from Within," 65–66.

104. Donald E. Worcester, *The Apaches: Eagles of the Southwest* (Norman: University of Oklahoma Press, 1979), 135–40, 213, 223–24.

105. James Burnham, *Struggle for the World* (New York: John Day, 1947), 222.

106. Stevenson, *Call to Greatness*, 99.

107. Delmer Daves Papers, Box 21, Folders 15, 16 (n.d.).

108. Josh Zeitz, "How FDR Invented the Four Freedoms," *Politico Magazine*, July 4, 2015, www.politico.com/magazine/story/2015/07/roosevelt-four-freedoms-119728.

109. Martin M. Winkler, "The Roman Empire in American Cinema after 1945," *Classical Journal* 93, no. 2 (December 1997–January 1998): 167–96.

110. Winkler, "The Roman Empire in American Cinema," 187.

111. *Daily Palo Alto*, May 22, 1925, 1.

112. Rasner, Wulf, and Bühler, "Gespräche mit Delmer Daves," 30; and Cobos, "Una conversación con Delmer Daves," 615.
113. Koppes, "From New Deal to Termination," 556.
114. Delmer Daves Papers, Box 31, Folder 5 (n.d.).
115. Delmer Daves, Columbia Oral History Program, 8.
116. Delmer Daves, Columbia Oral History Program, 21–23.
117. E.g., Sarris, *The American Cinema*, 86; and Quinlan, *Quinlan's Film Directors*, 42.
118. Frederick Lamster, *Souls Made Great through Love and Adversity: The Film Work of Frank Borzage* (Metuchen, NJ: Scarecrow Press, 1981), 7.
119. Sherwood, *The Petrified Forest*, 175.
120. Sherwood, *The Petrified Forest*, 116.
121. Thomson, *The New Biographical Dictionary of Film*, 641.
122. Quinlan, *Quinlan's Film Directors*, 226.
123. Frank Nugent, review of *The Petrified Forest*, New York Times, February 7, 1936, 14.
124. Kenneth J. Bindas, "Neon in the Desert: Robert Sherwood's *The Petrified Forest* (1936) and the Return of Hope," *Journal of Popular Film and Television* 27, no. 1 (Spring 1999): 24, 29.
125. Sherwood, *The Petrified Forest*, 7.
126. Sherwood, *The Petrified Forest*, 7.
127. Sherwood, *The Petrified Forest*, 9.
128. Screenplay for *The Stuff of Heroes*, Delmer Daves Papers, Box 11, Folder 1 (March 5, 1940); and Daves's notes for the screenplay, Delmer Daves Papers, Box 11, Folders 21 (February 1, 1940) and 24 (February 2, 1940).
129. Notes for *The Stuff of Heroes*, Delmer Daves Papers, Box 11, Folder 9d (February 8, 1940).
130. William Beaudine, dir., *How Baxter Butted In*, Warner Bros., 1925; based on a short story by Harold Titus, "The Stuff of Heroes," *American Magazine*, August 1924.
131. Notes for *The Stuff of Heroes*, Delmer Daves Papers, Box 10, Folder 21c, 4 (February 1, 1940).
132. Notes for *The Stuff of Heroes*, Delmer Daves Papers, Box 10, Folder 24e, 1 (February 22, 1940).
133. Notes for *The Stuff of Heroes*, Delmer Daves Papers, Box 10, Folder 24e, 3 (February 22, 1940).
134. Delmer Daves Papers, Box 11, Folder 9a (n.d.).
135. Letter from Hal B. Wallis to Delmer Daves, Delmer Daves Papers, Box 11, Folder 9 (February 19, 1940).
136. Delmer Daves Papers, Box 11, Folders 9a, 9b, 9e, 9f (n.d.).
137. Notes for *The Stuff of Heroes*, Delmer Daves Papers, Box 10, Folder 24e, 2–3 (February 22, 1940).
138. Adrian Danks, "This Room Is My Castle of Quiet: The Collaboration of Delmer Daves and Glenn Ford," in *ReFocus: The Films of Delmer Daves*, ed. Matthew Carter and Andrew Nelson (Edinburgh: Edinburgh University Press, 2016), 111.
139. Pheasant-Kelly, "Delmer Daves' *3:10 to Yuma*," 152; and David H. Murdoch, *The American West: The Invention of a Myth* (Cardiff: Welsh Academic Press, 2001), 7.
140. White, "Trying to Ameliorate the System from Within," 75.

141. Walker, "The Westerns of Delmer Daves," 125.

142. Detailed in Suzanne Finstad, *Warren Beatty: A Private Man* (London: Aurum Press, 2005), 295–96.

143. Gay P. Zieger and Robert H. Zieger, "Unions on the Silver Screen: A Review-Essay on *F.I.S.T.*, *Blue Collar*, and *Norma Rae*," *Labor History* 23, no. 1 (Winter 1982): 67–78.

144. The film was directed by Herbert Biberman, written by Michael Wilson, and produced by Paul Jarrico.

145. Deborah Silverton Rosenfelt, "Commentary," in *Salt of the Earth*, by Michael Wilson (New York: Feminist Press, 1978), 108.

146. Pauline Kael, *I Lost It at the Movies* (Boston: Little, Brown, 1965), 331–32.

147. Rosenfelt, "Commentary," 113.

148. Donald L. Barlett and James B. Steele, *America: What Went Wrong?* (Kansas City: Andrews and McMeel, 1992), 95–97, 106–7.

149. White, "Trying to Ameliorate the System from Within," 72.

150. White, "Trying to Ameliorate the System from Within," 71–72.

151. Keith Buchanan, "The Geography of Empire, part 3: The Economic Pattern of Empire," *Spokesman*, no. 20 (December 1971–January 1972): 49–55.

152. Walker, "The Westerns of Delmer Daves," 154.

153. Stevenson, *Call to Greatness*, 98.

154. Tavernier, "Chronique hollywoodienne," 239.

155. Howard Thompson, review of *Treasure of the Golden Condor*, *New York Times*, May 23, 1953, 19.

CHAPTER THREE

1. Harry M. Benshoff and Sean Griffin, *America on Film: Representing Race, Class, Gender and Sexuality at the Movies* (Chichester, W. Susx., England: Wiley-Blackwell, 2004), 54–55.

2. Brown v. Board of Education of Topeka, 347 U.S. 483 (1954).

3. Judith Crist, *The Private Eye, the Cowboy and the Very Naked Girl* (New York: Holt, Rinehart and Winston, 1968), 3–6.

4. Basinger, "The World War II Combat Film," 30–39, 41.

5. E.g., Frank Krutnik, Steve Neale, Brian Neve, and Peter Stanfield, eds., *"Un-American" Hollywood: Politics and Film in the Blacklist Era* (New Brunswick, NJ: Rutgers University Press, 2007), 176–77.

6. K. R. M. Short, "Hollywood Fights Anti-Semitism, 1940–1945," in *Film and Radio Propaganda in World War II*, ed. K. R. M. Short (London: Croom Helm, 1983), 168.

7. Tucker, *Dance Floor Democracy*, xii.

8. Bette Davis with Michael Herskowitz, *This 'n That: A Memoir* (London: Sidgwick and Jackson, 1987), 128.

9. Kevin Starr, *Embattled Dreams: California in War and Peace, 1940–1950* (New York: Oxford University Press, 2002), 168.

10. Sequences in Daves's initial screenplay of *Hollywood Canteen*, Delmer Daves Papers, Box 17, Folder 6 (October 15, 1943).

11. Tucker, *Dance Floor Democracy*, 300.

12. Review of *Kings Go Forth*, *Los Angeles Mirror News*, quoted in McNally, *When Frankie Went to Hollywood*, 88.

13. Joe David Brown, *Kings Go Forth* (London: Pan Books, 1958), 112.

14. McNally, *When Frankie Went to Hollywood*, 86–87.

15. Daniel J. Leab, *From Sambo to Superspade: The Black Experience in Motion Pictures* (Boston: Houghton Mifflin, 1976), 212.

16. Doherty, *Projections of War*, 122–23.

17. For example, in Morella, Epstein, and Griggs, *The Films of World War II*, 158.

18. Gerber, "In Search of Al Schmid," 26–27.

19. Memorandum from Albert Maltz to Jerry Wald, Delmer Daves Papers, Box 19, Folder 5 (December 2, 1944).

20. Butterfield, *Al Schmid, Marine*, 83.

21. Comments by Lieutenant Commanders Hopkins and Eggert, Delmer Daves Papers, Box 26, Folder 9 (September 12, 1945; September 21, 1945).

22. Rieupeyrout, "Rencontre avec Delmer Daves," 11.

23. Military Intelligence Service, *Soldier's Guide to the Japanese Army*, Special Series no. 27, US Department of War, November 15, 1944, 1–14.

24. Sandra Wilson, "Film and Soldier: Japanese War Movies in the 1950s," *Journal of Contemporary History* 48, no. 3 (2013): 537–40.

25. Wilson, "Film and Soldier," 540, 542–43, 554.

26. John F. Lane, "Moments of Truth: Interview with Francesco Rosi," *Films and Filming* 16, no. 12 (September 1970): 10.

27. Benshoff and Griffin, *America on Film*, 70, 83.

28. Krutnik et al., *"Un-American" Hollywood*, 176–77.

29. Thomas A. Guglielmo, "Fighting for Caucasian Rights: Mexicans, Mexican Americans, and the Transnational Struggle for Civil Rights in World War II Texas," *Journal of American History* 92, no. 4 (March 2006): 1212–17.

30. Memorandum from Albert Maltz, Delmer Daves Papers, Box 19, Folder 5 (December 2, 1944).

31. Tully's *The Bird of Paradise* was first performed in 1912.

32. Christopher Balme, "Selling the Bird: Richard Walton Tully's *The Bird of Paradise* and the Dynamics of Theatrical Commodification," *Theatre Journal* 57, no. 1 (March 2005): 10–12, 20.

33. Toni Morrison, *Playing in the Dark: Whiteness and the Literary Imagination* (London: Picador, 1993), 47.

34. Philip J. Deloria, *Playing Indian* (New Haven, CT: Yale University Press, 1998), 5.

35. Deloria, *Playing Indian*, 106–7.

36. Deloria, *Playing Indian*, 103–4.

37. Vine Deloria Jr., *Custer Died for Your Sins: An Indian Manifesto* (1969; Norman: University of Oklahoma Press, 1989), 8.

38. Deloria, *Custer Died for Your Sins*, 30.

39. Deloria, *Custer Died for Your Sins*, 3–5.

40. Morrison, *Playing in the Dark*, 82.

41. Morrison, *Playing in the Dark*, 34–35.

42. Edward A. Freeman, *Some Impressions of the United States* (London, Longmans, Green, and Company, 1883), 150–51.

43. Frederick Jackson Turner, "The Significance of the Frontier in American History," *Proceedings of the State Historical Society of Wisconsin*, December 14, 1893.

44. Turner, "The Significance of the Frontier."

45. Turner, "The Significance of the Frontier."

46. Theodore Roosevelt, *The Winning of the West*, vol. 1, *From the Alleghanies to the Mississippi, 1769–1776* (New York: G. P. Putnam's Sons, 1889), chap. 1.

47. Laura Ingalls Wilder, *Little House on the Prairie* (1935; London, Egmont, 2000), 132, 177.

48. Wilder, *Little House on the Prairie*, 132, 143, 147.

49. John E. O'Connor, "The White Man's Indian," *Film and History* 23, nos. 1–4 (1993): 21–22.

50. Richard Slotkin, *Regeneration through Violence: The Mythology of the American Frontier, 1600–1860* (New York: Harper Perennial, 1996), 4.

51. Angela Aleiss, "Native Americans: The Surprising Silents," *Cinéaste* 9, no. 3 (1995): 34–35.

52. Aleiss, "Native Americans: The Surprising Silents," 34.

53. For example, Autry in *Back in the Saddle* (1941) and *The Cowboy and the Indians* (1949), and Rogers in *North of the Great Divide* (1950).

54. O'Connor, "The White Man's Indian," 21–22.

55. Kenneth Roberts, *Northwest Passage* (London: Collins, 1938), 122.

56. Steven M. Leuthold, "Native American Responses to the Western," *American Indian Culture and Research Journal* 19, no. 1 (1995): 158–59.

57. Philip French, review of *Little Big Man*, *Sight and Sound* 40, no. 2 (Spring 1971): 102.

58. Melvyn Stokes, *American History through Hollywood Film: From the Revolution to the 1960s* (London: Bloomsbury, 2013), 140.

59. Bosley Crowther, review of *Broken Arrow*, *New York Times*, July 21, 1950, 15.

60. *Hollywood Reporter*, review of *Broken Arrow*, vol. 109, no. 24 (June 12, 1950): 3–4.

61. André Bazin, "The Evolution of the Western," in *What Is Cinema?*, vol. 2, trans. Hugh Gray (Berkeley: University of California Press, 1971), 150–51.

62. *Variety*, "*Broken Arrow* Leading Philly," vol. 179, no. 7 (July 26, 1950): 14–15; *Variety*, "Arrow Ace Pic in Cleve," vol. 179, no. 11 (August 23, 1950): 12; and *Variety*, "August's Top Twelve Winners," vol. 179, no. 13 (September 6, 1950): 4.

63. Edwin R. Sweeney, *Cochise: Chiricahua Apache Chief* (Norman: University of Oklahoma Press, 1991), 384–86.

64. John Prebble, *My Great Aunt Appearing Day and Other Stories* (London: Secker and Warburg, 1958).

65. Don Tollefson, "Delmer Daves on Film: Past, Present, and Future," *Stanford Daily*, March 2, 1972, 6.

66. Wicking, "Interview with Delmer Daves," 59.

67. Albert Turner, review of *Cowboy*, *Films in Review* 9, no. 3 (1958): 143.

68. Terry Mort, *The Wrath of Cochise* (London: Constable, 2014), 274.

69. Frank Manchel, "Cultural Confusion: A Look Back at Delmer Daves's *Broken Arrow*," *Film and History* 23, nos. 1–4 (1993): 58–69.

70. John E. O'Connor, *The Hollywood Indian: Stereotypes of Native Americans in Films* (Trenton: New Jersey State Museum, 1980), 54.

71. Wicking, "Interview with Delmer Daves," 59.

72. Walker, "The Westerns of Delmer Daves," 147.

73. Bourget, "Social Implications in the Hollywood Genres," 50–58.

74. Manchel, "Cultural Confusion," 65.

75. David Parkinson, "Subjects and Stories," in *The Graham Greene Film Reader: Mornings in the Dark*, ed. David Parkinson (Manchester: Carcanet Press, 1993), 409.

76. John Higham, *Writing American History: Essays on Modern Scholarship* (Bloomington: Indiana University Press, 1972), 119, 127.

77. John A. Price, "The Stereotyping of North American Indians in Motion Pictures," *Ethnohistory* 20, no. 2 (Spring 1973): 153–54, 167.

78. Robert M. Utley and Wilcomb E. Washburn, *Indian Wars* (Boston: Houghton Mifflin, 1987).

79. Oliver Otis Howard, *Famous Indian Chiefs I Have Known* (New York: Century Company, 1908), 131–32.

80. Dee Brown, *Bury My Heart at Wounded Knee: An Indian History of the American West* (London: Arena, 1987), 166–72.

81. Belton, *American Cinema/American Culture*, 261.

82. Tollefson, "Delmer Daves on Film," 6.

83. Mort, *The Wrath of Cochise*, xiv, 13, 209, 304.

84. Howard, *Famous Indian Chiefs I Have Known*, 114, 130–32.

85. Edwin R. Sweeney, ed., *Making Peace with Cochise: The 1872 Journal of Captain Joseph Alton Sladen* (Norman: University of Oklahoma Press, 1991), 64, 70, 75, 82–83.

86. Howard, *Famous Indian Chiefs I Have Known*, 119, 128–29, 133–34.

87. Sweeney, *Making Peace with Cochise*, 98–101.

88. E.g., Wicking, "Interview with Delmer Daves," 55, 63.

89. Richard Whitehall, "A Summer Place," *Films and Filming* 9, no. 8 (May 1963): 50.

90. Wakeman, *World Film Directors*, 198.

91. Walker, "The Westerns of Delmer Daves," 137.

92. Fredrik Gustafsson, "Delmer Daves Writes a Letter," Fredrik on Film, September 29, 2013, http://fredrikonfilm.blogspot.co.uk/2013/09/. Daves's letter, to the Swedish Film Institute and reproduced in this blog, is dated July 3, 1968.

93. Walker, "The Westerns of Delmer Daves," 140.

94. Galatians 3:13.

95. Berns, "Changing Societies," 172–73.

96. White, "Trying to Ameliorate the System from Within," 69.

97. Jaskulski, "Bent, or Lifted Out by Its Roots," 81–87.

98. Jaskulski, "Bent, or Lifted Out by Its Roots," 82.

99. Bryan Forbes, *A Divided Life* (London: Heinemann, 1992), 2–4.

100. Brown, *Bury My Heart at Wounded Knee*, 219–40; and Walker, "The Westerns of Delmer Daves," 129.

101. Brown, *Bury My Heart at Wounded Knee*, 219–21.

102. Lenihan, *Showdown*, 43.

103. Bertrand Tavernier, "Extraits d'une correspondance avec Delmer Daves," *Positif* 50, no. 52 (March 1963): 117.

104. Walker, "The Westerns of Delmer Daves," 129.

105. Bourget, "Social Implications in the Hollywood Genres," 50–58.

106. Walker, "The Westerns of Delmer Daves," 131.

107. Vine Deloria Jr., "Stereotyping: The Movie Indian and the Movie Jew," in *The Black Man on Film: Racial Stereotyping*, ed. Richard A. Maynard (Rochelle Park, NJ: Hayden Book Company, 1974), 113.

108. Rieupeyrout, "Rencontre avec Delmer Daves," 14.

109. Sobchack, "Round-Up in Sun Valley," 157–65.

110. Ken Nolley, "The Representation of Conquest," in *Hollywood's Indian: The Portrayal of the Native American in Film*, ed. Peter C. Rollins and John E. O'Connor (Lexington: University Press of Kentucky, 1998), 77.

111. Angela Aleiss, "Hollywood Addresses Postwar Assimilation: Indian/White Attitudes in *Broken Arrow*," *American Indian Culture and Research Journal* 11, no. 1 (1987): 72–74; and Delmer Daves Papers, Box 28, Folders 12, 16, 17 (May 12, 1949), and Folder 20 (May 5, 1949).

112. Morris E. Opler, *An Apache Life-Way: The Economic, Social, and Religious Institutions of the Chiricahua Indians* (Chicago: University of Chicago Press, 1941), 21–22, 53–55, 395–96.

113. Ralph E. Friar and Natasha A. Friar, "White Man Speak with Split Tongue," in *The Pretend Indian: Images of Native Americans in the Movies*, ed. Gretchen M. Bataille and Charles L. P. Silet (Ames: Iowa State University Press, 1980), 95.

114. Edward Buscombe, *"Injuns!" Native Americans in the Movies* (London: Reaktion Books, 2006), 102.

115. Delmer Daves Papers, Box 28, Folder 6 (May 9, 1949), and Folder 8 (August 28, 1949).

116. Delmer Daves Papers, Box 34, Folder 1 (n.d.).

117. Opler, *An Apache Life-Way*, 82–134; and James L. Haley, *Apaches: A History and Culture Portrait* (Garden City, NY: Doubleday, 1981), 135–43.

118. Aleiss, "Hollywood Addresses Postwar Assimilation," 72–74; Opler, *An Apache Life-Way*, 123–24; and Haley, *Apaches: A History and Culture Portrait*, 143.

119. Opler, *An Apache Life-Way*, 157–63; and Haley, *Apaches: A History and Culture Portrait*, 143–44.

120. Stokes, *American History through Hollywood Film*, 140–41.

121. E.g., Richard Slotkin, *Gunfighter Nation: The Myth of the Frontier in the Twentieth Century* (Norman: University of Oklahoma Press, 1998), 376.

122. Delmer Daves Papers, Box 38, Folder 21 (April 22, 1954).

123. Jean-Claude Philippe, "Delmer Daves Believes in Friendship," *Télérama*, March 29, 1964, 59.

124. Angela Aleiss, *Making the White Man's Indian: Native Americans and Hollywood Movies* (Westport, CT: Praeger, 2005), 91.

125. Delmer Daves Papers, Box 27, Folder 32 (May 12, 1949), and Box 38, Folder 21 (May 19, 1954).

126. Rasner, Wulf, and Bühler, "Gespräche mit Delmer Daves," 29–30.

127. Taft, "Dialogues with a Director," 46–51.

128. Price, "The Stereotyping of North American Indians," 164–65.

129. Description of Cochise in Sweeney, *Cochise: Chiricahua Apache Chief*, 262; a photograph of Naiche is reproduced on page 394. There are no known photographs of Cochise.

130. Lawrence J. Quirk, *James Stewart: Behind the Scenes of a Wonderful Life* (New York: Applause Books, 1997), 202.

131. Although Cody's supposed Native American ancestry is inaccurate, he was married to an American Indian, adopted children from the Dakota and Maricopa tribes, and espoused American Indian causes.

132. Kevin Brownlow, *The War, the West, and the Wilderness* (London: Secker and Warburg, 1972), 384.

133. Price, "The Stereotyping of North American Indians," 165.

134. Nobel K. Chissell, "Indian Actors Workshop: Great Oaks from Little Acorns Grow," *Indians Illustrated* 1, no. 5 (June 1968): 6–8.

135. Stokes, *American History through Hollywood Film*, 140–41.

136. Aleiss, *Making the White Man's Indian*, 91–92.

137. Deloria, "Stereotyping," 106–8.

138. Wicking, "Interview with Delmer Daves," 63.

139. Rick Worland and Edward Countryman, "The New Western American Historiography and the Emergence of the New American Westerns," in *Back in the Saddle Again: New Essays on the Western*, ed. Edward Buscombe and Roberta Pearson (London: British Film Institute, 1998), 188–89.

140. Alexandra Keller, "Historical Discourse and American Identity in Westerns since the Reagan Administration," *Film and History* 33, no. 1 (2003): 48.

141. Slotkin, *Gunfighter Nation*, 368, 374.

142. Don Miller, "New Words on Old Westerns," *Focus on Film*, no. 11 (Autumn 1972): 34–35.

143. *Time*, review of *Broken Arrow*, July 30, 1950, 38–39.

144. May, *The Big Tomorrow*, 2, 284.

145. Walker, "The Westerns of Delmer Daves," 129.

146. Murray Schumach, *The Face on the Cutting Room Floor: The Story of Movie and Television Censorship* (1964; New York: Da Capo Press, 1975), 140–41.

147. Stokes, *American History through Hollywood Film*, 140–41.

148. Jaskulski, "Bent, or Lifted Out by Its Roots," 86.

149. White, "Trying to Ameliorate the System from Within," 69.

150. Tavernier, "The Ethical Romantic," 49; and Tavernier, "Chronique hollywoodienne," 239.

151. Jaskulski, "Bent, or Lifted Out by Its Roots," 82, 93.

152. Walker, "The Westerns of Delmer Daves," 130.

153. William Indick, *The Psychology of the Western: How the American Psyche Plays Out on Screen* (Jefferson, NC: McFarland, 2008), 65–66.

154. Caroline Lejeune, review of *Broken Arrow*, *Observer*, August 27, 1950, 6.

155. Marubbio, *Killing the Indian Maiden*, 65–71.

156. Walker, "The Westerns of Delmer Daves," 134.

157. Memorandum from Darryl F. Zanuck, Delmer Daves Papers, Box 36, Folder 4 (January 11, 1954).

158. Walker, "The Westerns of Delmer Daves," 139–40.

159. Buscombe, *"Injuns!,"* 127–30.

160. Joanna Hearne, "The 'Ache for Home': Assimilation and Separatism in Anthony Mann's *Devil's Doorway*," in *Hollywood's West: The American Frontier in Film, Television, and History*, ed. Peter C. Rollins and John E. O'Connor (Lexington: University Press of Kentucky, 2005), 130.

161. White, "Trying to Ameliorate the System from Within," 66, 70.

162. Treatment of "Early Western Version," Delmer Daves Papers, Box 31, Folder 9 (April 9, 1951).

163. Aleiss, *Making the White Man's Indian*, 48.

164. Anti-miscegenation legislation applying to American Indians was repealed in Oregon in 1951, in Idaho and Nevada in 1959, and in North Carolina, South Carolina, Georgia, Texas, Virginia, and Tennessee in 1967.

165. Loving v. Virginia, 388 U.S. 1 (1967).

166. Philip French, *Westerns: Aspects of a Movie Genre and Westerns Revisited* (Manchester: Carcanet Press, 2005), 48–50.

167. *Variety*, July 12, 1944, 1, 32.

168. Interview with Delmer Daves, in Slotkin, *Gunfighter Nation*, 726n36.

169. Delmer Daves, Columbia Oral History Program, 34.

170. White, "Trying to Ameliorate the System from Within," 68.

171. Gerald D. Nash, *Creating the West: Historical Interpretations, 1890–1990* (Albuquerque: University of New Mexico Press, 1991), 79–80.

172. Higham, *Writing American History*, 119, 127.

173. Patricia Nelson Limerick, *The Legacy of Conquest: The Unbroken Past of the American West* (New York: W. W. Norton, 1988).

174. Limerick, *The Legacy of Conquest*, 17–23.

175. Stephen Handzo, "Through the Devil's Doorway: The Early Westerns of Anthony Mann," *Bright Lights* 1, no. 4 (Summer 1976): 6.

176. Worland and Countryman, "The New Western American Historiography," 188–89.

177. Manchel, "Cultural Confusion," 59.

178. Kenneth R. Philp, "John Collier and the American Indian," in *The Walter Prescott Webb Memorial Lectures: Essays on Radicalism in Contemporary America*, ed. Leon B. Blair (Austin: University of Texas Press, 1972), 67–69, 78.

179. Buscombe, *"Injuns!,"* 108–9.

180. Aleiss, "Hollywood Addresses Postwar Assimilation," 72–75.

181. David Murray, *Modern Indians: Native Americans in the Twentieth Century* (Durham, England: British Association for American Studies, 1982), 34–39.

182. Aleiss, *Making the White Man's Indian*, 91–92.

183. Mort, *The Wrath of Cochise*, xiv, 300.

184. Howard Mantell, "Counteracting the Stereotype," *American Indian* 5, no. 4 (Fall 1950): 19–20.

185. Tom Ryan, *The Films of Douglas Sirk: Exquisite Ironies and Magnificent Obsessions* (Jackson: University Press of Mississippi, 2019), 147–48.

186. Walker, "The Westerns of Delmer Daves," 136.

187. Aleiss, *Making the White Man's Indian*, 91.

188. Delmer Daves Papers, Box 36, Folders 7, 8 (n.d.); Box 36, Folder 9 (July 1, 1954).

189. Treatment of a Western version of "Bali Story," Delmer Daves Papers, Box 31, Folder 9 (April 9, 1951).

190. Freeman, *Some Impressions of the United States*, 150–51.

191. K. Tsianina Lomawaima, "Hm! White Boy! You Got No Business Here!," in *American Indians*, ed. Nancy Shoemaker (Malden, MA: Blackwell, 2001), 208–35.

192. Walker, "The Westerns of Delmer Daves," 141.

193. Jack Weatherford, *Indian Givers: How the Indians of the Americas Transformed the World* (New York: Fawcett Columbine, 1988), 133–43.

194. Higham, *Writing American History*, 122.

195. Higham, *Writing American History*, 105.

196. Higham, *Writing American History*, 122.

197. Philp, "John Collier and the American Indian," 73–74.

198. Philp, "John Collier and the American Indian," 70.

199. Philp, "John Collier and the American Indian," 67.

200. Gabriella Treglia, "Using Citizenship to Retain Identity: The Native American Dance Bans of the Assimilation Era, 1900–1933," *Journal of American Studies* 47, no. 3 (2012): 777–800.

201. Treglia, "Using Citizenship to Retain Identity," 787–88.

202. Rieupeyrout, "Rencontre avec Delmer Daves," 14.

203. Trudy Griffin-Pierce, *Chiricahua Apache Enduring Power: Naiche's Puberty Ceremony Paintings* (Tuscaloosa: University of Alabama Press, 2006), 33, 136–38.

204. Griffin-Pierce, *Chiricahua Apache Enduring Power*, 161.

205. The legislation also applied to Alaska Natives, Aleuts, and Native Hawaiians.

206. Koppes, "From New Deal to Termination," 544.

207. James S. Olson and Raymond Wilson, *Native Americans in the Twentieth Century* (Urbana: University of Illinois Press, 1986), 162–69.

208. Francis Parkman, *The Conspiracy of the Pontiac*, vol. 1, 10th ed. rev. (London: Macmillan, 1885), xiv.

209. Limerick, *The Legacy of Conquest*, 194.

210. Benshoff and Griffin, *America on Film*, 98.

211. Burnham, *Struggle for the World*, 182, 189.

212. Jentleson, *American Foreign Policy*, 154–55.

213. Krutnik et al., *"Un-American" Hollywood*, 213.

214. Worland and Countryman, "The New Western American Historiography," 182.

215. From an interview with William McKinley in the *Christian Advocate*, January 22, 1903, 17.

216. John Nickel, "Disabling African American Men: Liberalism and Race Message Films," *Cinema Journal* 44, no. 1 (Fall 2004): 27–40.

217. Tuska, *The American West in Film*, 238.

218. Jaskulski, "Bent, or Lifted Out by Its Roots," 93.

219. Griffin-Pierce, *Chiricahua Apache Enduring Power*, xiii.

220. Nelson, "Don't Be Too Quick to Dismiss Them," 55–57.

221. Jaskulski, "Bent, or Lifted Out by Its Roots," 87.

222. Captain Jack, synopsis, Delmer Daves Papers, Box 39, Folder 11 (March 20, 1939).

223. Howard, *Famous Indian Chiefs I Have Known*, 158–60.

224. Jaskulski, "Bent, or Lifted Out by Its Roots," 89.

225. Wicking, "Interview with Delmer Daves," 55.

226. Herbert L. Jacobson, "Cowboy, Pioneer, and American Soldier," *Sight and Sound* 22, no. 4 (April–June 1953): 189–90.

227. *Christian Century*, review of *Broken Arrow*, September 13, 1950, 1087.

228. E.g., Jaskulski, "Bent, or Lifted Out by Its Roots," 93.

229. Joyce Appleby, "Recovering America's Historic Diversity: Beyond Exceptionalism," *Journal of American History* 79, no. 2 (September 1992): 420.

230. Appleby, "Recovering America's Historic Diversity," 425.

231. Appleby, "Recovering America's Historic Diversity," 427, 431.

CHAPTER FOUR

1. Carl Boggs and Tom Pollard, "Postmodern Cinema and the Demise of the Family," *Journal of American Culture* 26, no. 4 (December 2003): 445.

2. Kate Weigand, "The Red Menace, the Feminine Mystique, and the Ohio Un-American Activities Commission: Gender and Anti-Communism in Ohio, 1951–1954," *Journal of Women's History* 3, no. 3 (Winter 1992): 70.

3. Ferdinand Lundberg and Marynia F. Farnham, *Modern Woman: The Lost Sex* (New York: Harper and Brothers, 1947), 25.

4. Marjorie Rosen, "Popcorn Venus; or, How the Movies Have Made Women Smaller than Life," in *Sexual Stratagems: The World of Women in Film*, ed. Patricia Erens (New York: Horizon Press, 1979), 26.

5. Laura Mulvey, "Visual Pleasure and Narrative Cinema," *Screen* 16, no. 3 (Autumn 1973): 6–18.

6. Rosen, "Popcorn Venus," 21.

7. Betty Friedan, *The Feminine Mystique* (1963; London: Penguin, 1965), 9, 23.

8. Schlesinger, "The Crisis of American Masculinity," 63.

9. Lundberg and Farnham, *Modern Woman*, 235–37.

10. Leslie Fishbein, "*The Snake Pit* (1948): The Sexist Nature of Sanity," in *Hollywood as Historian: American Film in a Cultural Context*, ed. Peter C. Rollins, rev. ed. (Lexington: University Press of Kentucky, 1998), 154–57.

11. Wini Breines, *Young, White, and Miserable: Growing Up Female in the Fifties* (Boston: Beacon Press, 1992), 6–7, 10–11, 33–34.

12. Lundberg and Farnham, *Modern Woman*, 166.

13. Susan M. Hartmann, "Women's Employment and the Domestic Ideal," in *Not June Cleaver: Women and Gender in Postwar America, 1945–1960*, ed. Joanne Meyerowitz (Philadelphia: Temple University Press, 1994), 85–86.

14. June Whitney, quoted in Michael Barson, *Better Dead than Red: A Nostalgic Look at the Golden Years of Russiaphobia, Red-Baiting, and Other Commie Madness* (London: Plexus Books, 1992), 99–100. Whitney was writing for *Look* magazine in 1954.

15. Emily S. Rosenberg, "'Foreign Affairs' after World War II: Connecting Sexual and International Politics," *Diplomatic History* 18, no. 1 (Winter 1994): 63–68.

16. Gavin Lambert, "Female Grotesques," *Films and Filming* 21, no. 10 (July 1975): 6.

17. Lucas, "Saloon Girls and the Ranchers' Daughters," 307.

18. David Meuel, *Women in the Films of John Ford* (Jefferson, NC: McFarland, 2014), 144, 149.

19. Meuel, *Women in the Films of John Ford*, 11.

20. Meuel, *Women in the Films of John Ford*, 106–7.

21. Joseph McBride, *Hawks on Hawks* (Berkeley: University of California Press, 1982), 96.

22. Wood was nominated for an Oscar for her performance in *Rebel without a Cause* (1955).

23. *Monthly Film Bulletin*, review of *Never Let Me Go*, vol. 20, no. 232 (May 1953): 73–74.

24. Dixon, *The Early Film Criticism of François Truffaut*, 149.

25. Rui Nogueira, "Writing for the Movies: Wendell Mayes," *Focus on Film*, no. 7 (Summer 1971): 38.

26. Coursodon, "Delmer Daves," 83.

27. Terence Pettigrew, *The Bogart File* (London: Golden Eagle Press, 1977), 110–13.

28. Kevin Gough-Yates, "The Heroine: Part One," *Films and Filming* 12, no. 8 (May 1966): 23.

29. *Variety*, review of *Stranded*, vol. 119, no. 2 (June 26, 1935): 23.

30. Leyland J. Axelson, "The Marital Adjustment and Marital Role Definitions of Husbands of Working and Nonworking Wives," *Marriage and Family Living* 25, no. 2 (May 1963): 195.

31. Memorandum from Herman Wouk to Delmer Daves, Delmer Daves Papers, Box 69, Folder 21 (December 3, 1962).

32. Robert L. Griswold, *Fatherhood in America: A History* (New York: Basic Books, 1993): 157–59.

33. Crowther, review of *To the Victor*, 11.

34. Pomp, "Home on the Range," 140–41.

35. E.g., Molly Haskell, *Holding My Own in No Man's Land: Women and Men and Film and Feminists* (Oxford: Oxford University Press, 1997), 21–34; and Kathrina Glitre, *Hollywood Romantic Comedy: States of the Union, 1934–1965* (Manchester: Manchester University Press, 2006), 159–80.

36. Haskell, *Holding My Own in No Man's Land*, 26–27.

37. Glitre, *Hollywood Romantic Comedy*, 160–62.

38. *Monthly Film Bulletin*, review of *A Kiss in the Dark*, vol. 17, no. 195 (March–April 1950): 49.

39. Whitehall, "On the 3:10 to Yuma," 54.

40. Jane Clarke and Diana Simmonds, "Introduction: A Chorus of Derision," in *Move Over Misconceptions: Doris Day Reappraised*, edited by Jane Clarke and Diana Simmonds (London: British Film Institute, 1980), 2–3.

41. Glitre, *Hollywood Romantic Comedy*, 162.

42. Benshoff and Griffin, *America on Film*, 239.

43. Mulvey, "Visual Pleasure and Narrative Cinema," 13.

44. *Monthly Film Bulletin*, review of *The Thrill of It All*, vol. 30, no. 358 (November 1963): 162.

45. Letter from Sloan Wilson to Delmer Daves, Delmer Daves Papers, Box 51, Folder 6 (January 16, 1959).

46. Jympson Harman, "It's Time the Censor Changed His Ideas," *Evening News* (London), January 7, 1960, 4.

47. Correspondence from the PCA, Delmer Daves Papers, Box 51, Folder 6 (December 16, 1958; July 14, 1959).

48. Delmer Daves Papers, Box 51, Folder 6 (December 16, 1958).

49. E.g., *Monthly Film Bulletin*, Review of *A Summer Place*, vol. 27, no. 313 (February 1960): 22; and Harman, "It's Time the Censor Changed His Ideas," 4.

50. Boggs and Pollard, "Postmodern Cinema and the Demise of the Family," 449.

51. Boggs and Pollard, "Postmodern Cinema and the Demise of the Family," 445.

52. Howard Thompson, review of *A Summer Place*, *New York Times*, October 23, 1959, 24.

53. Ryan, *The Films of Douglas Sirk*, 9, 230.

54. Ryan, *The Films of Douglas Sirk*, 173, 205, 9, 6.

55. Michael Stern, *Douglas Sirk* (Boston: Twayne Publishers, 1979), 23–30.

56. *Time*, review of *A Summer Place*, November 9, 1959, 58.

57. Thompson, review of *A Summer Place*, 24.

58. Janice M. Irvine, *Talk about Sex: The Battles over Sex Education in the United States* (Berkeley: University of California Press, 2002), 12.

59. *Time*, review of *A Summer Place*, 58.

60. Ira Lurvey and Selise Eiseman, "Divorce Goes to the Movies," *University of San Francisco Law Review* 30, no. 4 (1996): 1210–13.

61. Lurvey and Eiseman, "Divorce Goes to the Movies," 1218.

62. Roderick Phillips, *Putting Asunder: A History of Divorce in Western Society* (Cambridge: Cambridge University Press, 1988), 626.

63. George Levinger, "Sources of Marital Dissatisfaction among Applicants for Divorce," *American Journal of Orthopsychiatry* 36, no. 5 (1966): 803–7.

64. Phillips, *Putting Asunder*, 620–24.

65. George Levinger, "A Social Psychological Perspective on Marital Dissolution," *Journal of Social Issues* 32, no. 1 (Winter 1976): 44.

66. Carol A. Brown et al., "Divorce: Chance of a New Lifetime," *Journal of Social Issues* 32, no. 1 (Winter 1976): 119.

67. Brown et al., "Divorce: Chance of a New Lifetime," 119–33.

68. *Divorce in the Family*, shooting script, Delmer Daves Papers, Box 1, Folder 11 (June 11, 1932).

69. *Divorce in the Family*, shooting script, Delmer Daves Papers, Box 1, Folder 11 (June 11, 1932).

70. O'Hara with Nicoletti, *'Tis Herself*, 291–92.

71. Gough-Yates, "The Heroine: Part One," 27.

72. John Bowlby, *Maternal Care and Mental Health*, 2nd ed. (Geneva: World Health Organization, 1952), 46.

73. *Monthly Film Bulletin*, review of *The Battle of the Villa Fiorita*, 131.

74. Judson T. Landis, "The Trauma of Children When Parents Divorce," *Marriage and Family Living* 22, no. 1 (February 1960): 7–13.

75. Åse Skard, "Maternal Deprivation: The Research and Its Implications," *Journal of Marriage and Family* 27, no. 3 (August 1965): 343.

76. William Johnson, "Coming to Terms with Color," *Film Quarterly* 20, no. 1 (Fall 1966): 10.

77. Francis Ivan Nye, "Child Adjustment in Broken and Unhappy Unbroken Homes," *Marriage and Family Living* 19, no. 4 (November 1957): 356–61.

78. Skard, "Maternal Deprivation," 343.

79. Skard, "Maternal Deprivation," 341.

80. Kitses, *Horizons West*, 21.

81. Jacqueline Levitin, "The Western: Any Good Roles for Women?," in *Feminist Film Criticism: Film and Cultural Studies*, Film Reader, vol. 5, ed. Jae Alexander and Lolita Raclin Rodgers (Evanston, IL: Northwestern University Press, 1982), 95–96.

82. Levitin, "The Western: Any Good Roles for Women?," 98.

83. Levitin, "The Western: Any Good Roles for Women?," 95.

84. Carter, "This Is Where He Brought Me," 199–221.

85. Walker, "The Westerns of Delmer Daves," 132.

86. Lucas, "Saloon Girls and the Ranchers' Daughters," 312–13.

87. Levitin, "The Western: Any Good Roles for Women?," 98–101.

88. Lucas, "Saloon Girls and the Ranchers' Daughters," 312, 316–18.

89. Walter C. Metz, "'Have You Written a Ford, Lately?' Gender, Genre, and the Film Adaptations of Dorothy Johnson's Western Literature," *Literature/Film Quarterly* 31, no. 3 (Summer 2003): 10, 15–16.

90. Rosen, "Popcorn Venus," 335.

91. For example, an analysis of 1950 census returns detailed in Paul C. Glick, *American Families: A Demographic Analysis of Census Data on American Families at Mid-Century* (New York: John Wiley and Sons, 1957), 110–12, 154.

92. Thomas Poffenberger, "Individual Choice in Adolescent Premarital Sex Behavior," *Marriage and Family Living* 22, no. 4 (November 1960): 325–26.

93. Eugene Gilbert, "Why Today's Teenagers Seem So Different," *Harper's Magazine*, November 1959, 79.

94. Walker, "The Westerns of Delmer Daves," 138.

95. Robert O. Blood Jr., "Romance and Premarital Intercourse: Incompatibles?," *Marriage and Family Living* 14, no. 2 (May 1952): 105, 108.

96. Georganne Scheiner, "Look at Me, I'm Sandra Dee: Beyond a White, Teen Icon," *Frontiers: A Journal of Women Studies* 22, no. 2 (2001): 98, 106.

97. Pomp, "Home on the Range," 140.

98. Vance Packard, *The Sexual Wilderness: The Contemporary Upheaval in Male-Female Relationships* (London: Pan Books, 1970), 127–31.

99. Robert R. Bell and Jay B. Chaskes, "Premarital Sexual Experience, 1958 and 1968," *Journal of Marriage and Family* 32, no. 1 (February 1970): 81–84.

100. Albert Ellis, "In Defense of *The American Sexual Tragedy*," *Journal of Marriage and Family* 27, no. 1 (February 1965): 113.

101. Walter Stokes, "Our Changing Sex Ethics," *Marriage and Family Living* 24, no. 3 (August 1962): 269.

102. Bosley Crowther, review of *Rome Adventure*, New York Times, March 16, 1962, 25.

103. Letter from Delmer Daves to Mr. P. Davis, Delmer Daves Papers, Box 51, Folder 7 (May 2, 1960).

104. Rickie Solinger, *Wake Up Little Susie: Single Pregnancy and Race before Roe v. Wade* (New York: Routledge, 1992), 16–17.

105. Ellis, "In Defense of *The American Sexual Tragedy*," 113.

106. Ira L. Reiss, "The Double Standard in Premarital Sexual Intercourse: A Neglected Concept," *Social Forces* 34, no. 3 (March 1956): 224.

107. Reiss, "The Double Standard in Premarital Sexual Intercourse," 225.

108. Robert R. Bell, *Premarital Sex in a Changing Society* (Englewood Cliffs, NJ: Prentice Hall, 1966), 75.

109. Michael Schofield, *The Sexual Behaviour of Young People* (London: Allen Lane, 1973), 193–96.

110. Poffenberger, "Individual Choice in Adolescent Premarital Sex Behavior," 325–26.

111. Rosen, "Popcorn Venus," 320.

112. Pomp, "Home on the Range," 140.

113. Lester A. Kirkendall, "Values and Premarital Intercourse: Implications for Parent Education," *Marriage and Family Living* 22, no. 4 (November 1960): 317–24.

114. Robert R. Bell and Jack V. Buerkle, "Mother and Daughter Attitudes to Premarital Sexual Behavior," *Marriage and Family Living* 23, no. 4 (November 1961): 390–92.

115. Scheiner, "Look at Me, I'm Sandra Dee," 99.

116. Mulvey, "Visual Pleasure and Narrative Cinema," 12.

117. Scheiner, "Look at Me, I'm Sandra Dee," 98, 106n55.

118. Nogueira, "Writing for the Movies: Wendell Mayes," 38.

119. *Mothers and Daughters*, first and second drafts of screenplay, Delmer Daves Papers, Box 60, Folders 1, 2 (April 12, 1961).

120. Kevin Gough-Yates, "The Heroine: Part Two," *Films and Filming* 12, no. 9 (June 1966): 27–28; and Kevin Gough-Yates, "The Heroine: Part Three," *Films and Filming* 12, no. 10 (July 1966): 39.

121. Friedan, *The Feminine Mystique*, 297–98.

122. Tavernier, "The Ethical Romantic," 48.

123. Lucas, "Saloon Girls and the Ranchers' Daughters," 310.

124. Oakley, *God's Country*, 117.

125. Steven Cohan, *Masked Men: Masculinity and the Movies in the Fifties* (Bloomington: Indiana University Press, 1997): 50–51.

126. Louis Lyndon, "Uncertain Hero: The Paradox of the American Male," *Women's Home Journal*, November 1956, 41–43, 107, quoted in Cohan, *Masked Men*, 34–35.

127. Helen Mayer Hacker, "The New Burdens of Masculinity," *Marriage and Family Living* 19, no. 3 (August 1957): 227–29.

128. Schlesinger, "The Crisis of American Masculinity," 63–65.

129. Arthur Schlesinger Jr., *The Vital Center: The Politics of Freedom* (1949; New York: Da Capo Press, 1988), 151.

130. Schlesinger, *The Vital Center*, 126.

131. Arthur Schlesinger Jr., *The Politics of Hope and the Bitter Heritage* (1963–1967; Princeton, NJ: Princeton University Press, 2008), 112.

132. Schlesinger, *The Vital Center*, 14, 37, 41.

133. Schlesinger, *The Politics of Hope*, 16, 19, 37, 48.

134. K. A. Cuordileone, "'Politics in an Age of Anxiety': Cold War Political Culture and the Crisis in American Masculinity, 1949–1960," *Journal of American History* 87, no. 2 (September 2000): 515–45.

135. Cuordileone, "Politics in an Age of Anxiety," 544.

136. Quoted in Robert D. Dean, "Masculinity as Ideology: John Kennedy and the Domestic Politics of Foreign Policy," *Diplomatic History* 22, no. 1 (Winter 1998): 46.

137. Dean, "Masculinity as Ideology," 29–62.

138. George F. Kennan, *Memoirs, 1925–1950* (Boston: Little, Brown, 1967), 547–59.

139. Kennan, *Memoirs*, 550, 552, 553, 556.

140. Frank Costigliola, "'Unceasing Pressure for Penetration': Gender, Pathology, and Emotion in George Kennan's Formulation of the Cold War," *Journal of American History* 83, no. 4 (March 1997): 1333.

141. Kennan, *Memoirs*, 563.

142. Kennan's "Preparedness as Part of Foreign Relations" (January 8, 1948), quoted in David Mayers, *George Kennan and the Dilemmas of US Foreign Policy* (New York: Oxford University Press, 1988), 123, 348n47.

143. Theodore Roosevelt, *Ranch Life and the Hunting Trail* (1988; Memphis: General Books, 2012), 20.

144. Hacker, "The New Burdens of Masculinity," 227–28, 232.

145. Serge Chauvin, "Le Lien et le passage: Delmer Daves westernien," in *Delmer Daves: La Morale des pionniers*, ed. Jean-Pierre Garcia and Dominique Païni (Amiens: Éditions Vol de Nuit, 1999), 31.

146. Wendy C. Peek, "The Romance of Competence: Rethinking Masculinity in the Western," *Journal of Popular Film and Television* 30, no. 4 (Winter 2003): 208–19.

147. Walker, "The Westerns of Delmer Daves," 157.

148. Stephen J. Mexal, "Two Ways to Yuma: Locke, Liberalism, and Western Masculinity in *3:10 to Yuma*," in *The Philosophy of the Western*, ed. Jennifer L. McMahon and B. Steve Csaki (Lexington: University Press of Kentucky, 2010), 71.

149. White, "Trying to Ameliorate the System from Within," 71, 74.

150. R. W. B. Lewis, *The American Adam: Innocence, Tragedy, and Tradition in the Nineteenth Century* (1955; Chicago: University of Chicago Press, 1966), 5.

151. Jonathan Mitchell, *Revisions of the American Adam: Innocence, Identity and Masculinity in Twentieth-Century America* (London: Bloomsbury, 2011), 1.

152. Mitchell, *Revisions of the American Adam*, 4.

153. Mitchell, *Revisions of the American Adam*, 5, 42–43.

154. Peek, "The Romance of Competence," 208–19.

155. Hacker, "The New Burdens of Masculinity," 228–33.

156. Hacker, "The New Burdens of Masculinity," 228.

157. Carol A. MacCurdy, "Masculinity in *3:10 to Yuma*," *Quarterly Review of Film and Video* 26, no. 4 (August 2009): 280.

158. John Esther, "Avoiding Labels and Lullabies: An Interview with James Mangold," *Cinéaste* 33, no. 1 (Winter 2007): 30.

159. McBride, *Hawks on Hawks*, 130.

160. Elmore Leonard, "Three-Ten to Yuma," in *The Killers*, ed. Peter Dawson, 2nd ed. (New York: Bantam Books, 1974), 116, 126–28.

161. Hacker, "The New Burdens of Masculinity," 227, 232.

162. E.g., MacCurdy, "Masculinity in *3:10 to Yuma*," 280–83; Mexal, "Two Ways to Yuma," 69–81; and Simon Petch, "Return to Yuma," *Film Criticism* 32, no. 2 (Winter 2007–2008): 49–56.

163. MacCurdy, "Masculinity in *3:10 to Yuma*," 283.

164. Petch, "Return to Yuma," 64.

165. E.g., MacCurdy, "Masculinity in *3:10 to Yuma*," 282–83, 291; and Petch, "Return to Yuma," 65.

166. Slavoj Žižek, *Welcome to the Desert of the Real* (London: Verso, 2002), 74.

167. Kevin Gough-Yates, "The Hero: Part Two," *Films and Filming* 12, no. 4 (January 1966): 12–13.

168. William Savage Jr., *The Cowboy Hero: His Image in American History and Culture* (Norman: University of Oklahoma Press, 1979), 95–96.

169. Friedan, *The Feminine Mystique*, 331.

170. Mellen, *Big Bad Wolves*, 149–51.

171. Peek, "The Romance of Competence," 218.

172. David Riesman, "Permissiveness and Sex Roles," *Marriage and the Family* 21, no. 3 (August 1959): 213.

CONCLUSION

1. Margaret Mead, *And Keep Your Powder Dry* (New York: Morrow Quill, 1965), 114, 254.

2. Delmer Daves, "Nimbus beyond the Footlights," in *Stanford Mosaic: Reminiscences of the First Seventy Years at Stanford University*, ed. Edith R. Mirrielees (Stanford, CA: Stanford University Press, 1962), 131.

3. Rieupeyrout, "Rencontre avec Delmer Daves," 17.

4. Wicking, "Interview with Delmer Daves," 60.

5. Tollefson, "Delmer Daves on Film," 6.

6. Tavernier, "The Ethical Romantic," 46.

7. Daves, "Nimbus beyond the Footlights," 131.

8. Jonathan Kirshner, *Hollywood's Last Golden Age: Politics, Society, and the Seventies Film in America* (Ithaca, NY: Cornell University Press, 2012), 2–4, 10–11, 37–41.

9. Kirshner, *Hollywood's Last Golden Age*, 45–47.

10. Kirshner, *Hollywood's Last Golden Age*, 5.

11. Kirshner, *Hollywood's Last Golden Age*, 2.

12. Deloria, *Playing Indian*, 132.

13. Max Tessier, "*La Route des ténèbres*," *Cinéma* 159 (September–October 1971): 138.

FILMOGRAPHY

FILMS FOR WHICH DAVES HAD SOLE OR JOINT WRITING CREDIT AND TO WHICH REFERENCE HAS BEEN MADE IN THE TEXT

So This Is College (1929). MGM. Screenplay by Delmer Daves and Al Boasberg. Directed by Sam Wood.

Divorce in the Family (1932). MGM. Story by Delmer Daves and Maurice Rapf. Screenplay by Delmer Daves. Directed by Charles Reisner.

Clear All Wires (1933). MGM. Screenplay by Bella and Samuel Spewack, with Delmer Daves. Directed by George W. Hill.

Dames (1934). Warner Bros. Screenplay by Delmer Daves and Robert Lord. Directed by Ray Enright and Busby Berkeley.

Flirtation Walk (1934). First National Pictures. Screenplay by Delmer Daves. Directed by Frank Borzage and Bobby Connelly.

Miss Pacific Fleet (1935). Warner Bros. Screenplay by Peter Milne, Lucille Newmark, and (uncredited) Delmer Daves. Directed by Ray Enright.

Shipmates Forever (1935). Warner Bros. Story and screenplay by Delmer Daves. Directed by Frank Borzage.

Stranded (1935). Warner Bros. Screenplay by Delmer Daves. Produced and directed by Frank Borzage.

The Petrified Forest (1936). Warner Bros. Screenplay by Delmer Daves and Charles Kenyon. Directed by Archie L. Mayo.

The Go-Getter (1937). Warner Bros. Screenplay by Delmer Daves. Directed by Busby Berkeley.

Love Affair (1939). RKO Radio Pictures. Screenplay by Delmer Daves and Donald Ogden Stewart. Produced and directed by Leo McCarey.

It All Came True (1940). Warner Bros. Screenplay by Michael Fessier and Lawrence Kimble with uncredited work by Delmer Daves. Directed by Lewis Seiler.

You Were Never Lovelier (1942). Columbia Pictures. Screenplay by Delmer Daves, Michael Fessier, and Ernest Pagano. Directed by William A. Seiter.

Stage Door Canteen (1943). Sol Lesser Productions. Written by Delmer Daves. Produced and directed by Frank Borzage.

White Feather (1955). Twentieth Century Fox. Screenplay by Delmer Daves and Leo Townsend. Directed by Robert D. Webb.

An Affair to Remember (1957). Twentieth Century Fox. Screenplay by Delmer Daves and Leo McCarey. Directed by Leo McCarey.

FILMS FOR WHICH DAVES HAD CREDIT FOR DIRECTION

Pride of the Marines (1945; in Great Britain, *Forever in Love*). Warner Bros. Screenplay by Albert Maltz. Directed by Delmer Daves.
To the Victor (1948). Warner Bros. Screenplay by Richard Brooks. Directed by Delmer Daves.
A Kiss in the Dark (1949). Warner Bros. Screenplay by Everett Freeman and Harry Kurnitz. Directed by Delmer Daves.
Broken Arrow (1950). Twentieth Century Fox. Screenplay by Albert Maltz (credited to Michael Blankfort). Directed by Delmer Daves.
Return of the Texan (1952). Twentieth Century Fox. Screenplay by Dudley Nichols. Directed by Delmer Daves.
Never Let Me Go (1953). MGM. Screenplay by Ronald Millar and George Froeschel. Directed by Delmer Daves.
Demetrius and the Gladiators (1954). Twentieth Century Fox. Screenplay by Philip Dunne. Directed by Delmer Daves.
3:10 to Yuma (1957). Columbia Pictures. Screenplay by Halsted Welles. Directed by Delmer Daves.
Cowboy (1958). Columbia Pictures. Screenplay by Edmund R. North (and Dalton Trumbo, uncredited). Directed by Delmer Daves.
The Badlanders (1958). MGM. Screenplay by Richard Collins. Directed by Delmer Daves.
Kings Go Forth (1958). Frank Ross, United Artists. Screenplay by Merle Miller. Directed by Delmer Daves.
The Hanging Tree (1959). Warner Bros. Screenplay by Wendell Mayes and Halsted Welles. Directed by Delmer Daves.

FILMS FOR WHICH DAVES HAD DIRECTING AND SCREENWRITING CREDIT

Destination Tokyo (1943). Warner Bros. Screenplay by Delmer Daves and Albert Maltz. Directed by Delmer Daves.
Hollywood Canteen (1944). Warner Bros. Screenplay and directed by Delmer Daves.
The Very Thought of You (1944). Warner Bros. Screenplay by Alvah Bessie and Delmer Daves. Directed by Delmer Daves.
The Red House (1947). Sol Lesser Productions. Screenplay and directed by Delmer Daves.
Dark Passage (1948). Warner Bros. Screenplay and directed by Delmer Daves.
Task Force (1949). Warner Bros. Screenplay and directed by Delmer Daves.
Treasure of the Golden Condor (1953). Twentieth Century Fox. Screenplay and directed by Delmer Daves.
Jubal (1956). Columbia Pictures. Screenplay by Russell S. Hughes and Delmer Daves. Directed by Delmer Daves.

The Last Wagon (1956). Twentieth Century Fox. Screenplay by James Edward Grant, Gwen Bagni Gielgud, and Delmer Daves. Directed by Delmer Daves.

FILMS FOR WHICH DAVES WORKED AS PRODUCER, WRITER, AND DIRECTOR

Bird of Paradise (1951). Twentieth Century Fox. Produced, written, and directed by Delmer Daves.
Drum Beat (1954). Warner Bros. Produced by Delmer Daves and Alan Ladd. Written and directed by Delmer Daves.
A Summer Place (1959). Warner Bros. Produced, written, and directed by Delmer Daves.
Parrish (1961). Warner Bros. Produced, written, and directed by Delmer Daves.
Susan Slade (1961). Warner Bros. Produced, written, and directed by Delmer Daves.
Rome Adventure (1962; in Great Britain, *Lovers Must Learn*). Warner Bros. Produced, written, and directed by Delmer Daves.
Spencer's Mountain (1963). Warner Bros. Produced, written, and directed by Delmer Daves.
Youngblood Hawke (1964). Warner Bros. Produced, written, and directed by Delmer Daves.
The Battle of the Villa Fiorita (1965). Warner Bros. Produced, written, and directed by Delmer Daves.

BIBLIOGRAPHY

Aleiss, Angela. "Hollywood Addresses Postwar Assimilation: Indian/White Attitudes in *Broken Arrow*." *American Indian Culture and Research Journal* 11, no. 1 (1987): 67–79.

Aleiss, Angela. *Making the White Man's Indian: Native Americans and Hollywood Movies.* Westport, CT: Praeger, 2005.

Aleiss, Angela. "Native Americans: The Surprising Silents." *Cinéaste* 9, no. 3 (1995): 34–35.

Anderson, Lindsay. "The Director's Cinema?" *Sequence*, no. 12 (Autumn 1950): 6–11, 37.

Anderson, Thom. "Red Hollywood." In *Literature and the Visual Arts in Contemporary Society*, edited by Suzanne Ferguson and Barbara Groseclose, 141–96. Columbus: Ohio State University Press, 1985.

Appleby, Joyce. "Recovering America's Historic Diversity: Beyond Exceptionalism." *Journal of American History* 79, no. 2 (September 1992): 419–31.

Axelson, Leyland J. "The Marital Adjustment and Marital Role Definitions of Husbands of Working and Nonworking Wives." *Marriage and Family Living* 25, no. 2 (May 1963): 189–95.

Balme, Christopher B. "Selling the Bird: Richard Walton Tully's *The Bird of Paradise* and the Dynamics of Theatrical Commodification." *Theatre Journal* 57, no. 1 (March 2005): 1–20.

Barlett, Donald L., and James B. Steele. *America: What Went Wrong?* Kansas City: Andrews and McMeel, 1992.

Barson, Michael. *Better Dead than Red: A Nostalgic Look at the Golden Years of Russiaphobia, Red-Baiting, and Other Commie Madness.* London: Plexus Books, 1992.

Basinger, Jeanine. "The World War II Combat Film: Definition." In *The War Film*, edited by Robert Eberwein, 30–52. New Brunswick, NJ: Rutgers University Press, 2005.

Bazin, André. "The Evolution of the Western." In *What Is Cinema?* Vol. 2, translated by Hugh Gray, 149–57. Berkeley: University of California Press, 1971.

Bean, Robin. Review of *Lovers Must Learn*. *Films and Filming* 8, no. 10 (July 1962): 37.

Bean, Robin. Review of *Parrish*. *Films and Filming* 7, no. 12 (September 1961): 30.

Bean, Robin. Review of *Spencer's Mountain*. *Films and Filming* 9, no. 11 (August 1963): 24–25.

Beaudine, William, dir. *How Baxter Butted In*. Warner Bros., 1925.

Bell, Robert R. *Premarital Sex in a Changing Society*. Englewood Cliffs, NJ: Prentice Hall, 1966.

Bell, Robert R., and Jack V. Buerkle. "Mother and Daughter Attitudes to Premarital Sexual Behavior." *Marriage and Family Living* 23, no. 4 (November 1961): 390–92.

Bell, Robert R., and Jay B. Chaskes. "Premarital Sexual Experience, 1958 and 1968." *Journal of Marriage and Family* 32, no. 1 (February 1970): 81–84.

Belton, John. *American Cinema/American Culture*. 2nd ed. New York: McGraw-Hill, 2005.

Benshoff, Harry M., and Sean Griffin. *America on Film: Representing Race, Class, Gender and Sexuality at the Movies*. Chichester, W. Susx., England: Wiley-Blackwell, 2004.

Beresford, Bruce. "John Ford: Decline of a Master." *Film* 56 (Autumn 1969): 4–7.

Berns, Fernando G. "Changing Societies: *The Red House, The Hanging Tree, Spencer's Mountain*, and Post-War America." In *ReFocus: The Films of Delmer Daves*, edited by Matthew Carter and Andrew Nelson, 166–83. Edinburgh: Edinburgh University Press, 2016.

Bessie, Alvah. *Inquisition in Eden*. Berlin: Seven Seas Books, 1967. (First published, New York: Macmillan, 1965.)

Bindas, Kenneth J. "Neon in the Desert: Robert Sherwood's *The Petrified Forest* (1936) and the Return of Hope." *Journal of Popular Film and Television* 27, no. 1 (Spring 1999): 21–31.

Blood, Robert O., Jr. "Romance and Premarital Intercourse: Incompatibles?" *Marriage and Family Living* 14, no. 2 (May 1952): 105–8.

Bodnar, John. *Blue-Collar Hollywood: Liberalism, Democracy, and Working People in American Film*. Baltimore: Johns Hopkins University Press, 2003.

Bogdanovich, Peter. *Picture Shows: Peter Bogdanovich on the Movies*. London: George Allen and Unwin, 1975.

Boggs, Carl, and Tom Pollard. "Postmodern Cinema and the Demise of the Family." *Journal of American Culture* 26, no. 4 (December 2003): 445–63.

Bourget, Jean-Loup. "Social Implications in the Hollywood Genres." In *Film Genre Reader II*, edited by Barry Keith Grant, 50–58. Austin: University of Texas Press, 1995.

Bowlby, John. *Maternal Care and Mental Health*. 2nd ed. Geneva: World Health Organization, 1952.

Breines, Wini. *Young, White, and Miserable: Growing Up Female in the Fifties*. Boston: Beacon Press, 1992.

Brown, Carol A., Roslyn Feldberg, Elizabeth M. Fox, and Janet Kohen. "Divorce: Chance of a New Lifetime." *Journal of Social Issues* 32, no. 1 (Winter 1976): 119–33.

Brown, Dee. *Bury My Heart at Wounded Knee: An Indian History of the American West*. London: Arena, 1987. (First published, New York: Holt, Rinehart and Winston, 1970.)

Brown, Joe David. *Kings Go Forth*. London: Pan Books, 1958.

Brownlow, Kevin. *The War, the West, and the Wilderness*. London: Secker and Warburg, 1972.

Buchanan, Keith. "The Geography of Empire, part 3: The Economic Pattern of Empire." *Spokesman*, no. 20 (December 1971–January 1972): 49–59.

Burnett, Charles. "Anger Management." *Sight and Sound* 21, no. 4 (April 2011): 11.

Burnham, James. *Struggle for the World*. New York: John Day, 1947.

Buscombe, Edward. *100 Westerns*. London: British Film Institute, 2006.

Buscombe, Edward. *"Injuns!" Native Americans in the Movies*. London: Reaktion Books, 2006.

Butterfield, Roger. *Al Schmid, Marine*. New York: W. W. Norton, 1944.

Cameron, Ian. "Films, Directors and Critics." *Movie* 2 (September 1962): 4–7.

Carr, Edward Hallet. *What Is History?* London: Macmillan, 1961.

Carruthers, Susan L. "Between Camps: Eastern Bloc 'Escapees' and Cold War Borderlands." *American Quarterly* 57, no. 3 (September 2005): 911–42.

Carter, Matthew. "'This Is Where He Brought Me: 10,000 Acres of Nothing!' The Femme Fatale and Other Film Noir Tropes in Delmer Daves' *Jubal*." In *ReFocus: The Films of Delmer Daves*, edited by Matthew Carter and Andrew Nelson, 199–221. Edinburgh: Edinburgh University Press, 2016.

Carter, Matthew, and Andrew Nelson. "Introduction: No One Would Know It Was Mine; Delmer Daves, Modest Auteur." In *ReFocus: The Films of Delmer Daves*, edited by Matthew Carter and Andrew Nelson, 1–47. Edinburgh: Edinburgh University Press, 2016.

Carter, Matthew, and Andrew Nelson, eds. *ReFocus: The Films of Delmer Daves*. Edinburgh: Edinburgh University Press, 2016.

Carter, Paul A. *Another Part of the Fifties*. New York: Columbia University Press, 1983.

Cawelti, John G. *The Six-Gun Mystique*. Bowling Green, OH: Bowling Green State University Popular Press, 1975.

Ceplair, Larry, and Steven Englund. *The Inquisition in Hollywood: Politics in the Film Community, 1930–1960*. New York: Anchor/Doubleday, 1980.

Chafe, William H. *The Unfinished Journey: America since World War II*. 3rd ed. New York: Oxford University Press, 1995.

Chauvin, Serge. "Le Lien et le passage: Delmer Daves westernien." In *Delmer Daves: La Morale des pionniers*, edited by Jean-Pierre Garcia and Dominique Païni, 31–42. Amiens: Éditions Vol de Nuit, 1999.

Chissell, Noble K. "Indian Actors Workshop: Great Oaks from Little Acorns Grow." *Indians Illustrated* 1, no. 5 (June 1968): 6–8.

Christensen, Terry, and Peter J. Haas. *Projecting Politics: Political Messages in American Films*. Armonk, NY: M. E. Sharpe, 2005.

Christian Century. Review of *Broken Arrow*. September 13, 1950, 1087.

Clarke, Jane, and Diana Simmonds. "Introduction: A Chorus of Derision." In *Move Over Misconceptions: Doris Day Reappraised*, edited by Jane Clarke and Diana Simmonds, 1–5. London: British Film Institute, 1980.

Cobos, Juan. "Una conversación con Delmer Daves." *Film Ideal* 106 (October 1962): 612–17.

Cohan, Steven. *Masked Men: Masculinity and the Movies in the Fifties*. Bloomington: Indiana University Press, 1997.

Cohen, Karl F. *Forbidden Animation: Censored Cartoons and Blacklisted Animators in America*. Jefferson, NC: McFarland, 1997.

Corkin, Stanley. *Cowboys as Cold Warriors: The Western and U.S. History*. Philadelphia: Temple University Press, 2004.

Corliss, Richard. "Screenwriters Symposium." *Film Comment* 6, no. 4 (Winter 1970–1971): 86–100.

Costigliola, Frank. "'Unceasing Pressure for Penetration': Gender, Pathology, and Emotion in George Kennan's Formulation of the Cold War." *Journal of American History* 83, no. 4 (March 1997): 1309–39.

Coursodon, Jean-Pierre. "Delmer Daves." In *American Directors*, vol. 1, edited by Jean-Pierre Coursodon with Pierre Sauvage, 81–88. New York: McGraw Hill, 1983.

Coyne, Michael. *The Crowded Prairie: American National Identity in the Hollywood Western*. London: I. B. Tauris, 1998.

Crist, Judith. *The Private Eye, the Cowboy and the Very Naked Girl*. New York: Holt, Rinehart and Winston, 1968.

Crowther, Bosley. Review of *3:10 to Yuma*. *New York Times*, April 29, 1957, 22.

Crowther, Bosley. Review of *Broken Arrow*. *New York Times*, July 21, 1950, 15.

Crowther, Bosley. Review of *Dark Passage*. *New York Times*, September 6, 1947, 11.

Crowther, Bosley. Review of *Pride of the Marines*. *New York Times*, August 25, 1945, 7.
Crowther, Bosley. Review of *Return of the Texan*. *New York Times*, February 14, 1952, 23.
Crowther, Bosley. Review of *Rome Adventure*. *New York Times*, March 16, 1962, 25.
Crowther, Bosley. Review of *Task Force*. *New York Times*, October 1, 1949, 8.
Crowther, Bosley. Review of *To the Victor*. *New York Times*, April 17, 1948, 11.
Cuordileone, K. A. "'Politics in an Age of Anxiety': Cold War Political Culture and the Crisis in American Masculinity, 1949–1960." *Journal of American History* 87, no. 2 (September 2000): 515–45.
Danks, Adrian. "This Room Is My Castle of Quiet: The Collaboration of Delmer Daves and Glenn Ford." In *ReFocus: The Films of Delmer Daves*, edited by Matthew Carter and Andrew Nelson, 102–17. Edinburgh: Edinburgh University Press, 2016.
Daves, Delmer. "Closing the Gap." *Action* 5, no. 2 (January–February 1970): 25–26.
Daves, Delmer. Delmer Daves Papers. M0192. Department of Special Collections, Stanford University Libraries, Stanford, California.
Daves, Delmer. "John Garfield." *Positif*, no. 120 (October 1970): 1–3.
Daves, Delmer. "Nimbus beyond the Footlights." In *Stanford Mosaic: Reminiscences of the First Seventy Years at Stanford University*, edited by Edith R. Mirrielees, 128–33. Stanford, CA: Stanford University Press, 1962.
Daves, Delmer. *Reminiscences of Delmer Lawrence Daves*, transcript of a tape recording. Oral History Program at Columbia University, New York, Series 3, vol. 7, no. 322 (June 1959).
Daves, Delmer. "Responses d'amérique." *Cahiers du Cinéma*, nos. 150–151 (December 1963–January 1964): 38–41.
Daves, Delmer, et al. "Can Screen Writers Become Film Authors?" *Screen Writer* 3, no. 1 (June 1947): 34–38.
Daves, Michael. Radio conversation with John Mulholland. *Icons Radio Hour*, July 29, 2007.
Davis, Bette, with Michael Herskowitz. *This 'n That: A Memoir*. London: Sidgwick and Jackson, 1987.
Davis, John. "Notes on Warner Brothers Foreign Policy, 1918–1948." *Velvet Light Trap* 4 (Spring 1972): 23–33.
Dean, Robert D. "Masculinity as Ideology: John Kennedy and the Domestic Politics of Foreign Policy." *Diplomatic History* 22, no. 1 (Winter 1998): 29–62.
Deloria, Philip J. *Playing Indian*. New Haven, CT: Yale University Press, 1998.
Deloria, Vine, Jr. *Custer Died for Your Sins: An Indian Manifesto*. Norman: University of Oklahoma Press, 1989. (First published, New York: Macmillan, 1969.)
Deloria, Vine, Jr. "Stereotyping: The Movie Indian and the Movie Jew." In *The Black Man on Film: Racial Stereotyping*, edited by Richard A. Maynard, 106–13. Rochelle Park, NJ: Hayden Book Company, 1974.
Dick, Bernard F. *Anatomy of Film*. New York: St. Martin's Press, 1978.
Dick, Bernard F. Review of *ReFocus: The Films of Delmer Daves*, edited by Matthew Carter and Andrew Nelson. *Film and History* 48, no. 1 (Summer 2018): 70–71.
Dick, Bernard F. *The Star-Spangled Screen: The American World War II Film*. Lexington: University Press of Kentucky, 1985.
Dickens, Homer. *The Films of Gary Cooper*. New York: Citadel, 1970.

Dixon, Wheeler Winston. *The Early Film Criticism of François Truffaut*. Bloomington: Indiana University Press, 1993.

Doherty, Thomas. *Projections of War: Hollywood, American Culture, and World War II*. New York: Columbia University Press, 1993.

Donelan, Carol. "'Too Marvelous for Words': Bogart and Bacall's *Dark Passage* through Myth to the Enlightenment of Modernized Melodrama." *Film Criticism* 42, no. 1 (March 2018): 1–31.

Duning, George. "*3:10 to Yuma*." In *Film Music: From Violins to Video*, edited by James L. Limbacher, 111–12. Metuchen, NJ: Scarecrow Press, 1976.

Durgnat, Raymond. "This Damned Eternal Triangle: Films, Theatre, Literature Are Just Not Meant to Mix." *Films and Filming* 11, no. 3 (December 1964): 14–18.

Eberwein, Robert. *The Hollywood War Film*. Chichester, W. Susx., England: Wiley-Blackwell, 2010.

Effel, Jean. "Delmer Daves." *Cinéma* 92 (January 1965): 44–46.

Ellis, Albert. "In Defense of *The American Sexual Tragedy*." *Journal of Marriage and Family* 27, no. 1 (February 1965): 113–15.

Esther, John. "Avoiding Labels and Lullabies: An Interview with James Mangold." *Cinéaste* 33, no. 1 (Winter 2007): 28–30.

Evans, M. Stanton. *Blacklisted by History: The Untold Story of Senator Joe McCarthy and His Fight against America's Enemies*. New York: Three Rivers Press, 2007.

Eyles, Allen. Review of *Youngblood Hawke*. *Films and Filming* 11, no. 2 (November 1964): 29–30.

Eyles, Allen. "Suzanne Pleshette: Filmography." *Focus on Film*, no. 3 (May–August 1970): 57–58.

Films and Filming. Review of *Drum Beat*. Vol. 1, no. 6 (March 1955): 22.

Finstad, Suzanne. *Warren Beatty: A Private Man*. London, Aurum Press, 2005.

Fishbein, Leslie. "*The Snake Pit* (1948): The Sexist Nature of Sanity." In *Hollywood as Historian: American Film in a Cultural Context*, edited by Peter C. Rollins, 134–58. Rev. ed. Lexington: University Press of Kentucky, 1998.

Fonda, Henry, and Howard Teichmann. *Fonda: My Life as Told to Howard Teichmann*. London: Book Club Associates, 1982.

Forbes, Bryan. *A Divided Life*. London: Heinemann, 1992.

Ford, Peter. *Glenn Ford: A Life*. Madison: University of Wisconsin Press, 2011.

Freeman, Edward A. *Some Impressions of the United States*. London: Longmans, Green, and Company, 1883.

French, Philip. Review of *Little Big Man*. *Sight and Sound* 40, no. 2 (Spring 1971): 102–3.

French, Philip. *Westerns: Aspects of a Movie Genre and Westerns Revisited*. Manchester: Carcanet Press, 2005.

Friar, Ralph E., and Natasha A. Friar. "White Man Speak with Split Tongue." In *The Pretend Indians: Images of Native Americans in the Movies*, edited by Gretchen M. Bataille and Charles L. P. Silet, 92–97. Ames: Iowa State University Press, 1980.

Friedan, Betty. *The Feminine Mystique*. London: Penguin, 1965. (First published, New York: W. W. Norton, 1963.)

Garcia, Jean-Pierre, and Dominique Païni, eds. *Delmer Daves: La Morale des pionniers*. Amiens: Éditions Vol de Nuit, 1999.

Gardner, Joel. Interview with Albert Maltz, August 5, 1976. Text Encoding Initiative, University of California, Los Angeles.

Gerber, David A. "In Search of Al Schmid: War Hero, Blinded Veteran, Everyman." *Journal of American Studies* 29, no. 1 (April 1995): 1–32.
Gilbert, Eugene. "Why Today's Teenagers Seem So Different." *Harper's Magazine*, November 1959, 76–79.
Glick, Paul C. *American Families: A Demographic Analysis of Census Data on American Families at Mid-Century*. New York: John Wiley and Sons, 1957.
Glitre, Kathrina. *Hollywood Romantic Comedy: States of the Union, 1934–1965*. Manchester: Manchester University Press, 2006.
Gough-Yates, Kevin. "The Hero: Part Two." *Films and Filming* 12, no. 4 (January 1966): 11–16.
Gough-Yates, Kevin. "The Heroine: Part One." *Films and Filming* 12, no. 8 (May 1966): 23–27.
Gough-Yates, Kevin. "The Heroine: Part Two." *Films and Filming* 12, no. 9 (June 1966): 27–32.
Gough-Yates, Kevin. "The Heroine: Part Three." *Films and Filming* 12, no. 10 (July 1966): 39–43.
Griffin-Pierce, Trudy. *Chiricahua Apache Enduring Power: Naiche's Puberty Ceremony Paintings*. Tuscaloosa: University of Alabama Press, 2006.
Griswold, Robert L. *Fatherhood in America: A History*. New York: Basic Books, 1993.
Guest, Haden. "Festival Report: Cinema Ritrovato 2010." *Cinema Journal* 50, no. 3 (Spring 2011): 97–101.
Guglielmo, Thomas A. "Fighting for Caucasian Rights: Mexicans, Mexican Americans, and the Transnational Struggle for Civil Rights in World War II Texas." *Journal of American History* 92, no. 4 (March 2006): 1212–37.
Gustafsson, Fredrik. "Delmer Daves Writes a Letter." Fredrik on Film, September 29, 2013. http://fredrikonfilm.blogspot.co.uk/2013/09/.
Hacker, Helen M. "The New Burdens of Masculinity." *Marriage and Family Living* 19, no. 3 (August 1957): 227–33.
Haley, James L. *Apaches: A History and Culture Portrait*. Garden City, NY: Doubleday, 1981.
Halliwell, Martin. "'No Place to Go, See': Blindness and World War II Demobilization Narratives." *Journal of Literary and Cultural Disability Studies* 3, no. 2 (2009): 163–82.
Handzo, Stephen. "Through the Devil's Doorway: The Early Westerns of Anthony Mann." *Bright Lights* 1, no. 4 (Summer 1976): 4–15.
Hardwicke, Cedric. *A Victorian in Orbit: The Irreverent Memoirs of Sir Cedric Hardwicke*. Gateshead, Tyne and Wear, England: Northumberland Press, 1961.
Harman, Jympson. "It's Time the Censor Changed His Ideas." *Evening News* (London), January 7, 1960, 4.
Hartmann, Susan M. "Women's Employment and the Domestic Ideal." In *Not June Cleaver: Women and Gender in Postwar America, 1945–1960*, edited by Joanne Meyerowitz, 84–100. Philadelphia: Temple University Press, 1994.
Haskell, Molly. *Holding My Own in No Man's Land: Women and Men and Film and Feminists*. Oxford, Oxford University Press, 1997.
Hatch, Robert. Review of *Broken Arrow*. *New Republic*, July 31, 1950, 23.
Hearne, Joanna. "The 'Ache for Home': Assimilation and Separatism in Anthony Mann's *Devil's Doorway*." In *Hollywood's West: The American Frontier in Film, Television, and History*, edited by Peter C. Rollins and John E. O'Connor, 126–59. Lexington: University Press of Kentucky, 2005.
Hennebelle, Guy. "Si c'était a refaire." *Cinéma* 101 (December 1965): 36–37.

Herzberg, Bob. *Savages and Saints: The Changing Image of American Indians in Westerns.* Jefferson, NC: McFarland, 2008.

Higham, John. *Writing American History: Essays on Modern Scholarship.* Bloomington: Indiana University Press, 1972.

Hollywood Reporter. Review of *Broken Arrow.* Vol. 109, no. 24 (June 12, 1950): 3–4.

Hollywood Reporter. Review of *The Very Thought of You.* Vol. 80, no. 32 (October 16, 1944): 3.

Howard, Oliver Otis. *Famous Indian Chiefs I Have Known.* New York: Century Company, 1908.

Howe, Andrew. "Partial Rehabilitation: *Task Force* and the Case of Billy Mitchell." In *ReFocus: The Films of Delmer Daves,* edited by Matthew Carter and Andrew Nelson, 184–98. Edinburgh: Edinburgh University Press, 2016.

Hurd, Charles. *The Veteran's Program: A Complete Guide to Its Benefits, Rights and Options.* New York: McGraw Hill, 1946.

Hurewitz, Daniel. *Bohemian Los Angeles and the Making of Modern Politics.* Berkeley: University of California Press, 2007.

Huss, Roger. "Critics' Choice." *Cinema* (UK), no. 4 (October 1969): 2–5.

Indick, William. *The Psychology of the Western: How the American Psyche Plays Out on Screen.* Jefferson, NC: McFarland, 2008.

Irvine, Janice M. *Talk about Sex: The Battles over Sex Education in the United States.* Berkeley: University of California Press, 2002.

Jacobson, Herbert L. "Cowboy, Pioneer, and American Soldier." *Sight and Sound* 22, no. 4 (April–June 1953): 189–90.

James, Nick, ed. "The Greatest Films of All Time." *Sight and Sound* 22, no. 9 (September 2012): 40–71.

Jaskulski, Józef. "Bent, or Lifted Out by Its Roots: Daves' *Broken Arrow* and *Drum Beat* as Narratives of Conditional Sympathy." In *ReFocus: The Films of Delmer Daves,* edited by Matthew Carter and Andrew Nelson, 80–101. Edinburgh: Edinburgh University Press, 2016.

Jentleson, Bruce W. *American Foreign Policy: The Dynamics of Choice in the 21st Century.* 2nd ed. New York: W. W. Norton, 2004.

Johnson, William. "Coming to Terms with Color." *Film Quarterly* 20, no. 1 (Fall 1966): 2–22.

Jones, Dorothy B. "Communism and the Movies: A Study of Film Content." In *Report on Blacklisting: 1, Movies,* edited by John Cogley, 196–233. New York: *New York Times* and Arno Press, 1972. (First published, New York: Fund for the Republic, 1956.)

Joyner, C. Courtney. *The Westerners: Interviews with Actors, Directors, Writers and Producers.* Jefferson, NC: McFarland, 2009.

Kael, Pauline. *I Lost It at the Movies.* Boston: Little, Brown, 1965.

Keller, Alexandra. "Historical Discourse and American Identity in Westerns since the Reagan Administration." *Film and History* 33, no. 1 (2003): 47–54.

Kennan, George F. *Memoirs, 1925–1950.* Boston: Little, Brown, 1967.

Kirkendall, Lester A. "Values and Premarital Intercourse: Implications for Parent Education." *Marriage and Family Living* 22, no. 4 (November 1960): 317–24.

Kirshner, Jonathan. *Hollywood's Last Golden Age: Politics, Society, and the Seventies Film in America.* Ithaca, NY: Cornell University Press, 2012.

Kitses, Jim. *Horizons West: Directing the Western from John Ford to Clint Eastwood.* London: British Film Institute, 2004.

Koestler, Frances A. *The Unseen Minority: A Social History of Blindness in the United States*. New York: David McKay, 1976.

Koppes, Clayton R. "From New Deal to Termination: Liberalism and Indian Policy, 1933–1953." *Pacific Historical Review* 46, no. 4 (November 1977): 543–66.

Kovacs, Yves. "Mythologie du Western." *Études Cinématographiques* 2, nos. 12–13 (Winter 1961): 243–50.

Kreck, Joachim. *Delmer Daves*. Oberhausen, Germany: Will Wehling, 1972.

Krutnik, Frank, Steve Neale, Brian Neve, and Peter Stanfield, eds. *"Un-American" Hollywood: Politics and Film in the Blacklist Era*. New Brunswick, NJ: Rutgers University Press, 2007.

Kyne, Peter B. *The Go-Getter: A Story That Tells You How to Be One*. New York: Cosimo Classics, 2011. (First published, New York: Cosmopolitan Book Corporation, 1921).

Lambert, Gavin. "Female Grotesques." *Films and Filming* 21, no. 10 (July 1975): 6–7.

Lamster, Frederick. *Souls Made Great through Love and Adversity: The Film Work of Frank Borzage*. Metuchen, NJ: Scarecrow Press, 1981.

Landis, Judson T. "The Trauma of Children When Parents Divorce." *Marriage and Family Living* 22, no. 1 (February 1960): 7–13.

Lane, John F. "Moments of Truth: Interview with Francesco Rosi." *Films and Filming* 16, no. 12 (September 1970): 6–10.

Leab, Daniel J. *From Sambo to Superspade: The Black Experience in Motion Pictures*. Boston: Houghton Mifflin, 1976.

Lejeune, Caroline. Review of *Broken Arrow*. *Observer*, August 27, 1950, 6.

Lenihan, John H. *Showdown: Confronting Modern America in the Western Film*. Urbana: University of Illinois Press, 1985.

Leonard, Elmore. "Three-Ten to Yuma." In *The Killers*, edited by Peter Dawson, 112–28. 2nd ed. New York: Bantam Books, 1974.

Leuthold, Steven M. "Native American Responses to the Western." *American Indian Culture and Research Journal* 19, no. 1 (1995): 153–89.

Levinger, George. "A Social Psychological Perspective on Marital Dissolution." *Journal of Social Issues* 32, no. 1 (Winter 1976): 21–47.

Levinger, George. "Sources of Marital Dissatisfaction among Applicants for Divorce." *American Journal of Orthopsychiatry* 36, no. 5 (1966): 803–7.

Levitin, Jacqueline. "The Western: Any Good Roles for Women?" In *Feminist Film Criticism: Film and Cultural Studies*, Film Reader, vol. 5, edited by Jae Alexander and Lolita Raclin Rodgers, 95–108. Evanston, IL: Northwestern University Press, 1982.

Lewis, R. W. B. *The American Adam: Innocence, Tragedy, and Tradition in the Nineteenth Century*. Chicago: University of Chicago Press, 1966. (First published, 1955).

Limerick, Patricia Nelson. *The Legacy of Conquest: The Unbroken Past of the American West*. New York: W. W. Norton, 1988.

Link, Arthur S., and Richard L. McCormick. *Progressivism*. Wheeling, IL: Harlan Davidson, 1983.

Lomawaima, K. Tsianina. "Hm! White Boy! You Got No Business Here!" In *American Indians*, edited by Nancy Shoemaker, 208–35. Malden, MA: Blackwell, 2001.

Lord, Graham. *Niv: The Authorised Biography of David Niven*. London: Orion, 2003.

Lucas, Blake. "Saloon Girls and the Ranchers' Daughters: The Women in the Western." In *The Western Reader*, edited by Jim Kitses and Gregg Rickman, 301–20. New York: Limelight Editions, 1998.

Lundberg, Ferdinand, and Marynia F. Farnham. *Modern Woman: The Lost Sex*. New York: Harper and Brothers, 1947.

Lurvey, Ira, and Selise E. Eiseman. "Divorce Goes to the Movies." *University of San Francisco Law Review* 30, no. 4 (1996): 1209–18.

Lyndon, Louis. "Uncertain Hero: The Paradox of the American Male." *Women's Home Journal*, November 1956, 41–43, 107.

MacCurdy, Carol A. "Masculinity in *3:10 to Yuma*." *Quarterly Review of Film and Video* 26, no. 4 (August 2009): 280–92.

Maltz, Albert. Albert Maltz Papers, 1910–1985. Collection 02675. American Heritage Center, University of Wyoming, Laramie, Wyoming.

Maltz, Albert. "What Shall We Ask of Writers?" *New Masses*, February 12, 1946, 19–22.

Manchel, Frank. "Cultural Confusion: A Look Back at Delmer Daves's *Broken Arrow*." *Film and History* 23, nos. 1–4 (1993): 58–69.

Mantell, Howard. "Counteracting the Stereotype." *American Indian* 5, no. 4 (Fall 1950): 16–20.

Marubbio, M. Elise. *Killing the Indian Maiden: Images of Native American Women in Film*. Lexington: University Press of Kentucky, 2006.

May, Lary. *The Big Tomorrow: Hollywood and the Politics of the American Way*. Chicago: University of Chicago Press, 2000.

Mayers, David. *George Kennan and the Dilemmas of US Foreign Policy*. New York: Oxford University Press, 1988.

McBride, Joseph. *Hawks on Hawks*. Berkeley: University of California Press, 1982.

McCormick, Thomas J. *America's Half Century: United States Foreign Policy in the Cold War*. Baltimore: Johns Hopkins University Press, 1989.

McNally, Karen. *When Frankie Went to Hollywood: Frank Sinatra and American Male Identity*. Urbana: University of Illinois Press, 2008.

McNeill, Joe. *Arizona's Little Hollywood: Sedona and Northern Arizona's Forgotten Film History, 1923–1973*. Sedona, AZ: Northedge and Sons, 2010.

McVay Douglas. "The Five Worlds of John Ford." *Films and Filming* 8, no. 9 (June 1962): 14–17.

Mead, Margaret. *And Keep Your Powder Dry*. New York: Morrow Quill, 1965.

Mellen, Joan. *Big Bad Wolves: Masculinity in the American Film*. London: Elm Tree Books, 1978.

Metz, Walter C. "'Have You Written a Ford, Lately?' Gender, Genre, and the Film Adaptations of Dorothy Johnson's Western Literature." *Literature/Film Quarterly* 31, no. 3 (Summer 2003): 209–20.

Meuel, David. *Women in the Films of John Ford*. Jefferson, NC: McFarland, 2014.

Mexal, Stephen J. "Two Ways to Yuma: Locke, Liberalism, and Western Masculinity in *3:10 to Yuma*." In *The Philosophy of the Western*, edited by Jennifer L. McMahon and B. Steve Csaki, 69–87. Lexington: University Press of Kentucky, 2010.

Meyer, William R. *Warner Brothers Directors: The Hard-Boiled, the Comic, and the Weepies*. New Rochelle, NY: Arlington House, 1978.

Michel, Sonya. "American Women and the Discourse of the Democratic Family in World War II." In *Behind the Lines: Gender and the Two World Wars*, edited by Margaret Randolph

Higonnet, Jane Jenson, Sonya Michel, and Margaret Collins Weitz, 154–67. New Haven, CT: Yale University Press, 1987.
Military Intelligence Service. *Soldier's Guide to the Japanese Army*. Special Series no. 27. US Department of War, November 15, 1944.
Miller, Don. "New Words on Old Westerns." *Focus on Film*, no. 11 (Autumn 1972): 27–37.
Milne, Tom. Review of *Youngblood Hawke*. *Monthly Film Bulletin* 31, no. 371 (November 1964): 162.
Mitchell, Jonathan. *Revisions of the American Adam: Innocence, Identity and Masculinity in Twentieth-Century America*. London: Bloomsbury, 2011.
Monthly Film Bulletin. Review of *The Battle of the Villa Fiorita*. Vol. 32, no. 380 (November 1965): 130–31.
Monthly Film Bulletin. Review of *Dark Passage*. Vol. 15, no. 171 (March 1948): 32.
Monthly Film Bulletin. Review of *Drum Beat*. Vol. 22, no. 253 (February 1955): 19.
Monthly Film Bulletin. Review of *Jubal*. Vol. 23, no. 268 (May 1956): 61.
Monthly Film Bulletin. Review of *A Kiss in the Dark*. Vol. 17, no. 195 (March–April 1950): 49.
Monthly Film Bulletin. Review of *Lovers Must Learn*. Vol. 29, no. 341 (June 1962): 82.
Monthly Film Bulletin. Review of *Never Let Me Go*. Vol. 20, no. 232 (May 1953): 73–74.
Monthly Film Bulletin. Review of *Parrish*. Vol. 28, no. 330 (July 1961): 93–94.
Monthly Film Bulletin. Review of *Spencer's Mountain*. Vol. 30, no. 348 (January 1963): 121.
Monthly Film Bulletin. Review of *A Summer Place*. Vol. 27, no. 313 (February 1960): 22.
Monthly Film Bulletin. Review of *The Thrill of It All*. Vol. 30, no. 358 (November 1963): 161–62.
Monthly Film Bulletin. Review of *To the Victor*. Vol. 15, no. 178 (October 1948): 143.
More, Kenneth. *More or Less*. London: Hodder and Stoughton, 1978.
Morella, Joe, Edward Z. Epstein, and John Griggs. *The Films of World War II*. Secaucus, NJ: Citadel Press, 1973.
Morris, George. *John Garfield*. New York: Jove, 1977.
Morrison, Toni. *Playing in the Dark: Whiteness and the Literary Imagination*. London: Picador, 1993.
Mort, Terry. *The Wrath of Cochise*. London: Constable, 2014.
Moullet, Luc. "Sam Fuller: Sur les brisées de Marlowe." *Cahiers du Cinéma*, no. 93 (March 1959): 11–19.
Mowry, George E. *The California Progressives*. Chicago, Quadrangle Books, 1963. (First published, Berkeley: University of California Press, 1951.)
Mulvey, Laura. "Visual Pleasure and Narrative Cinema." *Screen* 16, no. 3 (Autumn 1973): 6–18.
Murdoch, David H. *The American West: The Invention of a Myth*. Cardiff: Welsh Academic Press, 2001.
Murray, David. *Modern Indians: Native Americans in the Twentieth Century*. Durham, England: British Association for American Studies, 1982.
Nacache, Jacqueline. "Au long des passages obscurs: sur *Dark Passage*, 1947." In *Delmer Daves: La Morale des pionniers*, edited by Jean-Pierre Garcia and Dominique Païni, 63–77. Amiens: Éditions Vol de Nuit, 1999.
Nash, Gerald D. *Creating the West: Historical Interpretations, 1890–1990*. Albuquerque: University of New Mexico Press, 1991.

Nelson, Andrew. "Don't Be Too Quick to Dismiss Them: Authorship and the Westerns of Delmer Daves." In *ReFocus: The Films of Delmer Daves*, edited by Matthew Carter and Andrew Nelson, 48–62. Edinburgh: Edinburgh University Press, 2016.

New York Times. Review of *The Battle of the Villa Fiorita*. May 27, 1965, 27–28.

New York Times Film Reviews 1913–1968. New York: New York Times and Arno Press, 1970.

Nickel, John. "Disabling African American Men: Liberalism and Race Message Films." *Cinema Journal* 44, no. 1 (Fall 2004): 25–47.

Nisbet, Robert A. "The Coming Problem of Assimilation." *American Journal of Sociology* 50, no. 4 (January 1945): 261–70.

Nogueira, Rui. "Writing for the Movies: Wendell Mayes." *Focus on Film*, no. 7 (Summer 1971): 36–42.

Nolley, Ken. "The Representation of Conquest." In *Hollywood's Indian: The Portrayal of the Native American in Film*, edited by Peter C. Rollins and John E. O'Connor, 73–90. Lexington: University Press of Kentucky, 1998.

Norris, Frank. *The Octopus: A Story of California*. New York: Doubleday and Page, 1901.

Nott, Robert. *He Ran All the Way: The Life of John Garfield*. New York: Limelight Editions, 2003.

Nugent, Frank. Review of *Dames*. *New York Times*, August 16, 1934, 20.

Nugent, Frank. Review of *The Petrified Forest*. *New York Times*, February 7, 1936, 14.

Nugent, Frank. Review of *Shipmates Forever*. *New York Times*, October 17, 1935, 29.

Nugent, Frank. Review of *Stranded*. *New York Times*, June 20, 1935, 16.

Nye, Francis Ivan. "Child Adjustment in Broken and Unhappy Unbroken Homes." *Marriage and Family Living* 19, no. 4 (November 1957): 356–61.

Oakley, J. Ronald. *God's Country: America in the Fifties*. New York: Dembner Books, 1986.

O'Connor, John E. *The Hollywood Indian: Stereotypes of Native Americans in Films*. Trenton: New Jersey State Museum, 1980.

O'Connor, John E. "The White Man's Indian." *Film and History* 23, nos. 1–4 (1993): 17–26.

O'Hara, Maureen, with John Nicoletti. *'Tis Herself: An Autobiography*. New York: Simon and Schuster, 2005.

Olson, James S., and Raymond Wilson. *Native Americans in the Twentieth Century*. Urbana: University of Illinois Press, 1986.

Opler, Morris E. *An Apache Life-Way: The Economic, Social, and Religious Institutions of the Chiricahua Indians*. Chicago: University of Chicago Press, 1941.

Packard, Vance. *The Sexual Wilderness: The Contemporary Upheaval in Male-Female Relationships*. London: Pan Books, 1970.

Parkinson, David. "Subjects and Stories." In *The Graham Greene Film Reader: Mornings in the Dark*, edited by David Parkinson, 409–18. Manchester: Carcanet Press, 1993.

Parkman, Francis. *The Conspiracy of the Pontiac*. Vol. 1. 10th ed. rev. London: Macmillan, 1885.

Pearsall, Sarah. "Women from the Colonial Era to 1900." In *The Columbia Companion to American History on Film: How Movies Portrayed the American Past*, edited by Peter C. Rollins, 303–9. New York: Columbia University Press, 2003.

Peek, Wendy C. "The Romance of Competence: Rethinking Masculinity in the Western." *Journal of Popular Film and Television* 30, no. 4 (Winter 2003): 206–19.

Petch, Simon. "Return to Yuma." *Film Criticism* 32, no. 2 (Winter 2007–2008): 48–69.

Pettigrew, Terence. *The Bogart File*. London: Golden Eagle Press, 1977.

Pheasant-Kelly, Fran. "Delmer Daves' *3:10 to Yuma*: Aesthetics, Reception, and Cultural Significance." In *ReFocus: The Films of Delmer Daves*, edited by Matthew Carter and Andrew Nelson, 149–65. Edinburgh: Edinburgh University Press, 2016.

Philippe, Jean-Claude. "Delmer Daves Believes in Friendship." *Télérama*, March 29, 1964, 59–61.

Phillips, Roderick. *Putting Asunder: A History of Divorce in Western Society*. Cambridge: Cambridge University Press, 1988.

Philp, Kenneth R. "John Collier and the American Indian." In *The Walter Prescott Webb Memorial Lectures: Essays on Radicalism in Contemporary America*, edited by Leon B. Blair, 63–80. Austin: University of Texas Press, 1972.

Poffenberger, Thomas. "Individual Choice in Adolescent Premarital Sex Behavior." *Marriage and Family Living* 22, no. 4 (November 1960): 324–30.

Pomerance, Murray. "Movies and the Specter of Rebellion." In *American Cinema of the 1960s: Themes and Variations*, edited by Barry Keith Grant, 172–92. New Brunswick, NJ: Rutgers University Press, 2009.

Pomp, Joseph. "Home on the Range: *Spencer's Mountain* as Revisionist Family Melodrama." In *ReFocus: The Films of Delmer Daves*, edited by Matthew Carter and Andrew Nelson, 135–48. Edinburgh: Edinburgh University Press, 2016.

Potter, Nicole. "Tales of the Red Menace." *Films in Review* 47, nos. 5–6 (September–October 1996): 29–33.

Powdermaker, Hortense. *Hollywood, the Dream Factory: An Anthropologist Looks at the Movie-Makers*. London: Secker and Warburg, 1951.

Poyato, Pedro. "An Essay on Subjectivity in Hollywood: *Dark Passage* (Delmer Daves, 1947) and Its Assimilation of Avant-Garde Features." *L'Atalante* 27 (January–June 2019): 91–104.

Pratt, George K. *Soldier to Civilian: Problems of Readjustment*. New York: McGraw Hill, 1944.

Prebble, John. *My Great Aunt Appearing Day and Other Stories*. London: Secker and Warburg, 1958.

Price, John A. "The Stereotyping of North American Indians in Motion Pictures." *Ethnohistory* 20, no. 2 (Spring 1973): 153–71.

Prior, Thomas M. Review of *The Very Thought of You*. *New York Times*, November 8, 1944, 16.

Quinlan, David. *Quinlan's Film Directors: The Ultimate Guide to the Directors of the Big Screen*. 2nd ed. London: B. T. Batsford, 1999.

Quirk, Lawrence J. *Claudette Colbert: An Illustrated Biography*. New York: Crown, 1985.

Quirk, Lawrence J. *James Stewart: Behind the Scenes of a Wonderful Life*. New York: Applause Books, 1997.

Rabourdin, Dominique. "Delmer Daves ou le secret perdu." *Cinéma* 72, no. 226 (October 1977): 53.

Rasner, Heinz-Gerd, Reinhard Wulf, and Wolf-Eckhart Bühler. "Gespräche mit Delmer Daves." *Filmkritik* 19, no. 217 (January 1975): 1–43.

Reiss, Ira L. "The Double Standard in Premarital Sexual Intercourse: A Neglected Concept." *Social Forces* 34, no. 3 (March 1956): 224–330.

Reynertson, A. J. *The Work of the Film Director*. London: Focal Press, 1970.

Riesman, David. "Permissiveness and Sex Roles." *Marriage and the Family* 21, no. 3 (August 1959): 211–17.

Rieupeyrout, Jean-Louis. "Rencontre avec Delmer Daves." *Cinéma* 53 (February 1961): 10–20.

Roberts, Kenneth. *Northwest Passage*. London: Collins, 1938.

Roosevelt, Theodore. *Ranch Life and the Hunting Trail*. Memphis: General Books, 2012. (First published, New York: Century Company, 1888.)

Roosevelt, Theodore. *The Winning of the West*. Vol. 1, *From the Alleghanies to the Mississippi, 1769–1776*. New York: G. P. Putnam's Sons, 1889.

Rosen, Marjorie. "Popcorn Venus; or, How the Movies Have Made Women Smaller than Life." In *Sexual Stratagems: The World of Women in Film*, edited by Patricia Erens, 13–30. New York, Horizon Press, 1979.

Rosenberg, Emily S. "'Foreign Affairs' after World War II: Connecting Sexual and International Politics." *Diplomatic History* 18, no. 1 (Winter 1994): 59–70.

Rosenfelt, Deborah Silverton. "Commentary." In *Salt of the Earth*, by Michael Wilson, 93–168. New York: Feminist Press, 1978.

Ross, Steven J. *Working-Class Hollywood: Silent Film and the Shaping of Class in America*. Princeton, NJ: Princeton University Press, 1999.

Rotha, Paul. *The Film Till Now: A Survey of World Cinema*. 3rd ed. London: Vision Press, 1960.

Russell, Harold. *Victory in My Hands*. London: John Lehmann, 1950.

Ryan, Tom. *The Films of Douglas Sirk: Exquisite Ironies and Magnificent Obsessions*. Jackson: University Press of Mississippi, 2019.

Salt, Barry. *Film Style and Technology: History and Analysis*. 2nd ed. London: Starword, 1992.

Sarris, Andrew. *The American Cinema: Directors and Directions, 1929–1968*. New York: Dutton, 1968.

Sarris, Andrew. "Notes on the Auteur Theory in 1962." *Film Culture*, no. 27 (Winter 1962–1963): 1–8.

Savage, William, Jr. *The Cowboy Hero: His Image in American History and Culture*. Norman: University of Oklahoma Press, 1979.

Sbardellati, John. *J. Edgar Hoover Goes to the Movies: The FBI and the Origins of Hollywood's Cold War*. Ithaca, NY: Cornell University Press, 2012.

Schatz, Thomas. *The Genius of the System: Hollywood Film-Making in the Studio Era*. London: Faber and Faber, 1998.

Scheiner, Georganne. "Look at Me, I'm Sandra Dee: Beyond a White, Teen Icon." *Frontiers: A Journal of Women Studies* 22, no. 2 (2001): 87–106.

Schell, Maximilian, dir. *My Sister Maria*. Rainbow Release, 2002.

Schlesinger, Arthur, Jr. "The Crisis of American Masculinity." *Esquire* 50, no. 5 (November 1958): 63–65.

Schlesinger, Arthur, Jr. *The Politics of Hope and the Bitter Heritage*. Princeton, NJ: Princeton University Press, 2008. (*The Politics of Hope* first published, 1963; *The Bitter Heritage* first published, 1967.)

Schlesinger, Arthur, Jr. *The Vital Center: The Politics of Freedom*. New York: Da Capo Press, 1988. (First published, Boston: Houghton Mifflin, 1949.)

Schofield, Michael. *The Sexual Behaviour of Young People*. London: Allen Lane, 1973.

Schumach, Murray. *The Face on the Cutting Room Floor: The Story of Movie and Television Censorship*. New York: Da Capo Press, 1975. (First published, New York: William Morrow, 1964.)

Scorsese, Martin, and Michael H. Wilson. *A Personal Journey with Martin Scorsese through American Movies*. London: Faber and Faber, 1997.

Sennwald, Andre. Review of *Flirtation Walk*. *New York Times*, November 29, 1934, 33.

Shain, Russell E. "Hollywood's Cold War." *Journal of Popular Film and Television* 3, no. 4 (Fall 1974): 334–49.

Sherwood, Robert E. *The Petrified Forest*. New York: Charles Scribner's Sons, 1935.

Short, K. R. M. "Hollywood Fights Anti-Semitism, 1940–1945." In *Film and Radio Propaganda in World War II*, edited by K. R. M. Short, 146–72. London: Croom Helm, 1983.

Simpson, Paul. *The Rough Guide to Westerns*. London: Rough Guides, 2006.

Skard, Åse. "Maternal Deprivation: The Research and Its Implications." *Journal of Marriage and Family* 27, no. 3 (August 1965): 333–43.

Slotkin, Richard. *Gunfighter Nation: The Myth of the Frontier in the Twentieth Century*. Norman: University of Oklahoma Press, 1998.

Slotkin, Richard. *Regeneration through Violence: The Mythology of the American Frontier, 1600–1860*. New York: Harper Perennial. 1996.

Sobchack, Vivian C. "Round-Up in Sun Valley." *Journal of Popular Film* 5, no. 2 (1976): 157–65.

Solinger, Rickie. *Wake Up Little Susie: Single Pregnancy and Race before Roe v. Wade*. New York: Routledge, 1992.

Starr, Kevin. *Embattled Dreams: California in War and Peace, 1940–1950*. New York: Oxford University Press, 2002.

Stern, Michael. *Douglas Sirk*. Boston: Twayne Publishers, 1979.

Stevenson, Adlai E. *Call to Greatness*. London: Rupert Hart-Davis, 1954.

Stewart, Donald Ogden. *By a Stroke of Luck! An Autobiography*. New York: Paddington Press, 1975.

Stokes, Melvyn. *American History through Hollywood Film: From the Revolution to the 1960s*. London: Bloomsbury, 2013.

Stokes, Walter R. "Our Changing Sex Ethics." *Marriage and Family Living* 24, no. 3 (August 1962): 269–72.

Strick, Philip. Review of *Susan Slade*. *Films and Filming* 8, no. 7 (April 1962): 32–33.

Sweeney, Edwin R. *Cochise: Chiricahua Apache Chief*. Norman: University of Oklahoma Press, 1991.

Sweeney, Edwin R., ed. *Making Peace with Cochise: The 1872 Journal of Captain Joseph Alton Sladen*. Norman: University of Oklahoma Press, 1991.

Taft, Joseph. "Dialogues with a Director." *Persimmon Hill* 5, no. 2 (1975): 40–53.

Tavernier, Bertrand. "Chronique hollywoodienne: Extraits d'une correspondence avec Delmer Daves." In *Amis Américains: Entretiens avec les grands auteurs d'Hollywood*, by Bertrand Tavernier, 229–45. Lyon: Institut Lumière; Arles: Actes Sud, 1993.

Tavernier, Bertrand. "The Ethical Romantic." *Film Comment* 39, no. 1 (January–February 2003): 42–49.

Tavernier, Bertrand. "Extraits d'une correspondance avec Delmer Daves." *Positif* 50, no. 52 (March 1963): 117–23.

Tessier, Max. "*La Route des ténèbres*." *Cinéma* 159 (September–October 1971): 138–40.

Thompson, Howard. Review of *A Summer Place*. *New York Times*, October 23, 1959, 24.

Thompson, Howard. Review of *Treasure of the Golden Condor*. *New York Times*, May 23, 1953, 19.
Thomson, David. *"Have You Seen . . . ?" A Personal Introduction to 1,000 Films*. London: Allen Lane, 2008.
Thomson, David. *The New Biographical Dictionary of Film*. 5th ed. London: Little, Brown, 2010.
Time. Review of *Broken Arrow*. July 30, 1950, 38–39.
Time. Review of *A Summer Place*. November 9, 1959, 58.
Titus, Harold. "The Stuff of Heroes." *American Magazine*, August 1924.
Tollefson, Don. "Delmer Daves on Film: Past, Present, and Future." *Stanford Daily*, March 2, 1972, 6.
Treglia, Gabriella. "Using Citizenship to Retain Identity: The Native American Dance Bans of the Assimilation Era, 1900–1933." *Journal of American Studies* 47, no. 3 (2012): 777–800.
Truffaut, François. *Hitchcock*. London: Panther, 1969.
Tucker, Sherrie. *Dance Floor Democracy: The Social Geography of Memory at the Hollywood Canteen*. Durham, NC: Duke University Press, 2014.
Turner, Albert. Review of *Cowboy*. *Films in Review* 9, no. 3 (1958): 143.
Turner, Frederick Jackson. "The Significance of the Frontier in American History." *Proceedings of the State Historical Society of Wisconsin*, December 14, 1893.
Tuska, John. *The American West in Film: Critical Approaches to the Western*. Lincoln: University of Nebraska Press, 1985.
Utley, Robert M., and Wilcomb E. Washburn. *Indian Wars*. Boston: Houghton Mifflin, 1987.
Variety. "Arrow Ace Pic in Cleve." Vol. 179, no. 11 (August 23, 1950): 12.
Variety. "August's Top Twelve Winners." Vol. 179, no. 13 (September 6, 1950): 4.
Variety. "*Broken Arrow* Leading Philly." Vol. 179, no. 7 (July 26, 1950): 14–15.
Variety. Review of *3:10 to Yuma*. Vol. 207, no. 11 (August 14, 1957): 6.
Variety. Review of *Stranded*. Vol. 119, no. 2 (June 26, 1935): 23.
Wakeman, John, ed. *World Film Directors*. Vol. 1, *1980–1945*. New York: H. W. Wilson, 1987.
Walker, Michael. "The Westerns of Delmer Daves." In *The Movie Book of the Western*, edited by Ian Cameron and Douglas Pye, 123–60. London: Studio Vista, 1996.
Weatherford, Jack. *Indian Givers: How the Indians of the Americas Transformed the World*. New York: Fawcett Columbine, 1988.
Weigand, Kate. "The Red Menace, The Feminine Mystique, and the Ohio Un-American Activities Commission: Gender and Anti-Communism in Ohio, 1951–1954." *Journal of Women's History* 3, no. 3 (Winter 1992): 71–94.
Wetta, Frank J., and Martin A. Novelli. "On Telling the Truth about War: World War II and Hollywood's Moral Fiction, 1945–1956." In *Why We Fought: America's Wars in Film and History*, edited by Peter C. Rollins and John E. O'Connor, 259–82. Lexington: University Press of Kentucky, 2008.
White, John. "Trying to Ameliorate the System from Within: Delmer Daves' Westerns from the 1950s." In *ReFocus: The Films of Delmer Daves*, edited by Matthew Carter and Andrew Nelson, 63–79. Edinburgh: Edinburgh University Press, 2016.
Whitehall, Richard. "The Heroes Are Tired." *Film Quarterly* 20, no. 2 (Winter 1966–1967): 12–24.
Whitehall, Richard. "On the 3:10 to Yuma." *Films and Filming* 9, no. 7 (April 1963): 51–54.

Whitehall, Richard. "A Summer Place." *Films and Filming* 9, no. 8 (May 1963): 48–51.
Wicking, Christopher. "Interview with Delmer Daves." *Screen* 10, nos. 4–5 (October 1969): 55–66.
Wilder, Laura Ingalls. *Little House on the Prairie*. London: Egmont, 2000. (First published, New York: Harper and Brothers, 1935.)
Wilmshurst, Clare, dir. *Epic: A Cast of Thousands*. BBC, 2011.
Wilson, Sandra. "Film and Soldier: Japanese War Movies in the 1950s." *Journal of Contemporary History* 48, no. 3 (2013): 537–55.
Winkler, Martin M. "The Roman Empire in American Cinema after 1945." *Classical Journal* 93, no. 2 (December 1997–January 1998): 167–96.
Wollen, Peter. *Signs and Meaning in the Cinema*. London: British Film Institute, 1998. (First published, London: Secker and Warburg, 1972.)
Wood, Robin. "Ideology, Genre, Auteur." *Film Comment* 13, no. 1 (January–February 1997): 46–51.
Wootton, Adrian, and Paul Taylor, eds. *David Goodis/Pulps Pictured: For Goodis' Sake!* London: British Film Institute, 1989.
Worcester, Donald E. *The Apaches: Eagles of the Southwest*. Norman: University of Oklahoma Press, 1979.
Worland, Rick, and Edward Countryman. "The New Western American Historiography and the Emergence of the New American Westerns." In *Back in the Saddle Again: New Essays on the Western*, edited by Edward Buscombe and Roberta Pearson, 182–96. London: British Film Institute, 1998.
Wright, Judith H. "Genre Films and the Status Quo." In *Film Genre Reader II*, edited by Barry Keith Grant, 41–49. Austin: University of Texas Press, 1995.
Zavattini, Cesare. "Some Ideas on the Cinema." *Sight and Sound* 23, no. 2 (October–December 1953): 64–69.
Zeitz, Josh. "How FDR Invented the Four Freedoms." *Politico Magazine*, July 4, 2015. https://www.politico.com/magazine/story/2015/07/roosevelt-four-freedoms-119728.
Zheutlin, Barbara, and David Talbot. "Albert Maltz: Portrait of a Hollywood Dissident." *Cinéaste* 8, no. 3 (Winter 1977–1978): 2–15, 59.
Zieger, Gay P., and Robert H. Zieger. "Unions on the Silver Screen: A Review-Essay on *F.I.S.T.*, *Blue Collar*, and *Norma Rae*." *Labor History* 23, no. 1 (Winter 1982): 67–78.
Žižek, Slavoj. "Guilty Pleasures." *Film Comment* 42, no. 1 (January–February 2006): 12–13.
Žižek, Slavoj. *Welcome to the Desert of the Real*. London: Verso, 2002.

INDEX

Page numbers in *italics* indicate illustrations.

Across the Wide Missouri (1951), 109–10
Aherne, Brian, 14
Aleiss, Angela, 91–92, 93, 104, 105, 106, 112, 115, 116, 117
Anderson, Judith, 131
Anderson, Thom, 59
Annie Get Your Gun (1950), 147
Anthony Adverse (1936), 158
Appleby, Joyce, 126
Arnold, Elliot, 95
Asphalt Jungle, The (1950), 32, 79, 147, 148
Astaire, Fred, 135
Astor, Mary, 131
Auteur theory, 4, 5, 6, 8–9, 12, 22, 23, 24, 33
Autry, Gene, 92
Avatar (2009), 118, 124
Awful Truth, The (1937), 142
Axelson, Leyland, 132–33

Bacall, Lauren, 29, 131, 132
Balme, Christopher, 90
Bancroft, Anne, 25, 130, 131
Barlett, Donald, 78
Barnes, Howard, 11
Basinger, Jeanine, 48, 84
Bataan (1943), 84
Bazin, André, 19, 94
Bean, Robin, 14, 15
Beatty, Warren, 12, 15, 76
Beguiled, The (1971), 21
Bell, Robert, 158, 160

Bellamy, Edward, 36
Belton, John, 9, 98
Ben-Hur (1959), 68
Benny, Jack, 44
Benshoff, Harry M., 82, 88, 122, 138
Beresford, Bruce, 12
Berkeley, Busby, 70
Berns, Fernando, 7, 101
Bessie, Alvah, 45, 58–59
Best Years of Our Lives, The (1946), 47, 51, 53
Big Jim McLain (1952), 56, 57, 61
Big Sky, The (1952), 110
Big Sleep, The (1946), 131
Bindas, Kenneth, 73
Bird of Paradise (1932), 90, 121
Blackboard Jungle (1955), 153
Black Knight, The (1954), 101
Blanding, Sarah, 159
Blitch, Iris, 140
Blood, Robert, 155
Blood Brother (1947 novel), 95, 109, 110
Bodnar, John, 53, 54
Body and Soul (1947), 88
Boetticher, Budd, 5
Bogart, Humphrey, 3, 23, 25, 29, 30, 32, 46, 72, 131, 132
Bogdanovich, Peter, 12
Boggs, Carl, 127, 140, 141
Bondi, Beulah, 140
Boone, Richard, 152
Borgnine, Ernest, 23, 25, 77

Borzage, Frank, 44, 71–72, 134
Bourget, Jean-Loup, 10, 96, 102
Bowlby, John, 145
Branagh, Kenneth, 22
Brazzi, Rossano, 144, 145
Breen, Joseph, 17
Breines, Wini, 129
Brennan, Walter, 152
Brent, George, 70
Bride Walks Out, The (1936), 130
Bronson, Charles, 25, 102
Brown, Carol, 143
Brown, Dee, 97, 102
Brown, Joe David, 86
Brownlow, Kevin, 106
Brown v. Board of Education, 82
Buchanan, Keith, 78–79
Buerkle, Jack, 160
Bühler, Wolf-Eckhart, 18, 24
Buñuel, Luis, 30
Burnett, Charles, 5
Burnham, James, 66, 123
Buscombe, Edward, 5, 104–5, 111, 115
Butterfield, Roger, 52, 87

Calamity Jane (1953), 147
Calhoun, Rory, 5
California Conquest (1952), 57
Cameron, Ian, 4
Cameron, Kate, 45, 46
Capra, Frank, 16–17
Carr, E. H., 9
Carruthers, Susan, 61
Carter, Matthew, 6, 7, 9, 23, 28, 35, 149
Carter, Paul, 55
Casablanca (1942), 19, 134
Catholic Legion of Decency, 17, 139
Ceplair, Larry, 57
Chafe, William, 38
Chandler, Jeff, 89, 94, 106
Charge at Feather River, The (1953), 111
Chavin, Serge, 166
Cheyenne Autumn (1964), 114
Chissell, Nobel, 106
Christensen, Terry, 37

CinemaScope, 6, 27, 28
Citizen Kane (1941), 19
Clark, Dane, 24, 44
Clarke, Jane, 137
Clément, Réné, 23
Cocteau, Jean, 30
Cody, "Iron Eyes," 106, 197n131
Cohan, Steven, 163
Cohn, Harry, 24
Colbert, Claudette, 15, 131, 154
Cold War, 12, 20, 43, 57, 61, 62, 63, 65, 67, 81, 103, 122, 123, 129, 164, 167
Collier, John, 115, 120
Collins, Richard, 59
Comes a Horseman (1978), 147
Cook, Pam, 9, 16
Cool Breeze (1972), 147, 149
Cooper, Gary, 3, 23, 49
Coppola, Francis Ford, 12, 181n12
Corkin, Stanley, 66
Costigliola, Frank, 165
Countryman, Edward, 107, 114
Coursodon, Jean-Pierre, 8, 14, 131
Covered Wagon, The (1924), 3
Coyne, Michael, 64
Cram, Mildred, 178n2
Crawford, Broderick, 137
Crawford, Joan, 44, 72, 129
Crisp, Donald, 174
Crist, Judith, 84
Crowther, Bosley, 28, 38, 40, 45, 48, 93, 134
Cruz, James, 3
Cukor, George, 17
Cuordileone, K. A., 164
Curtis, Tony, 86
Custer's Last Fight (1912), 92

Dana, Leora, 86, 131, *170*
Dances with Wolves (1990), 105, 107, 108, 118
Danks, Adrian, 74
Daves, Delmer: Arriflex camera, use of, 17, 30–31; attitudes towards American Indians, 5, 7–8, 40, 82, 93–103, 107–14; attitudes towards Japanese, 43, 48–49, 87–88; crane shots, use of, 6, 13, 27,

31–32, 34, 44, 76, 77; Directors Guild, 4, 59, 70; early life and career, 3, 4, 8, 36, 69, 95, 104; film festivals, 6; landscape, use of, 11–12, 26, 32–34, 76; methods of working, 12, 19–30; personal, social, and political beliefs and themes, 7–8, 15–16, 18, 35–36, 38, 40, 42, 43, 46, 49, 50–55, 57–58, 60–61, 63–66, 70–75, 77–81, 84–85, 89, 114–21, 122–26, 138–53, 154–63, 165–73; reviews of Daves's films, 4–5, 7, 11, 12, 14, 15, 28, 29, 38–39, 45–46, 48, 49, 62, 72, 80, 86, 93, 95, 108, 125, 131, 132, 134, 137, 139, 140–42, 144, 145, 157; style, 6, 11–13, 14–15, 20–28, 30–34, 44–45, 47–49, 76, 110; Screen Writers Guild, 70; subjective camera, use of, 17, 28–31, *29*

Works as director: *The Badlanders* (1958), 7, 13, 19, 32, 59, 77–80, 89, 124, 147–49; *Broken Arrow* (1950), 5, 6, 7, 8, 11, 12, 17, 18, 26, 31–32, 33, 35, 39, 40, 63, 64–66, *65*, 75, 82, 89, 93–99, 100, 101, 102, 103, 104–7, 108–13, 114–18, 120, *121*, 122, 123, 124–26, 166, 168, 176, 177; *Cowboy* (1958), 7, 18, 24, 33, 35, 59, 74–75, 95, 96, 165–68; *Demetrius and the Gladiators* (1954), 11, 26–28, 67, *68*, 68–69, 75, 83–84, 89, 131, 145–46; *The Hanging Tree* (1959), 5, 11, 13, 19, 21, 23, 25, 34, 41, 95, 101, 131, 149, 152–53, 162, 167, 177; *Kings Go Forth* (1958), 10, 18, 25, 31, 86–87, 112, 124, 131; *A Kiss in the Dark* (1949), 12, 137–38; *Never Let Me Go* (1953), 12, 17, 61–62, 105, 131; *Pride of the Marines* (1945), 4, 5–6, 11, 18, 19, 21, 25, 26, 35, 39, 47, 48–49, 50–55, 58, 59–60, 69, 84, 87, 88, 89, 102, 126, 152, 168, 172, 174, 177; *Return of the Texan* (1952), 45, 152, 167; *3:10 to Yuma* (1957), 4–5, 6, 9, 11, 12, 13, 18, 19–20, *21*, 23–26, 31, 34, 38, 41, 74, 95, 140, 150, 151, 167, 169–72, *170*, 176; *To the Victor* (1948), 11, 20, 33, 38–39, 40–41, 66–67, 89, 134, 172

Works as writer: *An Affair to Remember* (1957), 3, 140–41; *Clear All Wires* (1933), 82; *Dames* (1934), 3, 70, 154; *Divorce in the Family* (1932), 144; *Flirtation Walk* (1934), 3, 46, 132; *The Go-Getter* (1937), 50, 55, 70; *It All Came True* (1940), 101, 132; *Love Affair* (1939), 3, 4, 8, 19, 58, 140–41; *Miss Pacific Fleet* (1935), 46, 132; *Mothers and Daughters* (1961, unmade), 162, 173; *The Petrified Forest* (1936), 3, 58, 72–73, 135; *Shipmates Forever* (1935), 46, 61; *So This is College* (1929), 3, 135, 153, 175; *Stage Door Canteen* (1943), 44, 85; *Stranded* (1935), 55, 70–72, 73, 89, 132, 133–34, 136; *Stuff of Heroes* (1940, unmade), 55, 73–74; *White Feather* (1955), 59, 64, 94, 97–99, 107, 110, 112, 117, 119, 122, 150, 168; *You Were Never Lovelier* (1942), 45, 135

Works as writer and director: *The Battle of the Villa Fiorita* (1965), 11, 15–16, 32, 39, 144–47; *Bird of Paradise* (1951), 12, 18, 33, 89–90, 96, 105, 109, 119, 120, 121, 175, 176; *Dark Passage* (1948), 3, 5, 6, 10, 12, 17, 18, 20–21, 25, 26, 28–31, *29*, 32–33, 34, 36, 67, 80, 131, 132, 151–52; *Destination Tokyo* (1943), 4, 11, 20, 22, 26, 45, 46, 47–49, 58, 60, 140, 166, 173; *Drum Beat* (1954), 7, 28, 31, 33, 39–40, 41, 62–63, 64, 94, 97, 98, 101–3, 104, 105, 106, 109, 116, 117, 118, 124, 150; *Hollywood Canteen* (1944), 11, 44–46, 60, 85–86, 192n10; *Jubal* (1956), 6, 9, 13, 17, 41, 67–68, 95, 149–50, 167, *169*, 173; *The Last Wagon* (1956), 23, 32, 33–34, 40, 61, 66, 69, 81, 94, 97–98, 99–101, 108, 110–11, 113, *113*, 118, 119, 150, 151, 154, 155, 176–77; *Parrish* (1961), 11, 15, 32, 75–76, 136, 154, 159, 173; *The Red House* (1947), 4, 5, 18, 26, 35, 80, 154, 159, 174–75; *Rome Adventure* (1962), 10, 12, 14, 15, 80, 135,

153, 154, 156–57; *Spencer's Mountain* (1963), 3, 6, 7, 9, 11, 13, 14, 31, 35, 80, 84, 125, 126, 136, 154, 155, 159, 174, 175; *A Summer Place* (1959), 11, 14, 41–42, 139–44, 152, 155–56, 157, 158, 159–62, 173, 176; *Susan Slade* (1961), 14–15, 32, 155, 157, 158, 159, 161, 173; *Task Force* (1949), 30, 34, 39, 47, 49–50, 88, 96, 174; *Treasure of the Golden Condor* (1953), 17, 18, 32, 79, 80, 96, 105, 119, 124; *The Very Thought of You* (1944), 18, 34, 45, 46, 49, 58, 131, 140, 151, 160, 162; *Youngblood Hawke* (1964), 4, 11, 38, 76, 133
Daves, Michael, 24, 35
Davis, Bette, 44, 45, 85, 135
Davis, John, 46
Day, Doris, 136–37, 138–39
Dean, James, 164
Dean, Robert, 164
Dee, Sandra, 139, 155
Deloria, Philip, 90, 93, 176
Deloria, Vine, Jr., 90, 104, 106–7
DeMille, Cecil B., 57, 59, 91, 109
De Niro, Robert, 93
Destry Rides Again (1939), 130
Devil's Doorway (1950), 106, 107–8, 111, 114, 125, 129
Dick, Bernard, 9, 29, 48
Dickens, Homer, 5
Dickinson, Angie, 130
Dietrich, Marlene, 129, 130
Disney, Walt, 56, 61
Divorce American Style (1967), 142
Doherty, Thomas, 51
Donahue, Troy, 14, 15, 139, 156, 159, 173
Donelan, Carol, 25
Donlevy, Brian, 166
Dru, Joanne, 152
Drums Along the Mohawk (1939), 93, 97
Drury, James, 23
Duning, George, 25
Dunne, Philip, 83
Durgnat, Raymond, 31

Eastwood, Clint, 5, 104
Eberwein, Robert, 48
Egan, Richard, 139
Eiseman, Selise, 142
Eisenhower, Dwight G., 37, 141, 164, 186
Ellis, Albert, 156, 158
Emperor Jones, The (1933), 83
Englund, Steven, 57
Enrico, Roberto, 172
Epstein, Edward, 47
Evans, M. Stanton, 57
Every Girl Should be Married (1948), 127
Eviction, The (1907), 37
Ex-Convict, The (1905), 37
Eyles, Allen, 11, 12, 14

Farnham, Marynia, 127, 128, 129
Farr, Felicia, 21, 24, 40, 131, 149, 169
Father of the Bride (1950), 153
Father's Little Dividend (1951), 153
FBI Story, The (1959), 76
Fishbein, Leslie, 128
Fleming, Victor, 17
Fonda, Henry, 3, 13, 14, 93
Fonda, Jane, 15
Forbes, Bryan, 101–2
Ford, Constance, 139
Ford, Glenn, 13, 21, 22–23, 24, 25, 67, 166, 169, 170
Ford, John, 5, 12, 14, 18, 24, 25, 31, 33, 83, 93, 106, 109, 116, 123, 130, 152–53, 172, 174
Fort Apache (1948), 93, 166
Francis, Kay, 71
Franciscus, James, 12
Frankenheimer, John, 4
Franklin, Benjamin, 119
Freeman, Edward, 91, 117
French, Philip, 93, 112
French, Valerie, 149
Friar, Natasha, 104
Friar, Ralph, 104
Friedan, Betty, 128, 163, 173
From Here to Eternity (1953), 142
Fugitive, The (1963–1967 TV series), 3
Fuller, Samuel, 5

Gable, Clark, 3, 61, 62
Garbo, Greta, 129
Garfield, John, 6, 20, 24, 44, 45, 47, 58, 84
Garner, James, 138
Geer, Will, 65
Gentleman's Agreement (1947), 84, 88
Gerber, David, 21, 53, 87
Gilbert, Eugene, 154
Glitre, Kathrina, 137, 138
Godden, Rumer, 16
Golden Girls, The (TV series, 1985–1992), 142
Goldwyn, Sam, 4
Gone With the Wind (1939), 17
Gough-Yates, Kevin, 132, 145, 162, 172
Graduate, The (1967), 176
Grant, Cary, 3, 18, 30, 47, 173
Grant, James Edward, 61
Grapes of Wrath, The (1940), 18, 19, 130
Grease (1978), 155
Green Berets, The (1968), 123
Greene, Graham, 96
Griffin, Sean, 82, 88, 122, 138
Griffin-Pierce, Trudi, 120–21, 125
Griffith, David Wark, 91
Griggs, John, 47
Griswold, Robert, 134
Guadalcanal Diary (1943), 84, 87
Guest, Haden, 6
Guglielmo, Thomas, 89
Guicciardini, Francesco, 40

Haas, Peter J., 37
Hacker, Helen Mayer, 163–64, 165, 168–69, 171
Hagen, Jean, 148, 149
Haley, James, 105
Halliwell, Martin, 51, 54
Hamner, Earl, Jr., 7, 84, 125, 136
Hands of Orlac, The (1924), 30
Handzo, Stephen, 114
Harburg, E. Y., 44
Hardwicke, Sir Cedric, 16
Harman, Jypson, 139
Hartleben, Jerry, 25
Hartman, Susan, 129

Haskell, Molly, 137
Hatch, Robert, 7
Hathaway, Henry, 6
Hawks, Howard, 5, 14, 130, 170
Hayward, Susan, 69, 131, 145
Hayworth, Rita, 135
Hearne, Joanne, 111
Heflin, Van, 169, *170*
Henry V (1944 and 1989 versions), 22
Hepburn, Katherine, 44, 129
Herzberg, Bob, 63
Higham, John, 96, 114, 119
High Noon (1952), 170
Hitchcock, Alfred, 5, 6, 18, 30, 161
Hollywood Canteen, the, 44, 60, 85
Hollywood Studio System, 4, 8, 10, 16–19, 24, 35, 59, 76, 108
Home of the Brave (1949), 88, 124
Home of the Brave (2006), 54
Horne, Lena, 85
Howard, Leslie, 73
Howard, Oliver, 40, 66, 94, 97, 98, 101, 125, 151
Howe, Andrew, 39
How the West Was Won (1962), 107
HUAC (House Un-American Activities Committee), 55–56, 57, 58, 59, 60, 61, 67, 68, 69, 80
Hudson, Rock, 117
Hugueny, Sharon, 136
Hunter, Evan, 162
Hurewitz, Daniel, 61
Huss, Roger, 11
Huston, John, 79, 147

I Am a Fugitive from a Chain Gang (1932), 37
I Married a Communist (1949), 56, 129
Imitation of Life (1959), 141
Ince, Thomas, 91, 92
Indian Fighter, The (1955), 110
Indian Massacre, The (1912), 91
Indian Uprising (1952), 92, 118
Indick, William, 110
Iron Curtain, The (1948), 56

Iron Horse, The (1924), 93
Irvine, Janice, 142
I Was a Communist for the FBI (1951), 56

Jacobson, Herbert, 125
Jaeckel, Richard, 24–25
Jagger, Dean, 15
Jaskulski, Józef, 59, 101, 109, 124, 125
Jaws (1975), 155
Jentleson, Bruce, 56, 123
Johnny Guitar (1954), 129, 147
Johnson, Dorothy, 5, 152, 167
Johnson, Lyndon B., 112
Johnson, William, 146
Jones, Dorothy, 47, 59
Jourdan, Louis, 89
Jurado, Katy, 148

Kael, Pauline, 77
Kazan, Elia, 4
Keller, Alexandra, 107
Kelly, Claire, 148
Kennan, George, 164–65
Kennedy, Arthur, 139, 140
Kennedy, Douglas, 24
Kennedy, John F., 164
Kennedy, Robert F., 140
Kenyon, Charles, 72
Kern, Jerome, 135
King, Andrea, 85
Kirkendall, Lester, 159–60
Kirshner, Jonathan, 175–76
Kitses, Jim, 4, 9, 104, 147
Koch, Howard, 19
Koestler, Frances, 52, 54
Koppes, Clayton, 38, 122
Koster, Henry, 27
Kovacs, Yves, 40
Kramer vs. Kramer (1979), 142
Kreck, Joachim, 21
Krutnik, Frank, 88, 123

La Belle et le Bête (1946), 31
Ladd, Alan, 3, 23, 63, 77, 97, 101, 102, 148
Lady in the Dark, The (1944), 128

Lady in the Lake (1946), 28–29
Lambert, Gavin, 129
Lamster, Frederick, 72
Landis, Judson, 146
Lawton, Charles, Jr., 25
Leab, Daniel, 87
Legrand, Gérard, 5
Lejeune, Caroline, 110
Lemmon, Jack, 166
Lenihan, John, 63, 66
Leonard, Elmore, 170
Leone, Sergio, 13
Leroy, Mervyn, 76
Leslie, Joan, 45
Lesser, Sol, 18
Letter from an Unknown Woman (1948), 157
Leuthold, Steven, 92–93
Levinger, George, 143
Levitin, Jacqueline, 147, 150–51
Lewis, R. W. B., 168
Limerick, Patricia Nelson, 114, 122
Lindfors, Viveca, 41, 134, 135
Link, Arthur, 38
Little Big Man (1970), 93, 123
Little House on the Prairie (1935 novel), 91
Living on Velvet (1935), 134
Lomawaima, K. Tsianina, 118
Looking Backward (1887 novel), 36
Looking for Love (1964), 154
Lover Come Back (1961), 137
Love with the Proper Stranger (1963), 157
Loving v. Virginia (case, 1967), 112
Louis, Joe, 85
Lucas, Blake, 11, 129, 150, 151, 163
Lumet, Sidney, 4
Lundberg, Ferdinand, 127, 128, 129
Lurvey, Ira, 142
Lydia Bailey (1952), 83
Lyndon, Louise, 163

MacArthur, Douglas, 64
MacCurdy, Carol A., 169, 171
MacEwen, Walter, 23
Malden, Karl, 15, 75, 162
Malick, Terence, 174

INDEX

Maltby, Richard, 9, 16
Maltz, Albert, 8, 21–22, 35–36, 39, 58, 59, 60, 87, 89
Man Called Horse, A (1970), 124
Manchel, Frank, 95, 96, 115
Mangold, James, 167, 169–70
Manifest Destiny, 114, 122, 123
Man in the Gray Flannel Suit, The (1957), 129, 165
Mankiewicz, Joseph, 59
Mann, Anthony, 5, 14, 23, 107, 111
Mannequin (1937), 72
Man's Castle (1937), 71
Mantell, Howard, 116
Man Who Shot Liberty Valance, The (1962), 12, 152–53, 167, 172
Marshall, William, 83
Marubbio, M. Elise, 39, 110
Mature, Victor, 83
May, Lary, 108
Mayer, Louis B., 70
Mayes, Wendell, 19, 131, 162
Mayo, Archie, 73
McCarey, Leo, 19, 58, 61
McCarthy, Joseph, 56, 63, 65, 76, 80, 175, 177
McClusky, Clarence Wade, 39
McCormick, Richard, 38
McGuire, Dorothy, 139
McKinley, William, 123–24
McNally, Karen, 86
McVay, Douglas, 24
Mead, Margaret, 174
Mellen, Joan, 22, 37, 173
Menjou, Adolphe, 45, 135
Mercer, Johnny, 135
Metz, Walter, 152
Meuel, David, 130
Mexal, Stephen, 167
Meyer, William, 12
Michel, Sonya, 53, 54
Mildred Pierce (1945), 157
Miller, Don, 107–8
Minnelli, Vincente, 5
Mission to Moscow (1943), 43
Mitchell, Billy, 39

Mitchell, Jonathan, 168
Mogambo (1953), 130
Monroe, Marilyn, 148, 149
Montgomery, Robert, 28
Moorehead, Agnes, 25
Morella, Joe, 47
Morgan, Dennis, 40, 44–45, 49, 134, 135
Morris, George, 5–6
Morrison, Toni, 90, 93
Mort, Terry, 95, 98, 116
Mothers and Daughters (1961 novel), 162
Moullet, Luc, 8
Mowry, George, 36, 39
MPA (Motion Picture Alliance for the Preservation of American Ideals), 56, 59, 61, 70
Mulvey, Laura, 127, 138, 161–62
Murdoch, David, 74
Murray, David, 115
My Darling Clementine (1946), 18
My Son John (1952), 57, 61, 175

Nacache, Jacqueline, 3, 28
Nash, Gerald, 114
Nelson, Andrew Patrick, 6, 7, 9, 19, 23, 28, 35, 63, 125
New Land, The (1972), 102
Nickel, John, 124
Night of the Hunter, The (1955), 10
Nisbet, Robert, 50
Niven, David, 137
Nixon, Richard, 64, 121
Nolan, Lloyd, 14
Nolley, Ken, 104
Norris, Frank, 36, 39
North by Northwest (1959), 30
Northwest Passage (1938 novel), 92
Northwest Passage (1940), 92, 96
Nott, Robert, 5–6
Novelli, Martin, 48
Nye, Francis Ivan, 146

Oakley, J. Ronald, 37–38, 163
Occurrence at Owl Creek Bridge (1961), 172
O'Connor, John, 91, 92, 95

Octopus, The (1901 novel), 36, 39
O'Hara, Maureen, 16, 131, 144, 145
Olivier, Laurence, 22
Olson, James, 122
Once Upon a Time in the West (1968), 13
On the Waterfront (1953), 24
Opler, Morris, 104, 105
O'Sullivan, John, 122
Our Daily Bread (1934), 37
OWI (Office of War Information), 43, 46, 87

Packard, Vance, 155
Page, Geneviève, 76
Paget, Debra, 24, 69, 90, 94, 95, *121*
Parent Trap, The (1961), 142, 145
Parker, Eleanor, 24, 44, 47, 49, 131
Parkman, Francis, 122
Pavan, Marisa, 103
PCA (Production Code Administration/ Motion Picture Production Code), 10, 17–18, 34–35, 37, 39, 45, 46, 56, 72, 79, 80, 90, 101, 108, 109, 111, 112, 115, 139, 144, 149, 153, 155, 175, 176
Pearsall, Sarah, 40
Peek, Wendy C., 166, 168, 173
Petch, Simon, 171
Petrified Forest, The (1935 play), 58, 72–73
Pettigrew, Terence, 131–32
Pheasant-Kelly, Fran, 6, 7, 9, 20, 74
Philadelphia Story, The (1940), 142
Phillips, Roderick, 142, 143
Philp, Kenneth, 115, 120
Pillow Talk (1959), 137, 138
Pleshette, Suzanne, 12, 24, 131, 133, 135, 156–57
Poffenberger, Thomas, 153, 159
Point Blank (1967), 175–76
Politicians, The (1915), 37
Pollard, Tom, 127, 140, 141
Pomp, Joseph, 7, 9, 136, 155, 159
Porter, Cole, 44
Powdermaker, Hortense, 16, 19
Poyato, Pedro, 30
Pratt, George, 51, 53
Prebble, John, 94

Preminger, Otto, 17
Pretty Woman (1990), 138
Price, John, 96, 106
Prisoner of War (1954), 62
Progressive Movement/Progressive Party, 36, 38, 39
Psycho (1960), 30

Queen Kelly (1929), 3
Quiet Man, The (1952), 130
Quinlan, David, 11, 12, 15, 72
Quinn, Anthony, 84
Quirk, Lawrence, 15, 106

Rabourdin, Dominique, 6, 12
Rae Norma (1979), 76
Rancho Notorious (1952), 129
Random Harvest (1942), 53
Rasner, Heinz-Gerd, 18, 24
Reagan, Ronald, 56, 61, 62, 85, 121
Rear Window (1954), 161
Rebel Without a Cause (1955), 142, 153, 164, 165
Reisman, David, 173
Reiss, Ira, 158
Reynerston, A. J., 22
Reynolds, Debbie, 128
Ride Out for Revenge (1957), 92, 116
Rio Bravo (1959), 10, 130, 170
Rio Grande (1950), 123
Ritt, Martin, 4, 6
Robe, The (1953), 26, 27
Roberts, Julia, 138
Robertson, Dale, 152
Robeson, Paul, 83
Robinson, Edward G., 18, 80
Robinson, Jay, 68
Rogers, Ginger, 128
Rogers, Roy, 44, 92
Roosevelt, Franklin D., 38, 43, 59, 67, 73, 74, 87, 122
Roosevelt, Theodore, 91, 122, 165
Rosen, Marjorie, 127, 128
Rosenberg, Emily, 129
Rosenfelt, Deborah, 77, 78

Rosi, Francesco, 88
Ross, Steven, 56
Rotha, Paul, 22
Rusk, Dean, 112
Russell, Howard, 51
Russell, Rosalind, 129
Ryan, Tom, 117, 141

Saboteur (1942), 18
Salt, Barry, 27, 30
Salt of the Earth (1953), 76–79
Sarris, Andrew, 8–10, 12, 23, 31, 33
Savage, William, 173
Schatz, Thomas, 16, 19, 23
Scheiner, Georganne, 155, 161–62
Schell, Maria, 21, 23, 131
Schell, Maximilian, 23
Schlesinger, Arthur M., Jr., 38, 128, 164, 171
Schofield, Michael, 158
Schumach, Murray, 108
Scorsese, Martin, 4
Searchers, The (1956), 10, 111
Seconds (1966), 30
Selznick, David O., 17
Sergeant Rutledge (1960), 83
Seven Women (1966), 130
Shain, Russell, 56, 57
Shane (1953), 23, 172
Sheridan, Philip, 97
Sherwood, Robert, 58, 72–73
Short, K. R. M., 84
Siegel, Don, 21
Silverheels, Jay, 106
Simmonds, Diana, 137
Sinatra, Frank, 3, 86
Sirk, Douglas, 5, 15, 117, 141
Skard, Åse, 146–47
Sladen, Joseph, 98–99
Slotkin, Richard, 9, 91, 104, 107
Smith, Kent, 25
Snake Pit, The (1948), 128
Soldier Blue (1970), 93, 123
Solinger, Rickie, 157
Son of Fury (1942), 80, 124
Spielberg, Steven, 155

Spock, Benjamin, 127
Stagecoach (1939), 92, 97, 109, 147
Stanwyck, Barbara, 45, 130
Starr, Kevin, 85
Steele, James, 78
Steiger, Rod, 149
Steiner, Max, 25, 174
Stern, Michael, 141
Stevens, Connie, 14
Stevenson, Adlai E., 64–65, 67, 80
Stewart, Donald Ogden, 58, 178n2
Stewart, James, 3, 64, 65, 76, 94, *121*, 172
Stokes, Melvyn, 93, 105, 106, 107, 109
Stokes, Walter, 156
Stormy Weather (1943), 85
Strick, Philip, 14
Strode, Woody, 83
Suspicion (1941), 18
Sweeney, Edwin, 94, 106

Talbot, David, 22, 59
Tavernier, Bertrand, 6, 11, 12, 13, 14, 15, 26, 33, 34, 163
Taxi Driver (1976), 93
Taza, Son of Cochise (1953), 117
Ten Commandments, The (1956), 57
Tender Trap, The (1955), 128
Tessier, Max, 177
Thin Red Line, The (1998), 174
This is the Army (1943), 43, 85
Thomson, David, 7, 12, 13, 72
3.10 to Yuma (2007), 167
Thrill of It All, The (1963), 138
Ticket to Tomahawk, A (1950), 162–63
Tierney, Gene, 61, 131
Todd, Richard, 144
To Have and Have Not (1944), 131
Townsend, Leo, 59
Tracy, Spencer, 71, 72
Treglia, Gabriella, 120
Troell, Jan, 102
Truffaut, François, 6, 62, 131
Truman, Harry S., 64
Trumbo, Dalton, 35, 59
Tucker, Sherrie, 46, 60, 85

INDEX

Tully, Richard Walton, 90
Turner, Frederick Jackson, 91, 96, 102, 107, 114, 123
Tuska, John, 63, 124

Union Pacific (1939), 109
Up in Arms (1944), 43
Utley, Robert, 96–97

Vertigo (1958), 10
Vidor, King, 104
Vincent, Tom, 184n113
Visconti, Luchino, 23

Wagner, Robert, 94
Wakeman, John, 99
Wald, Jerry, 18, 60, 87
Walker, Michael, 6, 31, 62–63, 75, 79–80, 96, 99–100, 102, 103, 108, 109, 110, 111, 117, 118, 150, 154, 167
Walk the Proud Land (1956), 116
Wallace, Henry, 38
Waller, Fats, 85
Wallis, Hal, 74
Waltons, The (1972–1981 TV series), 3
Warlock (1959), 172
Warner, Jack, 4, 14, 17, 18, 22, 28, 58, 87
Washburn, Wilcomb, 96–97
Washington Merry-Go-Round (1932), 55
Waterloo Bridge (1940), 158
Wayne, John, 56, 61, 123, 130, 172
Weatherfield, Jack, 119
Weigand, Kate, 127
Weine, Robert, 30
Welles, Halstead, 19
Welles, Orson, 25
Wetta, Frank, 48

White, John, 7, 9, 35, 66, 74, 78, 101, 109, 111, 113, 167–68
Whitehall, Richard, 5, 99, 137
Whitney, June, 129
Widmark, Richard, 97, *113*
Wilde, Cornel, 79
Wilder, Laura Ingalls, 91
Wild One, The (1953), 142
Wilson, Dooley, 46
Wilson, Raymond, 122
Wilson, Sandra, 88
Wilson, Sloan, 139
Winchester 73 (1950), 111
Winkler, Martin, 68
Wizard of Oz, The (1939), 10, 19
Wollen, Peter, 7, 24
Wood, Natalie, 86, 131
Wood, Robin, 10
Wood, Sam, 3, 17
Worcester, Donald, 66
Worland, Rick, 107, 114
Wouk, Herman, 11, 133
Wright, Frank Lloyd, 141
Wright, Judith, 10
Wulf, Reinhard, 18, 24
Wyler, William, 47, 51
Wyman, Jane, 137, 138

Young, Loretta, 71

Zanuck, Darryl F., 5, 12–13, 17, 18, 26, 27, 32, 110, 111
Zavattini, Cesare, 34
Zheutlin, Barbara, 22, 59
Zieger, Gay, 76
Zieger, Robert, 76
Žižek, Slavoj, 5, 172

ABOUT THE AUTHOR

Photo courtesy of the author

Douglas Horlock has taught in elementary schools in England and America. He was also an inspector of schools in England and Wales. In the university sector, he taught education. He was program director of a degree course for trainee teachers and taught units that focused on curriculum planning for children with special educational needs and also gifted and talented students. He has also taught history, specializing in modern British and American cultural history, and has published articles in the *Historian* and the *Welsh Historian*. He has been a lifelong film fan, particularly of Hollywood's "Golden Age," and has a special interest in the Western genre.

www.ingramcontent.com/pod-product-compliance
Lightning Source LLC
Chambersburg PA
CBHW030619230426
43661CB00053B/2067